CONTEMPORARY ART

FROM CRESCENT MOON PUBLISHING

The Art of Andy Goldsworthy: Complete Works: Special Edition
by William Malpas

The Art of Andy Goldsworthy
by William Malpas

Andy Goldsworthy: Touching Nature
by William Malpas

Andy Goldsworthy In Close-Up
by William Malpas

Richard Long: The Art of Walking
by William Malpas

The Art of Richard Long: Complete Works: Special Edition
by William Malpas

Constantin Brancusi: Sculpting the Essence of Things
by James Pearson

Alison Wilding: The Embrace of Sculpture
by Susan Quinnell

Eric Gill: Nuptials of God
by Anthony Hoyland

The Erotic Object: Sexuality in Sculpture
From Prehistory to the Present Day
by Susan Quinnell

Minimal Art and Artists in the 1960s and After
by Laura Garrard

Land Art, Earthworks, Installations, Environments, Sculpture
by William Malpas

Land Art: A Complete Guide to Landscape, Environmental,
Earthworks, Nature, Sculpture and Installation Art
by William Malpas

Richard Long In Close-Up
by William Malpas

Land Art In Close-Up
by William Malpas

Colourfield Painting: Minimal, Cool, Hard Edge, Serial
and Post-Painterly Abstract Art From the Sixties to the Present
by Laura Garrard

Mark Rothko: The Art of Transcendence
by Julia Davis

Jasper Johns: Painting By Numbers
by L.M. Poole

Installation Art In Close-Up

Installation Art
In Close-Up

William Malpas

CRESCENT MOON

CRESCENT MOON PUBLISHING
P.O. Box 393
Maidstone
Kent, ME14 5XU
United Kingdom

First published 2007.
© William Malpas 2007.

Printed and bound in Great Britain.
Set in Garamond 9 on 14pt.
Designed by Radiance Graphics.

The right of William Malpas to be identified as the author of *Installation Art In Close-Up* has been asserted generally in accordance with sections 77 and 78 of the Copyright, Designs and Patents Act 1988.

British Library Cataloguing in Publication data

Malpas, William
Installation Art In Close-Up(Sculptors Series)
1. Sculpture – Criticism and interpretation
2. Sculpture, Modern – 20th century
I. Title

730. 9'2

ISBN 1-86171-053-4 (Pbk)
ISBN-13 978-186171-053-6 (Pbk)

ISBN 1-86171-107-7 (Hbk)
ISBN-13 978-186171-107-6 (Hbk)

CONTENTS

ACKNOWLEDGEMENTS

Thanks to Anthony d'Offay Gallery, London; Sperone Westwater, New York; Verlag der Buchhandlung Walther König, Köln; Thames & Hudson, London; Coracle Press, London; Karsten Schubert, London; Konrad Fischer Galerie, Düsseldorf; Hayward Gallery, London; Musée d'Art Moderne de la Ville de Paris; Phaidon Press, London; Tate Gallery, London; Tate Publishing.

Thanks to the copyright holders of the illustrations:
Tate Gallery, St Ives. Tate Modern, London. Museum of Modern Art, New York. Skystone Foundation. Chinati Foundation, Texas. Sculpture At Goodwood. Her Majesty's Stationery Office. Musée d'Art Moderne de la Ville de Paris. Saatchi Collection, London. Chris Drury. Andy Goldsworthy. David Nash. Richard Long. Hamish Fulton.

For quotations: University of California Press, Berkeley. Routledge, London. Methuen, London. Faber & Faber, London.

INTRODUCTION

INTRO. Installation art is a broad term, and as pretty much all contemporary art these days is installation art in some shape or form, it's not a very useful term. It can incorporate virtually anything.

An installation is the management of a whole space or environment – the floor, walls, ceiling, furnishings, lighting and doorways, as in Rebecca Horn's *Ballet of the Woodpecker*, a room full of mirrors, or Sylvia Stone's *Crystal Palace*. Artists aren't content any more to demurely hang paintings on walls or peacefully place sculptures on pedestals. Art exhibitions now are typically an art of environments, with TV monitors, computers, scaffolding, cables, cameras, supports, bones, wire mesh and a zillion other items installed everywhere (though video screens are the favourite installation media). At *Nine At Castelli* (1968), Bruce Nauman, Richard Serra, Eva Hesse and Keith Sonnier *et al* deployed a variety of materials, including aluminium, polythene, plastic, water, steel, latex rubber, acid, chicken wire, canvas, neon, cotton, copper, felt and flocking.[1]

The classic type of installation art developed out of the 1960s, out of performance art, Process art, ABC art, Minimal and Postminimal art. Even today one of the most common forms of installation art is a bunch of TV monitors hooked up together (or often a video projector) showing grainy video images of people accompanied by an atmospheric soundtrack.

In the 1960s and 1970s, it seemed as if every artist went through a Minimal period at some time in their career, as well as a painting-as-sculpture period, and a brush with performance art (and perhaps body art). Both a Conceptual art phase and an on-going installation art preoccupation were mandatory for contemporary artists, it seems. All contemporary art can be viewed as basically Conceptual art, and a increasing proportion of it is installation art.

Installation artists have used a myriad of tactics and materials in their art. Some installation artists used liquid to cover the floor area. Per Barclay also used pools of oil: in *Old Boathouse* (1990) an oil pool was set in a Norwegian boathouse beside the sea; in *The Jaguar's Cage* (1991), made a Turin Zoo, a large oil pool was set behind bars. Eve Laramee spread a rectangular mound of cobalt glass on the gallery floor in her *Requiem For a Blue Fluid* (1991). Michelangelo Pistoletto created an interior maze from large pieces of corrugated cardboard laid out across the whole gallery (*Labyrinth,* 1991). In *Monumental Ikebana* (1990) Hiroshi Teshigahara made a giant arched path from bamboo in a gallery space. For Vong Phaephanit's bamboo installation (*What Falls to the Ground Cannot Be Eaten*, 1991), a forest of bamboo sticks was hung from the ceiling of the London gallery, approached through a monumental black doorway. Anya Gallaccio made large installations using flowers: thousands of red roses in *Red On Green* (1992), 101 sunflowers in *Preserve Sunflower* (1991) and 1,600 zinnias in *Untitled* (1992). Gallaccio's flower-pieces emphasized beauty and decay, sensuality and death.

Recalling Wolfgang Laib's pollen floor pieces, Shelagh Wakely covered the marble floor of the British School at Rome with a layer of tumeric spice (*Curcuma sul Travertino*, 1991). In Rudolf Stingel's untitled floor-piece (New York), the entire gallery area was covered with a thick shagpile orange carpet. Gabriel Orozco worked like Andy Goldsworthy with snowballs – in *Planets of the Volcano* (1992) he placed small snowballs on top of some posts near Popocatepetl volcano. Anish Kapoor's *Void Field* (1990) had a Goldsworthyian flavour: each of twenty large pieces of sandstone had small holes bored in the top, which were painted black inside. Chris Jenning's *Vault* (1992) reacted to the Museum of Installation's space by filling it with curving metal rods which connected the walls and floor together. The thin rods curving through space recalling Goldsworthy's wall drawings. Bill Viola brought a whole tree into the Newport Harbor Art Museum in California for his *Theatre of Memory* (1985), the branches were hung with bells blown by electric fans. The tinkling tree faced a giant video image of hissing static. For *Post and Beam* (Cologne, 1991), Simon Unger made a mirror image of the ceiling of the gallery on the floor, complete with lighting and beams.

Giovanni Anselmo used stone like painted canvases, mounting thin slabs of granite on a Paris gallery wall like paintings (*Meeting of Two Works*, 1990).

LAND ART. Installation art is closely linked to land and environmental art. Land or garden art can include American earthworks (such as those by Michael Heizer and Walter de Maria); ephemeral interventions in the environment (such as those by Andy Goldsworthy, Christo and Michael Singer); architectural installations (such as those by Alice Aycock, Mary Miss and Nancy Holt); land art as performance art (Richard Long, Hamish Fulton, Christo); land art that involves landscaping and garden art (such as Alan Sonfist, Robert Irwin and Ian Hamilton Finlay); and sculpture or art parks. Many land/ environmental artworks have been included in this book.

Land art is related to, or a part of, Conceptual art (as is installation art). Much of land art exists only in photographs, memories, words, various texts which are not the land art itself. Works that can be seen and those that are hidden or 'invisible' have the same importance for the artist. One of the hallmarks of the 'ideal Conceptual work', as Mel Bochner said, is 'an exact linguistic correlative, that is, it could be described and experienced in its data and it could be infinitely repeatable'.[2] Land art is often Conceptual art: Christo's *Running Fence*, de Maria's *The New York Earth Room* and Robert Morris's steam pieces exist now only as photographs, memories and criticism. Many sculptors have spoken of the importance of the *making* of the sculpture, its actual construction, with real (and sometimes organic, living) materials. As Barry Flanagan put it: '[m]y work isn't centred in experience. The making of it is itself the experience'.[3] In some artists, the material employed also has a symbolic or added meaning, as in Joseph Beuys' *Fettecke* or 'fat corner', a sculpture with powerful autobiographical and semiotic associations. Beuys emphasized process, evolution, change: his sculpture, he said, was not 'fixed and finished. Processes continue in most of them: chemical reactions, fermentations, colour changes, decay, drying up. Everything is in a *state of change*'.[4]

CONTEXT. As art critics have pointed out, much of what makes art art or sculpture sculpture or an installation installation is that the object/ artwork/ installation is contextualized, physically as well as æsthetically and psychologically, as a sculpture or artwork or installation. Context is crucial (as the French philosopher Julia Kristeva said), for context carries so much meaning. Thus, a pile of bricks on a building site is... a pile of bricks; ordinary, unremarkable, just another cluster of objects in a planet covered with them. But a pile of bricks in an art gallery is... sculpture. This is what

Carl Andre explored with his *Equivalents* series. The *response*, affected by so much of culture, socialization, physical context, education, politics, and so on, makes objects sculptures.

LIGHT. Light is a key ingredient in installation art. Numerous artists have worked with light and lighting; light art has become a whole sub-genre of contemporary installation art. Some artists made light central to their art: James Turrell (with what he calls his 'skyspaces', environments which have openings onto the sky); Robert Irwin (who reworked gallery spaces with scrims, false walls and ceilings); Eric Orr (with his sound and light environments); Dan Flavin (with his famous fluorescent tubes); Bruce Nauman (who built narrow corridors lit by green fluorescents, as well as many neon tubing sculptures); Maria Nordman (who extended studio exteriors); and Nancy Holt (with her environmental sculptures based around celestial events). Other light artists include Douglas Wheeler, Hap Tivey, Susan Kaiser Vogel, Chryssa, Keith Sonnier, Stephen Antonakos, Nicolas Schöffer, Larry Bell, and DeWain Valentine. Sculptors, even the most traditional kind, have to work with light: sculptures are usually meant to be seen (even though sculpture is known as an art of touch).

Some of the artists who made light central to their work in the post-WW2 era were known as Minimal artists (Dan Flavin, Larry Bell and partly Bruce Nauman), while others were more usually categorized as installation or environmental artists (James Turrell, Robert Irwin and Eric Orr), although Turrell, Orr and Irwin utilized Minimal principles. Many of the major works of installation art have used light as the foundation of the piece. For instance, the mirrored boxes of Donald Judd and Robert Morris, or Larry Bell's decorated glass cubes, or Robert Smithson's *Non-site* sculptures. Some artists fitted lamps into their works (such as Morris with his half-circle floor sculpture). And many painters worked directly with light in their monochrome canvases, experimenting with optical effects (Jules Olitski, Agnes Martin), merging into Op Art (Morris Louis, Frank Stella), and the viewer's perception of colour and light.

Many artists have taken gallery spaces and reworked them, adding walls or scrims, or curtains, or false ceilings, or doorways, or new windows, or altering the floor with liquids or false floors. The forms of the additions to gallery spaces were often Minimal – smooth, undecorated, rectilinear partitions, doors, walls and scrims to hide, block or enhance spaces. Often these light and sound spaces look like empty gallery rooms: Eric Orr (*Light Space*, 1985), Hap Tivey's *Sodium Exchange* (1976), Susan Kaiser Vogel's *Point Conception* (1980), DeWain Valentine's *Curved Wall Spectrum* (1974, acrylic tubes hanging alone from gallery ceilings), Larry Bell's *Leaning Room II* (1988), Bruce Nauman's *Yellow Triangular Room* (1973), Douglas Wheeler's *All Gray Graduating Light* (1976), Maria Nordman's *6/ 21/ 79 One Day Only* (1979), James Turrell's *Second Meeting* (1988), and Robert Irwin's Kansas *Installation* (1979).

The forerunners of these light art spaces included Yves Klein's *Le Vide*, and the modernist light art of László Moholy-Nagy (*Light-Space Modulator*, 1923-30), Naum Gabo (*Kinetic Construction*) and Alexander Rodchenko (*Hanging Construction*, 1920-21). Some artists made the reconstituted gallery interior one of their trademarks, Robert Irwin being prominent among them.

In *Silence and the Ion Wind* installation (1980), Eric Orr constructed a series of dark rooms culminating in the *Golden Room* (described as 'an allusive structure for an elusive experience'), a space which was approached through an ion wind. In works such as *Wall Shadow, Sky Lights, Sound Tunnel, Zero Mass, Sunrise, Blood Shadow, The Stone Snake, Prime Matter* and *Blue Void,* Orr deployed sound, light, wind, sand, ice and shadow. For *Prime Matter* (1981), Orr created fog and flames from a twenty foot tall metal column (a larger version was constructed outside the Mitsui Fudosan Building in L.A. in 1991, as a permanent sculpture). Other Orr pieces include firing xenon lasers up into the sky on top of skyscrapers in Long Beach, California (a permanent installation, *Landmark Lumière*, 1991).

It's not possible to include more than a few of the works of the major installation artists here. There are zillions of works that we did not have space for. We have included many land artists, artists who are known for their land and environmental works, but who also created many important installations. The boundaries between categories such as installation art, land art, sculpture, performance art, and painting are continually shifting. Thus, we have included some painters, such as Mark Rothko, Barnett Newman and Frank Stella. They're not known are installation artists, but they did produce installations: Rothko with his Harvard murals and chapel in Houston, for instance.

NOTES

1. See R. Williams, 2000, 86.
2. "Mel Bochner on Malevich", interview with John Coplans, *Artforum*, June, 1974, 62.
3. B. Flanagan, "Sculpture Made Visible", *Studio International*, 178, 915, Oct, 1969.
4. J. Beuys, in *Documenta* 7, 2, Documenta, Kassel, 1982.

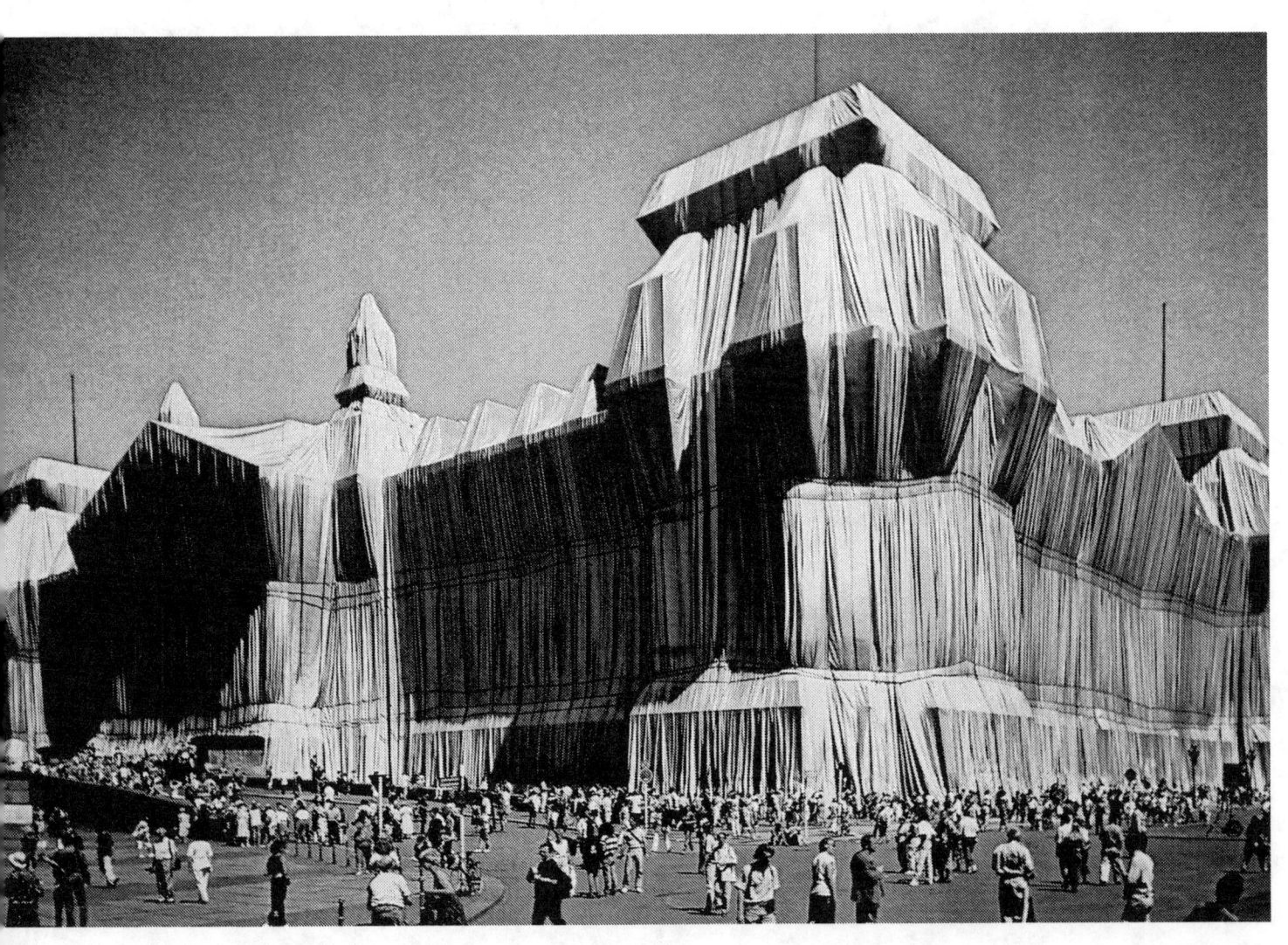

みどりいろの　おくがいとそうよう　エナメ

れんがのかべに　まかれた　一クォートの

ONE QUART EXTERIOR GREEN INDUSTRIAL ENAMEL THROWN ON A BR

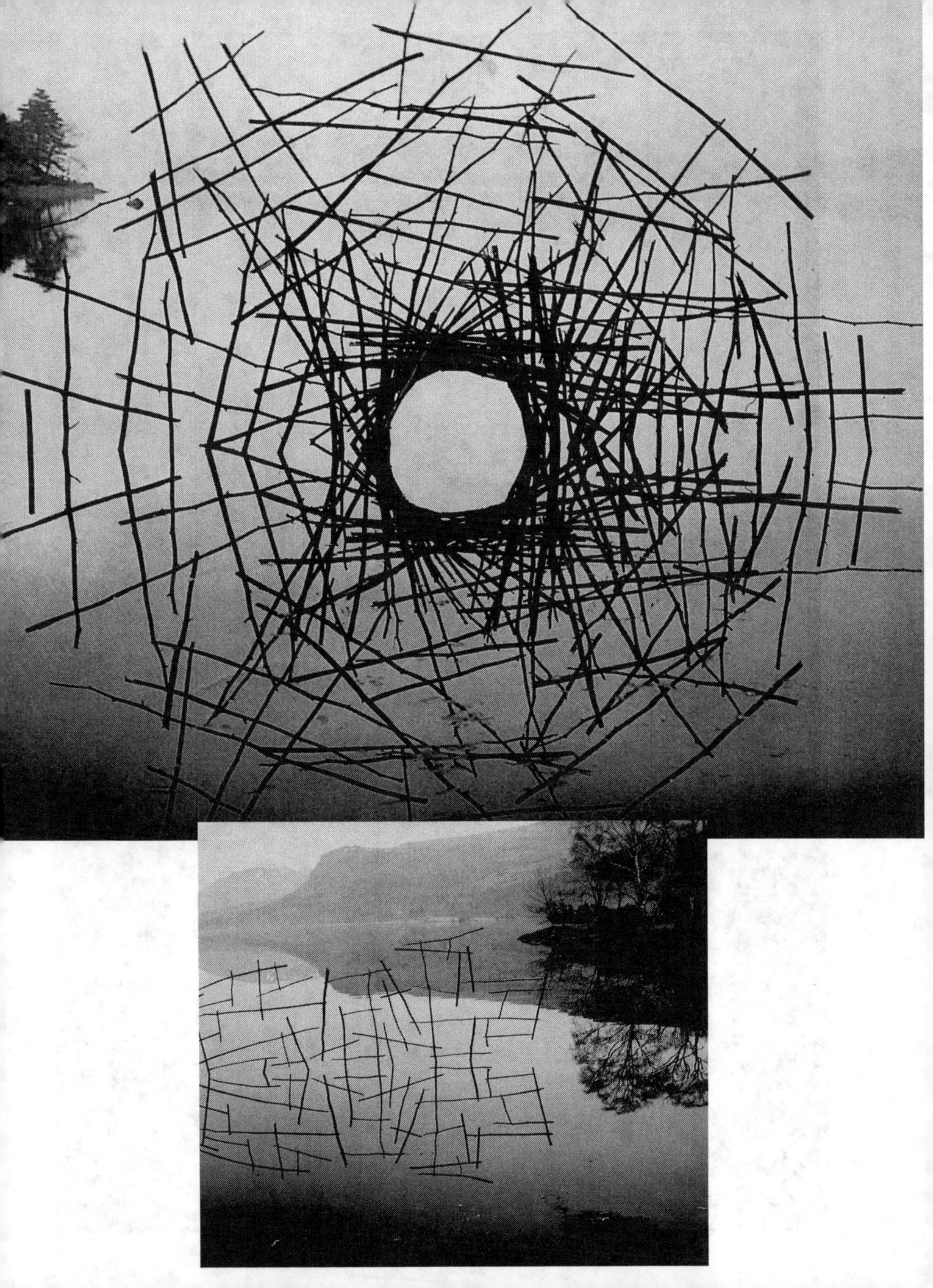

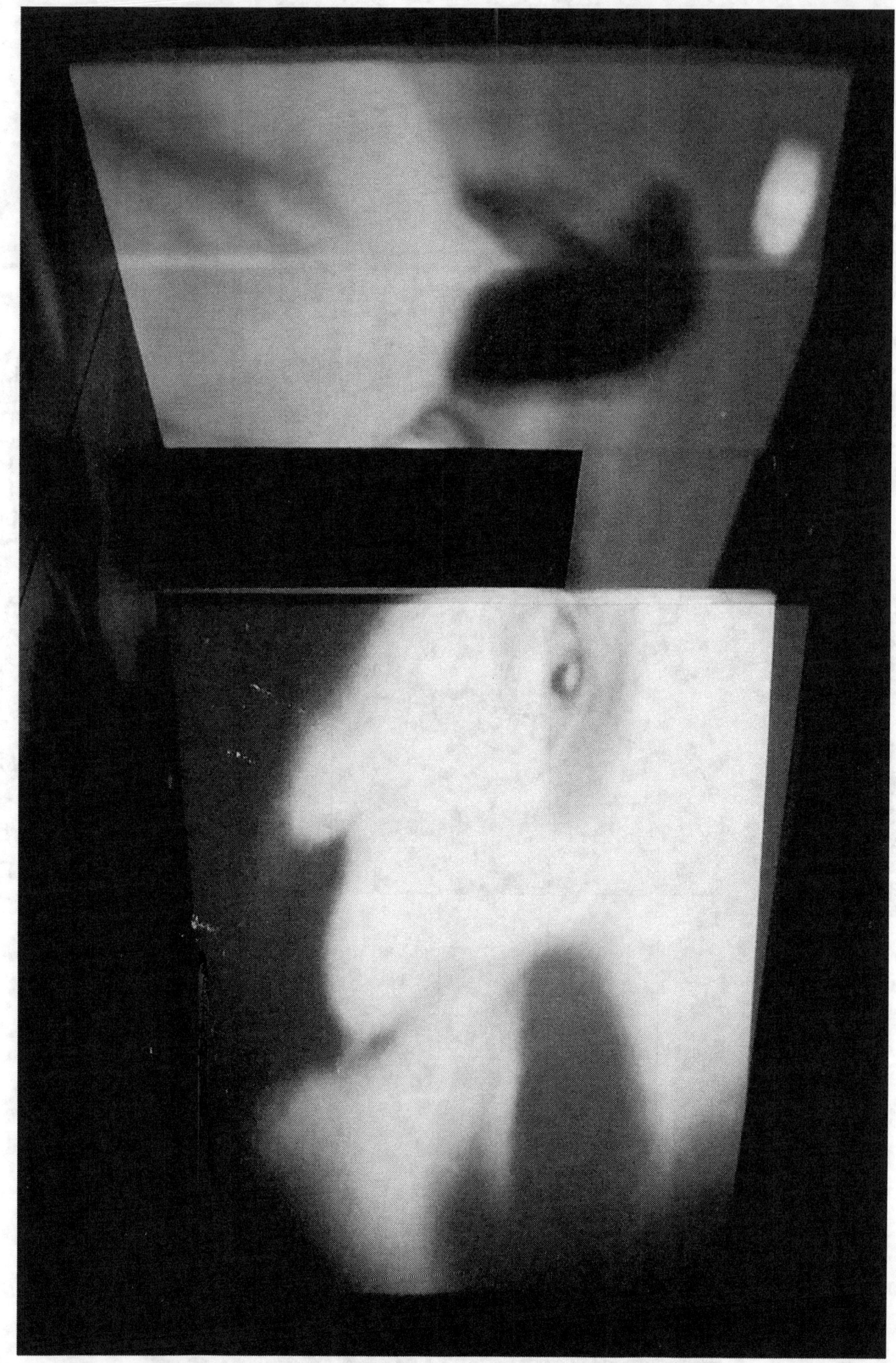

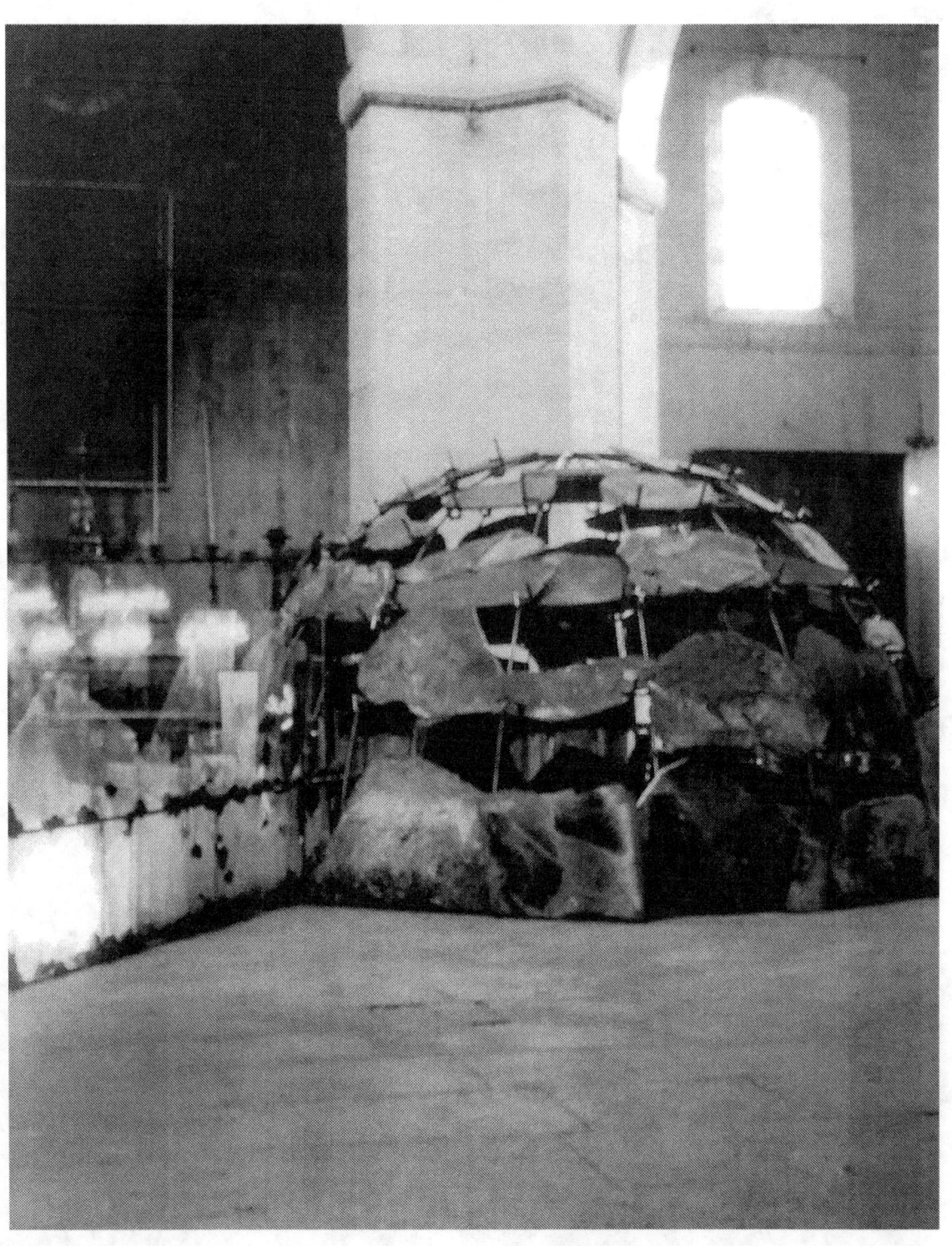

INSTALLATION ART IN CLOSE-UP

JEFF KOONS: *DOG*

One of the most famous of contemporary sculptures using living flowers was Jeff Koons' giant dog (*Puppy*, 1992), constructed in Arolsen with 17,000 flowers, and standing 11.5 metres tall. 'I decided I wanted to make an image that communicated warmth and love to people. A very spiritual piece. It just came to me to make the *Puppy* out of live flowers'.[1] Although Koons' art was known for its postmodern, camp, trashy chic, Koons likened the interior of the *Puppy* to a church: 'I wanted the piece to deal with the human condition, and this condition in relation to God. I wanted it to be a contemporary Sacred Heart of Jesus' (ibid.).

1. J. Koons, in A. Muthesiues, ed. *Jeff Koons*, Cologne, 1992.

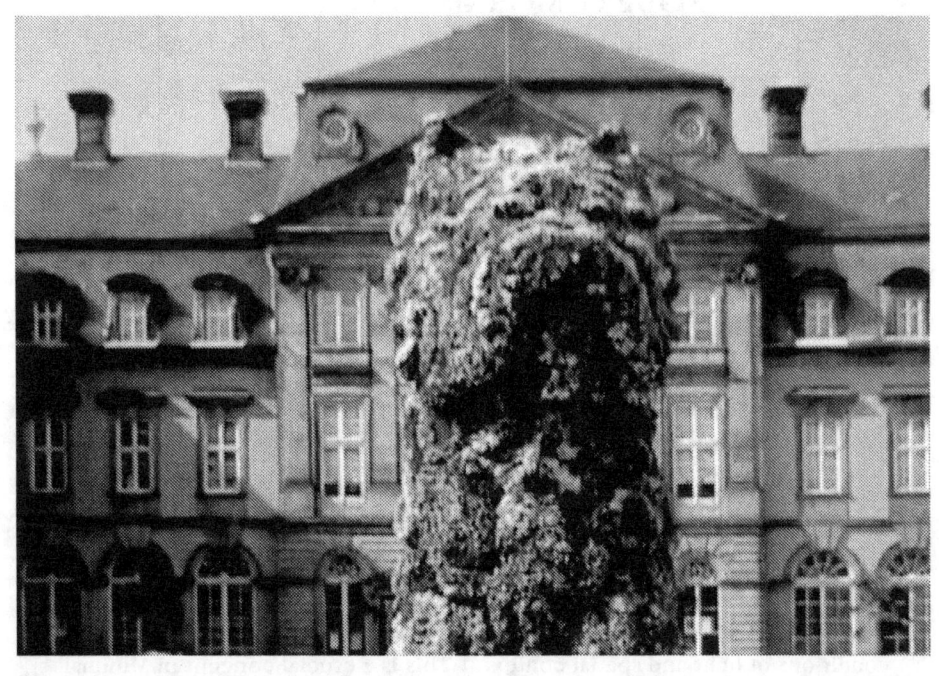

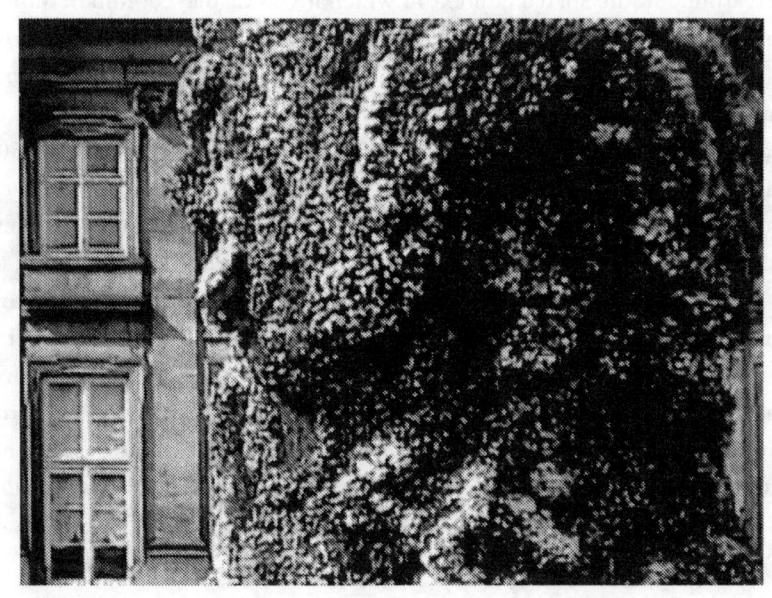

ROBERT MORRIS: *UNTITLED*

Robert Morris was one of the most eloquent theorists of Sixties and Minimal sculpture (along with Donald Judd and Carl Andre). Robert Morris had, like Donald Judd, begun in painting, but moved on to sculpture. Morris studied at Kansas City Art Institute, California School of Fine Arts and Hunter College, New York. In San Francisco in 1961 he worked with the dancer Anna Halprin. He was part of the Fluxus school, alongside Yoko Ono, Simone Forte, Walter de Maria and Henry Flynt. Morris wrote many artistic statements, the most famous probably being the articles published in *Artforum* entitled "Notes on Sculpture". For Robert Morris, one of the things that was new about 1960s sculpture was the object's relationship with the viewer. Before, Morris argued, the viewer related to the object as something separate; the new æsthetic put the viewer into the same space as the object. 'One is more aware than before that he himself is establishing relationships as he apprehends the object from various positions and under varying conditions of light and spatial context.'[1] This is a crucial concept in Minimal art, which is nearly always viewed in an object-viewer continuous space. Robert Morris's concept of 'objecthood' was central to his notion of sculpture. 'Morris wants to achieve presence through objecthood, which requires a certain largeness of scale, rather than through size alone' wrote Michael Fried (1967). Just as important as the object itself was the sense of space around it, the spatial context in which it was displayed. Robert Morris wanted to emphasize that 'things are in a space with oneself', rather than the notion that 'one is in a space surrounded by things' (ib., 127). The whole context of the object in its space ('the entire situation') was important to Morris's notion of the new sculpture. One might say the new, 1960s sculpture, like land art, was about the 'thing in itself', a notion borrowed from Existentialism, but also about the 'thing in its space'. Although Robert Morris denied being an 'environmental' artist, the context was important to his art.[2] For one critic, Morris's sculpture 'redirect[s] the entire environmental experience'.[3] Referring to Donald Judd's "Specific Objects" article, Robert Morris said he did not separate the two, he did not think that something must be either an object or an environment.[4] As he moved towards Postminimalism, Morris advocated doing away with a figure-ground relationship; instead, heterogeneous 'stuff' should be used, an 'accumulation of things or stuff' ("Notes on Sculpture", 4, 51).

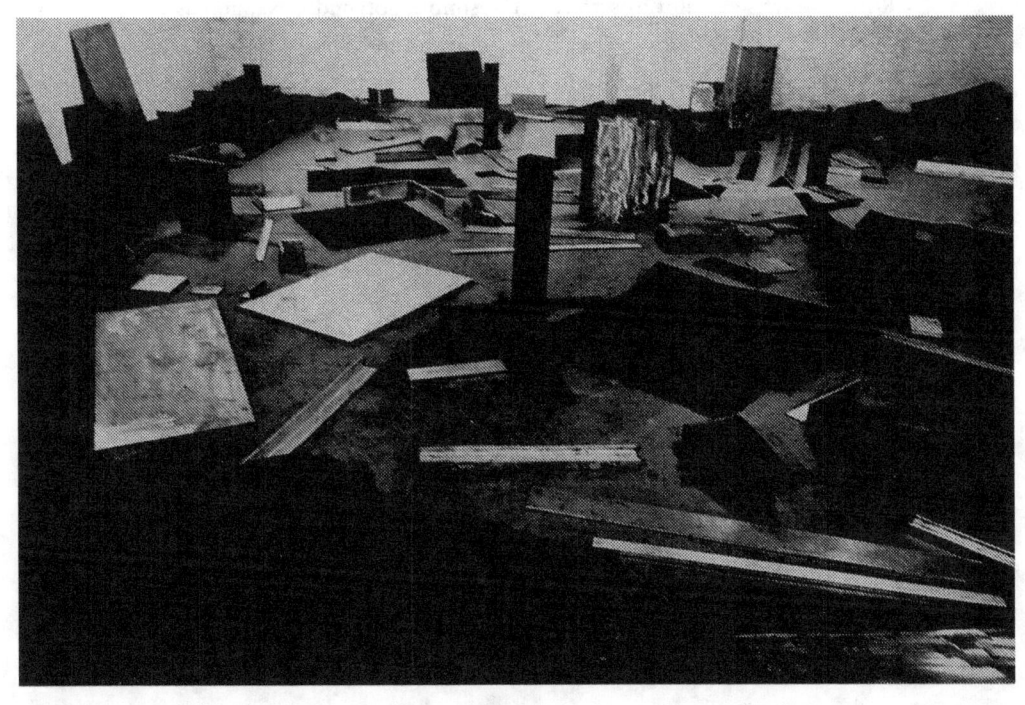

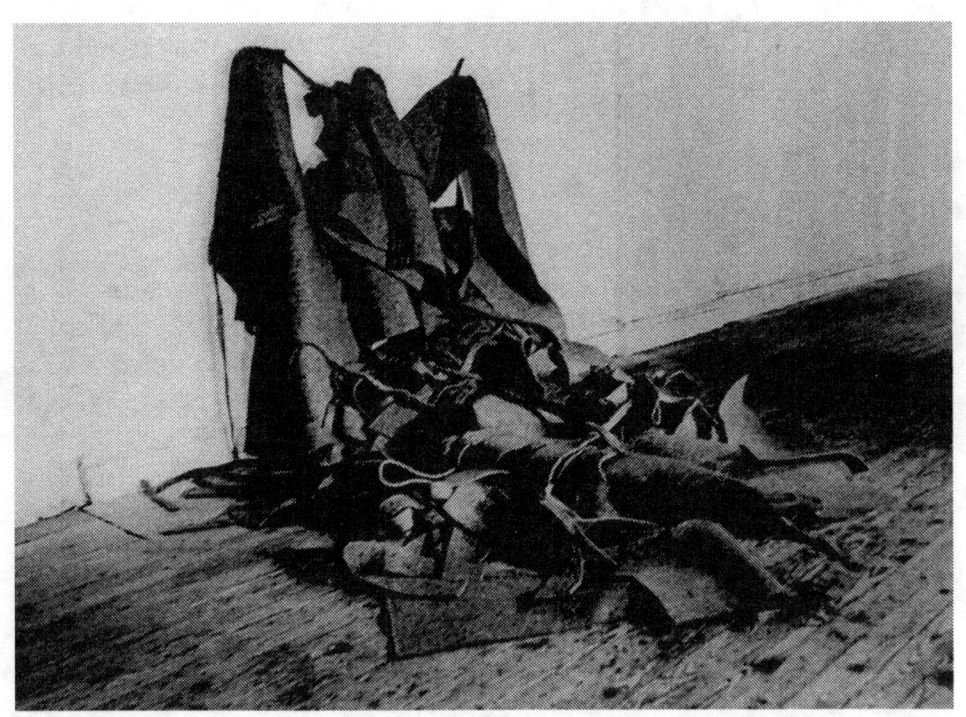

Robert Morris's sculptures were often simple polyhedrons, such as cubes, circles, ovals and beams. They were modular and serial. 'Unitary Objects' he termed them, recalling Judd's 'Specific Objects'. They appeared to be 'simple'; as with Donald Judd's sculptures, Morris's did not seem to be hiding anything. Yet just because they appeared 'simple' did not mean that their effects were simple: 'simplicity of shape does not necessarily equate with simplicity of experience' wrote Morris,[5] and Minimal art proved him right. Morris's art was by turns ironic, blank, unambiguously clear and frustratingly amorphous. Morris's *Battered Cubes* (1965/ 88, Margo Leaven Gallery, Los Angeles) were four boxes of painted steel that were set near each other. Each unit had a gently sloping outside face. His Unitary Objects were made in materials such as wood, concrete, wire mesh, aluminium and granite. Morris also made felt works which could not be arranged the same each time, which determinedly refused to be locked into the Minimalist æsthetic of straight edges and regularity. The felt was partly haphazard, relying on gravity, but it was also stiff enough to stay roughly where it was put. It was not final, but malleable.

1. R. Morris, quoted in M. Fried, 1967, in G. Battock, 1968, 126.
2. Friedman, 1966, 23.
3. D. Factor, 1966, 13.
4. In M. Compton, 1971, 16.
5. In D. Wheeler, 221.

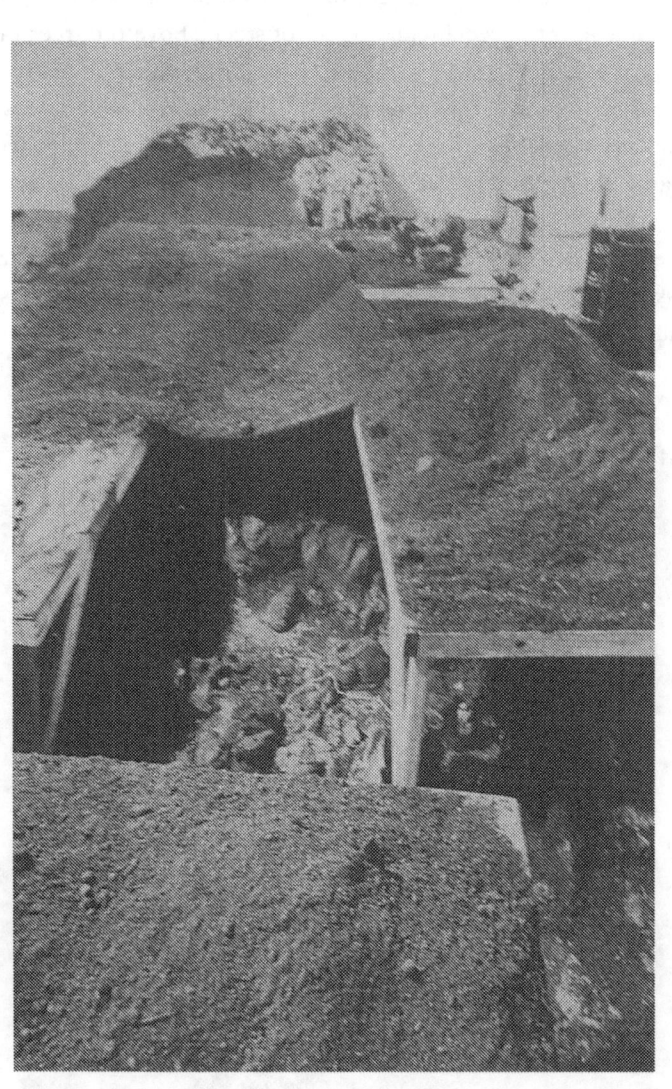

ROBERT MORRIS: *UNTITLED*

Robert Morris's *Untitled* (1968) was a pile of cotton waste and mirrors. The mirrors were seen sticking up in the cotton. An *Untitled* of 1969 comprised of little trees in soil set in rectangular boxes of steel; above the trees hung fluorescent 'grow' lamps. These works interfused the human or 'artificial' (the lamps and mirrors) with the 'natural' or organic (the cotton and trees). A number of Robert Morris's works were what appeared to be piles of concrete and wool, large oblong blocks piled up on top of each other. Robert Morris produced both indoor and outdoor versions of these sprawls of oblong blocks. Sometimes they looked like the stacks of timber at a wood merchants on the outskirts of a town, or the detritus that's thrown into heaps beside sidings at railway stations.

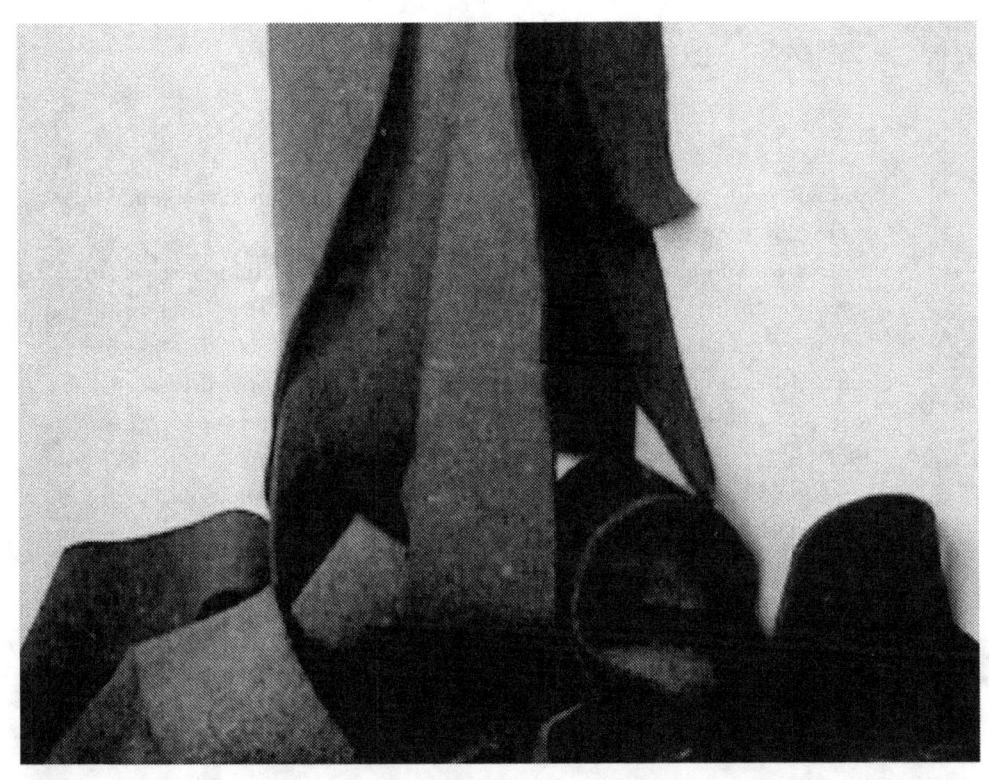

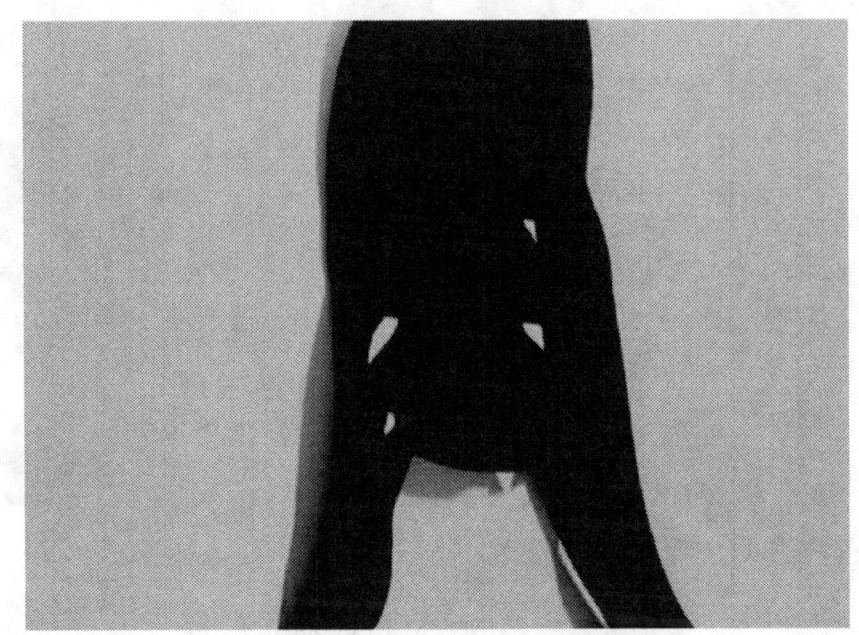

ROBERT MORRIS: *STEAM PIECE*

Among Robert Morris's stranger concepts was his 'mobile' mausoleum: in an aluminium tunnel 3 miles long a coffin made from iron and suspended from pulleys would be moved intermittently. An attendant with a magnet would shift the coffin using a magnet. By the entrance to the tube would be swooning maidens in marble, carved in the style of Canova.[1] 'If something is still capable of moving, is it dead?' Morris wondered.[2] Morris produced some works of a highly 'ephemeral' nature, such as his 'steam piece' (*Untitled*, 1968-69), which was made out of doors on a patch of grass. How the work turned out was dependent upon physicalities such as humidity, air pressure, wind speed and direction, and temperature. Clouds of steam drifted over the grass. British artist Rose Finn-Kelcey has also produced a steam work: her *Untitled* (1992, Chisenhalle Gallery, London) comprised of water placed on a sheet metal base, with an extractor hood hung above it. In between the two was a cloud of steam, made dramatic by the lighting.

1. B. Rose, 1965.
2. D. Sylvester, 1996, 243.

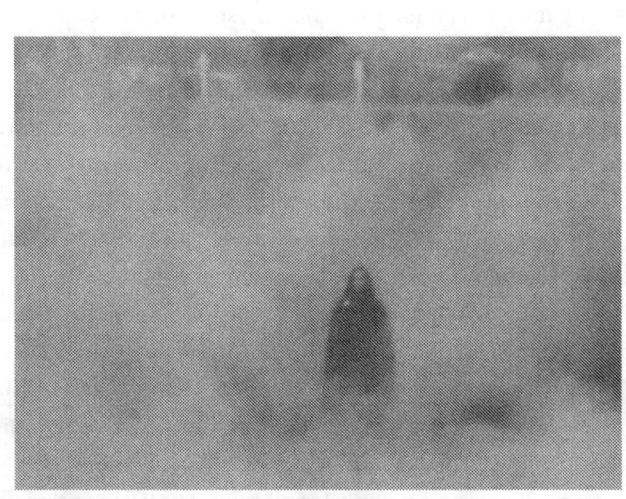

JAMES TURRELL: *RODEN CRATER PROJECT*

Contemporary artists, of all kinds, have made massive art. David Smith's *Wagon I* and his *Cubi* sculptures are huge, heavy, chunky, truly colossal pieces which dominate their surroundings. Donald Judd wrote: '[t]his scale is one of the most important developments in twentieth century art'.[1] One of the largest earthwork projects is James Turrell's *Roden Crater Project,* a series of tunnels and chambers in an Arizonan extinct volcano, begun in 1974 and funded by the Dia Foundation. The first stage of Turrell's project, which involved bulldozing 200,000 cubic yards of earth from the volcano's rim, 'so as to shape the sky'. Turrell also planned tunnels, pools and viewing chambers. Turrell said '[m]y art is made for one person. I like the solitary experience. Standing alone at night, perceiving the Roden Crater and the moon and stars, you really feel the vastness of the universe and yourself entering into it'.[2] There were spaces at Roden Crater where clouds were projected onto the floor during the day, which at night were related to the procession of equinoxes. Richard Long's art is not monolithic in scale, usually: but his works can stretch over many miles, far longer than even Christo's fences. The Abstract Expressionists, such as Helen Franken-thaler, Mark Rothko, Franz Kline and Barnett Newman, produced huge paintings, which swallow up the spectator when s/he moves close to them. One can get up close to a Morris Louis and be enveloped by it. Similarly, postwar sculptors have made massive works. Artists such as Christo made pieces that were 24 miles long. Even medium-sized pieces, such as Donald Judd's wooden boxes, are sometimes seen as monumental. A critic on *The New York Times* called Judd's 1977 installation at the Heiner Friedrich Gallery a 'majestic and finely measured presence'.[3]

1. *Complete Writings*, 200f.
2. In A. Benjamin, 47.
3. "Donald Judd", *The New York Times*, 1 Apl, 1977, C20.

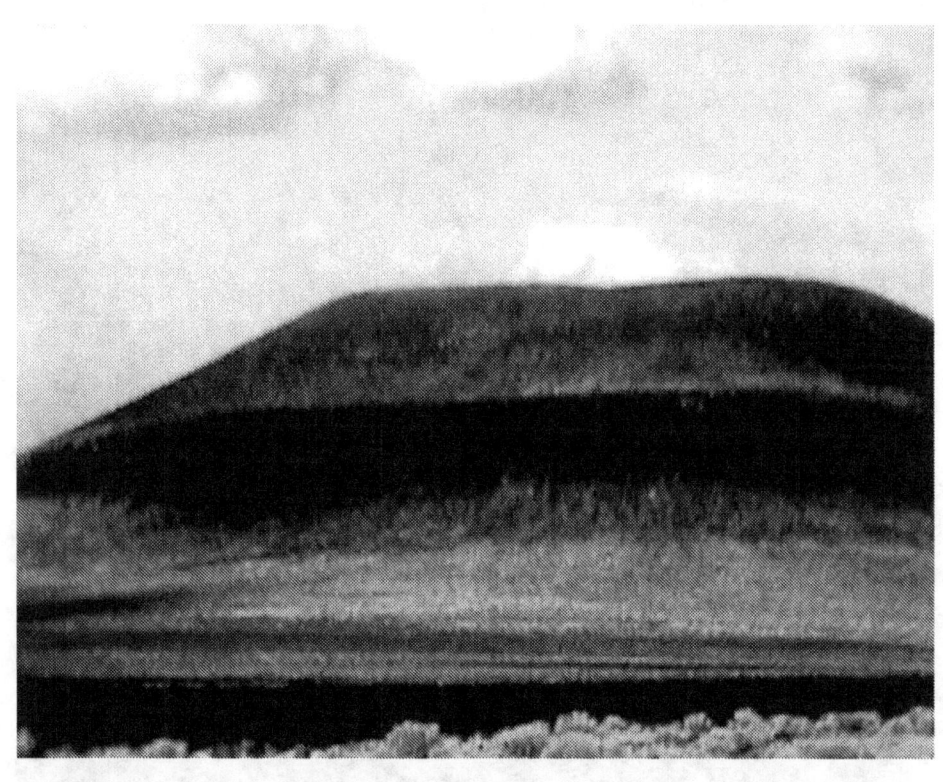

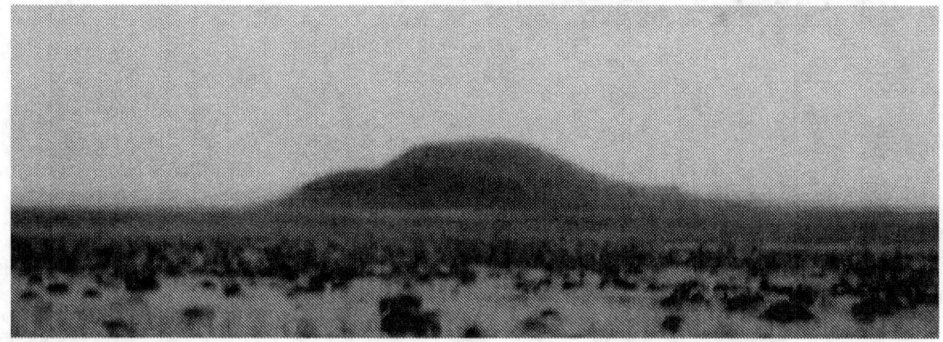

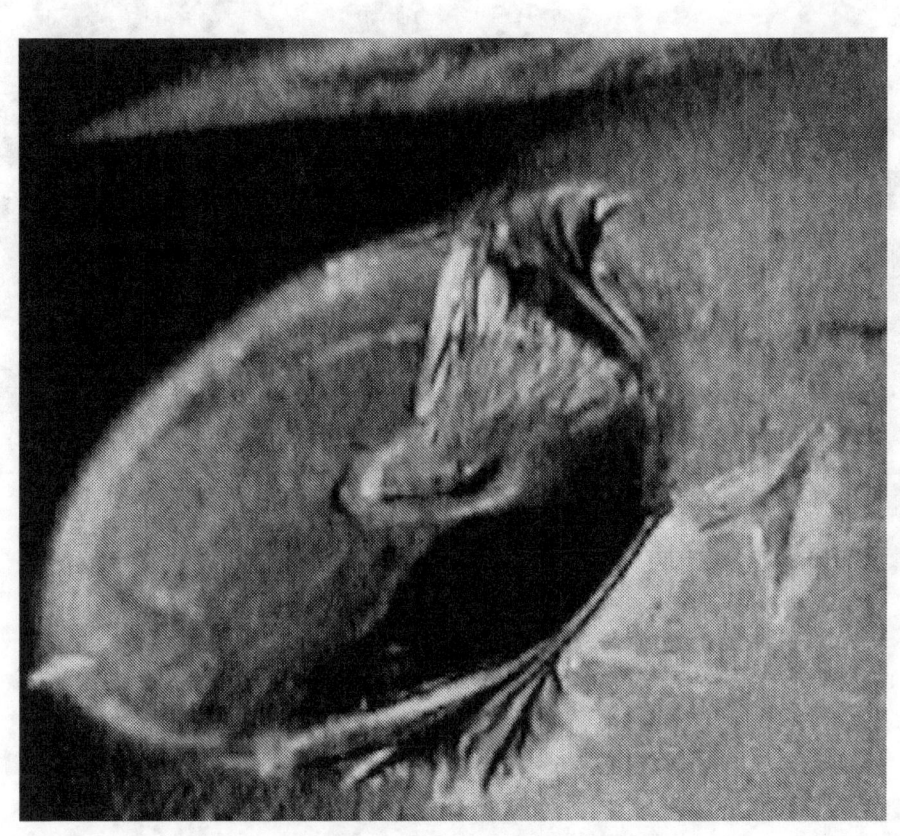

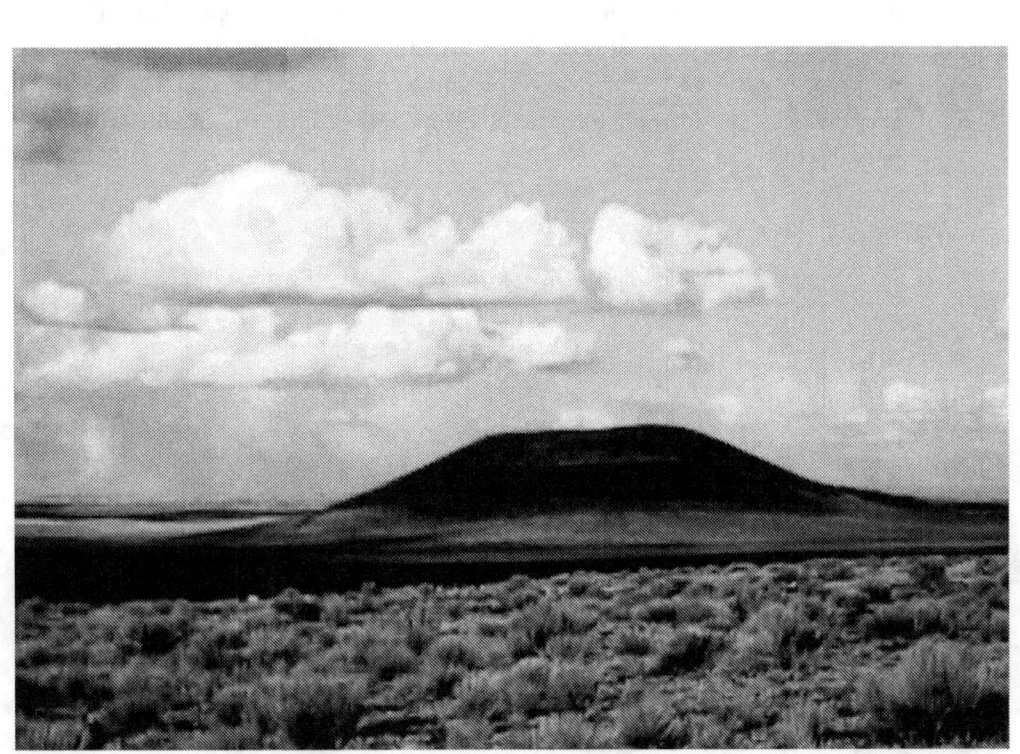

JAMES TURRELLL: *ROOM*

As well as his famous *Roden Crater Project*, James Turrell also made smaller works with light and space, such as *Porter Powell* (1967). In London in 1991, he created an empty blue room (*Rayzor*), using a mix of artificial and natural light. An ealier work, *Skyspace I* (1972), had a square section of the roof open to the sky. Turrell said he was influenced by painters such as Rothko, Monet and Cézanne, who explored light. Turrell said (in 1987) that the goal was not to turn an experience into art, but 'to set up a situation to which I take you and let you see. It becomes your experience… not taking from nature as much as placing you in contact with it' (1995, 77).

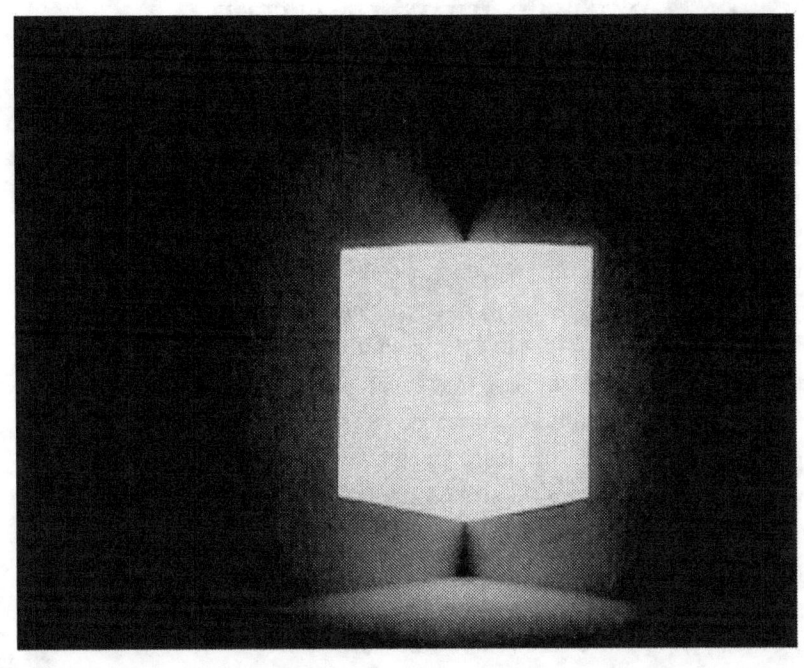

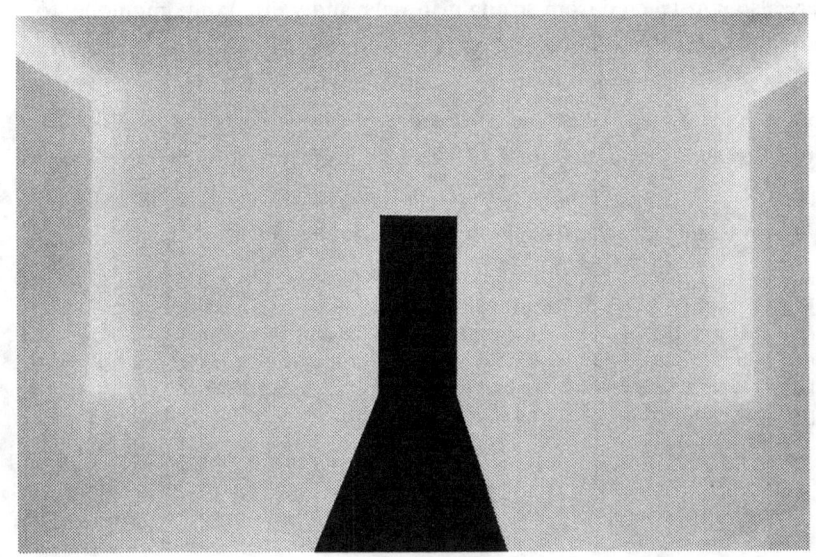

DONALD JUDD: *UNTITLED*

Donald Judd was one of the most learned of Minimal artists: he had a BA in philosophy and an MA in art history (at Columbia University). Judd's theorizing on art and Minimalism was influential in the Sixties (his famous articles included "Specific Objects" and "Local History"). Donald Judd's works at first seemed to be firmly fixed in a monotonous rectilinear view of the world. It seemed to be an arid, vacuous world of boxes and more boxes. Looking closer, one saw that there was a great sense of play and humour at work in the choice of materials (sometimes wood, sometimes steel, or glass, or copper, or lacquer, or Plexiglas). Sometimes Judd's serial boxes were open, and one could see inside them; at other times, Judd placed coloured Plexiglas over the end, and the interior was hidden or vaguely discernible; sometimes the boxes were sprayed with Harley Davidson motorbike lacquer and enamel, so they'd be bright green, or red. Using Plexiglas meant the colours would deepen across the row of boxes. The emphasis on hollowness meant there was nothing to hide; there was mystery, but no deliberate mystification on the part of the artist. Seemingly hollow and fragile, with their thin walls, Donald Judd's 'specific objects' were also constructed from strong materials, and were fixed, immobile, to the wall. The wall-mounted objects did not require a base; they seemed to float in space. They were unitary, modular: there was no single unit that stood out from the others. The gaps between each object was also regular. Hierarchy was avoided. There was in fact a lot going in Judd's works. Robert Hughes, in *American Visions*, defined Judd's work as the product of 'esthetic fanaticism' and uncompromising reductionism:

> Judd was the doyen of "high" Minimalism: inorganic materials (steel, tin, colored plastic, aluminium), blatantly artificial colors (Harley-Davidson red lacquer was a particular favourite), geometric rigidity (but without the Utopian overtones of earlier geometric abstraction), industrial process, and, in its refusal of touch, an address to the eye alone. (1997, 563-4)

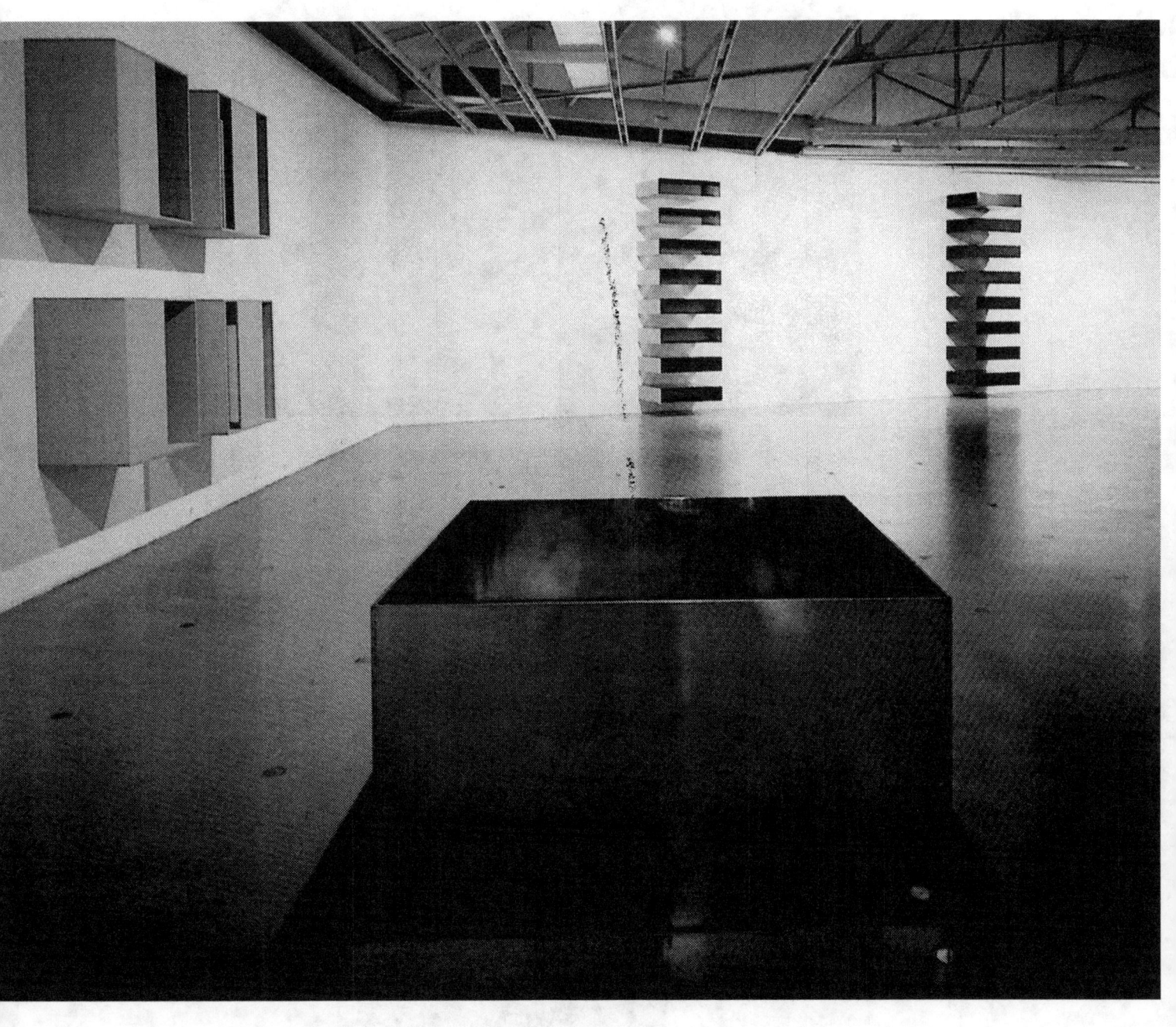

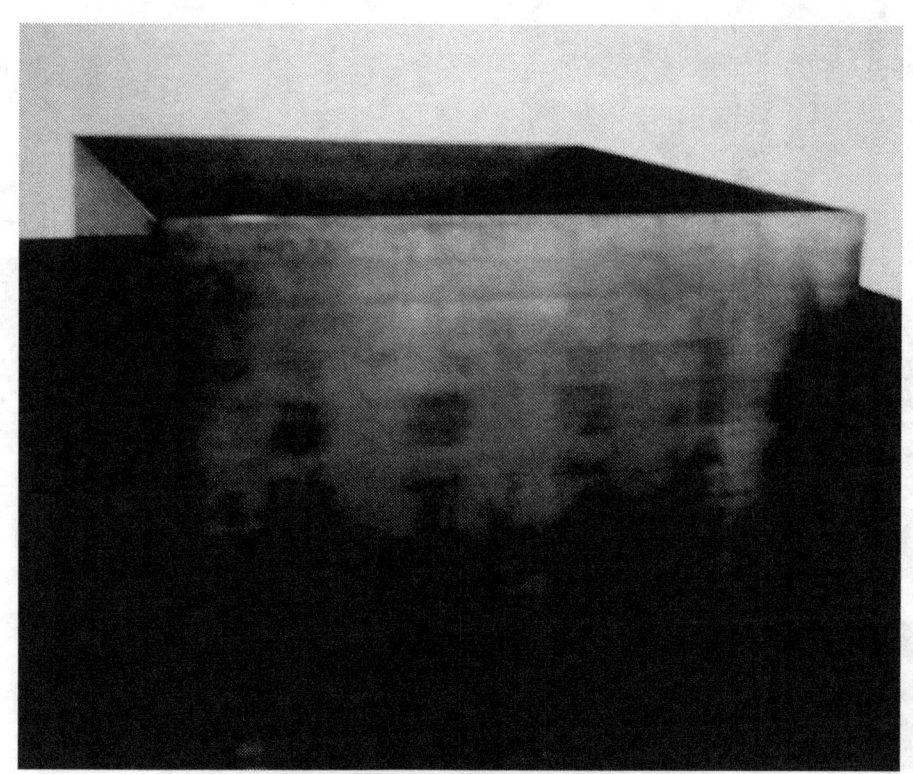

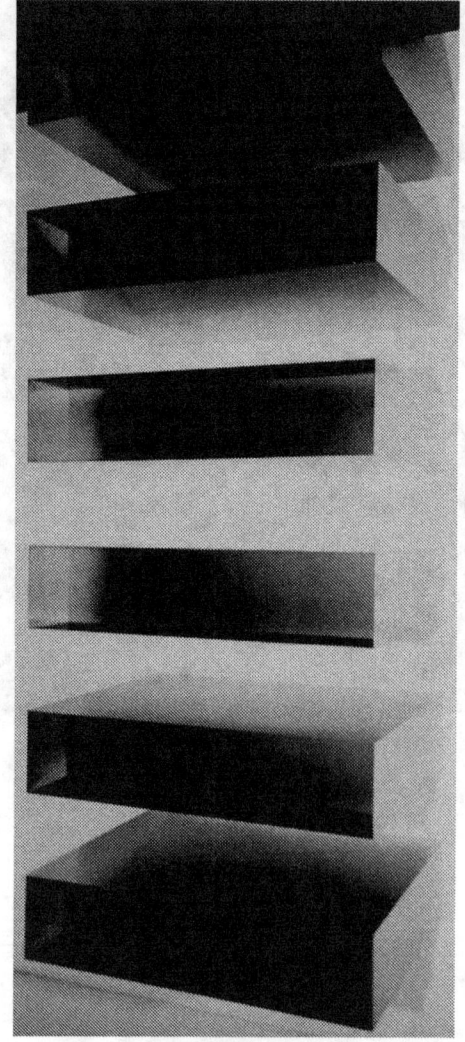

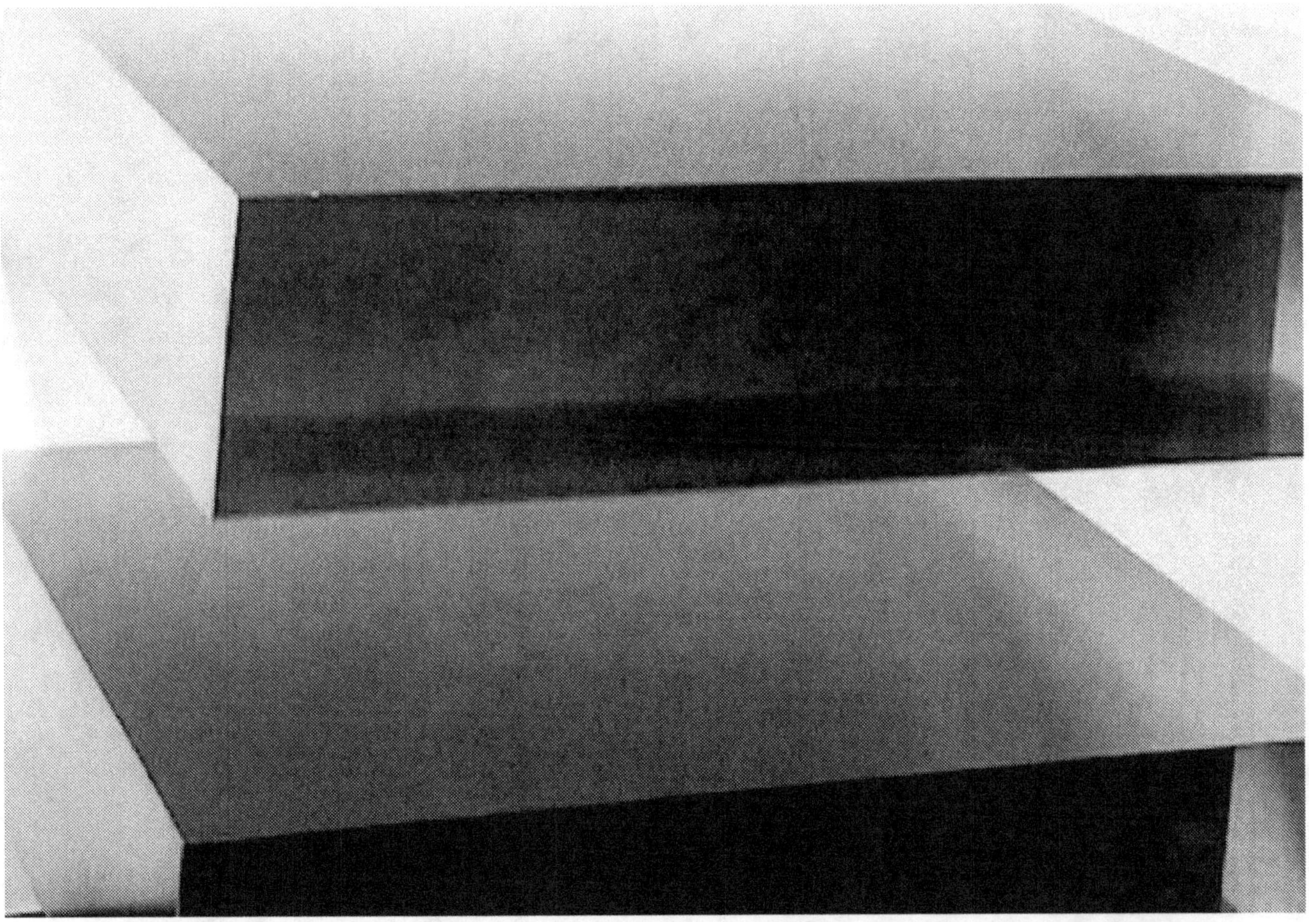

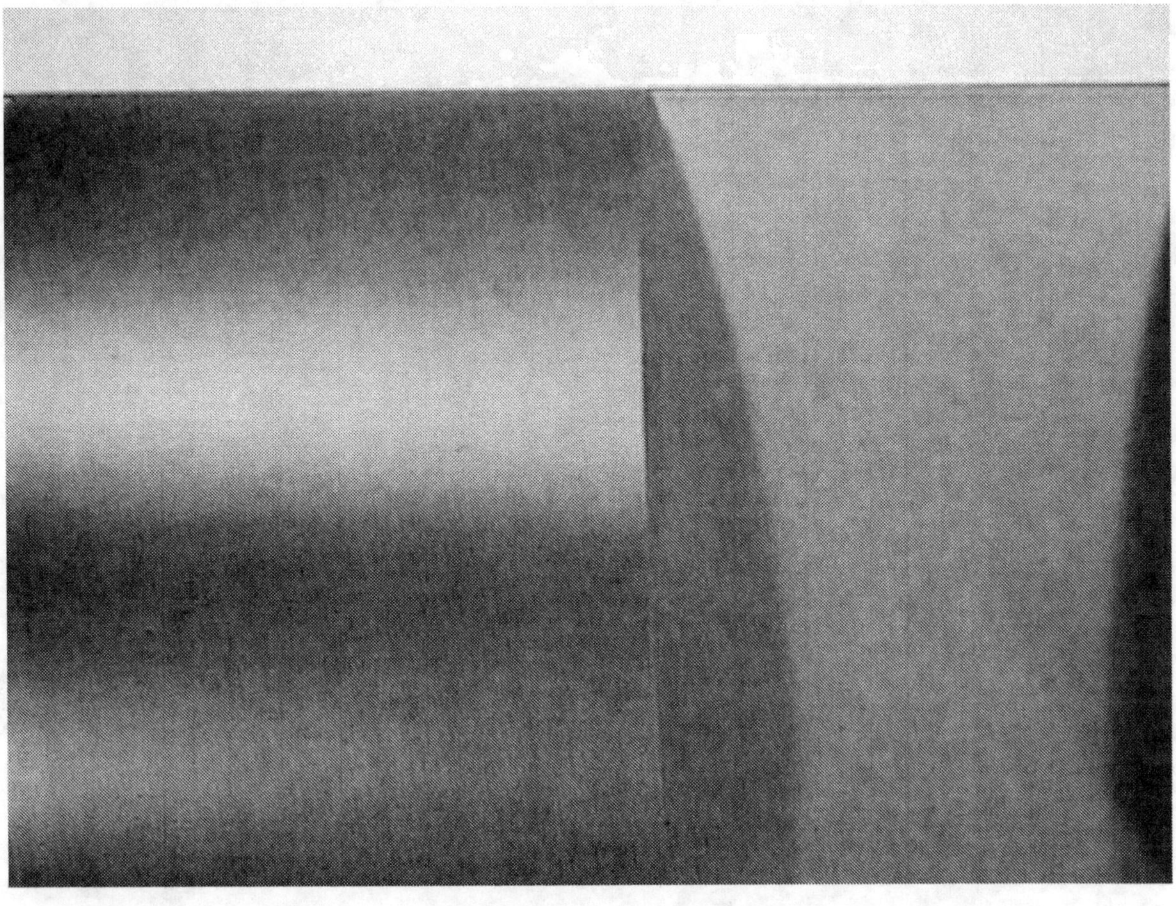

DONALD JUDD: *UNTITLED (MARFA)*

Many of Donald Judd's best Minimal works are housed in his permanent installation in Marfa, Texas. Marfa was a former military base (Fort Russell), which Judd redesigned. He installed his sculptures in the artillery sheds and the fields, as well as creating exhibition spaces for other artists' work. He designed a huge amount of furniture, fittings, structures and interiors at the Chinati Foundation, including tables, desks, beds, chairs, pergolas, pools, yards, walls, a library, a labyrinth of adobe walls, and the artists' compound.

One of the main works at Marfa is the epic *Untitled* (1980-86), one hundred large (41 x 51 x 72 inch) mill-aluminium boxes, each one apparently the same, yet each one different (some were open at the side, some on top; many had the signature Judd diagonal and right angle panels). The field of boxes was funded by the Dia Art Foundation, and made by the Lippincott Foundry, New Haven. The 1981 *Untitled* was a row of enormous hollow concrete boxes, separated into groups, and installed in the fields near the artillery sheds. Each module was eight feet high, with some eight feet wide and some 16 feet wide. This was Juddian Minimal box permutations on a grand scale.

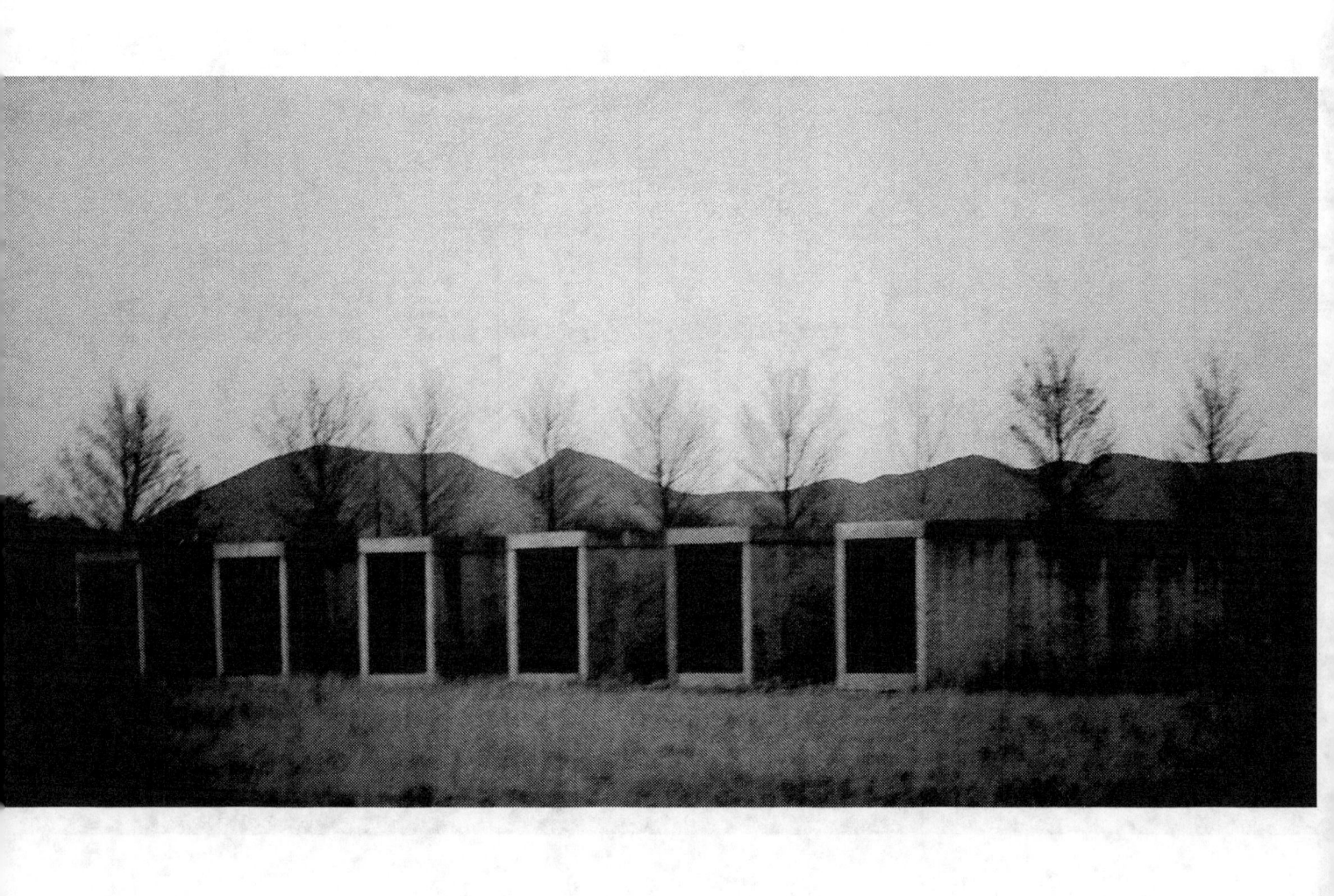

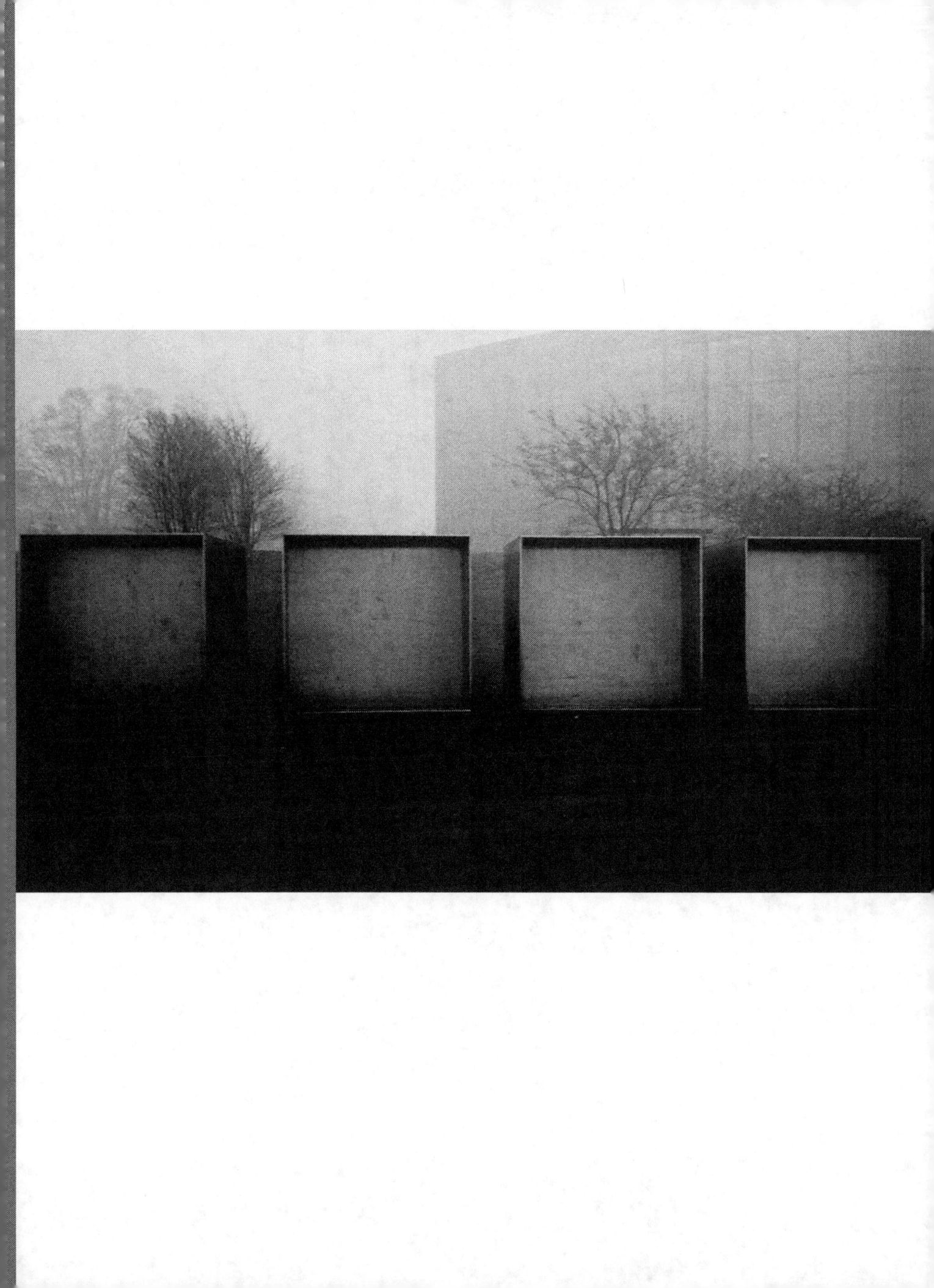

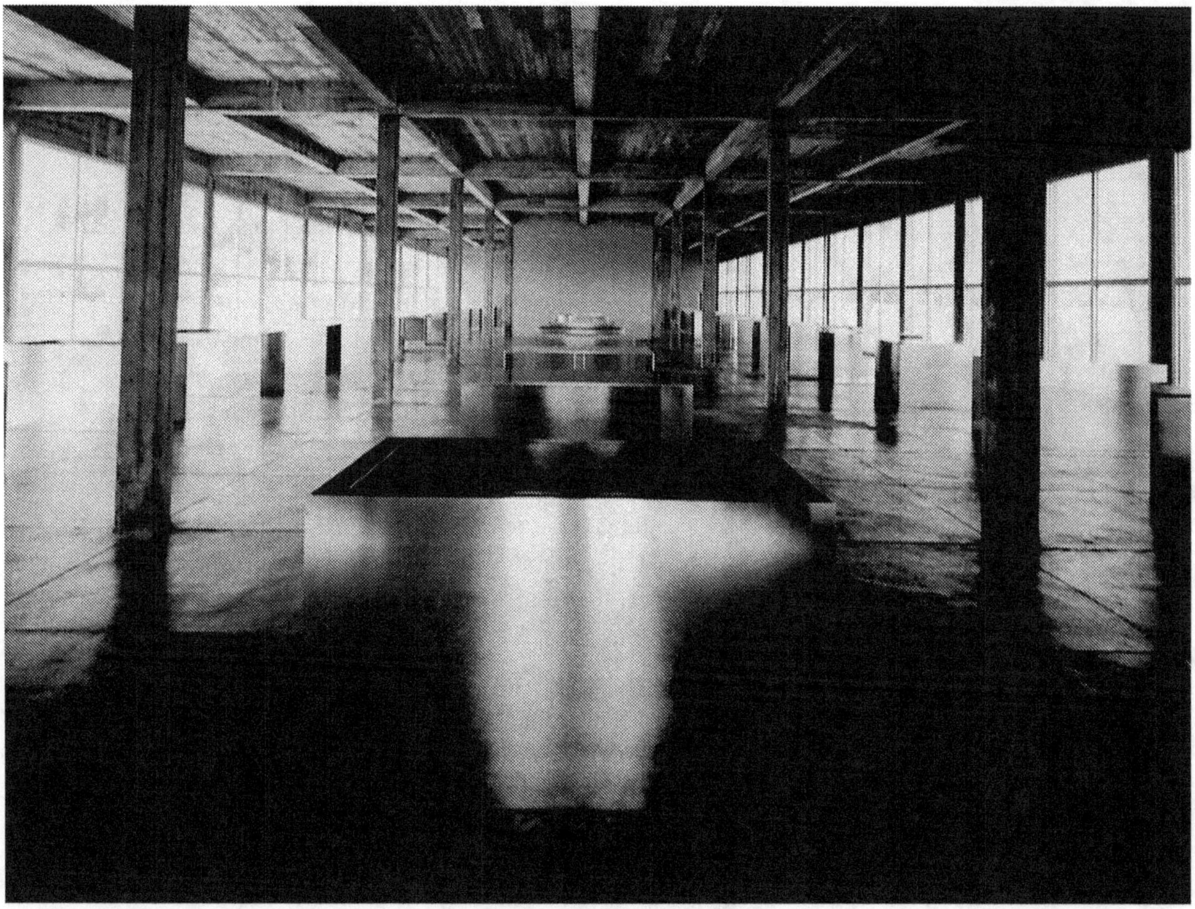

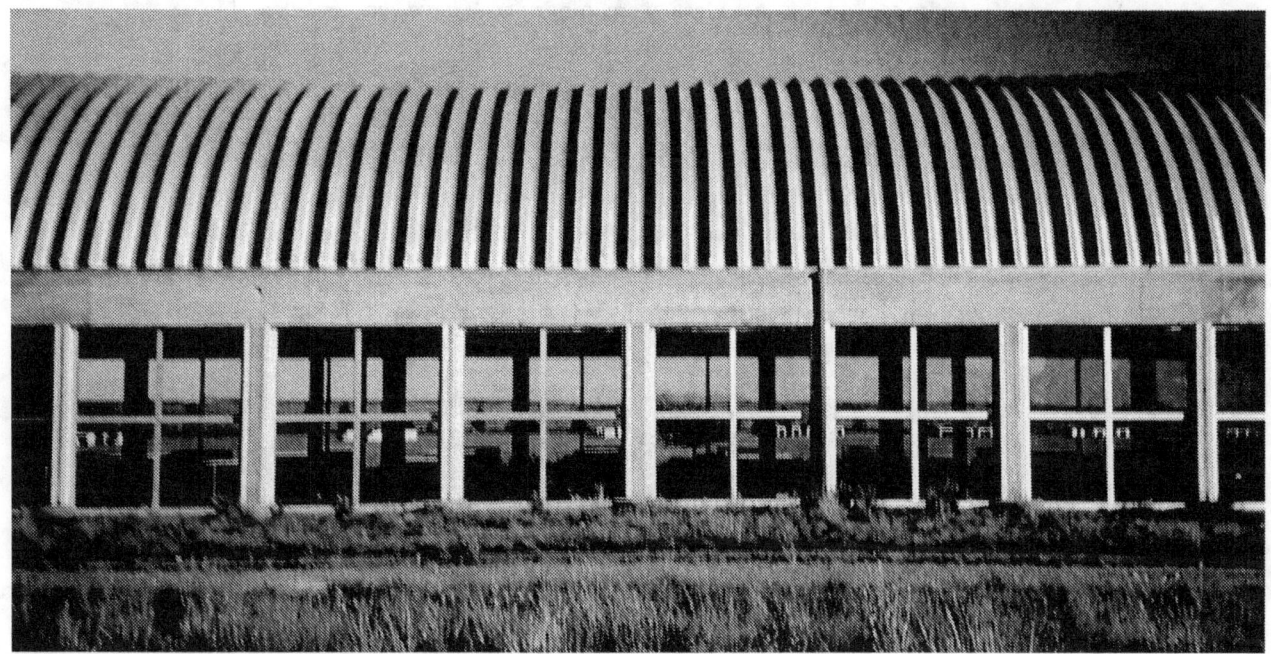

CARL ANDRE: *EQUIVALENT VIII*

Carl Andre's biography is often cited in accounts of his art. For a time Andre worked in Frank Stella's studio in Manhattan (they were students together at Andover). Andre worked on the railways, as a freight conductor and brakeman (in Newark, at the Pennsylvania Railroad) from 1960-64, and this is used to explain Carl Andre's use of modules and units which join together to form a work. Like Sol LeWitt and Donald Judd, Carl Andre takes one unit and multiplies them until he had a line or a square. In Carl Andre's art, only one type of unit is used in each work: bricks, metal plates, blocks of wood. Each work is made for the specific site. Simple rectilinear patterns, such as grids, are favoured. No glues are used, but simple joints. Gravity is one of the key means of construction: i.e., objects are placed on the floor, or on top of each other. The question of height is thus rarely introduced in Andre's sculpture.[1]

Before working on the railroad, Carl Andre was 'a wood-carving disciple of Brancusi', carving chunks out of wood beams. For a long time the shadow of Brancusi lay over Carl Andre's art. When he came to explain his floor-standing works, such as *Lever*, a line of firebricks, he said he was 'putting Brancusi's *Endless Column* on the ground instead of in the sky... Most sculpture is priapic with the male organ in the air. In my work, Priapus is down on the floor. The engaged position is to run along the earth' (in ib., 104). Carl Andre found that it was better if the wood in his sculptures was not carved. Therefore he stopped trying to 'improve it in any way'.[2] Andre has spoken in interviews that the best creative work is erotic. In a 1970 radio discussion (with Lucy Lippard, Douglas Huebler, Dan Graham and Jan Dibbets on WBAI FM), Andre said desires, not ideas, were important. 'I have very few ideas, but I have strong desires.... I agree with Dr Guillotine that all ideas are the same except in execution... You can't cut off desires except painfully'.[3] Nature was also crucial: Andre said he disliked Conceptual art because it was cut of from nature (ibid.). He said his art 'has never been conceptual in any way' (1984). 'The materiality, the presence of the work of sculpture in the world, essentially independent of any single individual, but rather the residue of many individuals and the dream, the experience of the sea, the trees and the stones – I'm interested in that kind of essential thing'.[4] 'I will try to have in my work only what is necessary to it' Andre said (1984).

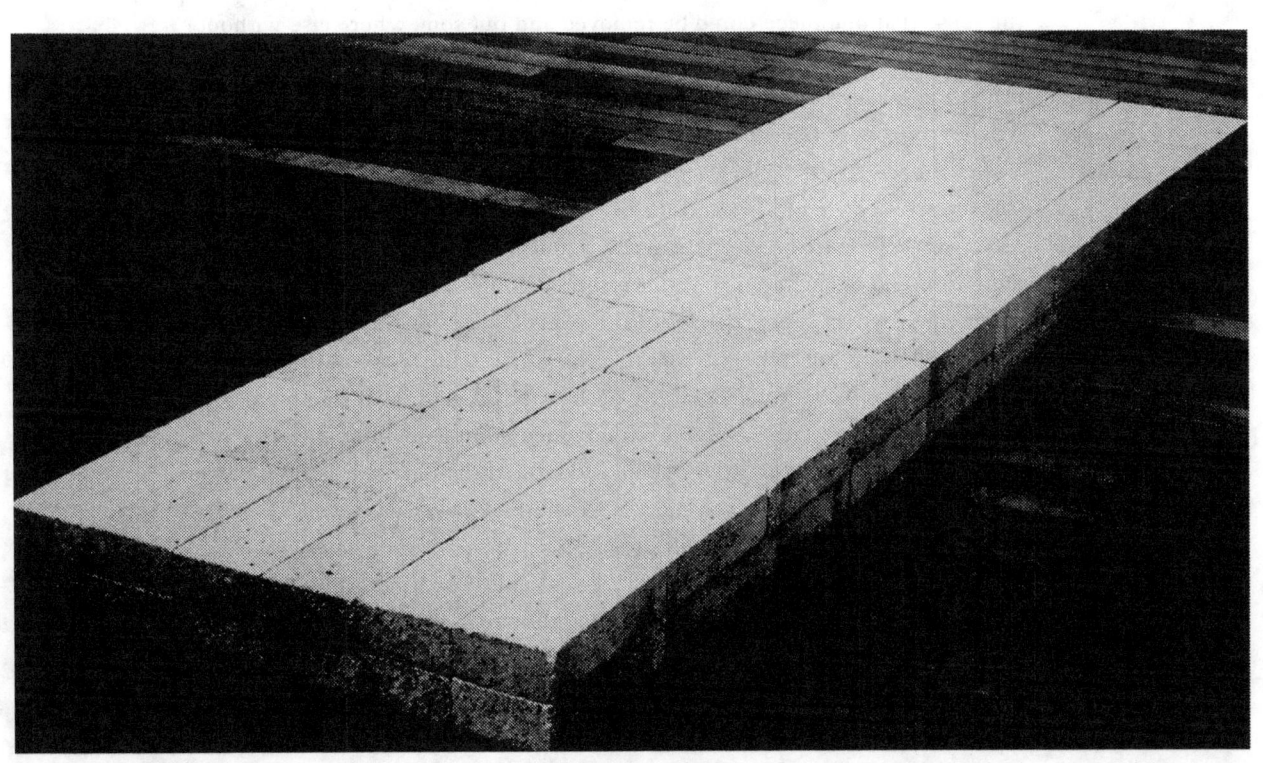

While he was in New Hampshire in 1965, canoeing on a lake, Andre (apparently) realized that sculpture ought to be level, like water. After this, most of his sculpture was floor-standing and flat. Spectators are invited to walk on his sculptures, offering a new relation with the work. Andre did not make boxes in the usual Minimal manner. Andre's sculptures were modular in the sense that one piece could be removed and put somewhere else without altering the whole (Andre's 'anaxial symmetry'). Lines of bricks or squares made from plates of metal were typical Andre works. Andre's use of materials was not 'poetic' or 'spiritual' in the usual sense of the word. In works such as *Cedar Piece* (1959, Basel), *Pyre* (1971, S. & C. Gilman), *Herm* (1976, Guggenheim), *Stile* (1975) and *Well*, which were made out of wood, Carl Andre was using materials as themselves, but 'not to evoke nature'.[5] Andre did not intend his materials to refer to other things, to be allusive in the art historical or lyrical sense. His Styrofoam planks were not alluding to marble, as some viewers mistakenly thought.[6] *Herm*, though, recalled the ancient Greek statues to the god Hermes, which were set on top of pillars beside roads. The phallic statues sometimes included genitals, which chimes with Andre's erotic view of art. Mel Bochner identified the characteristics of Carl Andre's art as being (1) strictly modular, (2) use of materials (wood, cement, bricks, steel) which spoke of 'density, rigidity, opacity, uniformity', (3) only one kind of unit is used in each work, (4) the typical geometric shape favoured by Andre is the grid, and sometimes the row or line.[7]

1. M. Bochner, "Serial Art Systems".
2. In Develing, 1969, 39.
3. L. Lippard, 1973, 157.
4. In L. Lippard, 1970, 7.
5. L. Lippard, 1965, 58.
6. C. Andre, 1970, 61.
7. 1967, in G. Battock, 1995, 94.

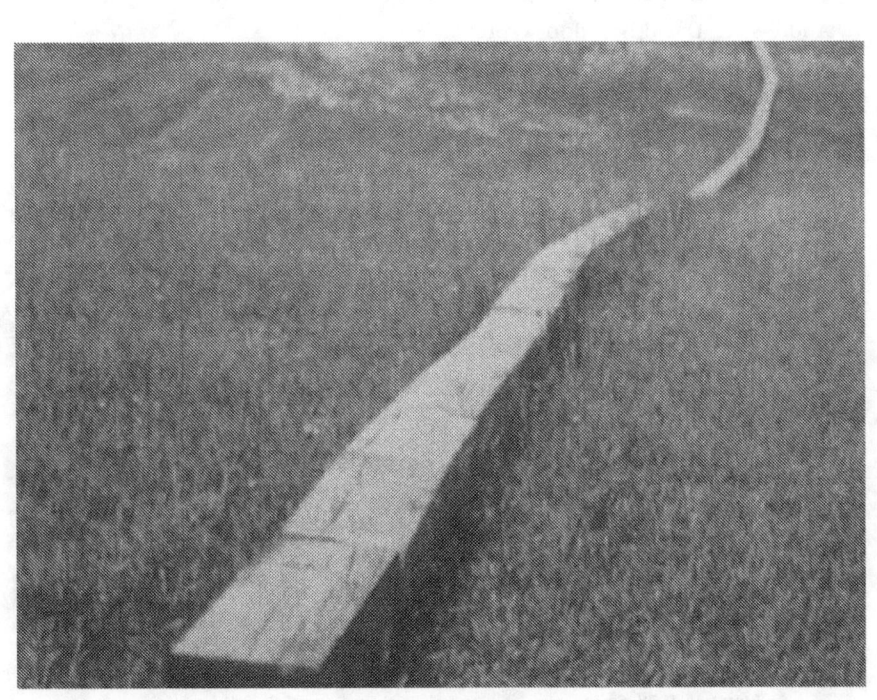

CARL ANDRE: *37 PIECES OF WORK*

The most sensual of Carl Andre's works are probably the metallic floor-pieces. Andre's floor-pieces bring out the tactile, visual nature of copper, aluminium and zinc. Andre's *37 Pieces of Work* is a good example of Minimal æsthetic permutations taken to extremes. It is a sculpture that is typical of Andre's art, David Bourdon wrote:

> Taken as a whole *37 Pieces of Work* consists of 1,296 plates, 216 each of aluminium, copper, steel, magnesium, lead and zinc. Each metal appears alone in individual six-foot square plains. Then alternates with another, checkerboard fashion, in every possible permutation. Since each of the six metals in the large piece was laid out in the alphabetical order of its chemical symbol, alternating successively with the others, there are two versions of each combination.[1]

37 Pieces of Work is a 432 inch wide 'floor-hugging' square, in which the colours of the copper, aluminium, lead, steel, zinc and magnesium is to the fore.

Many of Carl Andre's floor-pieces are similar (*Twelfth Copper Corner*, 1975, *Brooklyn Field*, 1966, Belgium, *8 Cuts*, 1967, Switzerland): the spectator is aware of the material first and foremost: the colour, mass, weight, size and texture of the metals.

1. D. Bourdon, 1978, 56.

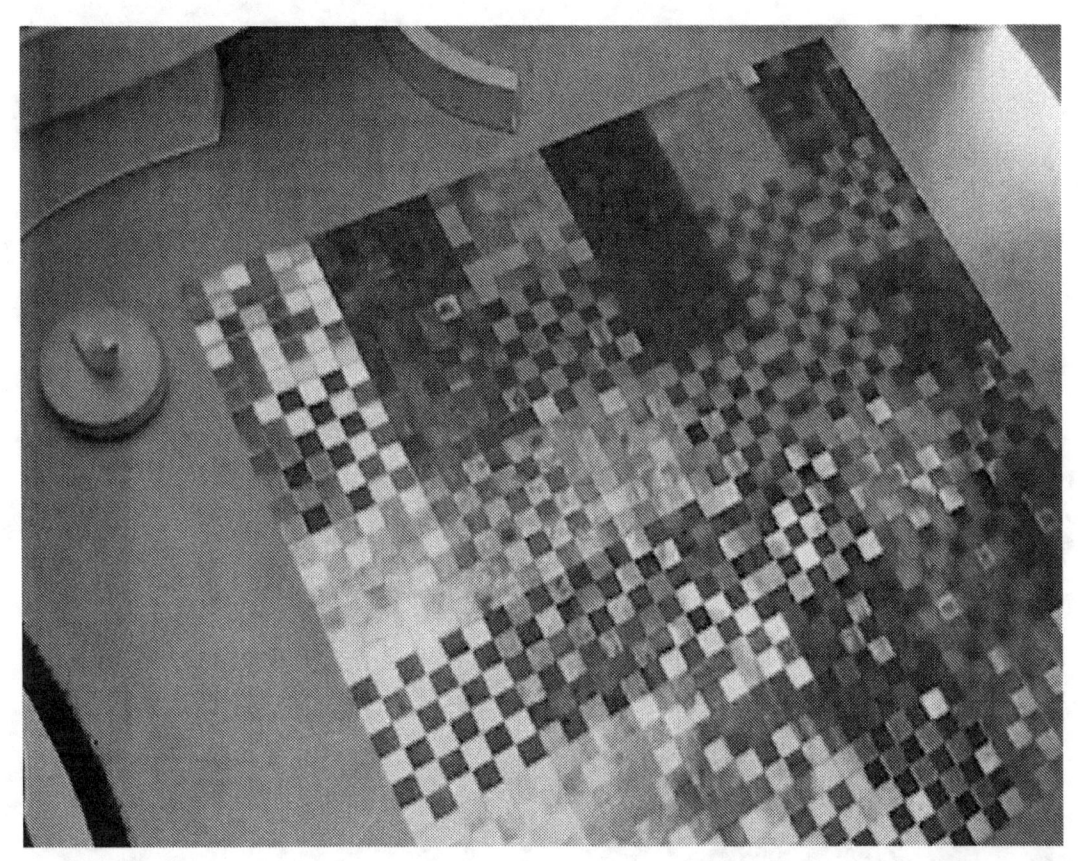

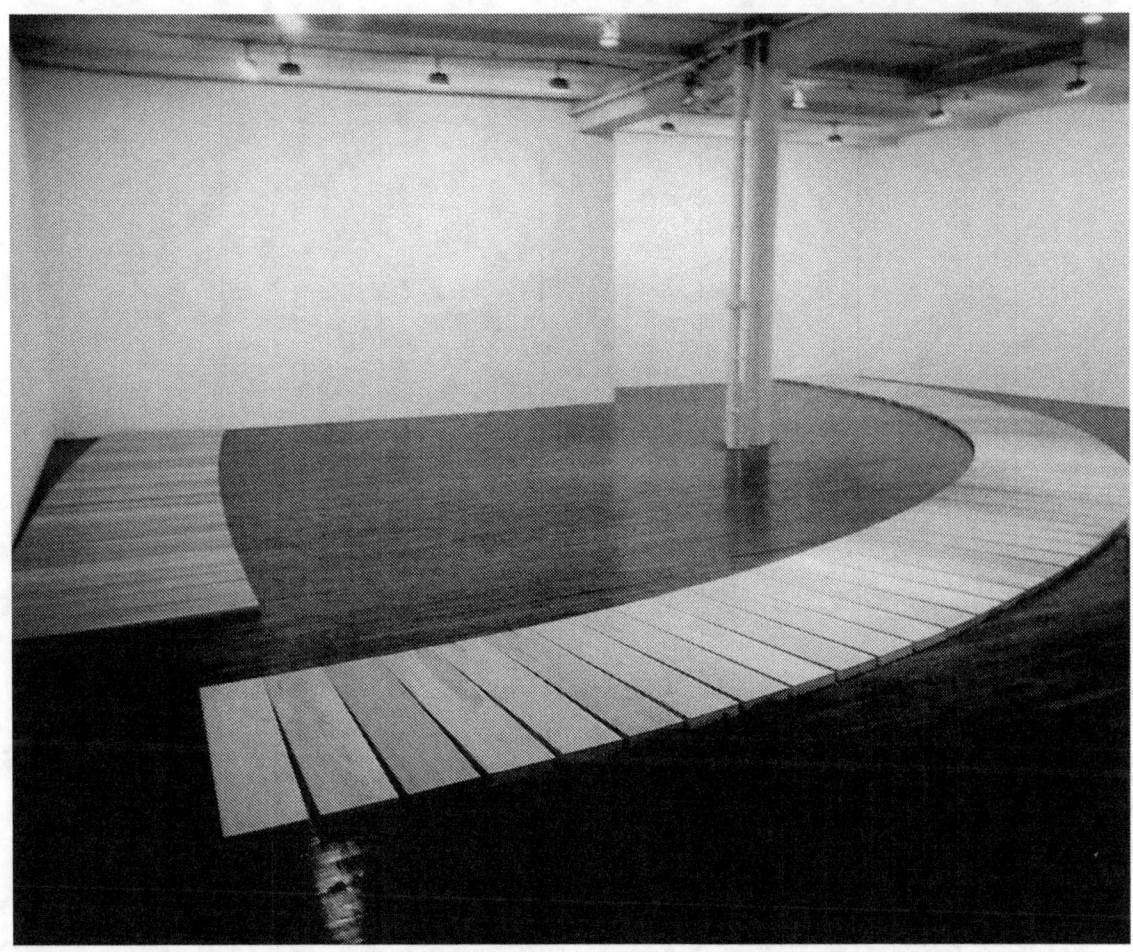

CARL ANDRE: *SIXTEENTH COPPER CARDINAL*

Carl Andre's works are extremely sensuous, with their shiny or dull surfaces of copper, zinc, steel or aluminium. A piece like Andre's *Sixteenth Copper Cardinal*, sixteen square copper slabs, is a work that could be described as luscious. People are used to marble and stone being beautiful, and also certain metals – bronze, silver and gold in particular have been central to sculpture for millennia. Why not zinc and copper, too? After all, much jewellery is made from copper. Carl Andre, like other Minimal sculptors, introduces the viewer to the sensuality of copper, bronze and zinc shaped into nothing more than... a simple shape, like a slab, put on the floor. Andre's slabs are not 'narrative' or anthropomorphic; they do not 'depict' animals or gods or people; but they are no less beautiful, as objects in their own right.

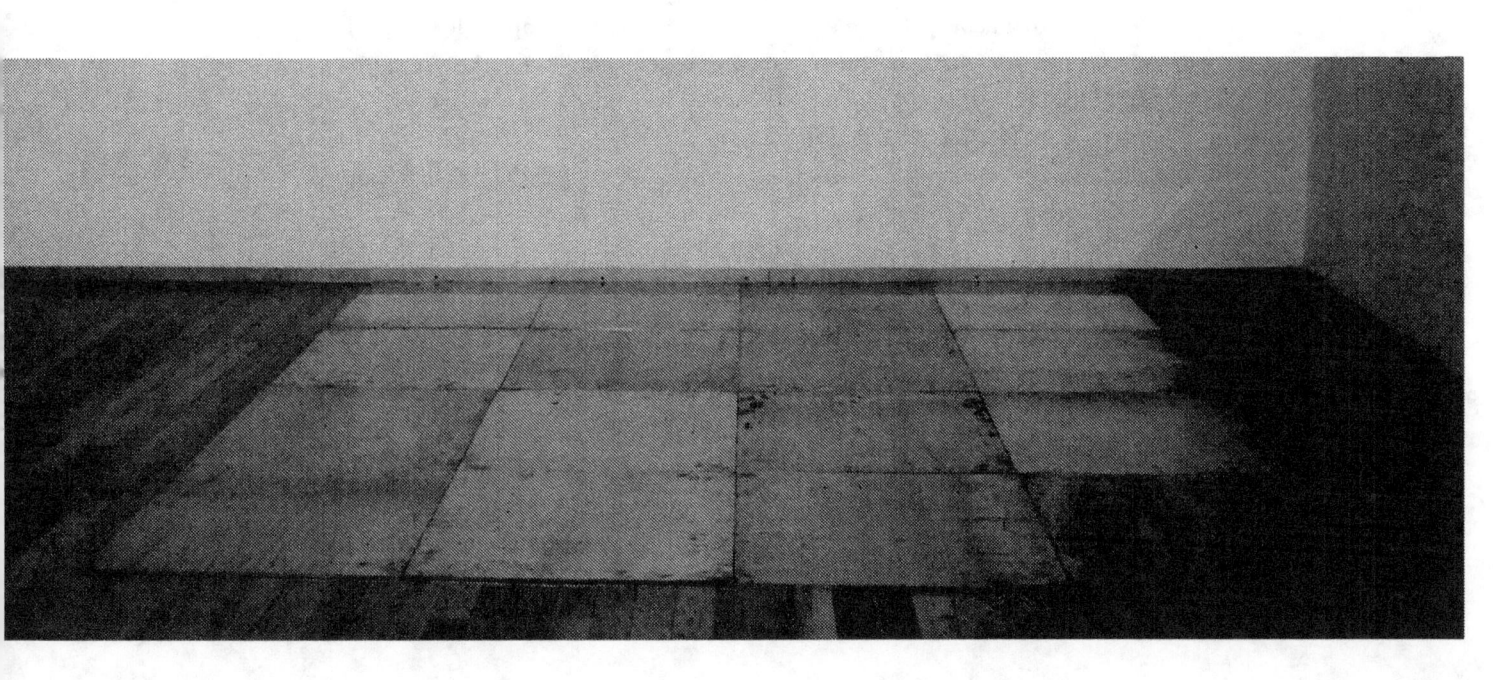

DAN FLAVIN: *UNTITLED*

Like Carl Andre's bricks or Eva Hesse's strands of rope, Dan Flavin's strip lights are made by people in factories. They are mass-produced household and business objects, not special or unique, like an 'original' oil painting. At first glance, it seems as if Flavin has simply bought a few fluorescent lamps and set them on a wall. Flavin's art seems to be founded on an act of Minimal literalism as infamous as Carl Andre placing some house bricks in a line and selling it to a gallery. Flavin's art draws attention to its operation: 'you are always aware of the fluorescents as running' remarked Kenneth Baker (1988, 100). Flavin's art is part of long tradition in 20th century art which explores (electrical) lighting in particular environments. As soon as different types of lighting were invented, artists started to experiment with them. Neon lamps, for example, have been a favourite with sculptors as with theatre and film designers, not to mention the denizens of commercial cities such as Hong Kong or Las Vegas, which are aglow at night with neon.

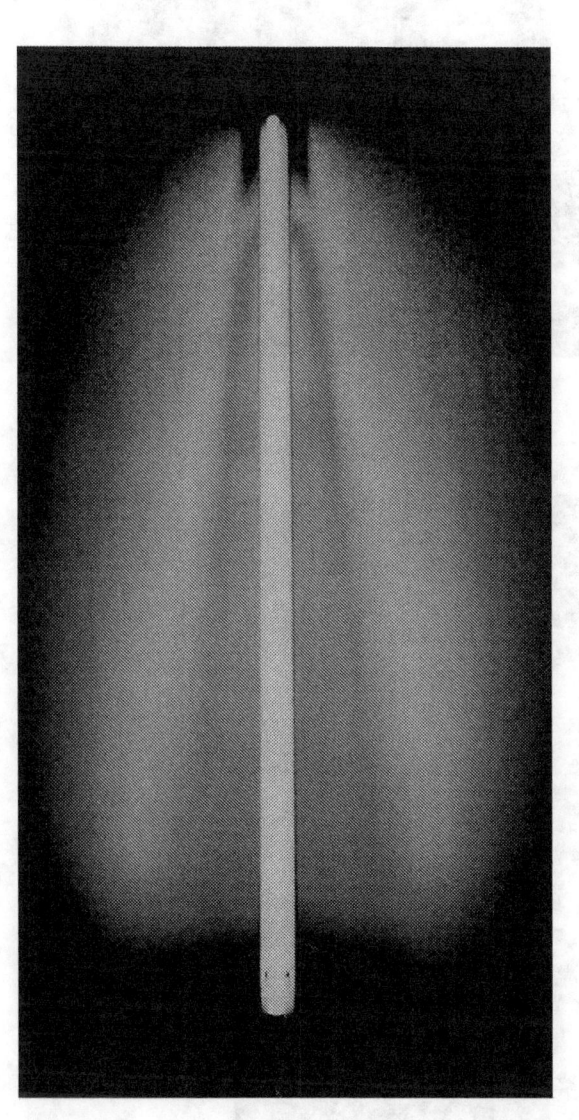
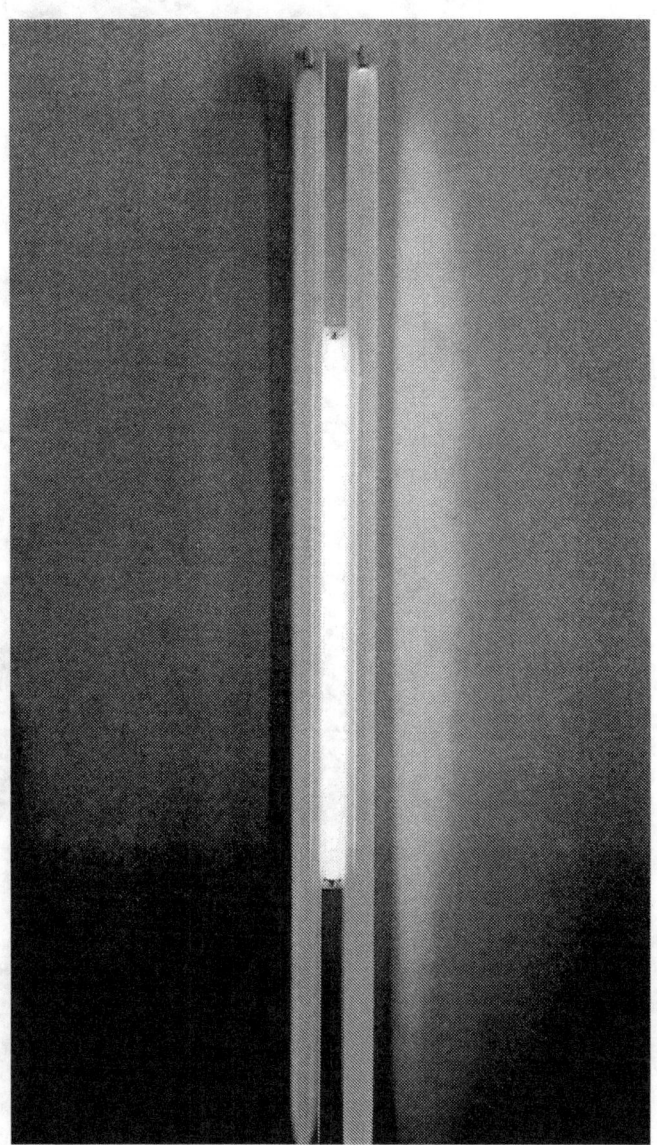

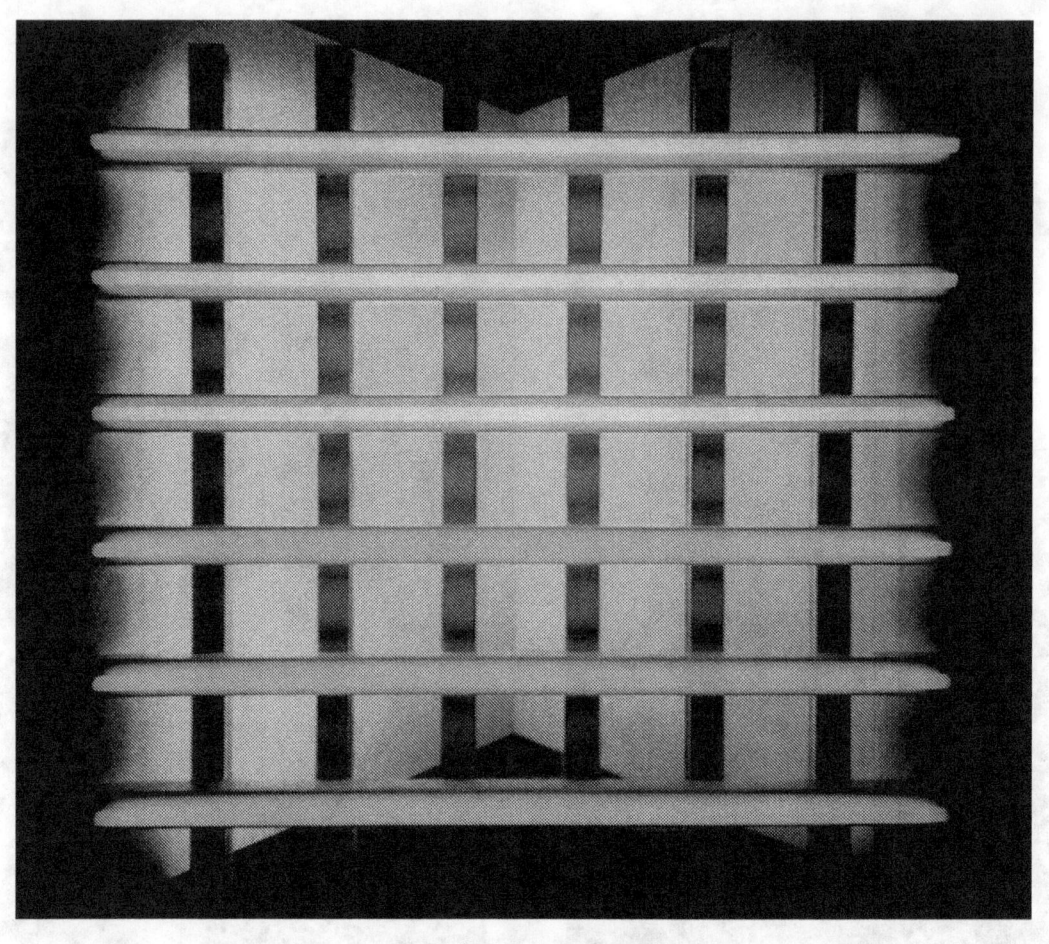

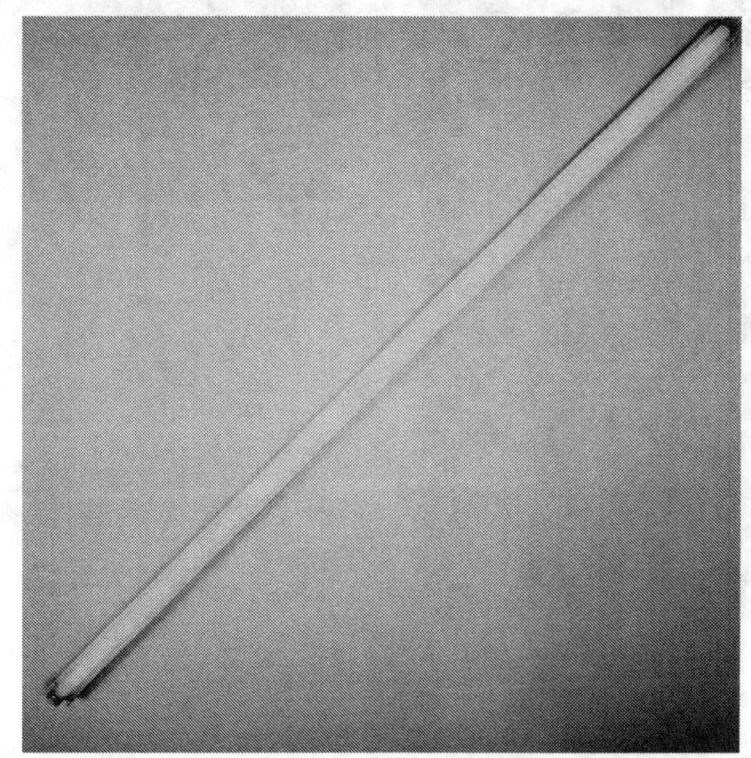

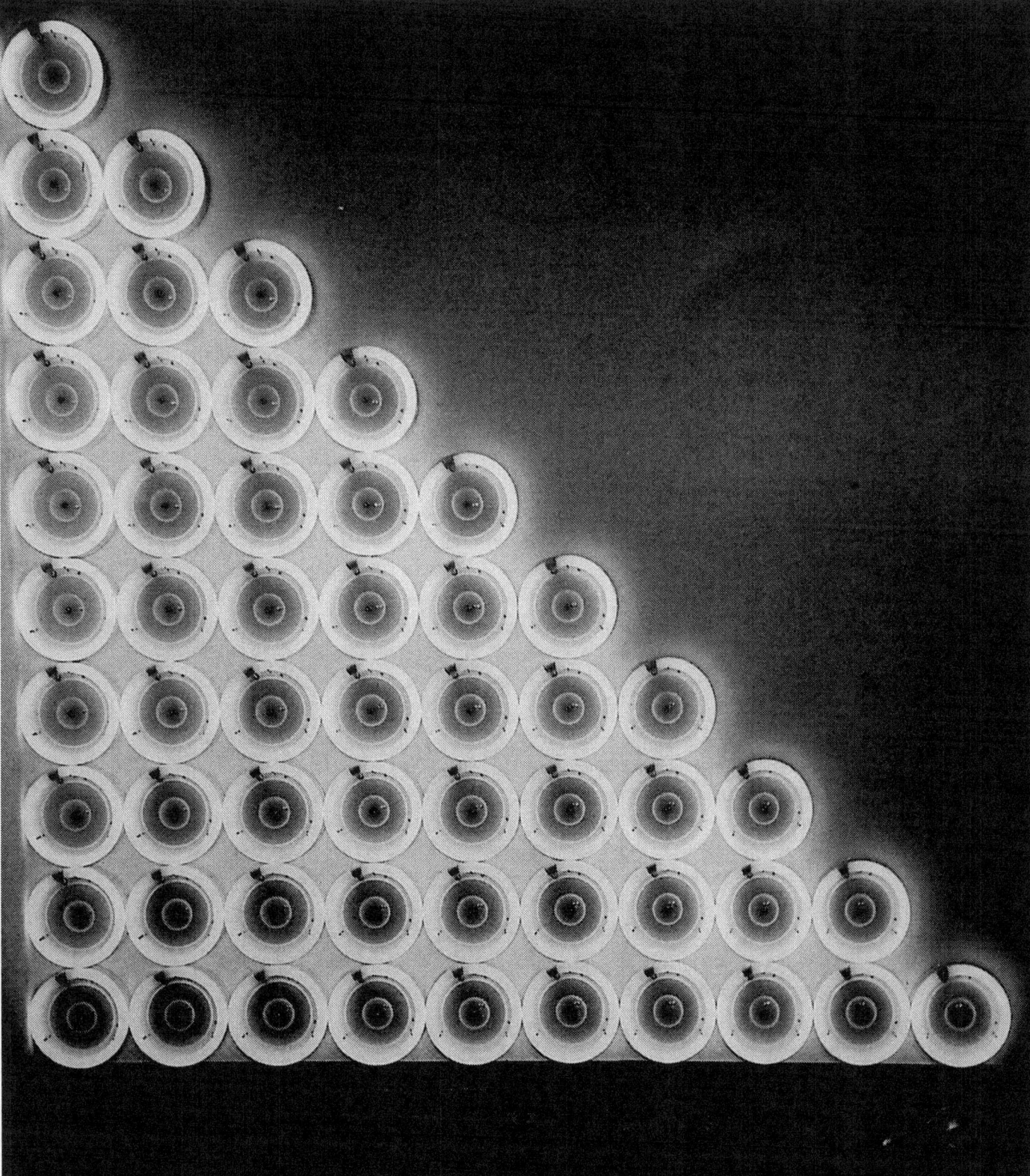

DAN FLAVIN: *UNTITLED (TO TRACY)*

Some of Dan Flavin's sculptures consist of nothing more than a strip light leaning against a wall (*Untitled*, 1976, Saatchi Collection), or a white fluorescent light mounted on a wall (*Diagonal of May 25, 1963*, Saatchi Collection). This latter early work was described in Flavin's notebook as 'the diagonal of personal ecstasy'. Flavin's Duchampian, post-Constructivist art of fluorescent lamps was in fact linked by the artist to spirituality, to the ability of light to transform a space, to light as a religious power. This is not something that might strike the viewer coming to Flavin's art afresh, that these ready-made fluorescent tubes are associated by the artist to light as a mystical presence. Some of Flavin's early works had distinctly religious connotations: *Icon V (Coran's Broadway Flesh)*, for example (1962, Heiner Friedrich, New York) or *The Nominal Three (to William of Ockham*, 1963*)*, which was an arrangement of six fluorescent tubes standing in three groups (of one, two and three lamps [1963, Giuseppe Panza di Biumo-Varese]). 'Flavin turns gallery space into gallery time' commented Robert Smithson (1979, 10). Sometimes Dan Flavin's luminism was an art of unexpected beauty – especially when Flavin set different coloured fluorescent lamps next to each other, as in *A Primary Structure* (1964, collection: the artist). Pale blue, red and yellow illumination merges on the wall, casting a ghostly light around the room.

One of Flavin's most significant shows was at the Guggenheim in 1992, where he took over the famous central rotunda with light installations, including a giant pink tower of fluorescents: *Untitled (To Tracy, To Celebrate the Love of a Lifetime*, 1992). Another big commission was the Munich subway installation (1998), an underground space that Flavin designed to be lit by his familiar coloured fluorescent lamps. One of the most impressive of Flavin's important commissions was the lighting design of the S. Maria Annunciata in Chiesa Rossa in Milan, made in 1996 via sponsorship from Dia Center for the Arts and Fondazione Prada. Flavin provided blue, gold, pink, green and ultraviolet light for the modern Italian church.

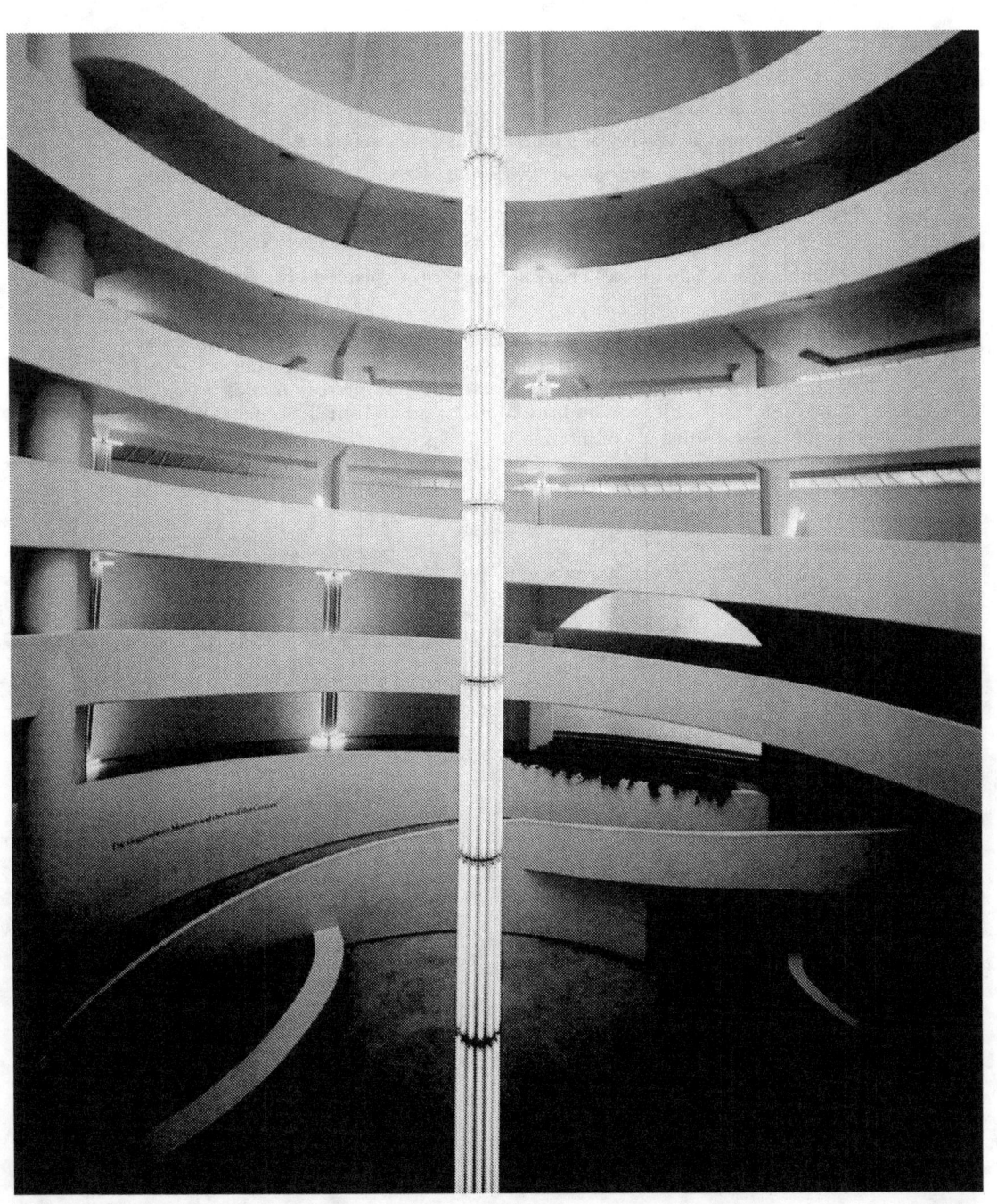

SOL LEWITT: *SIX-PART MODULAR CUBE*

Some might see some of Minimalist, Conceptual or mathematical art as too abstract, too unreal, too dry and clinical. But critics such as Robert Rosenblum claim that Conceptual art can be 'awesome'. Of Sol LeWitt's art, Rosenblum wrote that it 'elicits... an immediate awe that... has to be translated by the same feeble words – beautiful, elegant, exhilarating – that we use to register similar experiences with earlier art'.[1] Sol LeWitt explained his view thus:

> I wouldn't say that I wanted to like uninteresting things or to dislike interesting things. I think that's one way that you measure your response, if it interests you. 'Interests' means that it somehow makes a bridge between you and it, you and the object, you and the art object. If it hits home, it means that it's of interest.[2]

1. "Notes on Sol LeWitt", 1978, 15-16.
2. Quoted in F. Colpitt, 121.

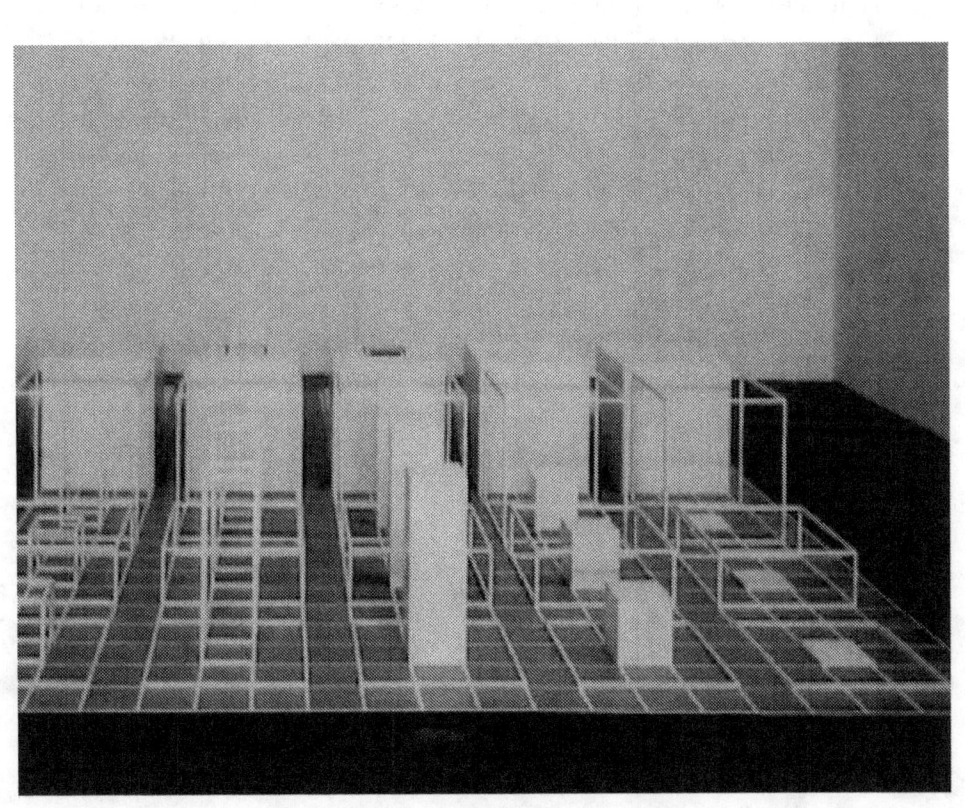

SOL LEWITT: *WALL DRAWING*

For Sol LeWitt, the idea was everything: rather than being seen as a Minimalist, LeWitt was much more a Conceptualist. The making of the art became a 'perfunctory affair' (D. Wheeler, 227). LeWitt espoused some of Conceptualism's and Process art's anti-art æsthetics: LeWitt deliberately used materials that were not 'sexy'. His basic format was an open modular cube, mathematical variations on the cube made from aluminium or wood (such as *Open Modular Cube* [1966, Art Gallery of Ontario, Toronto] or *47 Three-Part Variations on Three Different Kinds of Cubes* [1967/74, Allen Memorial Art Museum, Oberlin College] or the *Six-Part Modular Cube* [1976, San Diego]). LeWitt explored the permutations cubes could have set beside each other. Some of LeWitt's most impressive works were his huge wall drawings (such as *Wall Drawing: Part 1 with 10,000 Lines 6" Long*, 1971, private collection).

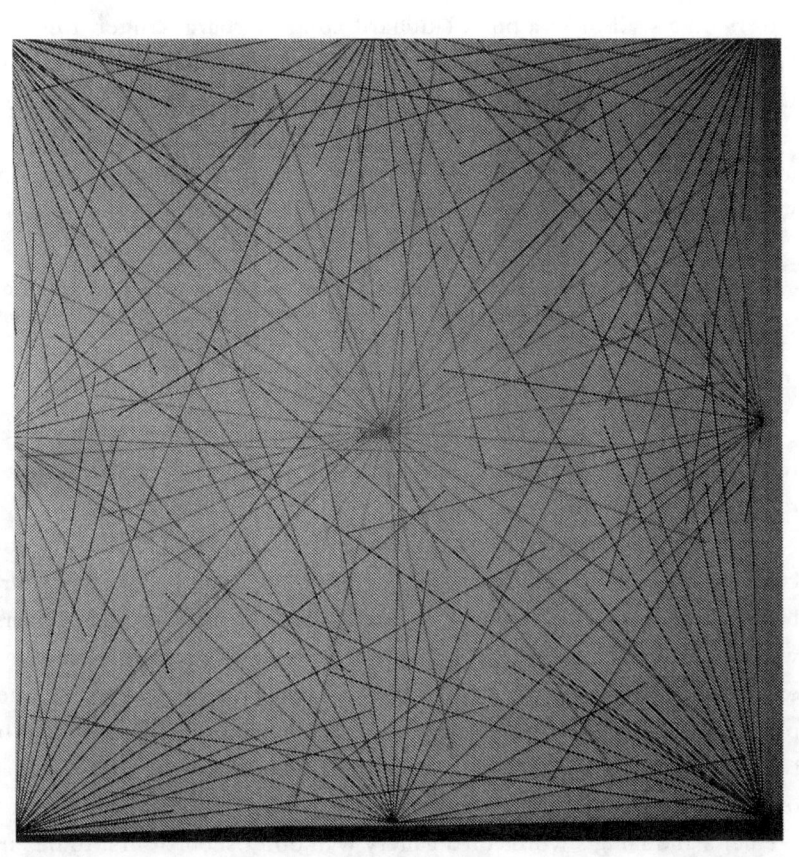

LAWRENCE WEINER: *BILLOWING CLOUDS*

Sixties Conceptual artist Lawrence Weiner produced text works, capital letters on a wall or in a book (Richard Long, Barbara Kruger, the Art & Language group and Michael Craig-Martin have also produced post-Conceptualist wall works). Weiner's solution to making sculpture was that a sculpture on a plinth has to be 'translated' into language, so that people can understand it. Sculpture is language, and words are language, therefore, Weiner reckons, words can be sculpture:

> when you see a piece of wood lying on the ground with a piece of stone on top of it, you must translate that in your own head into language. What I try to do is present language itself as a key to what sculpture is about... It is a presentation of a piece of sculpture in language.[1]

Weiner produces capital letters in short phrases which are about a viewer's relationship with an object. The words are a means or the expression of a relationship with something.

Billowing Clouds is a typical Lawrence Weiner artwork.[2] Richard Long comments that '[t]he discovery [Weiner] made that art does not necessarily have to be made, that was a great breakthrough'.[3] Weiner is right, of course: words alone can be sculpture, for poets have long known that language is an experience, not simply abstractions or concepts. Language really does affect people – otherwise why would they spend so much time consuming language? That is, they consume 40 hours of broadcasting per week – that's over a day and a half spent consuming television and radio per week. So Weiner's and Long's words on a gallery wall don't seem at first to be 'art'. They are not sensual and graspable, like a marble sculpture. Yet those words, whether photocopied on cheap paper or printed by high quality typography on deluxe paper, are 'art', they are communication, language, even sculpture. Conceptual art or Process art is 'possessed' by the viewer, in Weiner's system. Indeed, some Conceptual art requires the existence of the viewer to make the work work at all. The viewer brings the work alive.

1. Lawrence Weiner, in Lucie-Smith, 1987, 117.
2. L. Weiner, *Billowing Clouds...*, 1986, 86.2 x 17.5 in, Anthony d'Offay Gallery, London.
3. *Richard Long: In Conversation* 2, 24.

BILLOWING CLOUDS OF FERROUS OXIDE
SETTING APART A CORNER ON THE BOTTOM OF THE SEA

ROBERT SMITHSON: *NON-SITE WORKS*

Robert Smithson was the chief mouthpiece of American earth/ site æsthetics, and is probably the most important theoretician among all land artists. Smithson's theoretical statements were published in three essays. In "The Crystal Land" Smithson recounts a trip he made to a quarry with Donald Judd, the key Minimal artist. Smithson evokes the decayed nature of the quarry, those aspects of entropy which would feature in his own work ('cracked broken shattered earth, of fragmentation, corrosion, decomposition, disintegration, rock crisis, debris slides, mud flow avalanche' [*Writings*, 1979, 20]). In the second article, "Entropy and the New Monuments" (1966), Smithson discussed the important Minimal show *Primary Structures* at the Jewish Museum. Smithson's themes were entropy in nature and art; he used the science of crystals and minerals as paradigms of the new art. Smithson had collected crystals and rocks as a child. Crystallography, for Smithson, offered 'a way of dealing with nature without falling into the old trap of the biological metaphor' (R. Hobbs, 12). No wonder, then, that when Smithson saw Judd's pink plastic boxes he compared them to 'giant crystals from another planet'.[1] The dissolution of crystals also provided Smithson with another analogy for his theory of natural entropy. The third piece, "A Sedimentation of the Mind: Earth Projects" (1968), concerned notions of time and place. Rather than sculptors such as Anthony Caro and his ilk, who still clung to the old-fashioned ideas of beauty, Smithson spoke of artists such as Walter de Maria, Carl Andre, Michael Heizer, Dennis Oppenheim, Tony Smith and Douglas Huebler (*Writings*, 85). Smithson was also interested in science fiction: the poetic elements of his art thus form a continuum: between the industrial wastelands he visited for his 'non-site' sculptures and the desolate planets of science fiction; between chaos theory in the New Physics and its exploration in postmodern science fiction; between the forms of crystals and Minimal sculptures, and so on. Smithson's exaltation of lonely postindustrial sites was echoed in the speculative fictions of writers who evoked post- or near-Holocaust worlds.

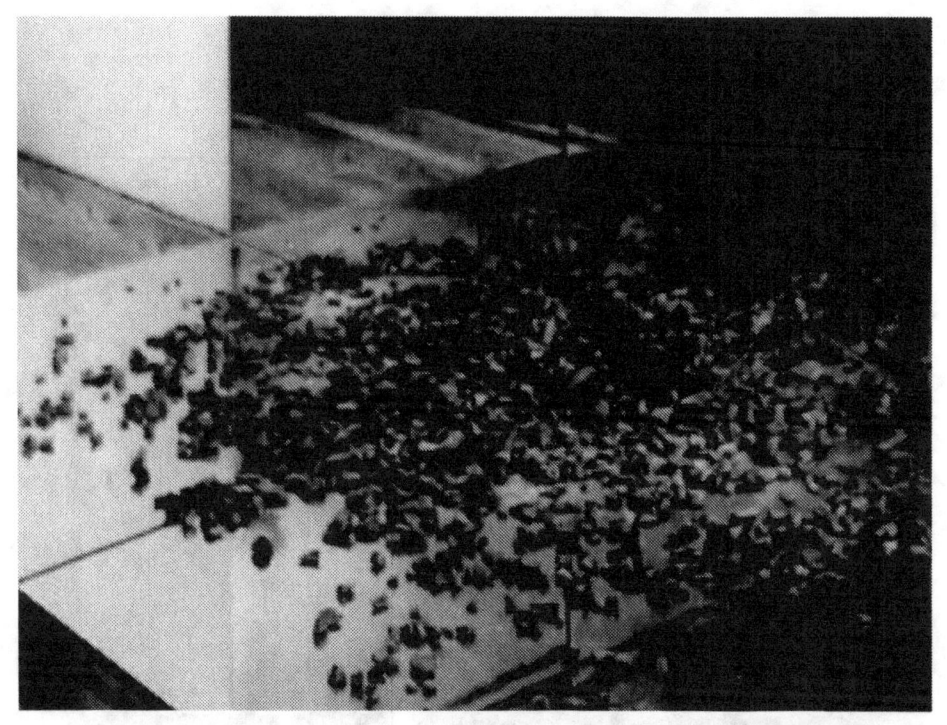

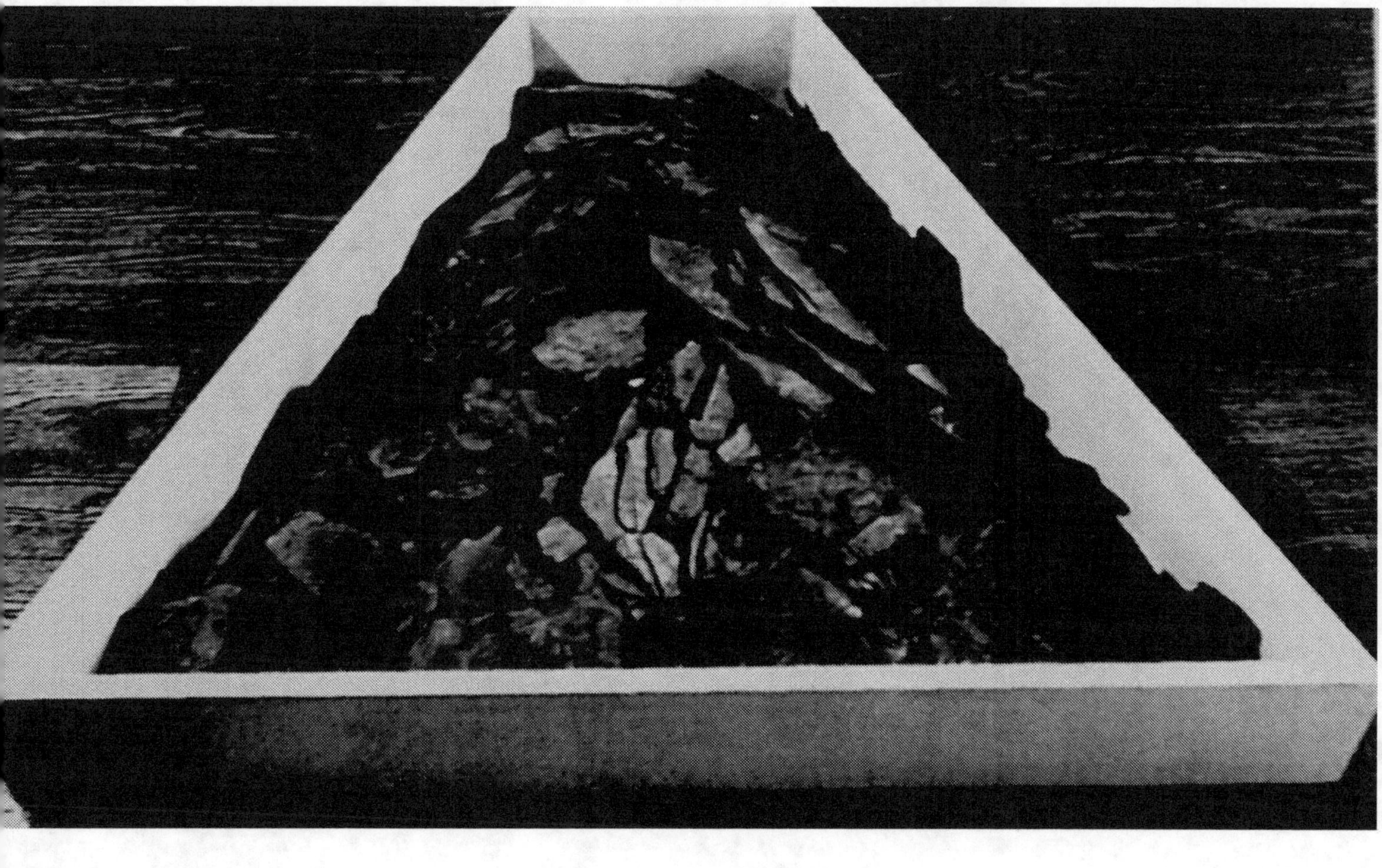

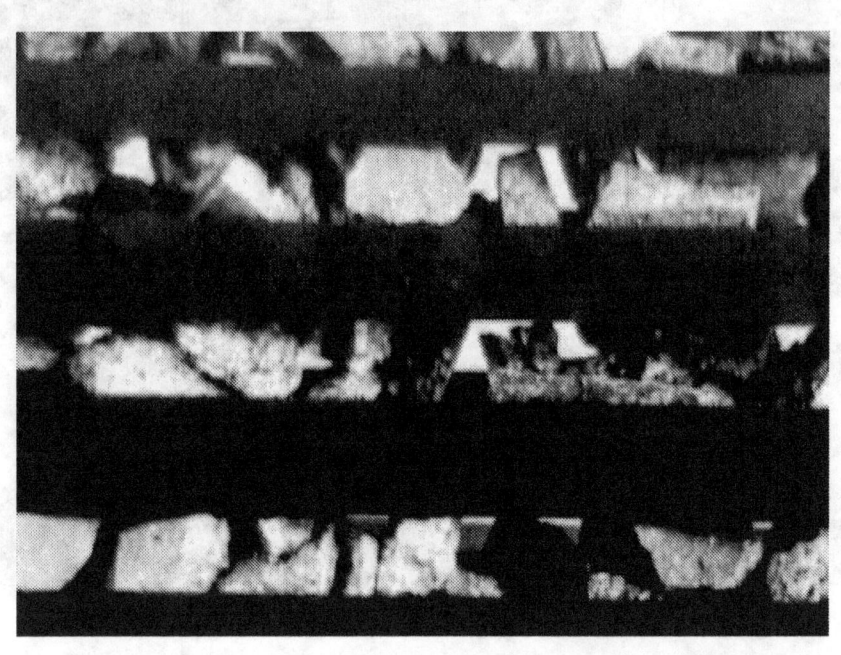

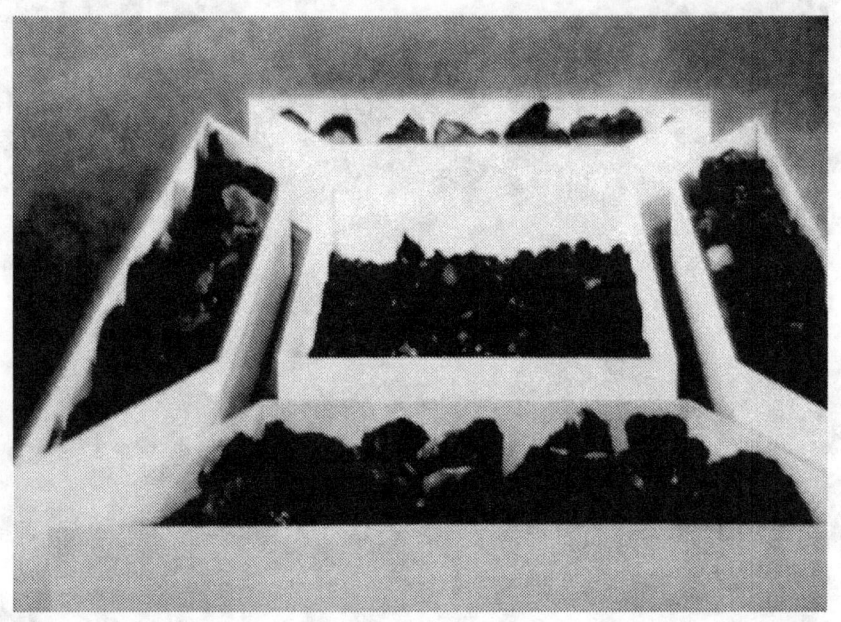

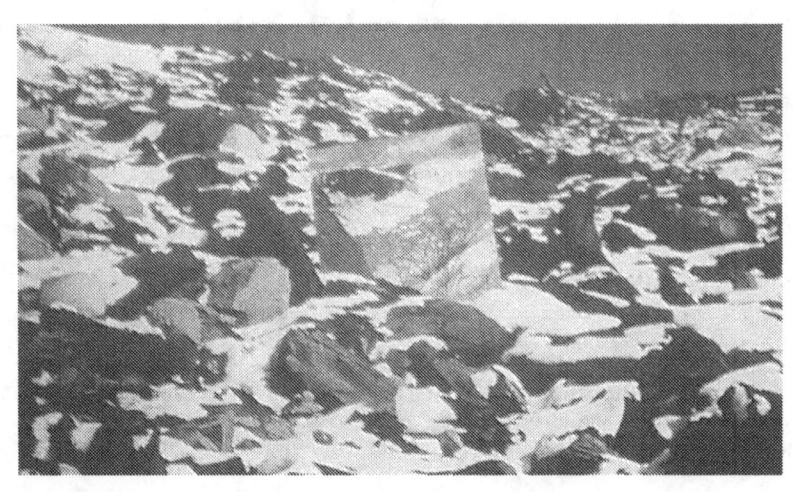

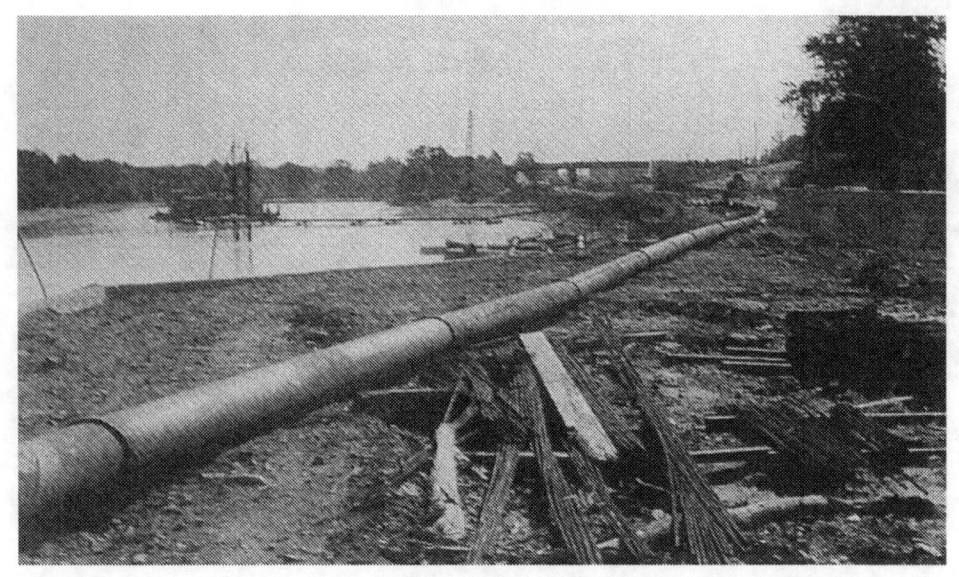

ROBERT SMITHSON: *NON-SITE WORKS*

Robert Smithson's theory of the 'non-site' was based on 'absence, a very ponderous, weighty absence'.[1] Smithson proposed a theory of a dialectic between absence and presence, in which the 'non-site' and 'site' are both interacting. In the 'non-site' work, presence and absence are there simultaneously. 'The land or ground from the Site is placed in the art (Non-Site) rather than the art is placed on the ground. The Non-Site is a container within another container – the room'.[2]

> In a sense my nonsites are rooms within rooms. Recovery from the outer fringes brings one back to the central point... The scale between indoors and outdoors, and how the two are impossible to bridge... What you are really confronted with in a non-site is the absence of the site. It is a contraction rather than an expansion of scale. One is confronted with a very ponderous, weighty absence... There is this dialectic between inner and outer, closed and open, center and peripheral.[3]

1. C. Robins, 1984, 82.
2. *Writings*, 1979, 115.
3. in L. Lippard, 1973, 88.

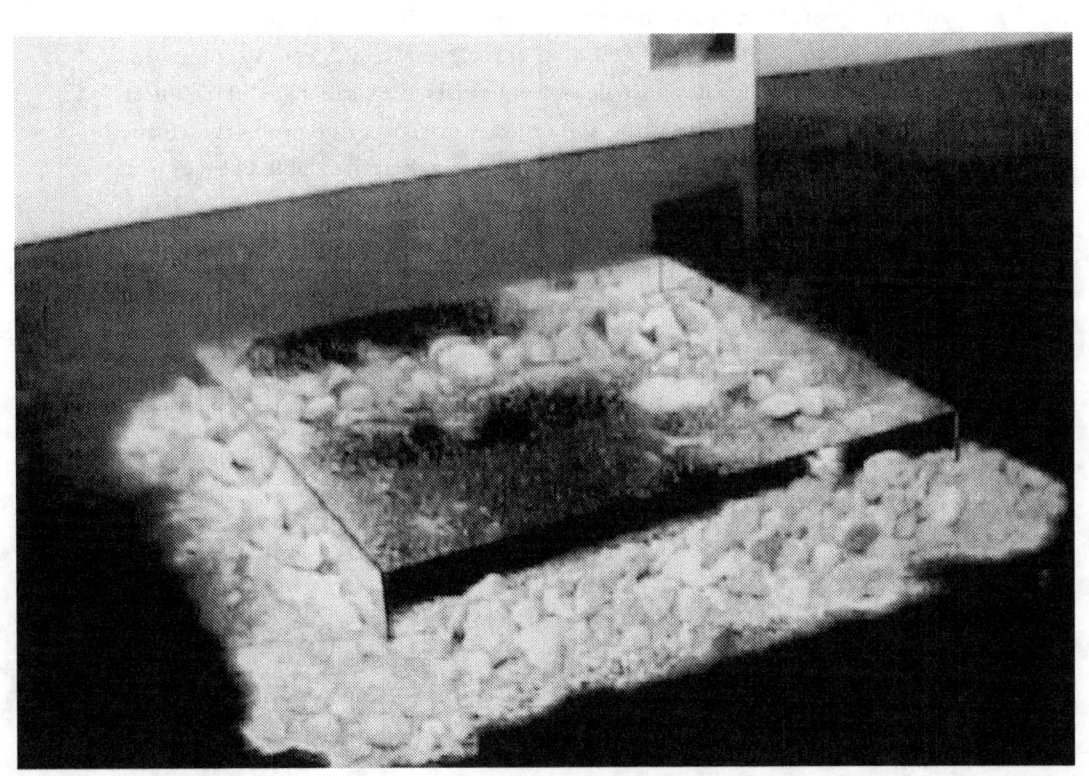

ROBERT SMITHSON: *MIRROR DISPLACEMENTS*

The 'non-site' works were permanent, gallery works. Robert Smithson's *Mirror Displacements* (1968) consisted of putting some mirrors in various settings and taking photographs of them before moving them somewhere else. *Mirror Displacements* was documented in Smithson's *Artforum* article "Incidents of Mirror Travel in the Yucatan" (1969). Sometimes Smithson put soil on top of the mirrors, to dirty them up, to sabotage 'the perfect reflections of the sky'. Smithson liked dirt, gravel, sand, sludge and sediment – indeterminate, malleable substances. Land artists often sabotaged the clinical nature of much of art – putting soil or grass or slate or horses in the clean, white gallery space. Of his Italian horse piece, where he stabled horses in a gallery, Jannis Kounellis said the aim was to increase awareness of the 'basic nature of a gallery, of its bourgeois origin', its economic and ideological aspects.[1]

1. C. Robins, 1984, 82.

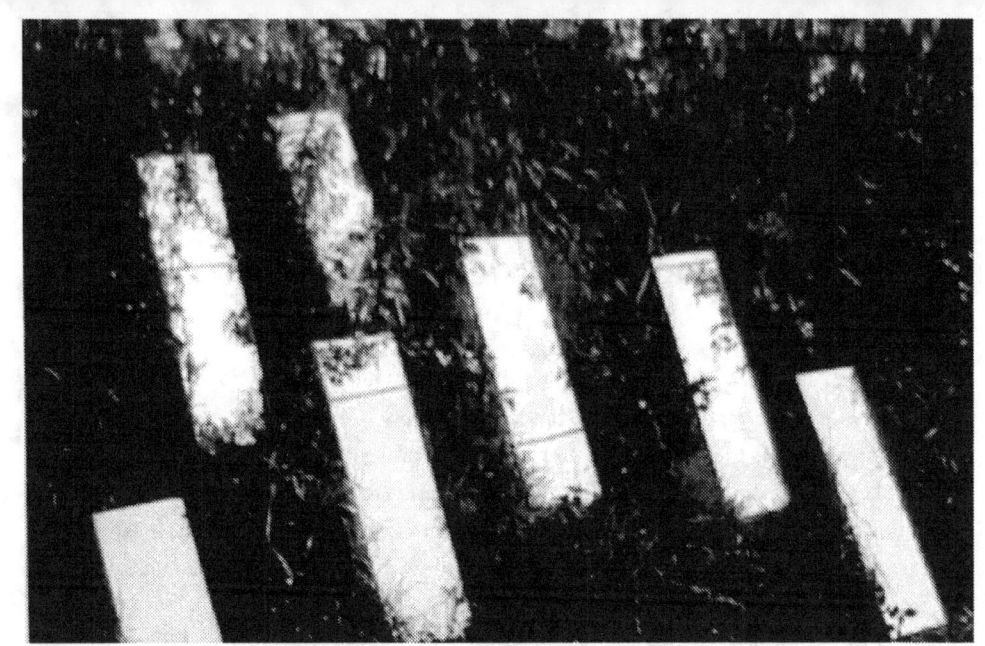

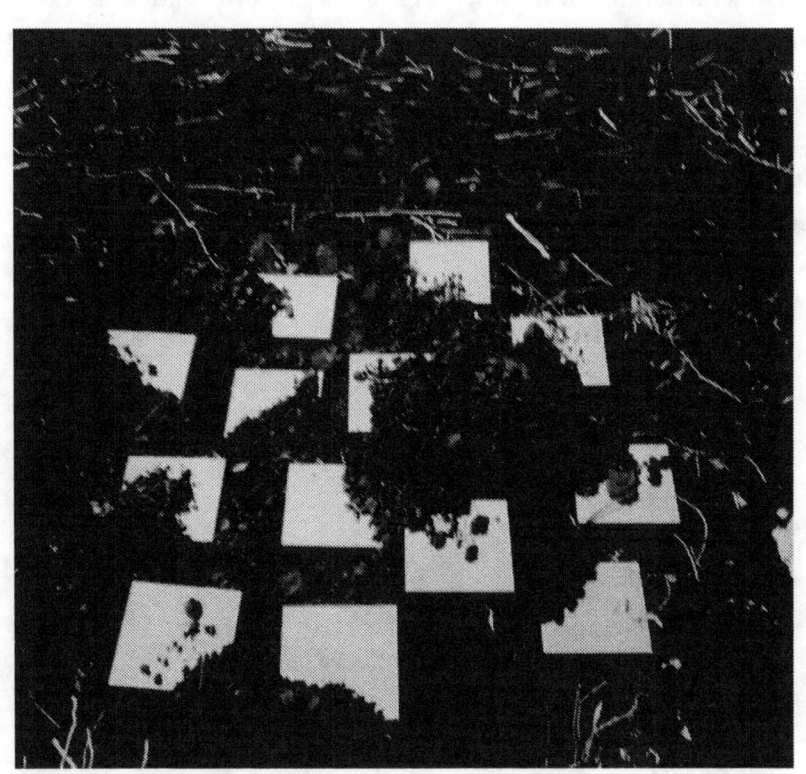

WALTER DE MARIA: *VERTICAL EARTH KILOMETER*

Walter de Maria made a dramatic land art gesture when he cut a 4.5 mile-long 6 foot-wide scar in the desert in Nevada with a bulldozer. Commentators have spoken of this cut as a 'wound' or 'scar' on the Earth (a wound in the body of the Earth in its Great Mother persona). The ultimate in ithyphallic, male land art must be de Maria's *Vertical Earth Kilometer*. At a cost of $500,000, de Maria sunk a 1-kilometre brass rod into the planet. Nothing can be seen of it except a 2 inch brass disc on the ground. The making of de Maria's work is perhaps far more interesting than the artwork itself. It must be the ultimate art statement/ non-statement. De Maria's *Vertical Earth Kilometer* remains practically invisible. It neatly melds two 1960s æsthetic movements: Conceptualism (wow, what an idea, sticking a kilometer of brass into the Earth!) and Minimalism (there's nothing to see of it except... a two-inch brass disc!). Yeah, that's *real art*, a kilometer-long piece of metal stuck into the ground with nothing of it showing except a tiny disc. Shown at Kassel Dokumenta 6 in 1977, de Maria's *Vertical Earth Kilometer* annoyed British artist Stuart Brisley so much he made *Survival in Alien Circumstances*. This was a hole in the earth dug with his bare hands, which Brisley lived in for 2 weeks, intending to mock de Maria's overblown American earthwork. In 1979 de Maria exhibited *The Broken Kilometer*: 500 brass roads each two metres in a New York gallery.

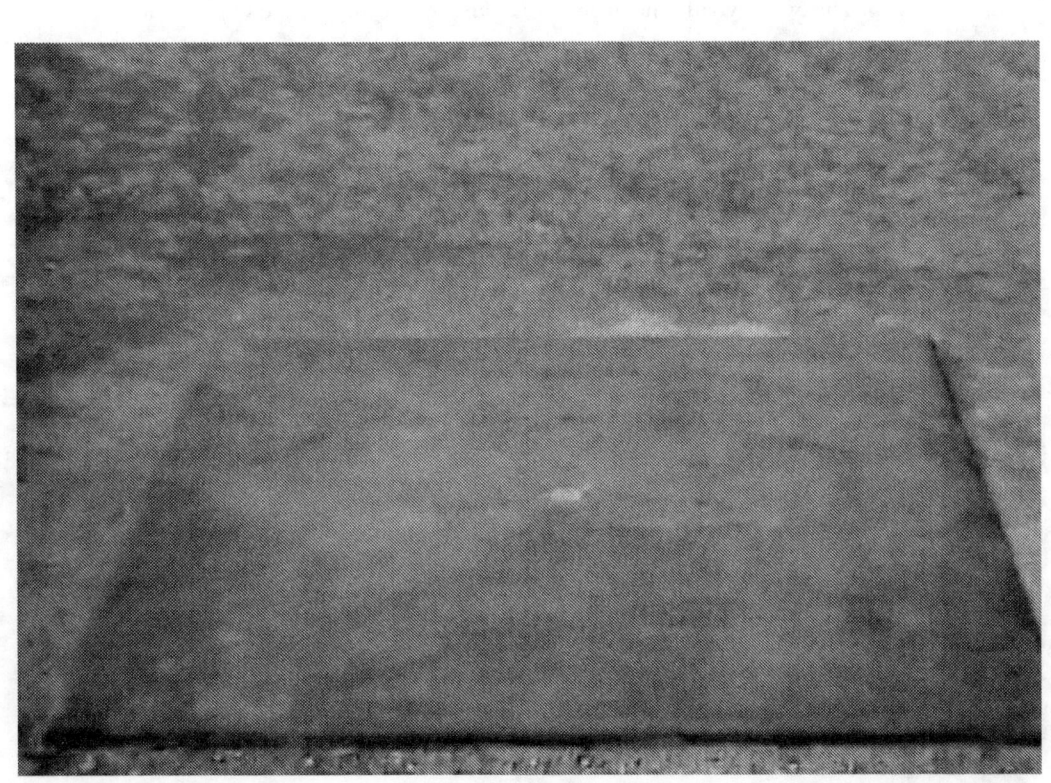

WALTER DE MARIA: *EARTH ROOM*

Walter de Maria's *Earth Room* was a gallery full of dark earth made in 1968 in Munich and later in New York (*The New York Earth Room*, SoHo Gallery, 1977). It consisted of 125 tons of soil, taking up 3,600 square feet, 22 inches deep. This was a vivid (and aromatic) example of bringing the Outside inside, one of land art's key projects. The contrasts were immediate, between the flat, clean, white, controlled gallery space and the 1,600 ft³ of uneven, 'dirty', dark, organic soil. Roberta Smith said it was a 'shock' to see the soil taking up the interior space usually reserved for things such as furniture and people. 'The dirt carried its own absence, was somehow a living substance' (1978, 104).

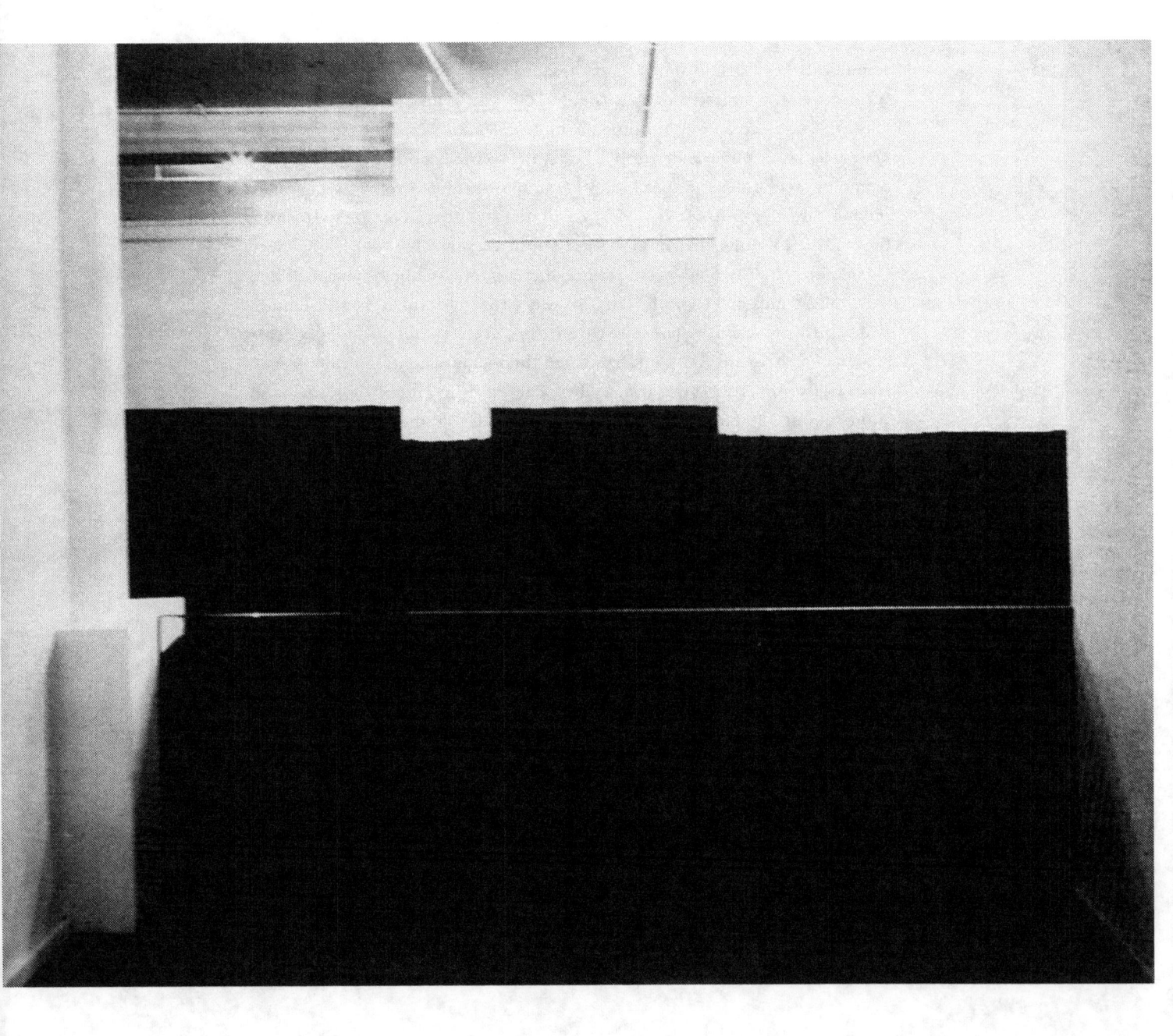

WALTER DE MARIA: *LIGHTNING FIELD*

Kenneth Baker calls de Maria's most famous work, the *Lightning Field,* the 'grandest Minimalist work of the 1970s' and 'the closest thing to a masterpiece to come out of Minimalism' (125-7). De Maria's firat *Lightning Field* was sited 40 miles from Flagstaff in Arizona, consisting of 2 inch diameter steel poles, 18 feet tall, 30 feet apart, in five rows of seven. The second, larger *Lightning Field* is a grid of 400 stainless steel poles, 16 along the width, 25 along the length, each about 20 feet high, set in the New Mexico desert.[1] The poles were set in concrete, one foot below land, able to withstand winds of 110 mph. The site was chosen for its flatness, isolation and lightning activity. The most lightning activity occurs during May-September; there are about 60 days when thunder and lightning can be seen from *Lightning Field* (de Maria, 1980). The poles in *Lightning Field* stand alone, about 220 feet apart. The tips of the poles define a plane in space parallel to sea level: the length of each pole varies according to the contours of the landscape. The *Lightning Field* is an exact, mathematically precise human site laid onto nature, where the poles are tiny mirrors which mark out and calibrate the landscape. The site looks like a scientific or industrial project – like a radio telescope site, say, or a military communications centre. *Lightning Field* is spectacular, with masculine and phallic connotations (lightning is related in symbolism to male creativity, sperm, fire, power and shamanism).

1. See D. Bourdon, 1968, 39-43, 72; M. Winton, 1970, 18-19; R. Smith, 1978, 102-5.

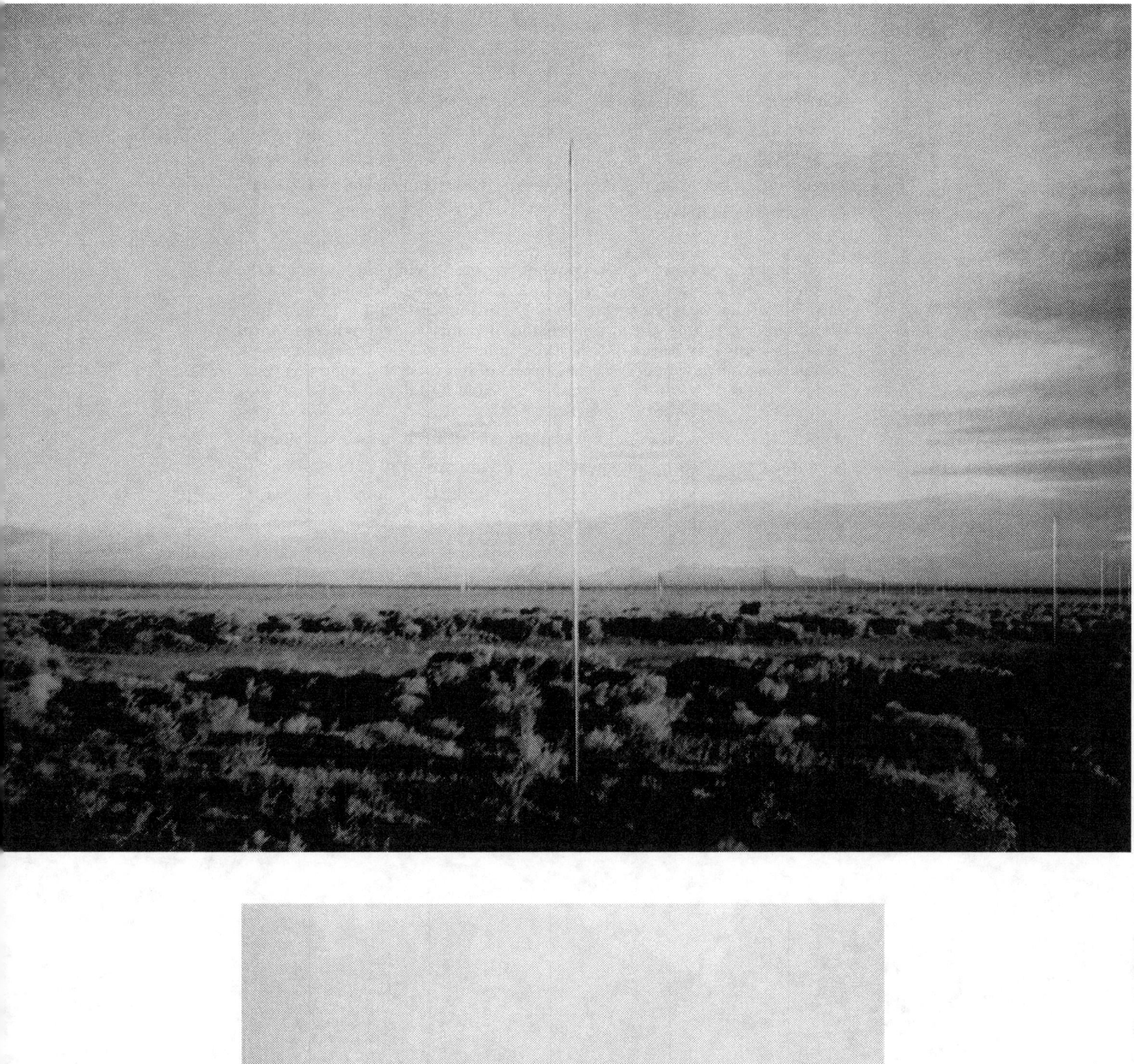

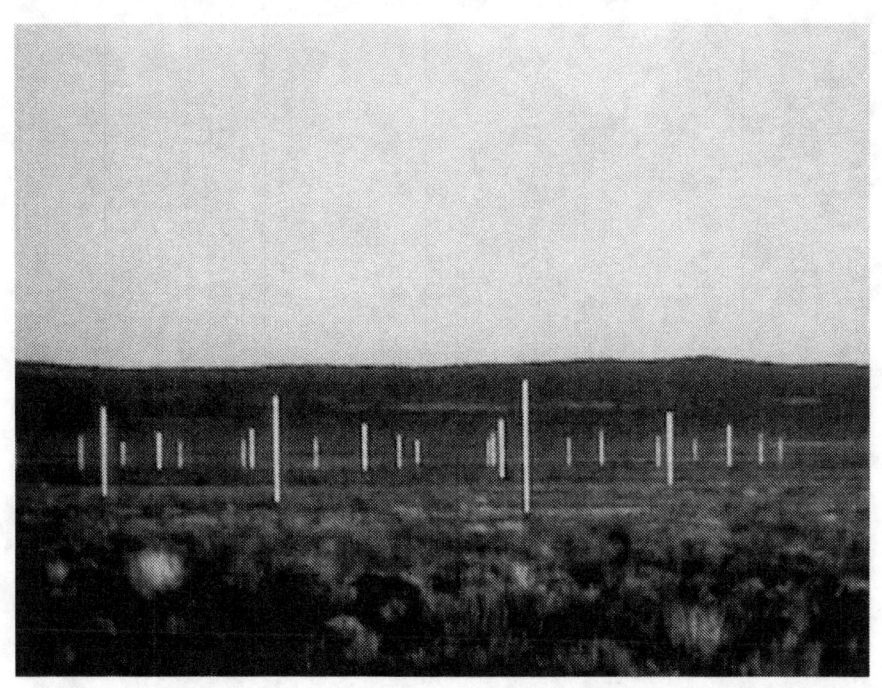

Lightning Field is ambiguously related to the Dia Art Foundation, which financed its construction. The site recalls technological experiments, while the poles themselves recall Brancusi's *Birds in Space*, and his *Endless Column*. Art critic Kenneth Baker relates de Maria's *Lightning Field* to issues of philosophy and politics:

> The piece also serves as an instrument for intensifying one's grasp of the beauty of the earth... The *Lightning Field* acquaints the visitor with the possibility that beauty may be the only conscionable and feasible refuge from history. That is, the apprehension of reality as everywhere *radiant with its being* may be the only bearable consciousness of life that does not entail repressing awareness of the horrors of our time. Beauty in this sense is just what the *Lightning Field* makes available... (127)

De Maria's *Lightning Field* attracts lightning, and a storm, as anyone knows, is about the most erotic and spectacular phenomenon in nature.[1] May to September is the season of the great storms in the area, sometimes 'two or three a week cross this field of poles'.[2]

1. See Peter Redgrove, *The Black Goddess and the Sixth Sense*, Bloomsbury, 1987; *The Cyclopean Mistress*, Bloodaxe, 1993. (De Maria himself thinks that a lightning strike is a 'false climax' to the work, which really needs to be seen over a period of time to appreciate its qualities).
2. H. Smagula, 290.

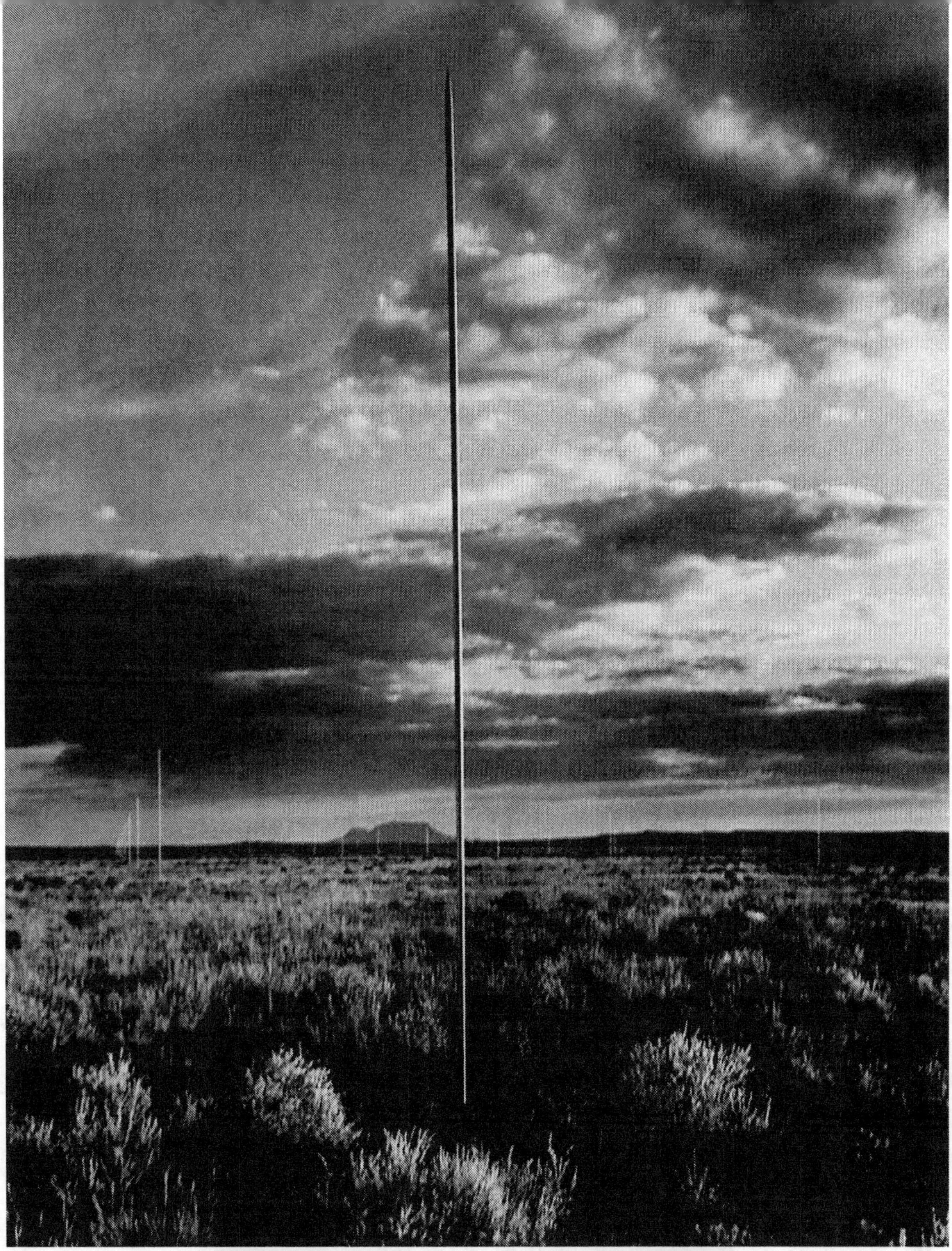

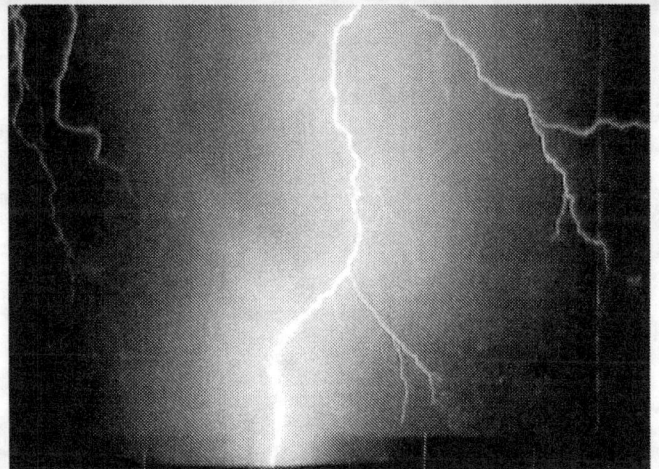

WALTER DE MARIA: *DRAWING*

Walter de Maria started out as a musician rather than, like many land artists, as a painter or sculptor. He played drums with the art rockers Velvet Underground. One of his early ideas (in 1962) for an earthwork was a mile-long pair of walls that would be 12 feet high and 12 feet apart. De Maria said that 'when you walk between, you can look up and see the sky'.[1] After the four and a half mile bulldozer square cut in the Earth, de Maria made a chalk drawing in the desert.

1. Quoted in H. Smagula, 289.

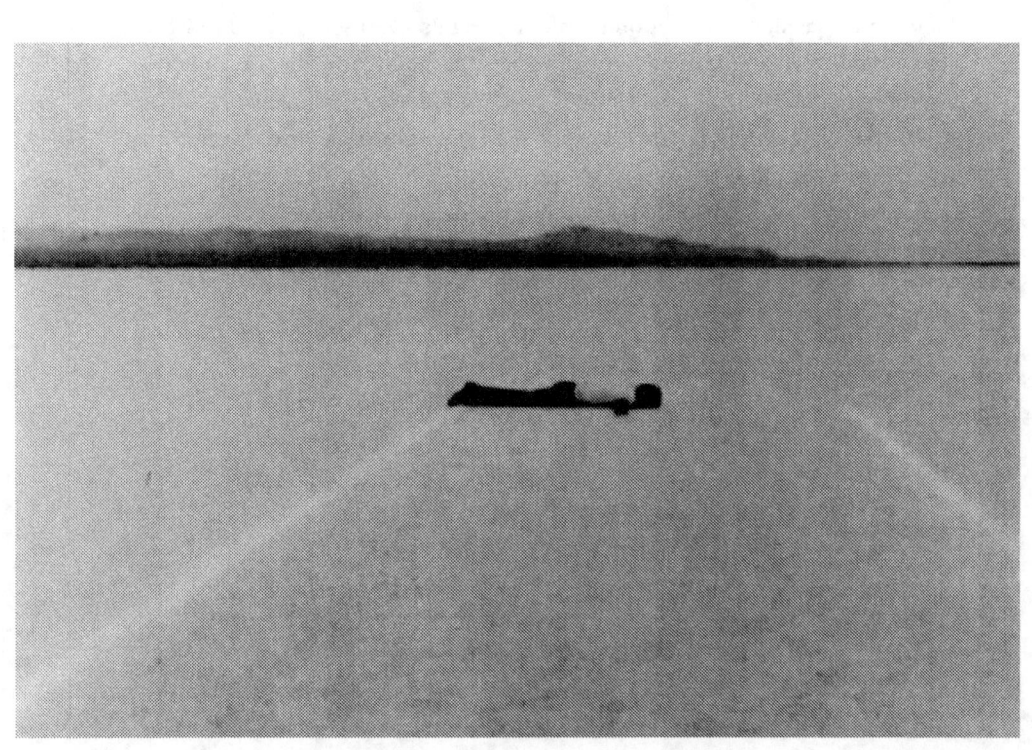

TONY CRAGG: *NEW STONES – NEWTON'S TONES*

Tony Cragg is known for his coloured spreads of found objects arranged in lines on the floor (such as his *New Stones*). Cragg's are works of found objects, all manner of objects, each given the same status, in a non-hierarchical fashion, laid out on the floor. Cragg's 1980 sculpture *Black and White Stack* contains bicycle tyres, tin cans, car radiator grills, the side of a child's cot, an ironing board. There is eroticism in Tony Cragg's work; Cragg has spoken of having 'an erotic response to the external world', something which, it seems, all artists have, or have to have, to be truly 'great' artists.[1]

1. Quoted in D. Wheeler, 324.

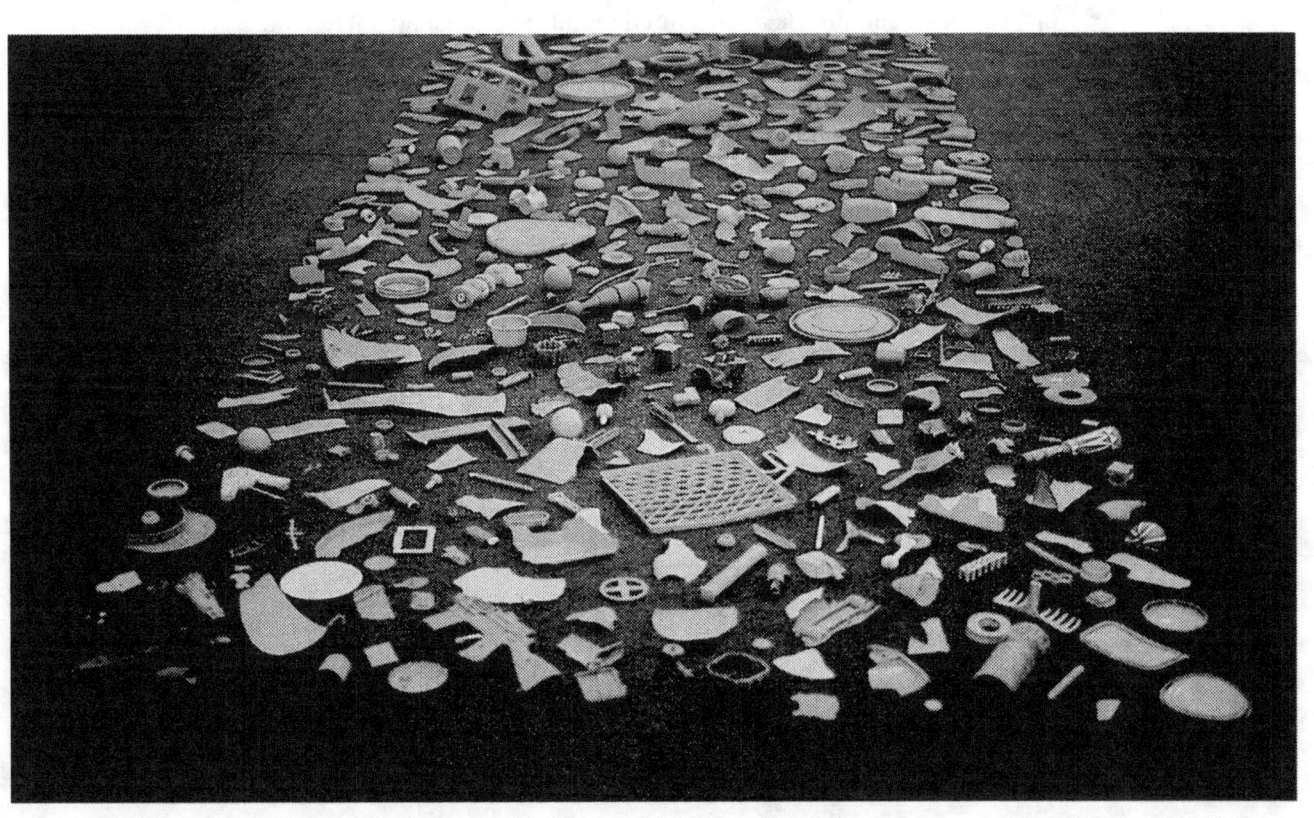

TONY CRAGG: *FIVE OBJECTS – FIVE COLOURS*

Tony Cragg's sculptures, like Bill Woodrow's and David Mach's, are not simply sensual modernist objects but ironic, postmodernist commentaries on the social and political uses of commodities. In Cragg, Mach and Woodrow familiar consumer durables and industrial materials are represented in an ironic, metaphoric and parodying manner.[1] Cragg, and other British sculptors who trawl the skips and trash yards of urban landscapes (Nash, Pope, Gormley, Woodrow), make ironic comments on scavenging and ecological recycling. Cragg is not interested, he says, 'in romanticizing an epoch in the distant past', but questioning the massive amount of commodity consumption in a late capitalist epoch:

> We consume, populating our environment with more and more objects, with no chance of understanding the making processes because we specialize in the production, but not in the consumption.[2]

1. J. Roberts, 1990, 111f.
2. T. Cragg, in E. Lucie-Smith, 1987, 130.

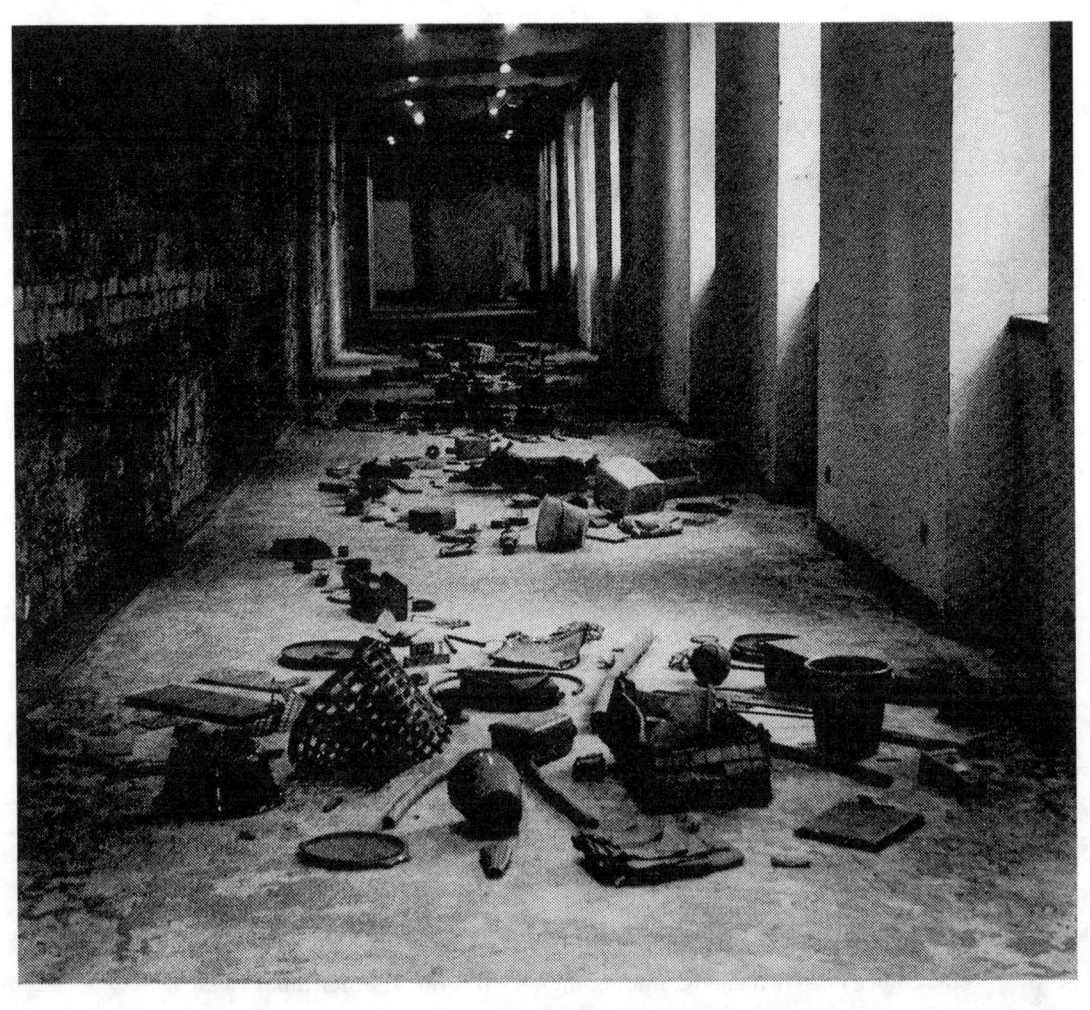

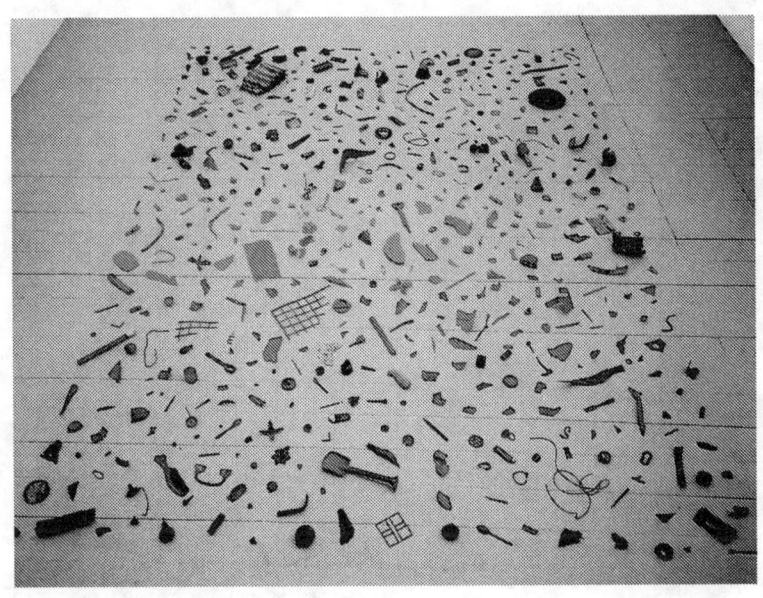

EVA HESSE

Eva Hesse, who died at the age of 34 in 1970, is a fascinating artist. She was part of the group that included Carl Andre, Robert Ryman, Sol LeWitt and Mel Bochner. She worked in series, like other Process artists. She called the repetitions 'sequels' and 'schemas'. Her artworks have immediate, challenging impact. They hang from ceilings, in rows, made of rubber, latex, cloth, wire, fibreglass, evoking organic forms in ambivalent, sensual ways.[1] Pieces such as *Ingeminate* offer up a mysterious affirmation of life in the form of two coils of cord connected by a long piece of surgical hose. *Sans II,* meanwhile, was a dozen rectangular 'compartments' made from fibreglass which hinted at some obscure systematization of flesh and organic form. Hesse wrote: '[i]f I can name the content…it's the total absurdity of life' (ib.). As Anna Chave noted, Hesse's forms resemble abstract 'breasts, clitorises, vaginas, fetuses, uteruses, fallopian tubes', articulating a new feminine sexual subjectivity, utilizing the female, not the male gaze.[2] In a 1968 statement, Hesse said, sounding like Ad Reinhardt:

> I remember I wanted to get to non-art, non connative, non anthropo-morphic, non geometric, non, nothing, everything, but of another kind, vision, sort. From a total other reference point. Is it possible? I have learned anything is possible.[3]

Sometimes loosely hanging, finding their own form, at other times Hesse's sculptures were bound with wire, as if 'making psychic models', as Robert Smithson said.[4]

1. In C. Nemser, 1970, 62.
2. A. Chave, in H. Cooper, 1992, 100f.
3. In L. Lippard, *Eva Hesse*, 1976.
4. Quoted in ib., 6.

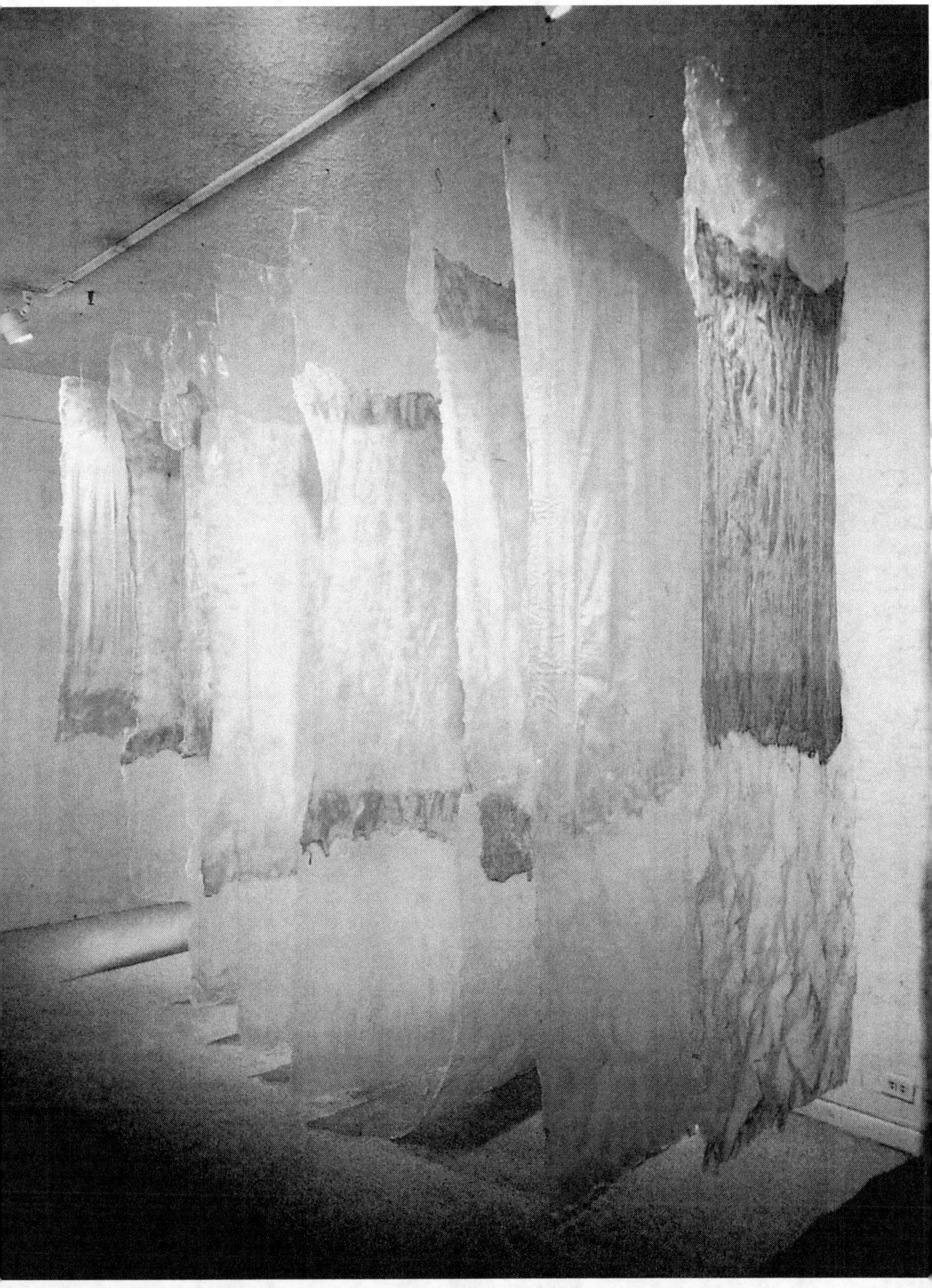

MICHAEL HEIZER: *DESERT CUTS*

Michael Heizer went on archælogical digs as a child with his father. He started out with the ambition to be a painter, which he studied at San Francisco. He made his first earthwork in 1967, and accompanied Smithson on geological expeditions. In 1968, Heizer collaborated with Smithson and Nancy Holt on a Super-8 film, *Mono-Lake*. (Heizer had invited Holt and Smithson to his parents' house at Lake Tahoe). Heizer's motorbike earthwork was entitled *Circular Surface Displacement*; it was made at Mono Lake.

Michael Heizer's other works include gouging huge holes in the ground and putting great chunks of rock in them. *Nine Nevada Depressions* (1968) was 5 cuts in the Blackrock desert, each one twelve feet long in an area 50 by 50 feet. *Munich Depression* (1969) was another cut, a line 15 feet deep.

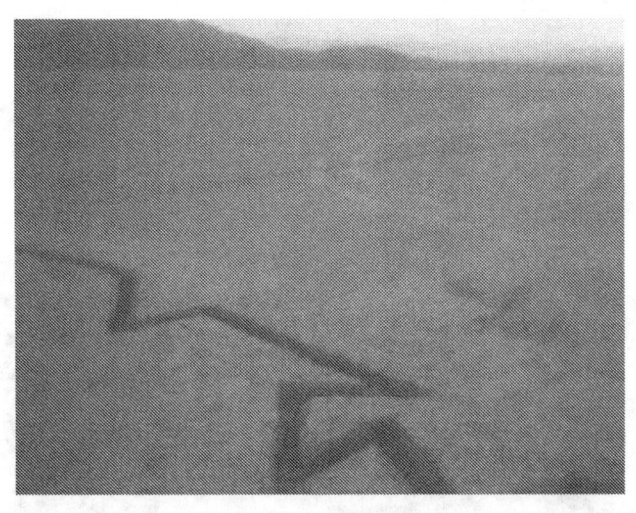

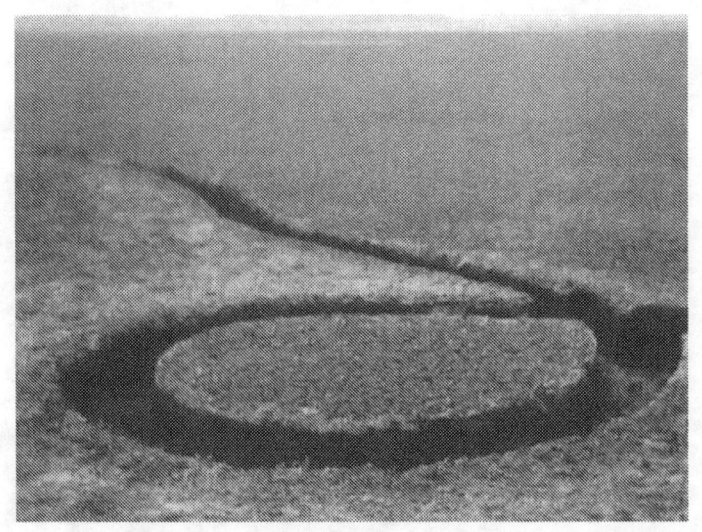

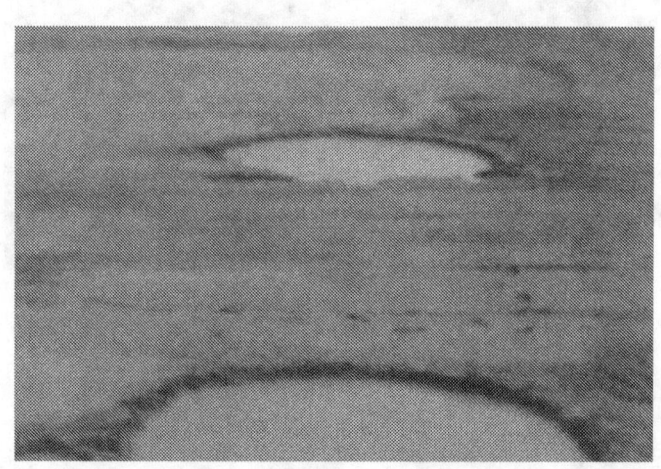

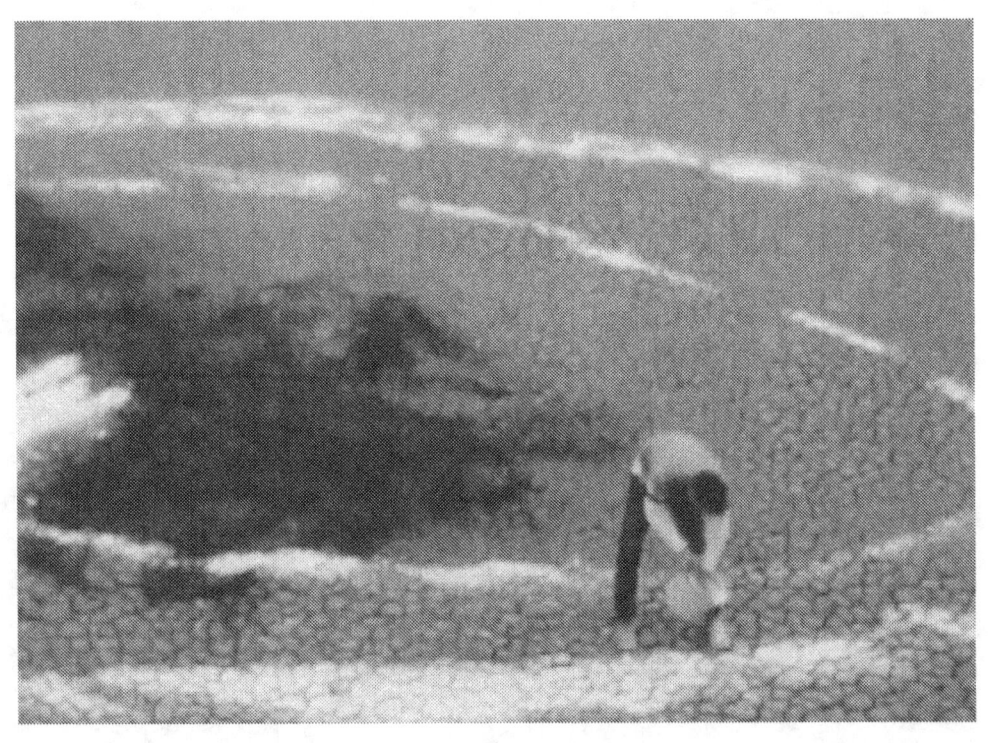

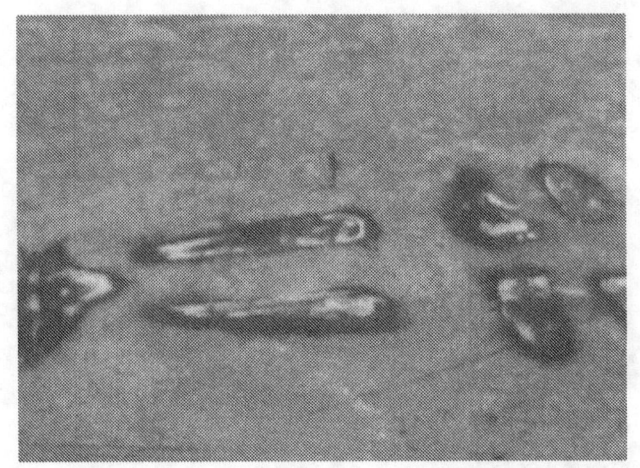

GORDON MATTA-CLARK

Gordon Matta-Clark was famous for transforming buildings by knocking enormous holes in them (*Conical Intersect*, 1975), or cutting a house in New Jersey in half (*Splitting*, 1974). But these were not sculpted spaces or physical gestures so much as Conceptual reorganizations of a structure. It's easy to discern the influence of Matta-Clark's interventions in houses and buildings (which he called 'unbuilding') on Andy Goldsworthy's holes and Rachel Whiteread's works (such as her impressions of rooms and houses). Matta-Clark bought up pieces of land in the borough of Queens (in 1973), in another Conceptual piece; none of them were big enough for housing of for much else (some were only 2 by 3 feet, tiny strips of land). *Reality Positions, Fake Estates* explored the notion of land ownership.

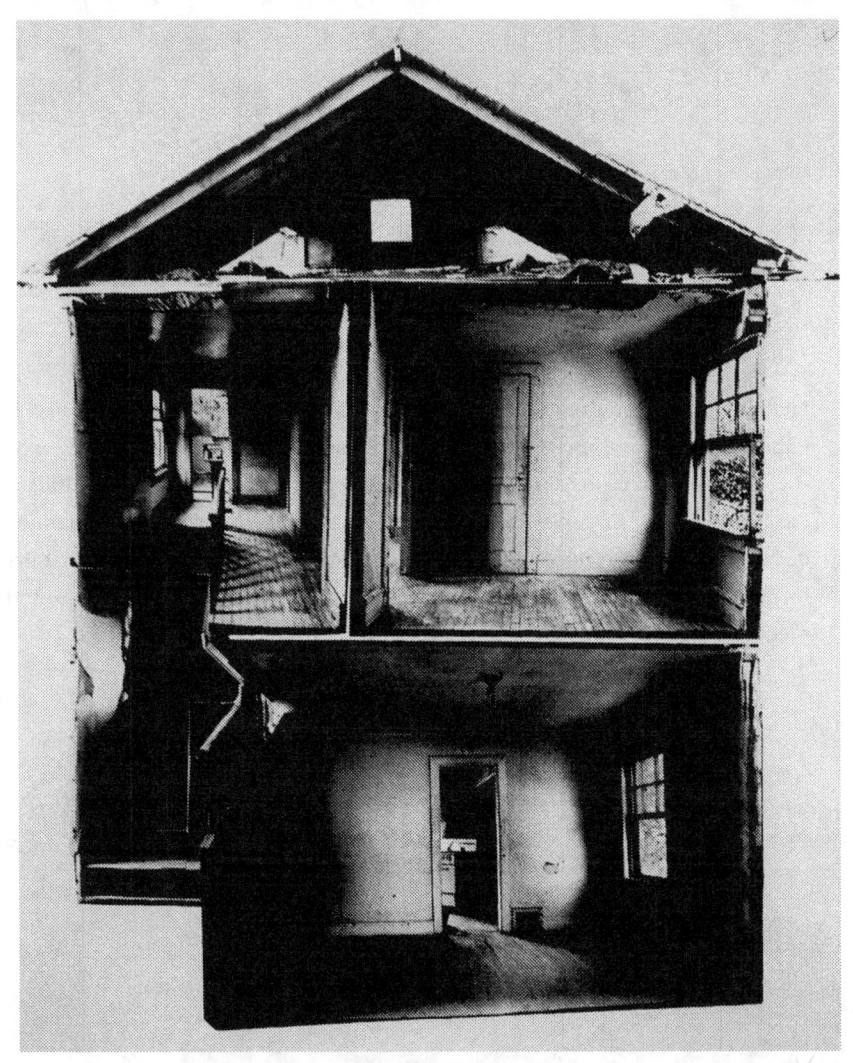

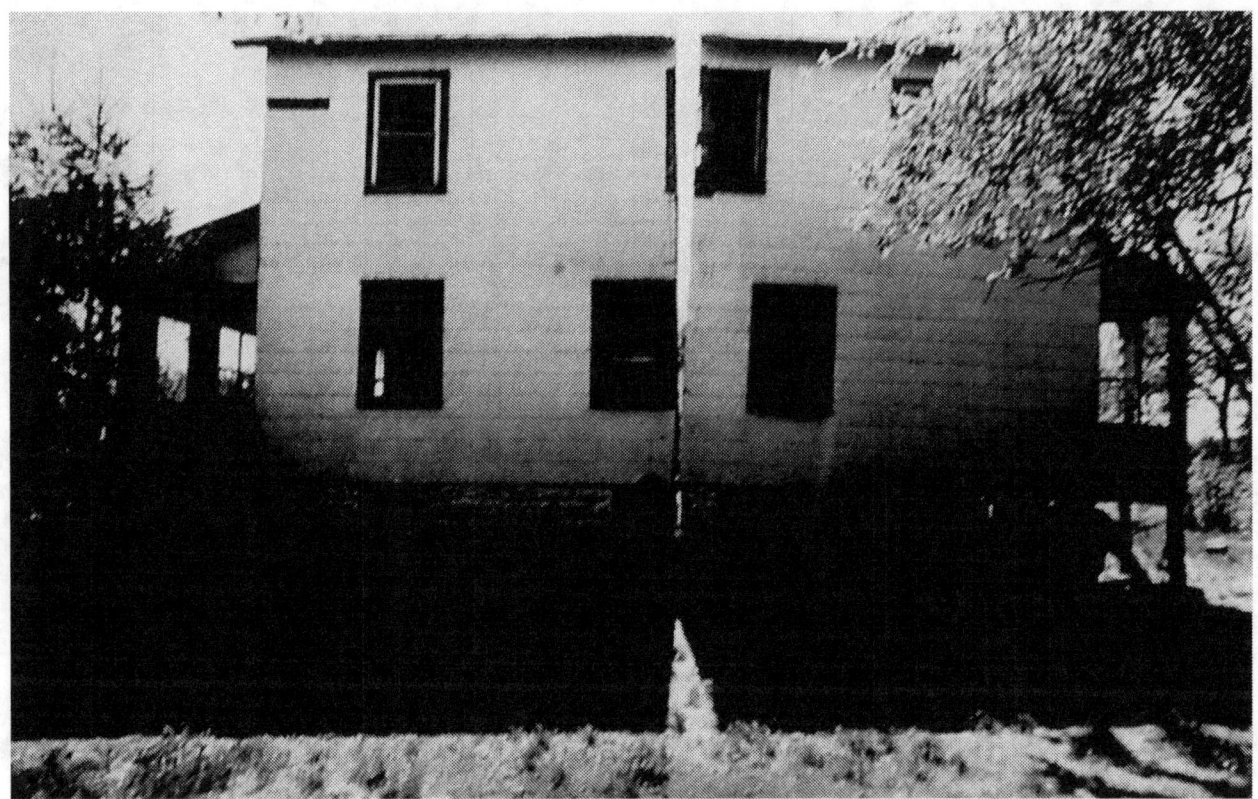

JACKIE WINSOR: *BURNT PIECE*

Jackie Winsor made the cube one of her major forms, but she fashioned her cubes from 'natural' materials, such as twine and wood. Winsor's cubes take the Minimal cube only as a starting point, because her series of cubes are explorations of the mysteries of being. Some of Winsor's works change or decay: the *Burnt Piece* cube burnt away, alchemically, when the artist fired its interior. As with the land artists, Winsor said: 'I was unable to see how the piece would look until the moment of completion' (D. Wheeler, 323).

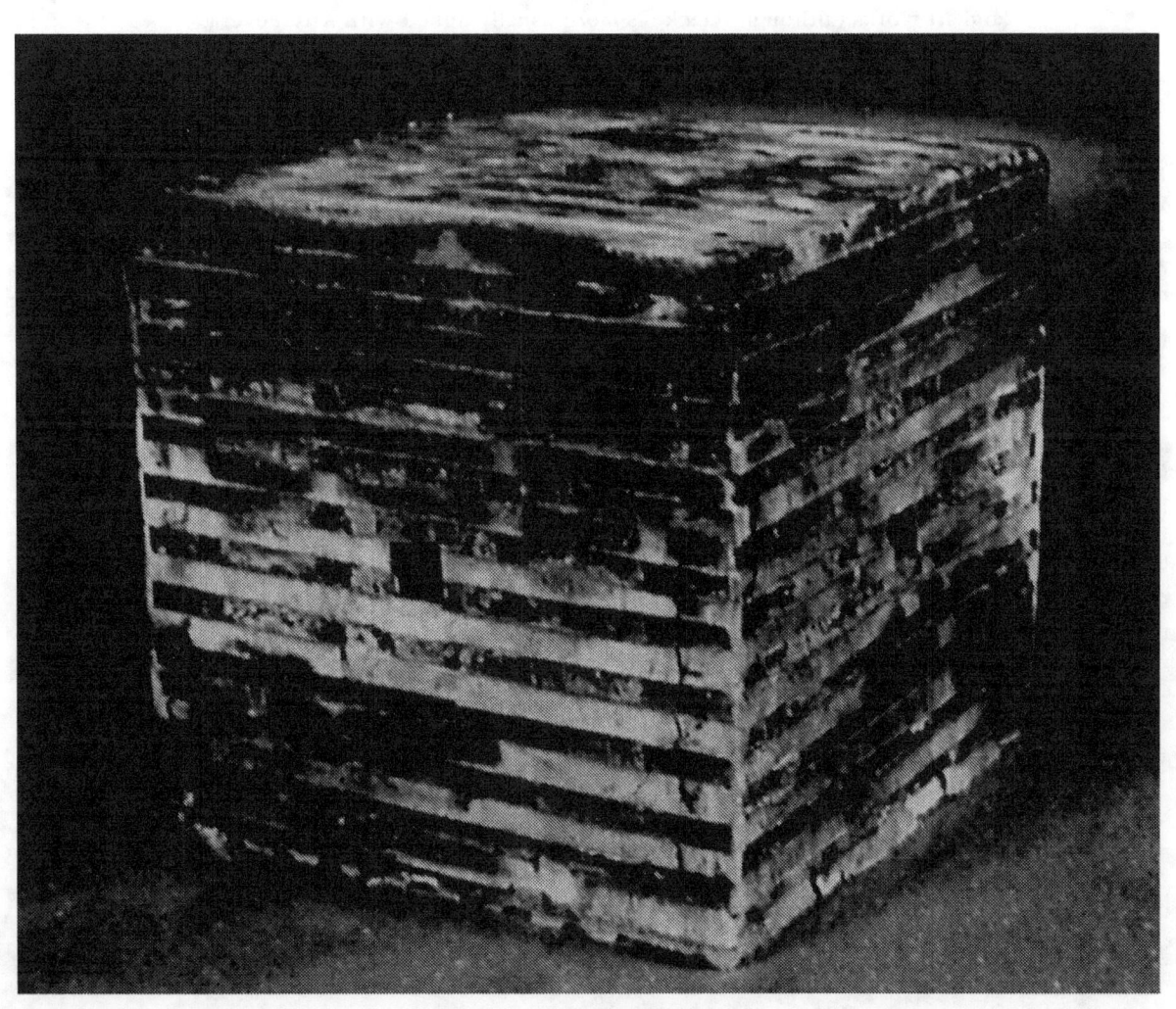

HANS HAACKE: *GRASS GROWS*

The German artist Hans Haacke has produced some of the most intriguing land art works (although Haacke is more usually linked with Arte Povera, Conceptual or process art, than land art). Many of Haacke's early works explored natural or organic systems. Later, Haacke moved on to social, economic and political systems (what Haacke called 'real-time systems'). Haacke's 1965 artistic statements included: 'make something that lives in time and makes the "spectator" experience time... articulate something natural'.[1] One of Haacke's tenets was 'the simpler the better'.

Grass Grows (1966 and 1969) was a mound of soil with grass growing out of it. Haacke later fashioned a row of beans growing along string suspended at an angle, in soil mounted on glass on the gallery floor (*Directed Growth*, 1972), and in tropical plants growing on a circular area of soil, *Rye in the Tropics* (1972). In *Sky Line* (1967) Haacke released white helium balloons over Central Park. Hans Haacke commented that 'in spite of my environmental and monumental thinking I am still fascinated by the nearly magic, self-contained quality of objects. My water levels, waves and condensation boxes are unthinkable without this physical separation from their surroundings'.[2]

1. H. Haacke, in J. Burnham, 1967.
2. H. Haacke, in ib.

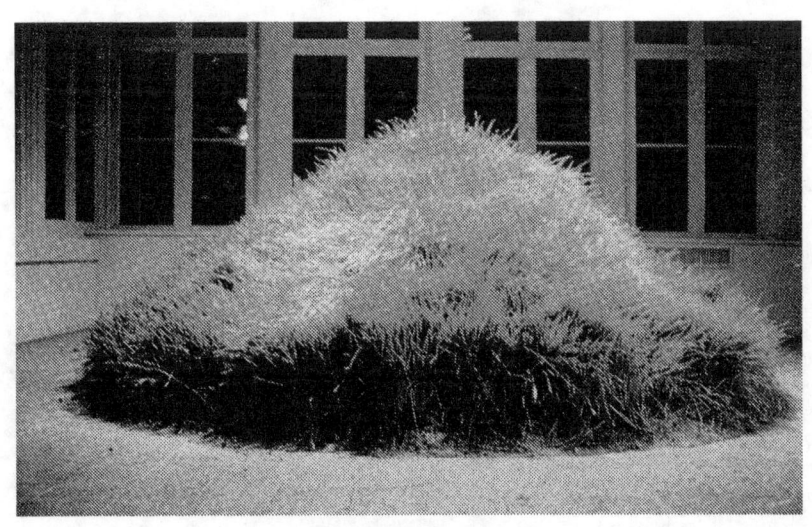

HANS HAACKE: *CONDENSATION CUBE*

Condensation Cube (1963-65) was a Plexiglas cube (a metre on each side) with water inside which condensed on the clear sides of the box, an exploration of process. 'It is changing freely, bound only by statistical limits' remarked Haacke of his 'Weather Box'.

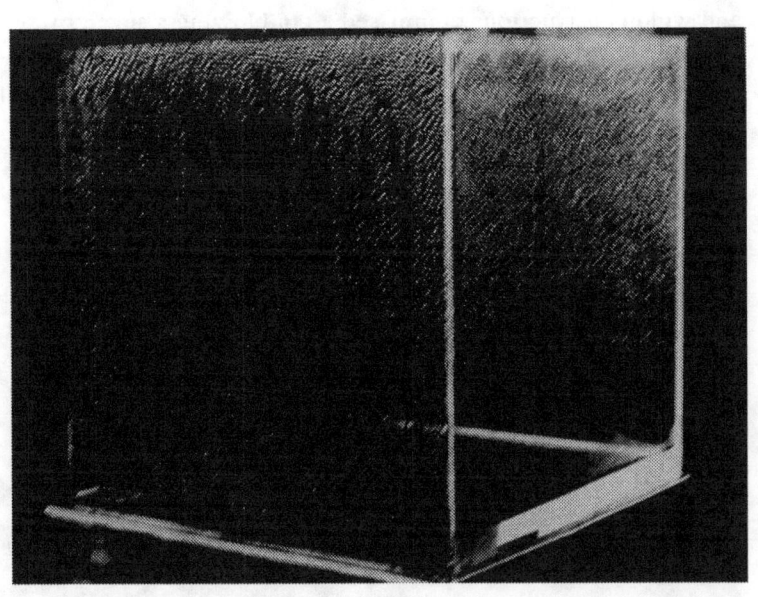

HANS HAACKE: *FOG, FLOODING, EROSION*

Many of Hans Haacke's most compelling artworks were made to explore the ephemeral qualities of ice, snow, fog, steam, smoke and water. *Fog, Flooding, Erosion* (1969) employed a sprinkler system to turn a lawn in Seattle (WA) into mud. *Fog Dripping From or Freezing On Exposed Surfaces* (Boston, 1971) and *Spray of Ithaca: Falls Freezing and Melting On Rope* (1969) explored water and fog freezing on waterfalls and trees. One of Haacke's air and wind constructions comprised a fan blowing a seven by seven foot chiffon sail hung parallel to the gallery floor. Another air sculpture was a balloon balanced above an air jet (a favourite with science and natural history museums). He had proposals for monumental-sized windmills and sails, all naturally powered by the winds. Haacke preferred to use unmechanical sources of energy.

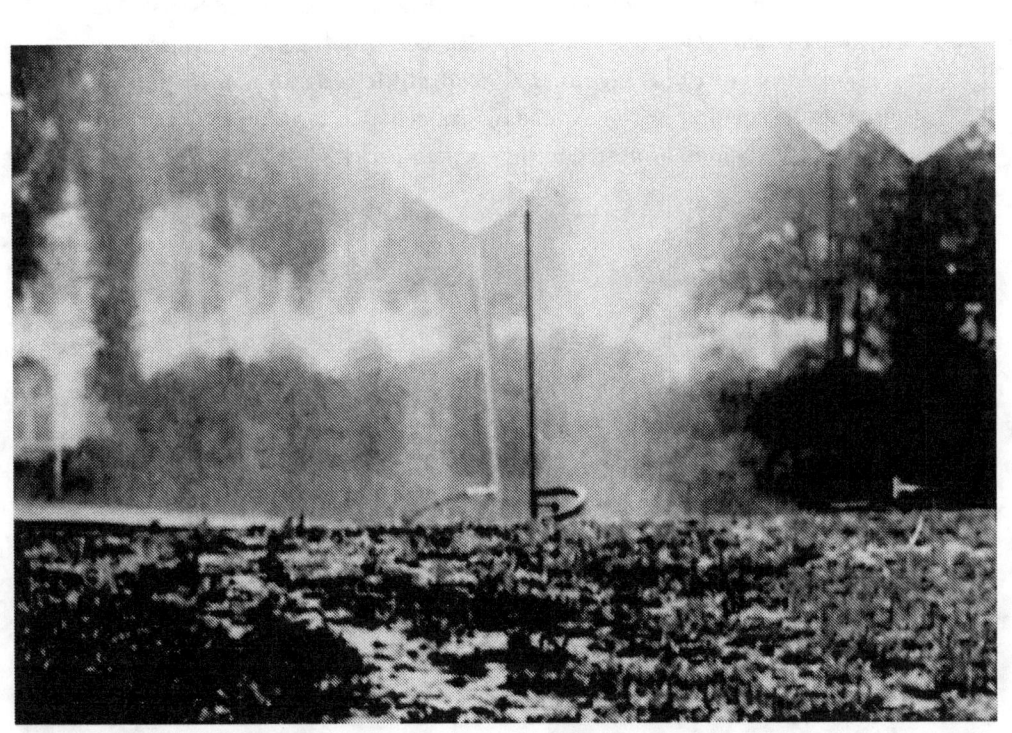

HANS HAACKE: *PETITION*

Hans Haacke later considered economic systems in works such as *Shapolsky et al, Manhattan Real Estate Holdings, a Real-Time Social System* (1971). For the *Information* show at Gotham's Museum of Modern Art (in 1971), Haacke exhibited a poll about Governor Rockefeller running for election, inviting visitors to vote. Haacke took on cultural institutions such as museums, landlords, and politicians such as President Reagan and British PM, Margaret Thatcher. On a few occasions Haacke's proposals were negated by the authorities of the Guggenheim, Wallraf-Richartz and Metropolitan museums, with works and shows being can-celled as a result. Other artists (such as Daniel Buren) protested in support of Haacke.

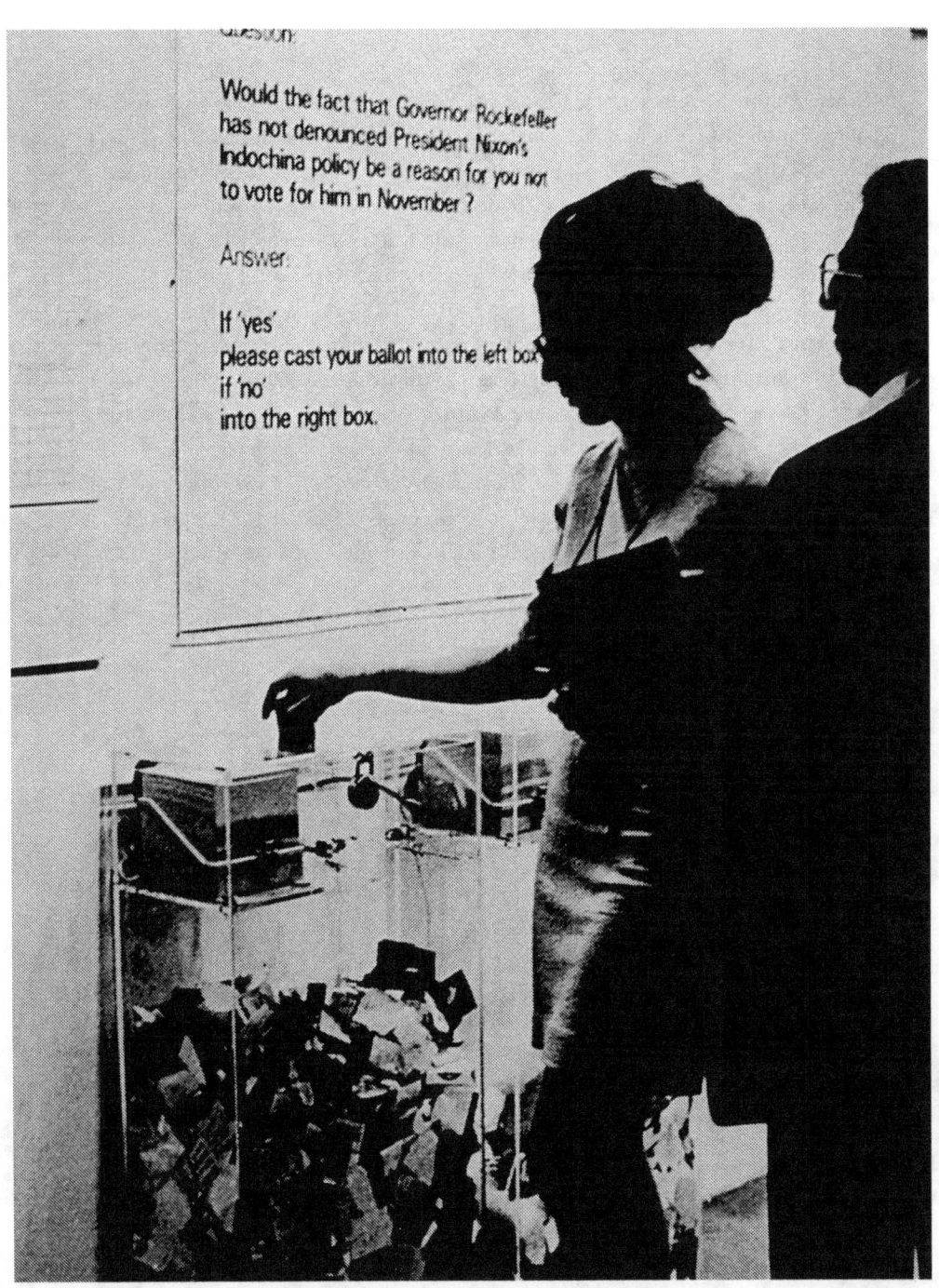

HAMISH FULTON: *ROCK FALL ECHO DUST*

Hamish Fulton is Richard Long's contemporary (he was born a year later than Long). Fulton is a companion of Long's many journeys and walks (and works). Fulton writes: '[m]y work is about the experience of walking' (echoing Long's ethics). Fulton continues: '[t]he framed artwork is about a state of mind – it cannot convey the experience of the walk.' What counts in Fulton's work may be the communication of a particular state of mind (in Zen fashion). The reduction to one or two words, like Zen *haiku*, the unfussy design of Fulton's text works, the lack of extra æsthetic paraphernalia, attest to his desire for clarity of communication. Fulton's *Seven Days (Whistling Elk): a seven day walk in the Rocky Mountains of Alberta Canada* (1978) is similar to Long's works: a large black and white photograph (of pieces of wood on soil, it seems to be) is set above a caption which is also the title of the work. Another Fulton artwork is a text piece, just like one of Long's text pieces: four words are printed in capitals in red and black: 'ROCK/ FALL/ ECHO/ DUST'.

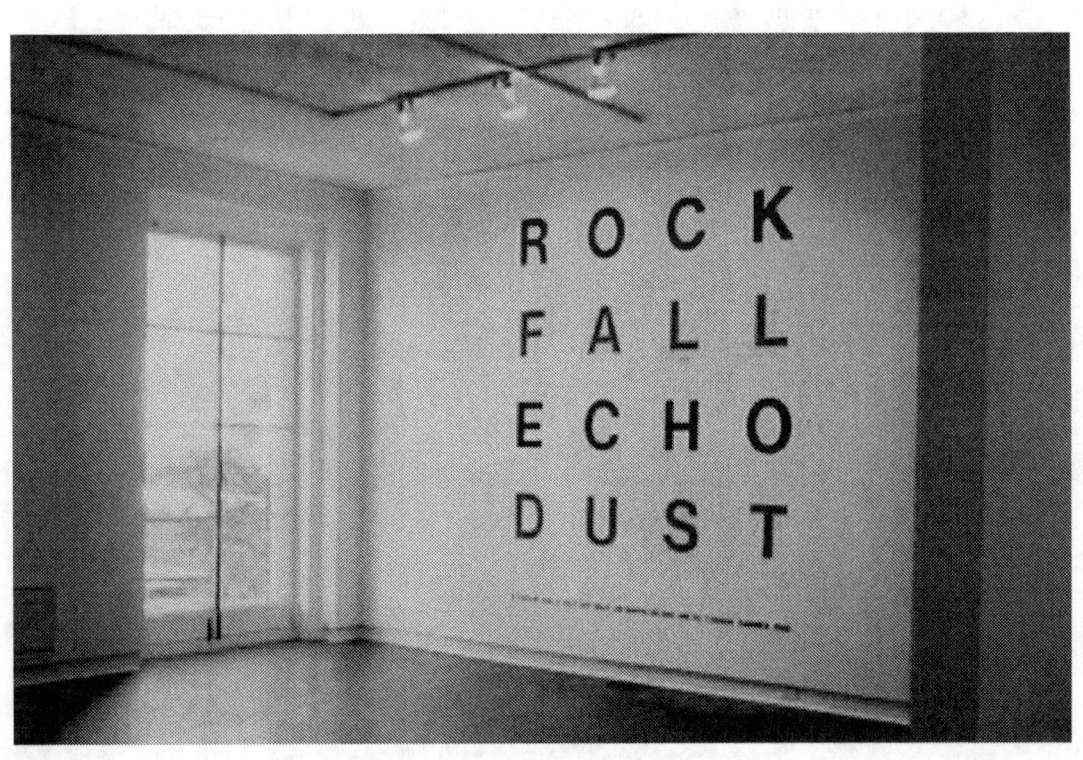

HAMISH FULTON: *NO TALKING*

Art possesses nature and yet does not possess nature: something always remains elusive. What's there, in nature, is no longer there in the artwork. As David Reason noted of Hamish Fulton's work: '[i]n the work, everything derives from what cannot be shown and shared – walking and camping in close relationship to a specific patch of the natural world.'[1] The viewer does not experience the real subject of the work, which is the walk. Instead, the viewer has to place her/ himself into the role played by the artist, as s/he walks in the landscape.

1. D. Reason: "Echo and Reflections", in S. Bann, 169.

NO TALKING
FOR SEVEN DAYS

ALKING FOR SEVEN DAYS IN A WOOD JANUARY FULL MOON CAIRNGORMS SCOT

RICHARD LONG: *STONE CIRCLES*

Some land artists, such as Richard Long, maintain that their stone circles are subjective, private, individual works, quite different from the public, social art of the prehistoric stones circles. The ancient stone rings were made by a group of people, a society, constructed, perhaps, according to the plans of a priestly elite. Land art circles are the work of one person, but a major contemporary artist is no less a member of the cultural, æsthetic élite. Prehistoric stone circles may have been made for religious rituals, perhaps connected with the position of certain astronomical bodies. Land art stone circles are for private consumption, for an onlooker who wanders into a gallery or a space then out again, back into the hurly burly and stench of the city. Yet the ancient sacred sites and land art/ Postminimal/ Arte Povera earthworks have much in common, because art and religion join at so many points.

Richard Long produces installations of stone circles for his exhibitions, as well as stone rows and lines, mud wall drawings and the like. One or two of Long's stone circles are small – *Circle of Standing Stones* (1983), which is 26 stones arranged in a circle of a half metre in diameter, *Cornwall Slate Circle* (1982), 34 stones in a 2 metre circle, and *Standing Stone Circle* (1982), 36 stones in a similar size circle. The small stone circles are often made of standing stones, and many of the outdoor circles are of this type (*Stones in Bolivia*, 1981, for instance). Long's use of standing stones, rather than ones laid flat, echoes prehistoric stone circles – for instance, the Scottish stone circle (*Stones and Stac Pollaidh*, 1981), or the Icelandic *Touchstone, Shelter From the Storm* (1982). Long's small stone circles are intimate works compared to the broad, large pieces. In Britain there are a number of small stone circles which produce similar atmospheres of human-scale and intimacy (such as the small circles on the ridges of hills in Dorset). 'I like simple, emotional, quiet, vigorous art' says Long.[1] While the large circles in the galleries of Western cities speak of polished, upmarket art, the small, 1.5 metre stone circles speak of small wayside shrines. The large gallery circles are planned and organized months in advance, but still look spontaneous. Long's small outdoor stone circles, though, are direct and spontaneous responses to a landscape.

1. In R. Fuchs, 236.

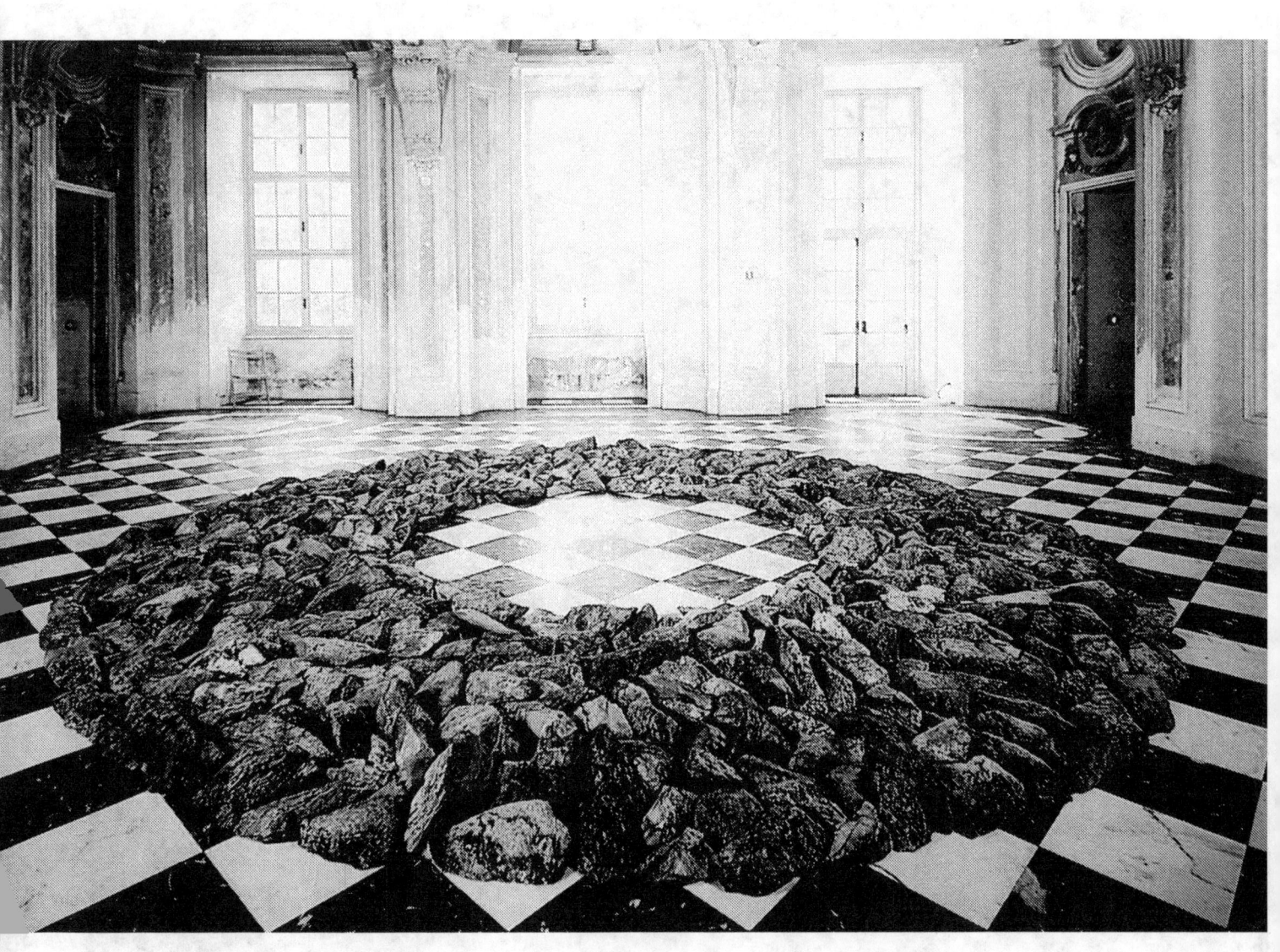

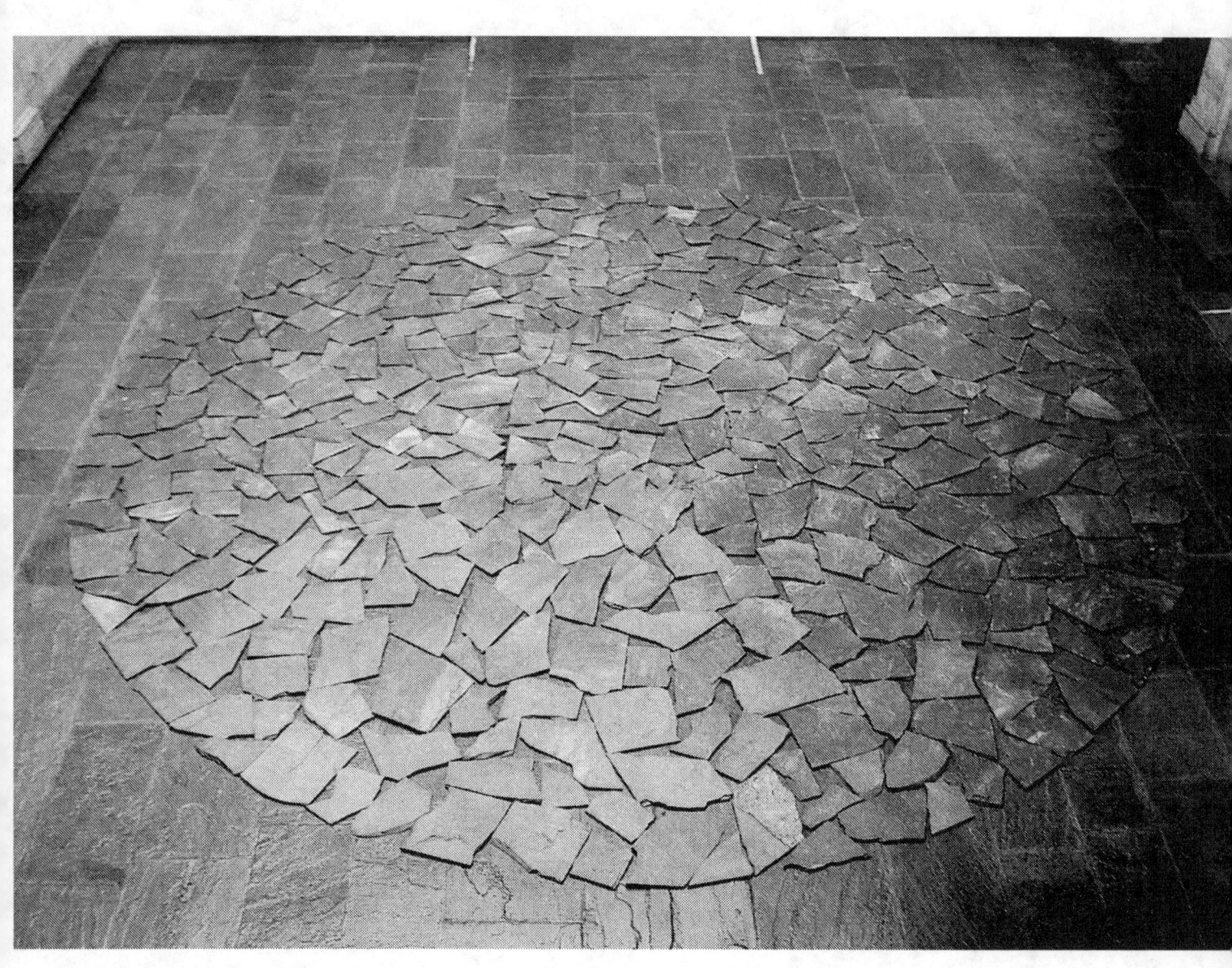

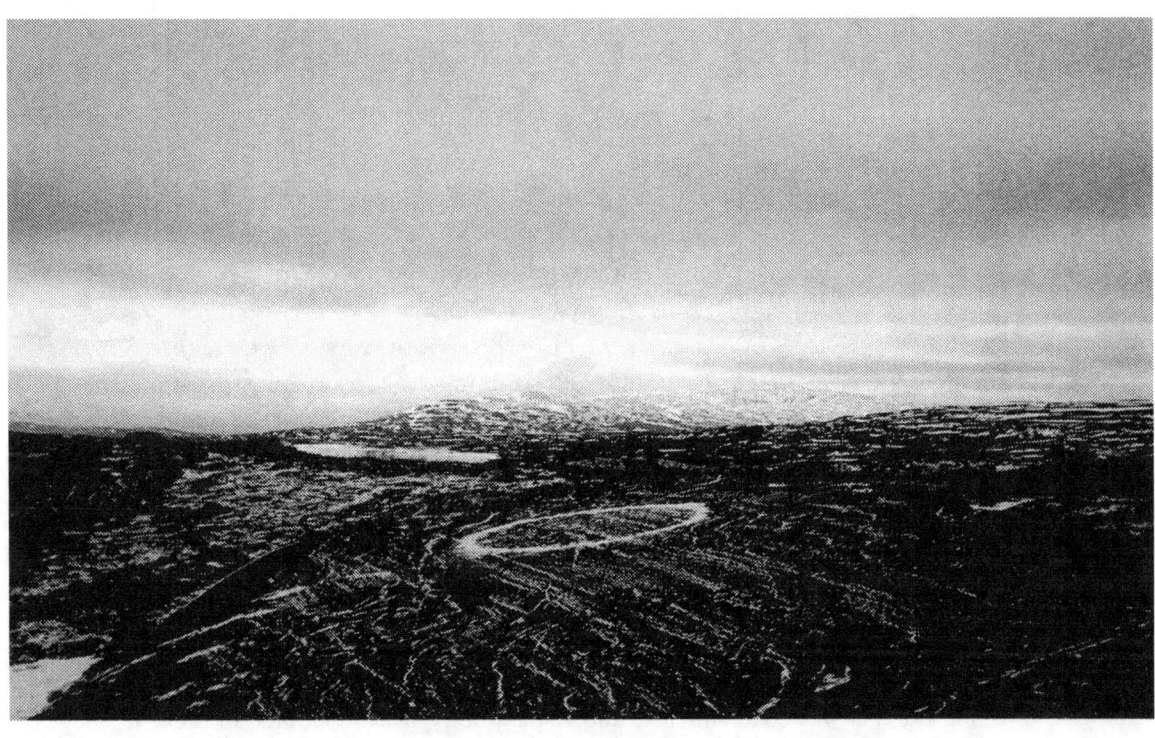

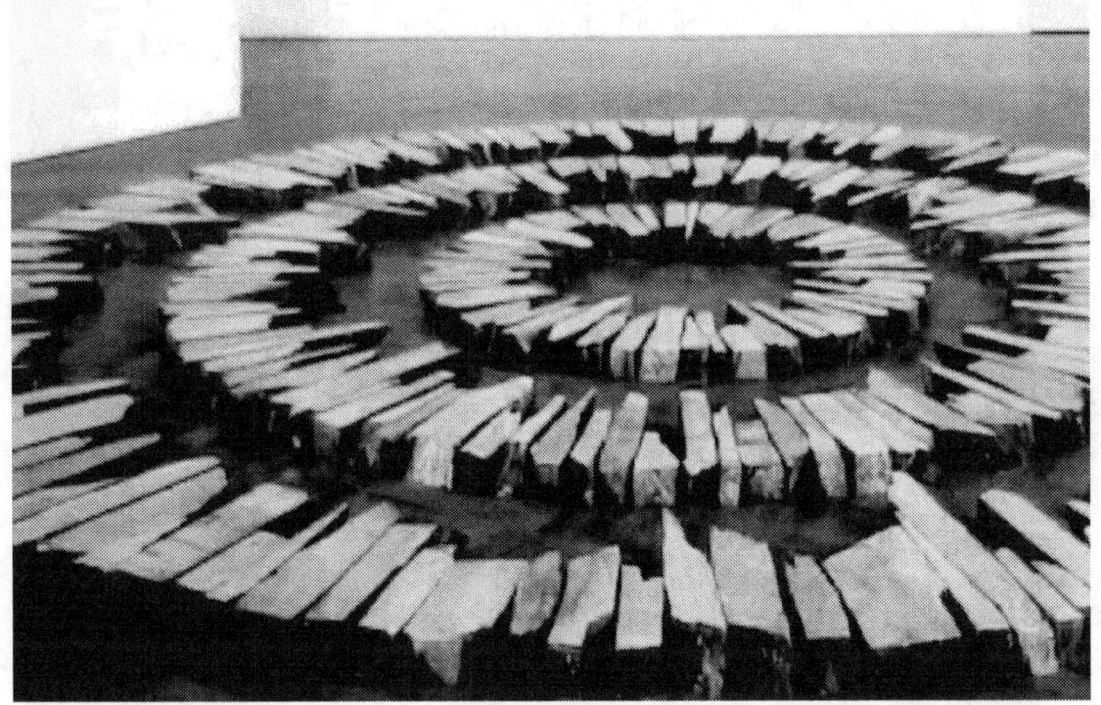

RICHARD LONG: *A FOUR DAY WALK*

Land art is meta-art, art about art, art that relies on other art to 'exist'. It's Conceptual, 'art as language'. Land art exists for a brief moment, then becomes myth, gossip, photography, words. Many of Richard Long's works are simply collections of words, printed in capitals, in Eric Gill's font, Gill Sans, on large pieces of paper. The text printed opposite is be very close to being a Richard Long artwork in itself (although he likes them printed larger). Long's exhibitions often comprise installations of textworks in frames on the walls beside stone or mud sculptures, on the floors (and occasionally the walls).

There's no picture, no map, no reference to anything other than itself. This work is simply these words. At the same time, Long's works have all sorts of readings. He chooses particular words, often plain words, or words used in simple phrases and clauses. The vocabulary Long employs – *road, grass, fields, mud* – is simple and direct, with few embellishments. Nevertheless, Long's text works echo concrete and visual poetry at many points. In the book *Mountains and Waters* there are works with distinctly 'poetic' titles: 'November Sunshine', 'A Spring Walk', 'In the Cloud', 'Dorset Song Lines', 'Walking Up Cedar Creek', 'Dartmoor Stones' and 'Mind Rock'. Long also uses descriptive words which are usually the province of poetry: for instance, a text work from Nepal (1983) reads like cut-up poetry, a poem with verbs and pronouns excised:

**GREAT HIMALAYAN TIME A LINE OF MOMENTS
MY FATHER STARLIT SNOW
HUMAN TIME FROZEN BOOTS**

A FOUR DAY WALK

A LINE OF GROUND 94 MILES LONG

ROAD STONY TRACK ROAD GRASS FIELD
ROAD BARE ROCK LANE ROAD STONY PATH
HEATHER BURNT MOOR STONY PATH ROAD
ROUGH GRASSLAND RIVERBED SHEEPTRACKS EARTH WALL
ROUGH GRASSLAND GRASS FIELDS BRAMBLES GRASS FIELD PATH
ROAD DUSTY LANE
ROAD GRASS FIELDS EARTH PATH ROAD
SAND BEACH CLIFF PATH ROAD ROCKS
CLIFF PATH SAND DUNES SAND PATH EARTH PATH
ROAD OLD RAILWAY TRACK MUD FLATS SEA WALL
MUD FLATS ROAD RIVERBANK ROAD

ENGLAND 1980

STONE WALK

FROM ONE STONE TO ANOTHER, PICKING UP AND CARRYING
EACH STONE TO THE PLACE OF THE NEXT STONE

STONE TO STONE ALLT TO BLANYOY
STONE TO STONE BLANYOY TO HAY BLUFF
STONE TO STONE HAY BLUFF TO TYMPA
STONE TO STONE TYMPA TO Y DÂS
STONE TO STONE Y DÂS TO GIST WEN
STONE TO STONE GIST WEN TO CORN DÛ
STONE TO STONE CORN DÛ TO PEN Y FAN
STONE TO STONE PEN Y FAN TO CRIBIN
STONE TO STONE CRIBIN TO WAUN FÂCH
STONE TO STONE WAUN FÂCH TO PENTWYNGLAS
STONE TO STONE PENTWYNGLAS TO TAL TRWNAU
STONE TO STONE TAL TRWNAU TO Y FAN
STONE TO STONE Y FAN TO TWYN TAL-Y-CEFN
STONE TO STONE TWYN TAL-Y-CEFN TO BLWCH-BACH
STONE TO STONE BWLCH-BACH TO BÂL-MAWR
STONE TO STONE BÂL-MAWR TO GARN-WEN
STONE TO STONE GARN-WEN TO SUGAR LOAF
STONE TO STONE SUGAR LOAF TO ALLT

A 101 MILE WALK IN THE BLACK MOUNTAINS AND BRECON
BEACONS

WALES 1984

SPRING WALK

PRIMROSES AT 3 MILES
FROGSPAWN AT 18 MILES
A CROW NEST-BUILDING AT 29 MILES
A FARMER SOWING AT 34 MILES
LADYBIRDS AT 38 MILES
SQUIRRELS AT 57 MILES
LAMBS AT 62 MILES
STICKY BUDS AT 67 MILES
A TREE PLANTED AT 70 MILES
A BUTTERFLY AT 85 MILES
BLOSSOM AT 104 MILES
DAFFODILS AT 112 MILES

AVON ENGLAND 1991

RICHARD LONG: *LINES*

Denying it or hinting at it, Richard Long's sculpture is definitely 'religious'/ 'mystical'/ 'spiritual'. Walking itself is sacred; making art is sacred; the allusions to stone circles are religious; circles themselves are religious; the awe with which viewers regard the sculpture has a religious aspect, and so on. Not all of Long's works are circles – there are always the lines. Long continued to make lines in the shape of a cross from time to time, such as in *Two Places* (Bolivia, 1972), where a small cross is made on marshland in a pile of stalks. Another cross was made in Iceland from some stones (*Stopping Place Stones*, 1974). The crosses are very much like geometric marks 'drawn' onto the landscape, as if to mark a place. Most of the single straight lines are short, like the crosses, such as *Walking Without Travelling* (Sahara, 1988). Occasionally, Long makes a square zigzag line: short right angles are marked upon bare soil, as in *Campfire Ash* (Bolivia, 1972 – all these works are from *Mountains and Waters*). Another zigzag line sculpture, in Antwerp in 1973, extends outwards to take over the gallery: each Long sculpture is made for a particular space, and expands to consume the gallery floor. The zigzag lines recall the Peruvian Nazca animals and symbols drawn on the lava plain (Long had walked along one of the desert lines in 1972: he also made sculptures which employed symbols such as the puma, condor, falcon, moon, sun and rain.)

The rows are really lines – Long calls them lines. *A Line in Ireland* (1974) is a short pile of flat rocks in a line, while *A Line in Australia* (1977) is a wider line, more like a row of red rocks.[1] *A Line in Scotland* (1981) is a row of small flattish rocks that were stood on end at Cul Mór, like a row of prehistoric standing stones. In *Ash Line* and *Bushfire Line* (both 1994, Australia), Long dropped wood ash in a short line in a forest. In Yorkshire in 1977, as in Bolivia in 1981, Long cleared a space each side of the line as he picked up rocks (ib., 124, 126). The opposite of this line is the 'negative' line, made by leaving a path through a tangle of rocks, as in *A Line in California* (1982).

1. *Richard Long*, 54-55.

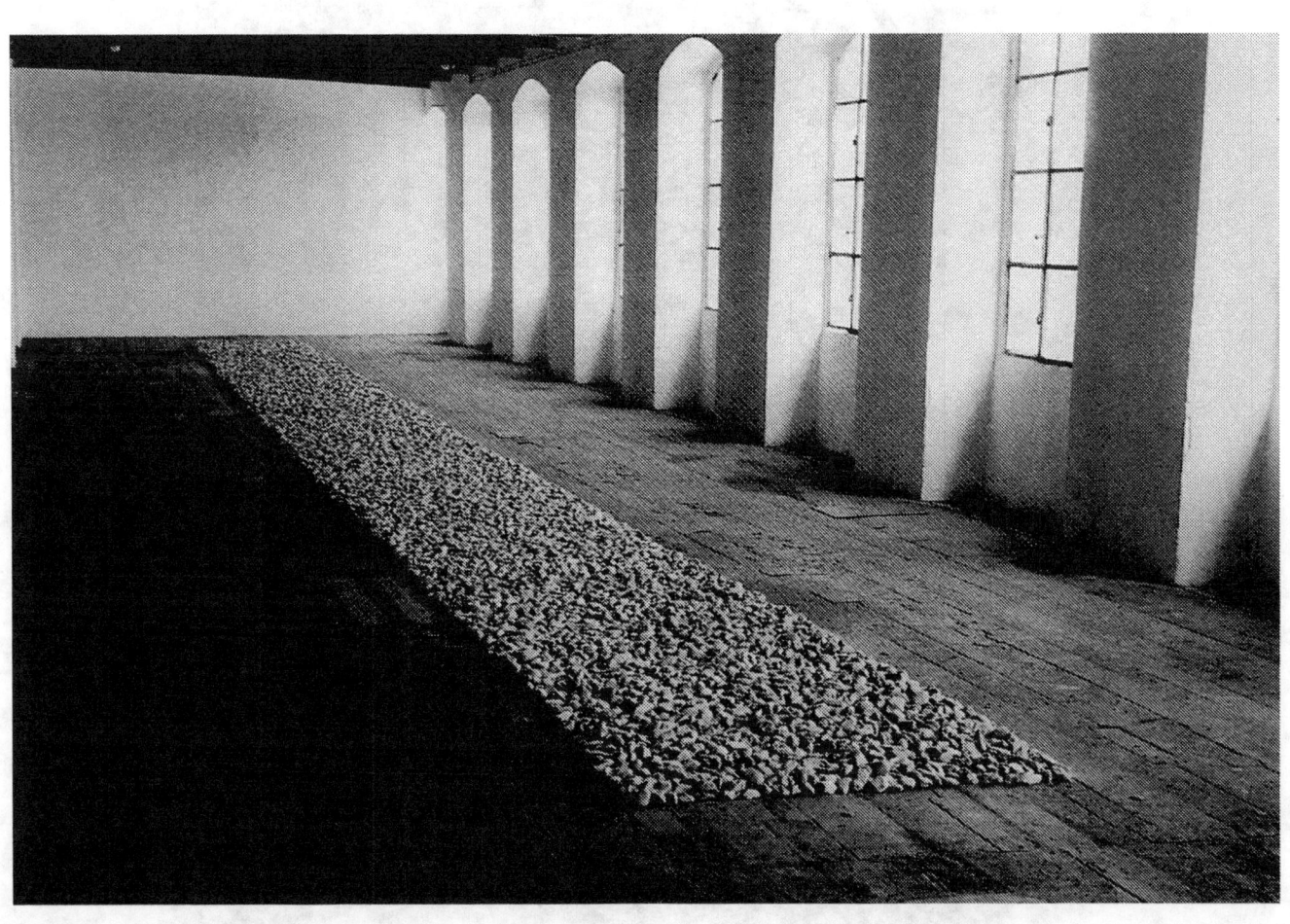

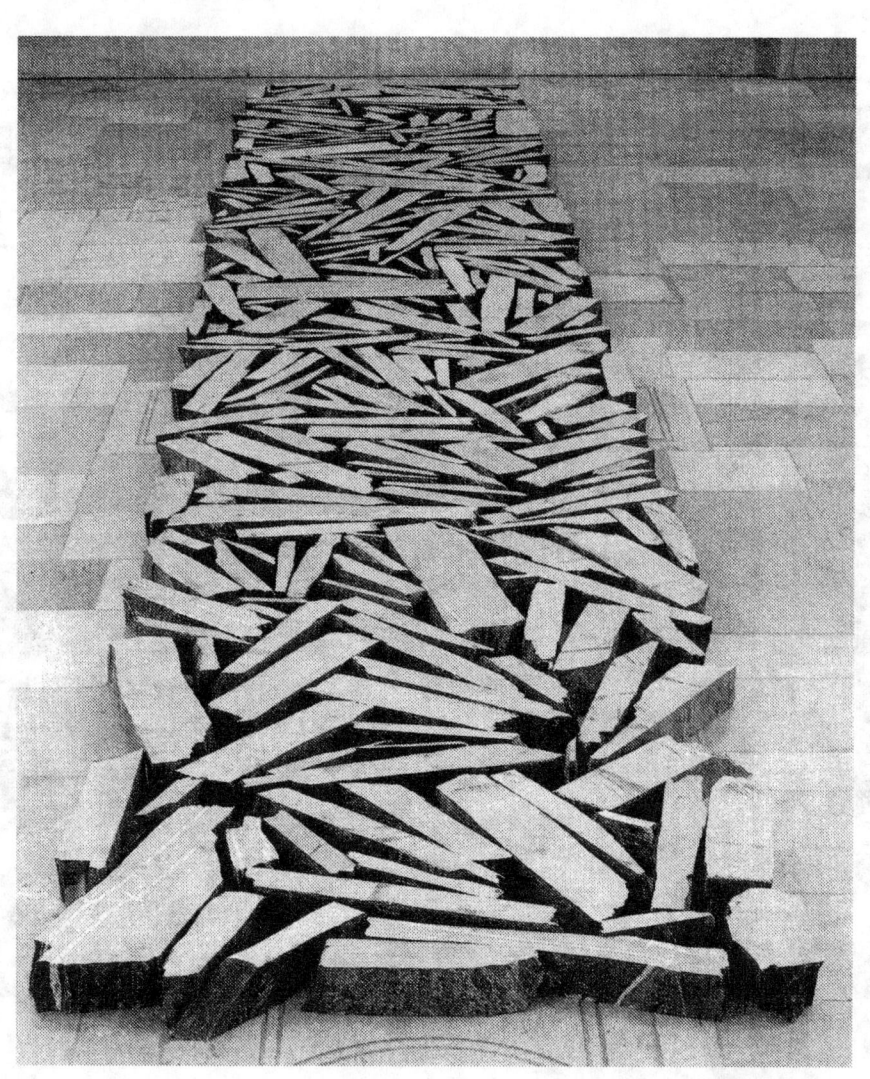

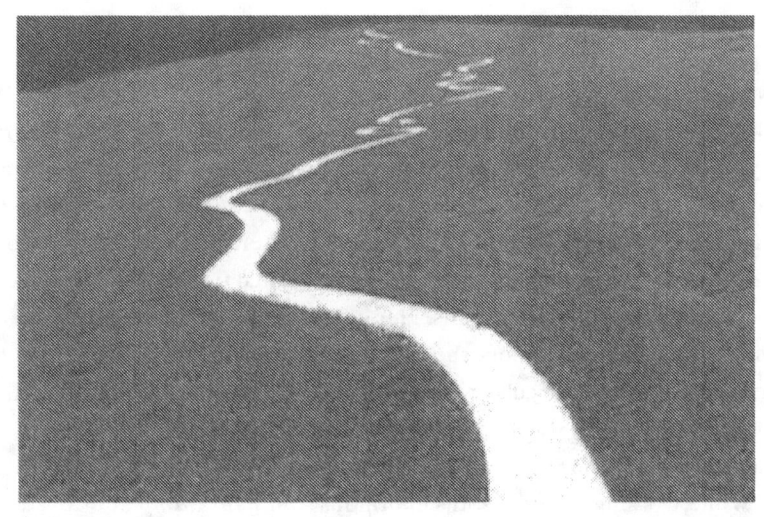

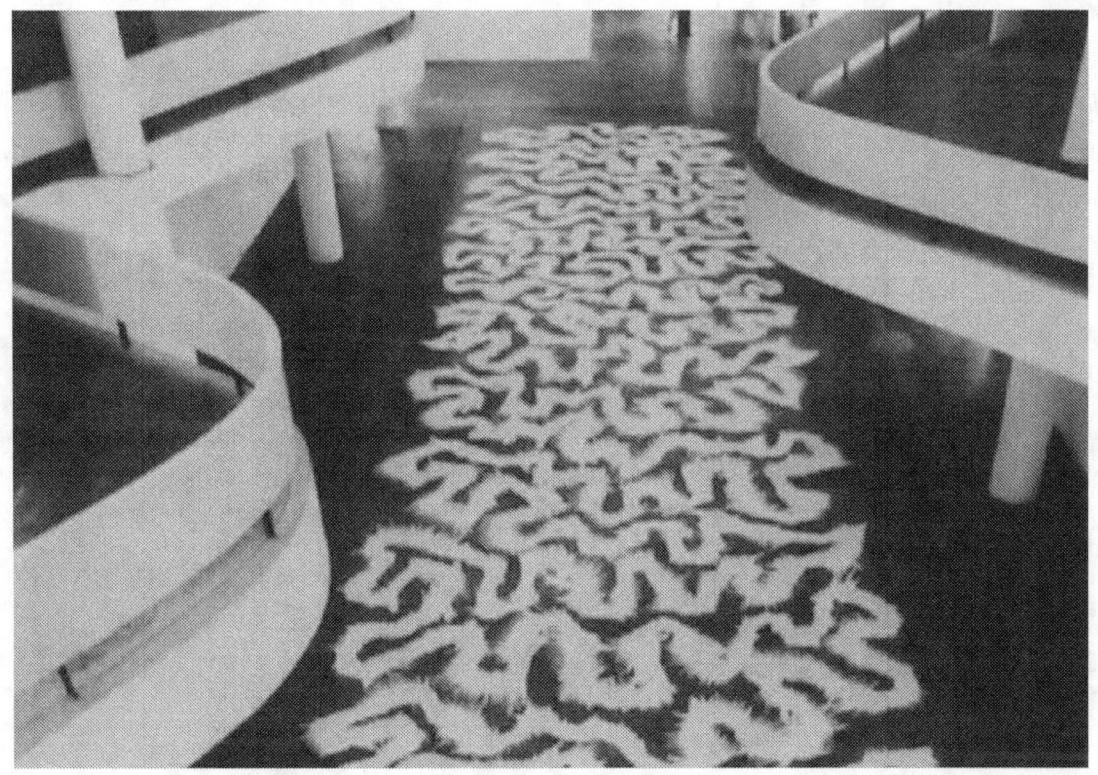

NANCY HOLT: *SUN TUNNELS*

Nancy Holt married the key earthwork artist, Robert Smithson, in 1963. She worked with him on his non-site projects, including the famous *Spiral Jetty* and *Amarillo Ramp*. Nancy Holt's art, with its large, heavy landscaping gestures (such as her *Dark Star Park*), is comparable with the male land artists. The globes and pools of water, though, are traditional 'feminine' volumes, here given a new, monumental turn. Holt's art concerns the movements of the heavens. Her sculptures focus the viewer on the motions of the earth, moon, sun and stars. Holt's art is concerned with the notion of time, in particular with geological time, the relation between time and the Earth. Holt was impressed by the desert when she visited it in the late 1960s with Smithson and Michael Heizer.

While working on Smithson's enormous *Amarillo Ramp* after his death in a plane crash, Holt developed the idea for the gigantic *Sun Tunnels*, 18ft long pipes that were 9 feet high with many holes punched in the side, to let light in.[1] She searched for a suitable site – a desert floor surrounded by low hills. The site she chose (and bought) was in the Great Basin Desert of Utah. *Sun Tunnels* was finished in 1976, with holes in the side of each concrete tube 7, 8, 9 and 10 inches diameter. The holes corresponded with star constellations (Capricorn, Draco, Columba and Perseus), as with *Hydra's Head*. During the day the sun creates points of light on the bottom of the tunnels that move. The moon also shines through the holes by night. The pipes were set about 32° North and South of true East and West, aligned with the rising and setting of the sun at the Summer and Winter solstices. *Sun Tunnels* links together the movements of celestial objects and the viewer on the planet. Holt said she had the idea for *Sun Tunnels* while being out in the desert and watching the sun rising and setting. The flat desert area evoked 'a sense of being on this planet, rotating in space, in universal time' (1977). It is a cosmological piece of land art, something of an observatory, like the Bronze Age stone circles of Europe. 'I wanted to bring the vast space desert back to human scale' (1977). The astronomical observatory has been an enduring theme in land art. Robert Morris, Michael Dan Archer, Julia Barton and Andy Goldsworthy have also made viewing sites.

1. See N. Holt, 1975, 1977; T. Castle, 1982.

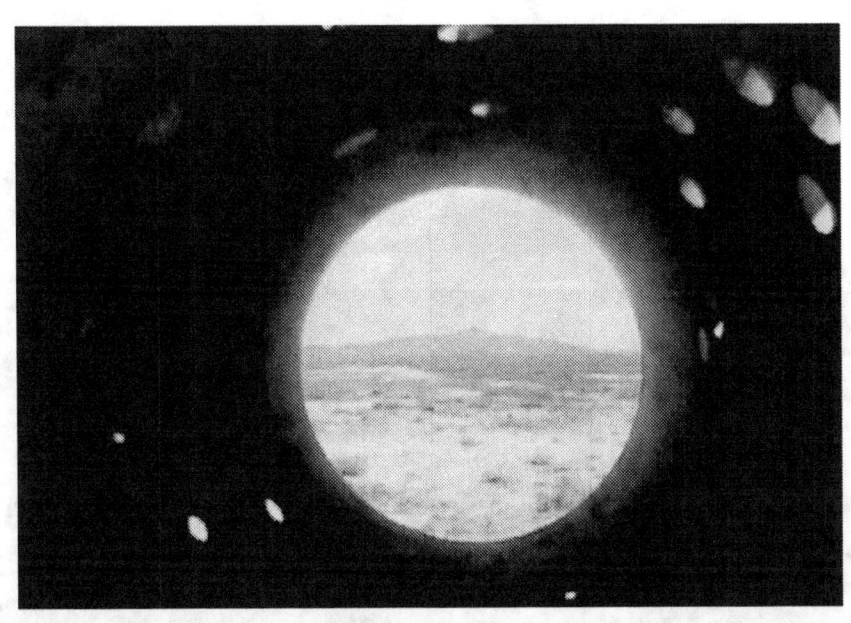

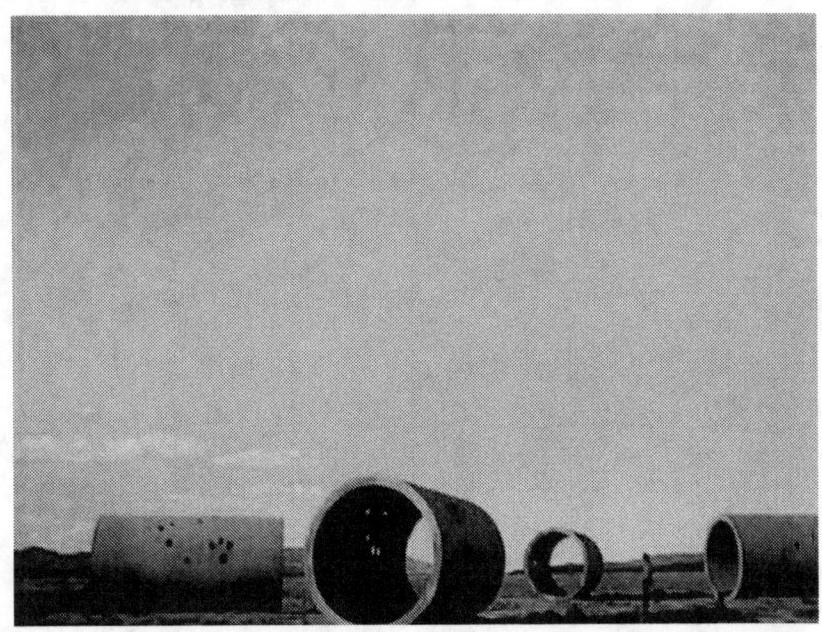

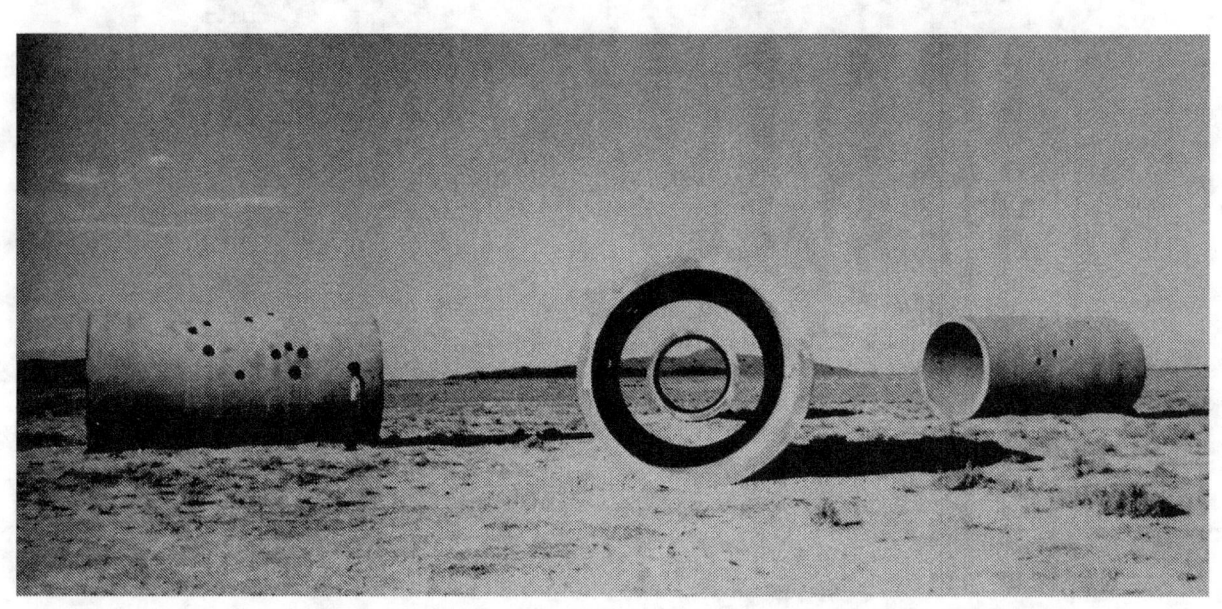

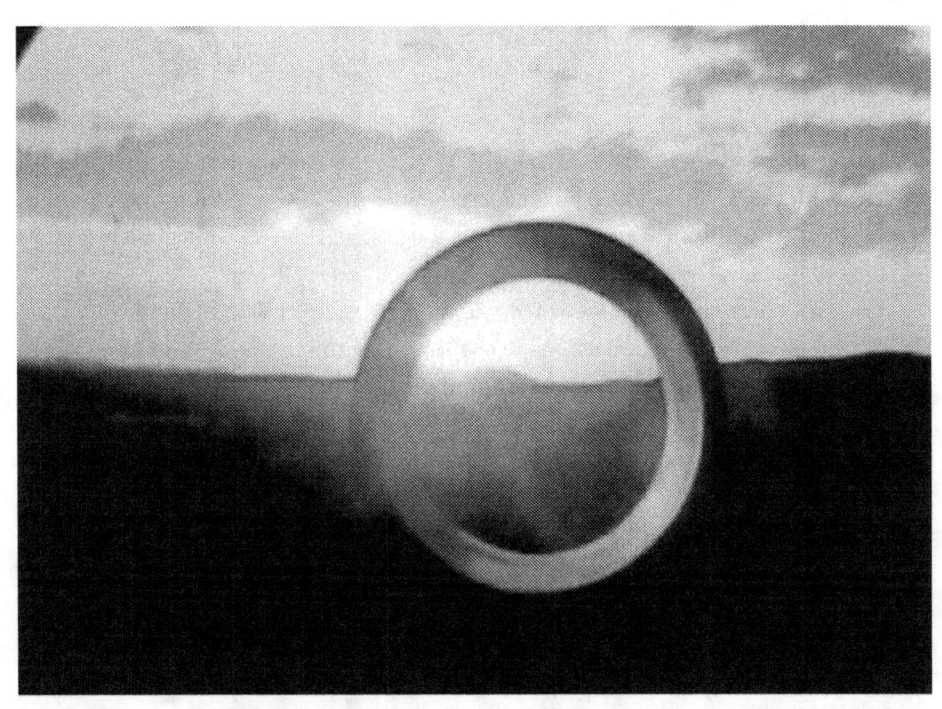

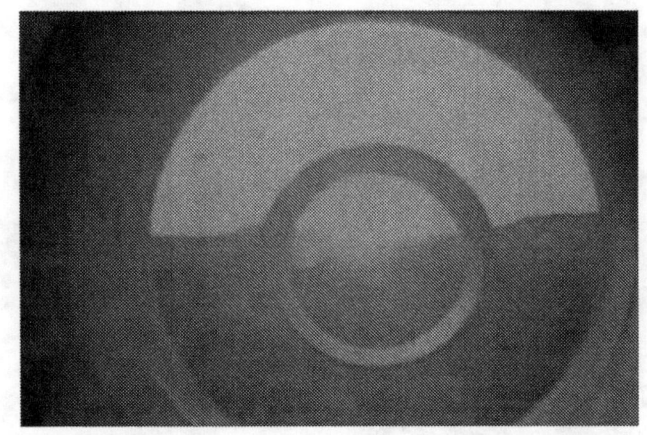

NANCY HOLT: *HYDRA'S HEAD*

Nancy Holt's *Hydra's Head* (1975) was another installation concerning the relation between the heavens and earth. Next to the Niagara River at Art Park, Lewiston, New York, Holt sank 6 concrete tubes into the soil. Each three foot pipe was filled with water, so they formed circular mirrors flush with the ground. Again, Holt based the position of the concrete pits on a constellation (Hydra). *Hydra's Head* combined the presence and noise of the rushing Niagara River with the reflections of the sky, stars and moon. Holt's concrete pipe sculptures use the prime symbol of change and all things cosmic, the circle. The *Sun Tunnels* are like enormous telescopes or astrolabes, while *Hydra's Head* evokes six fallen stars, the circles of water reflecting the sky and stars.

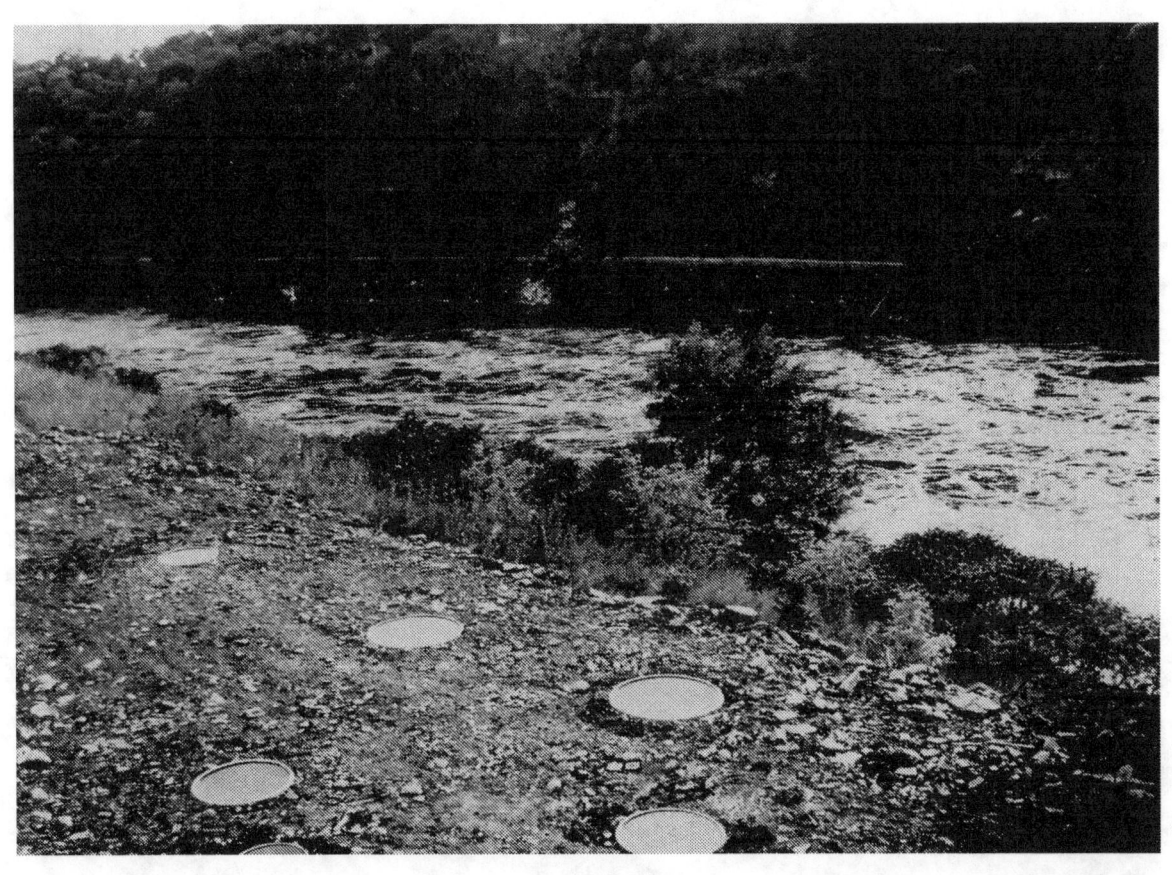

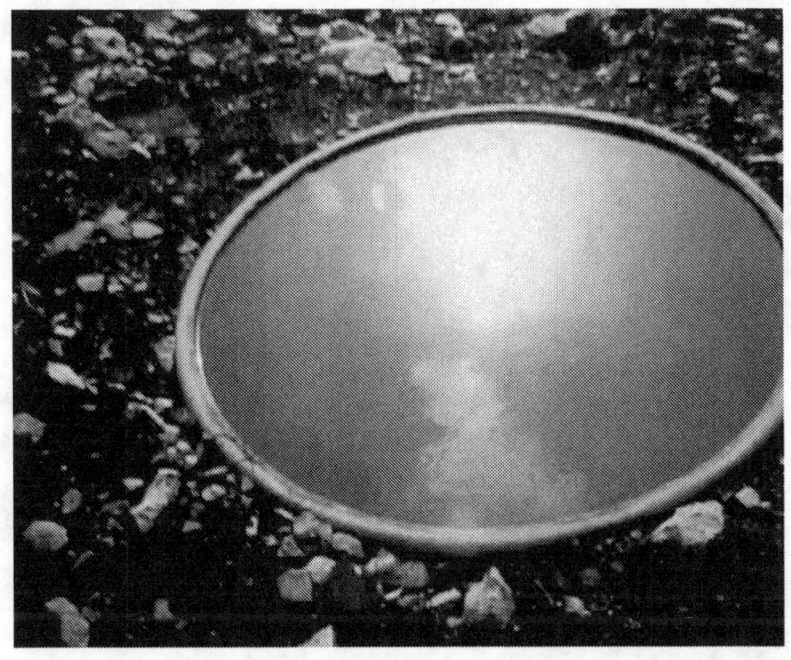

MARY MISS: *BATTERY PARK CITY ESPLANADE*

Mary Miss studied at the University of California at Santa Barbara. In summer 1963 she took sculpture at Colorado College. After graduating in 1966 from the University of California Miss studied at the Rinehard School of Sculpture at the Maryland Art Institute until 1968. Early works included a 'waterline': at Fountain Creek in Colorado Miss suspended a double knot of hemp rope 100 feet over a dry riverbed; every twenty feet were lines of rope. At War's Island in New York Miss threw 15 foot long wooden stakes into the water which were weighted with rocks. *Battery Park City Esplanade* (1985-87) is a typical Miss work, a big public commission in Gotham.

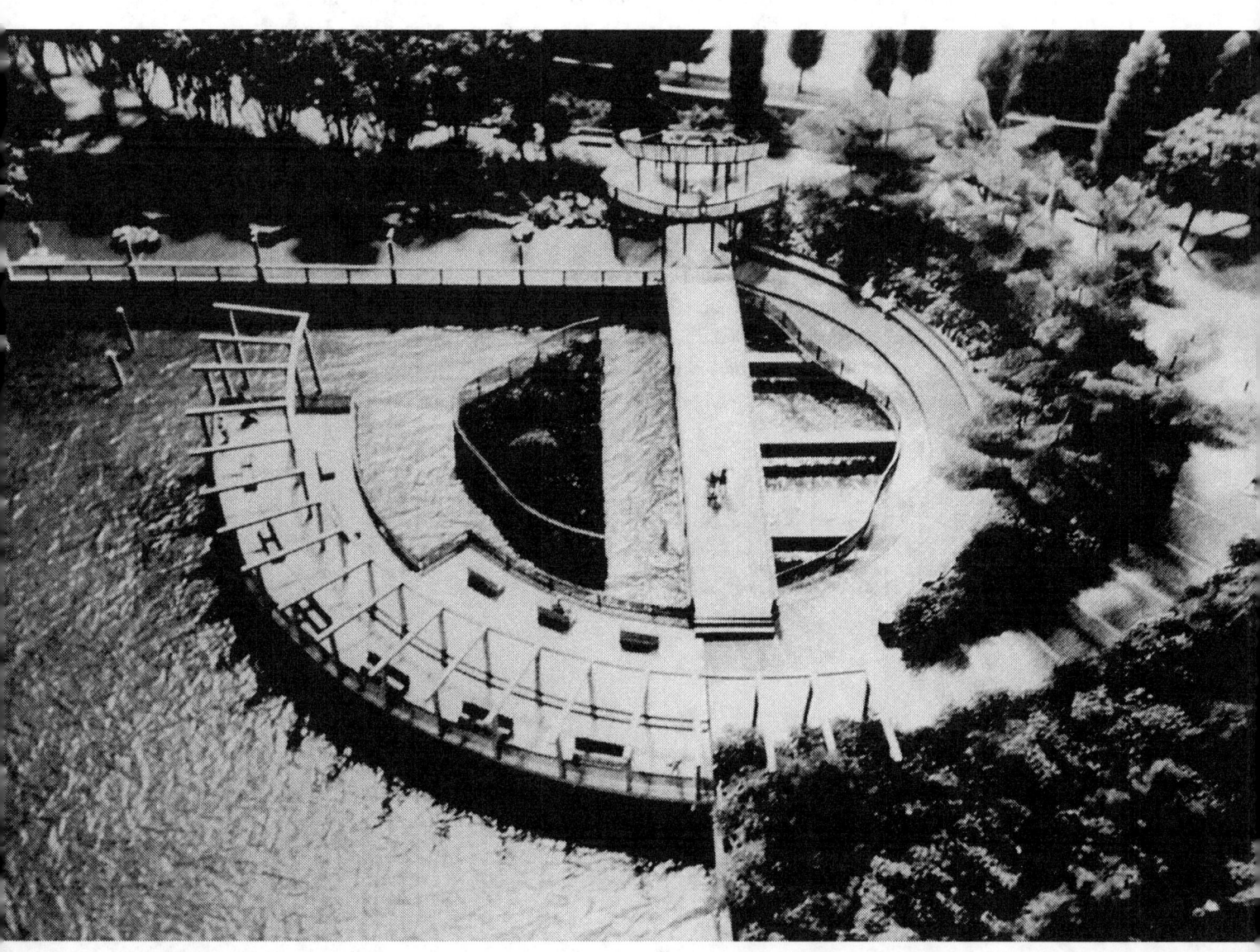

MARY MISS: *PERIMETERS/ PAVILION/ DECOYS*

Mary Miss's 1978 *Perimeters/ Pavilion/ Decoys* was constructed in Roslyn, New York, in a field that was part of the Nassau County Museum's ground. *Perimeters/ Pavillion/ Decoys* consists of three wooden towers, which look like tree houses with four platforms on stilts, two mounds of earth, and an underground space which's accessed by a ladder. The wooden towers are not for climbing on, but for viewing. The tallest is 18 by 10 by 10 feet. The subterranean atrium was for exploring through. It was a 16 ft^2 pit with a seven foot hole acting as an entrance; visitors climbed down a ladder to explore the various underground spaces, some with wooden, others with soil walls. *Perimeters/ Pavillion/ Decoys* was related to Pueblo Indian structures, Pompeiian and Mexican courtyards, and Mesopotamian brick complexes. The site explored the physical and psychological aspects of 'inside/ outside, above/ below, light/ dark, open/ closed, nature/ artifice'.[1] Miss's works are often large, spreading over a wide area of ground. In Illinois she created a 5-acre scale work.[2]

1. R. Onoratio, "Illusive Spaces: The Art of Mary Miss", *Artforum*, Dec, 1978, 32; see also K. Linker, "Mary Miss", *Mary Miss*, ICA, 1983.
2. See L. Anderson, 1973; M. Miss, 1981.

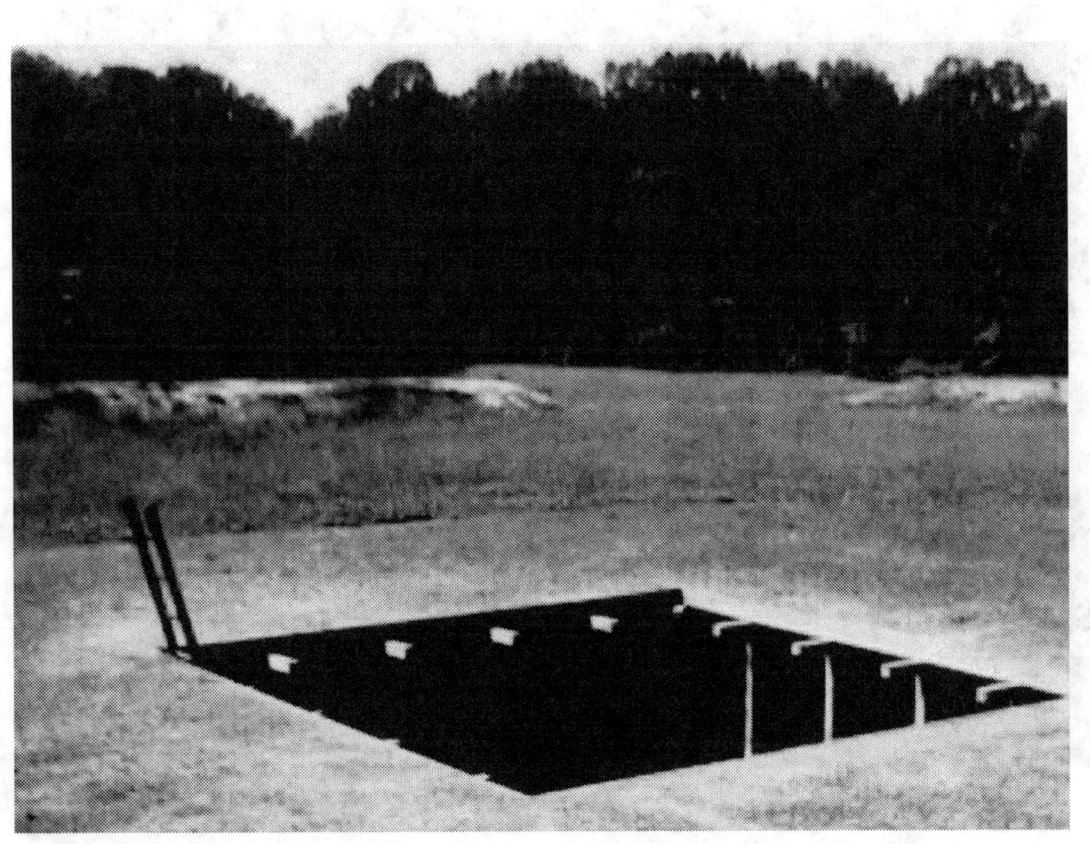

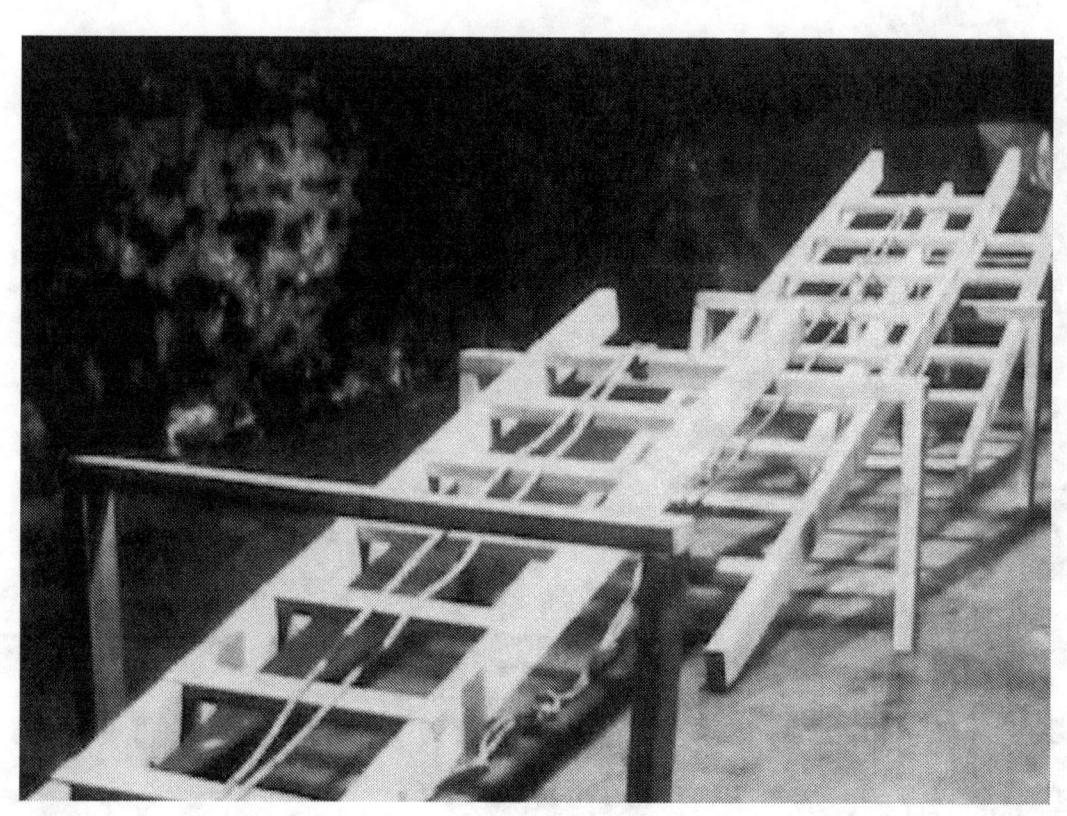

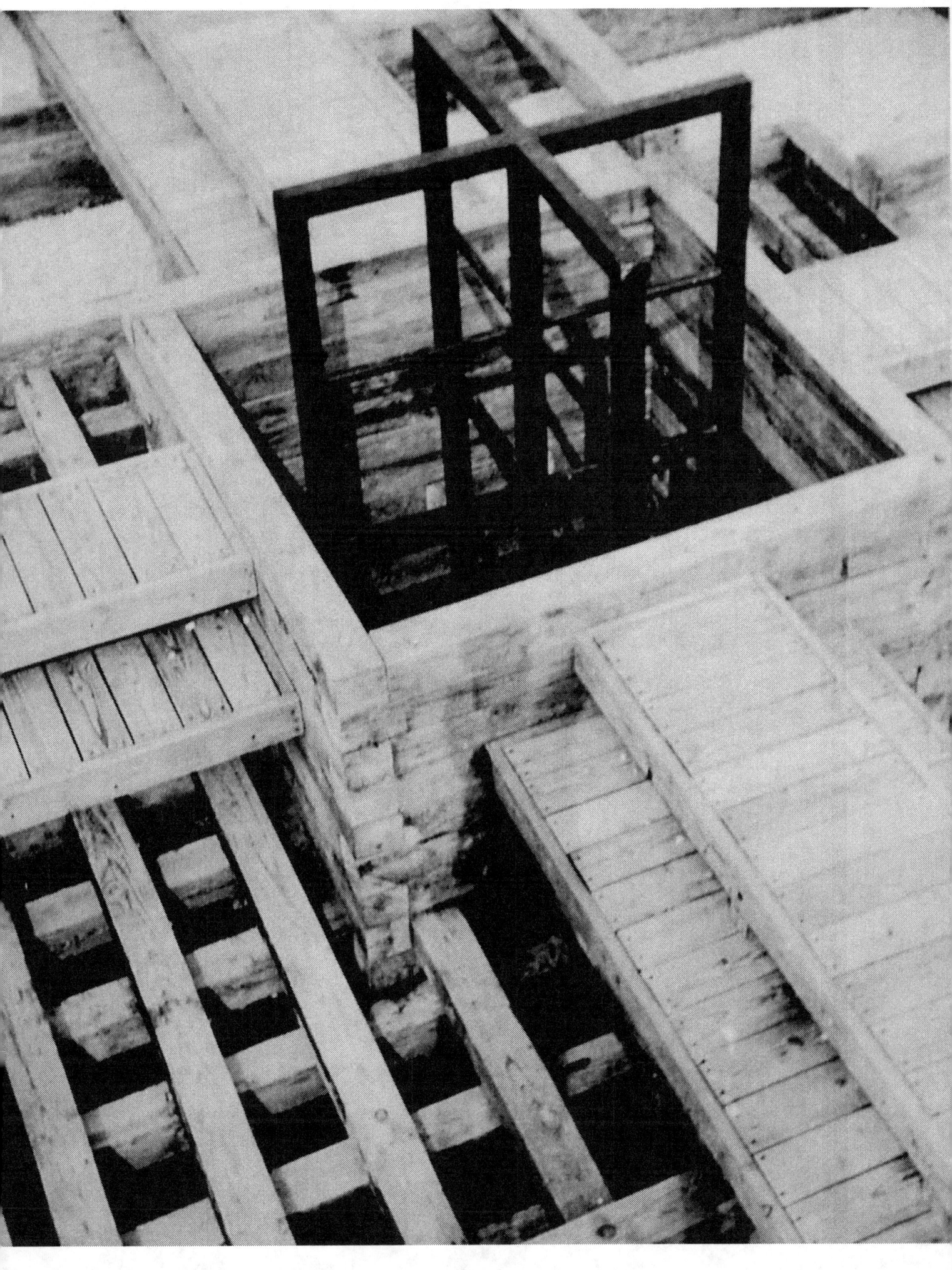

ALICE AYCOCK: *A SIMPLE NETWORK OF UNDERGROUND WALLS AND TUNNELS*

Alice Aycock's land artworks are much more ambiguous and deliberately problematic than Nancy Holt's or Carl Andre's works. Many of Aycock's land sculptures involve underground passages and spaces. In 1972 she constructed a series of underground spaces in *Low Building Made with Dirt Roof (For Mary)* in Pennsylvania. The spectator entered the 20 by 12 feet work through a doorway thirty inches high. The work was experienced by crawling through it. Aycock's intention was to evoke an experience of claustrophia, of being in a cellar. Aycock's works had titles such as *The Machine That Makes the World* (1979), *A Theory of Universal Causality* (1983) and *How to Catch and Manufacture Ghosts* (1979). Aycock's sculpture explored the rationality of machines and technology and irrationality of ghosts and magic (H. Risatti, 37).

Alice Aycock's *A Simple Network of Underground Walls and Tunnels* (1975) was made in a corn field at Far Hills, New Jersey. It consisted of 6 square wells in two rows of three excavated out of a 20 by 50 foot area. Two of the wells had 7 foot ladders that enabled the spectator to climb down and explore the dark connecting tunnels. Some of the wells were capped, others were open. The effect was a series of spaces that recalled 'ominous historical precedents, caves, catacombs, dungeons and beehive tombs' wrote Roberta Smith (1975, 68).

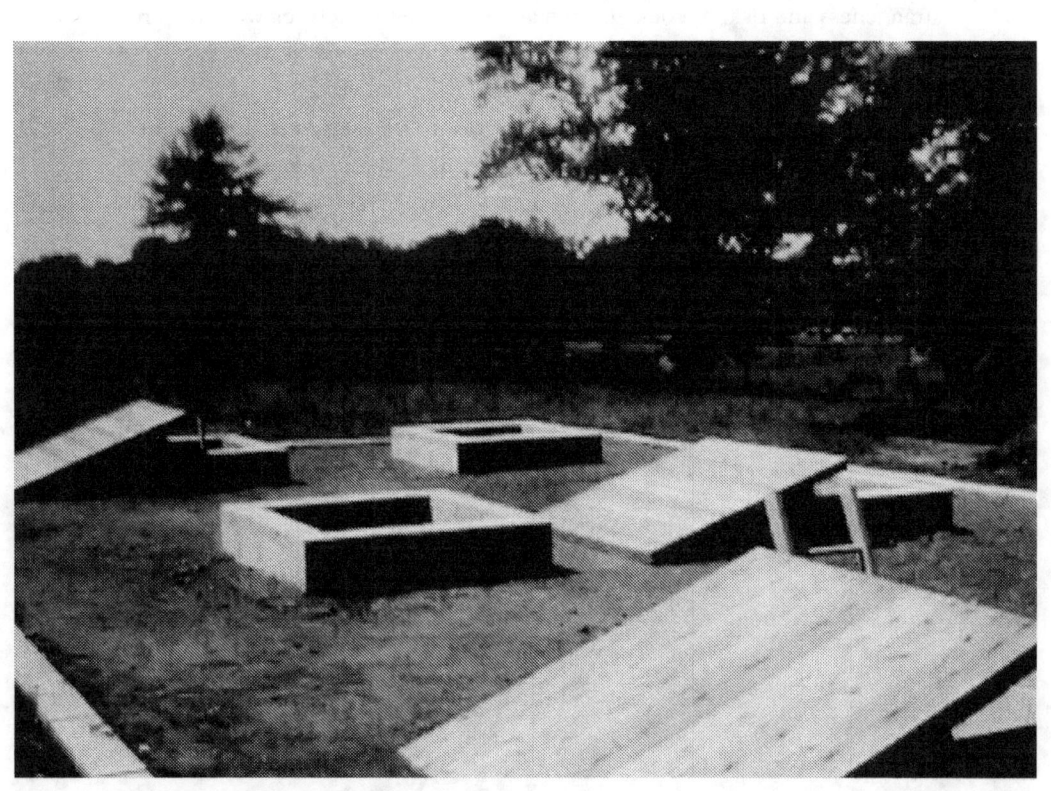

ALICE AYCOCK

Alice Aycock has spoken of the relations between her art and her own childhood dreams and fears. Her works recreate disturbing moments from her childhood, such as when she was trapped in a revolving barrel at an amusement park. Aycock's works deal with such moments of fear, confusion, strangeness and risk. Aycock also remarked that her structures were inspired by visits to the Pyramids in 1970 and the Greek tombs at Mycenae, and fantasies of being buried alive.

The structure *From the Series Entitled How To Catch and Manufacture Ghosts* (1980) was a much larger development of the earlier *How to Catch and Manufacture Ghosts*. It was a combination of steel, pipes, spheres and galvanized drums that drew inspiration from early experiments with electricity and magnetism, Marcel Duchamp's *Bachelor Apparatus*, Montgolfier's balloon launch pad, and an oil refinery on the New Jersey turnpike. A later work, *Tree of Life Fantasy: Synopsis of the Book of Questions Concerning the World Order and/ or the Order of Worlds* (1990-92), drew on influences from Renaissance illustrations of people walking into the sky to Heaven, DNA helices, ancient Indian observatories, and Walter Gropius's designs for theatres.

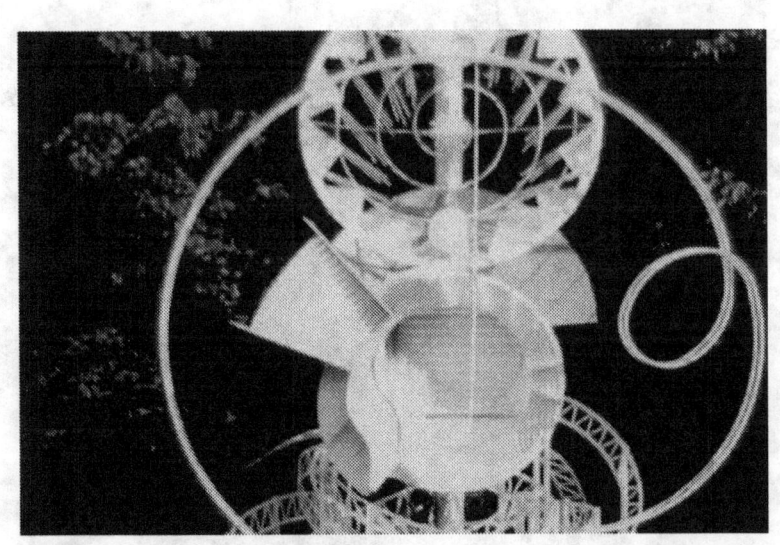

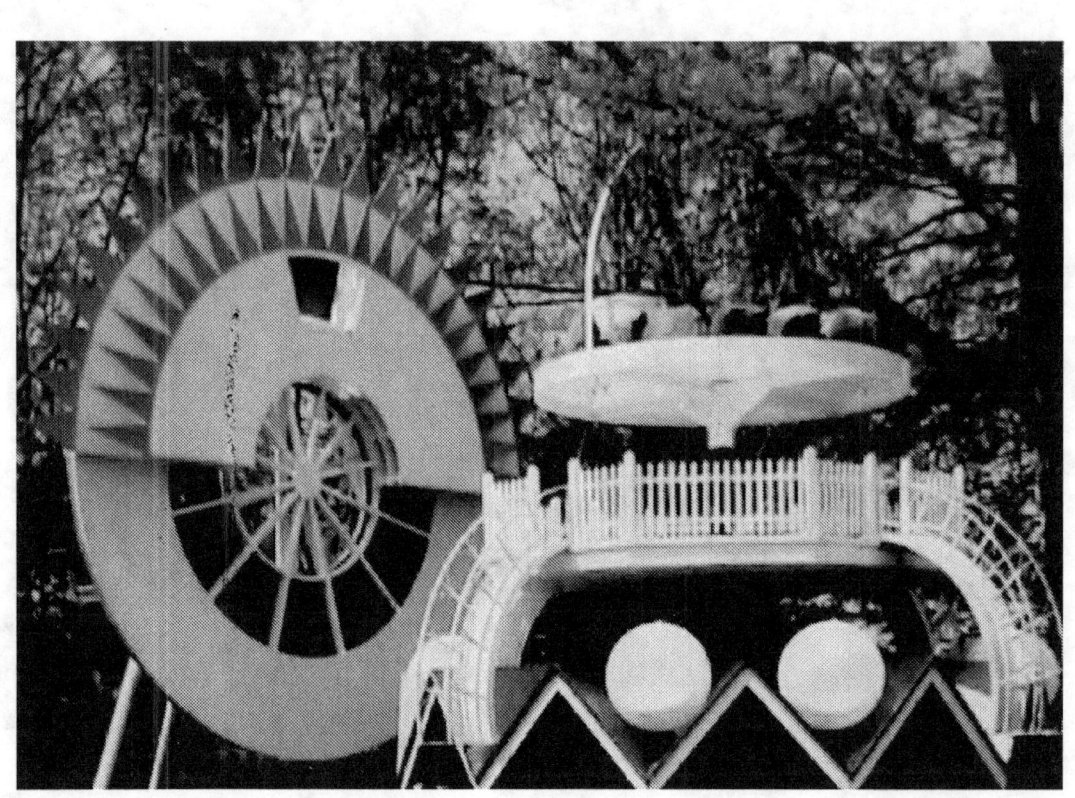

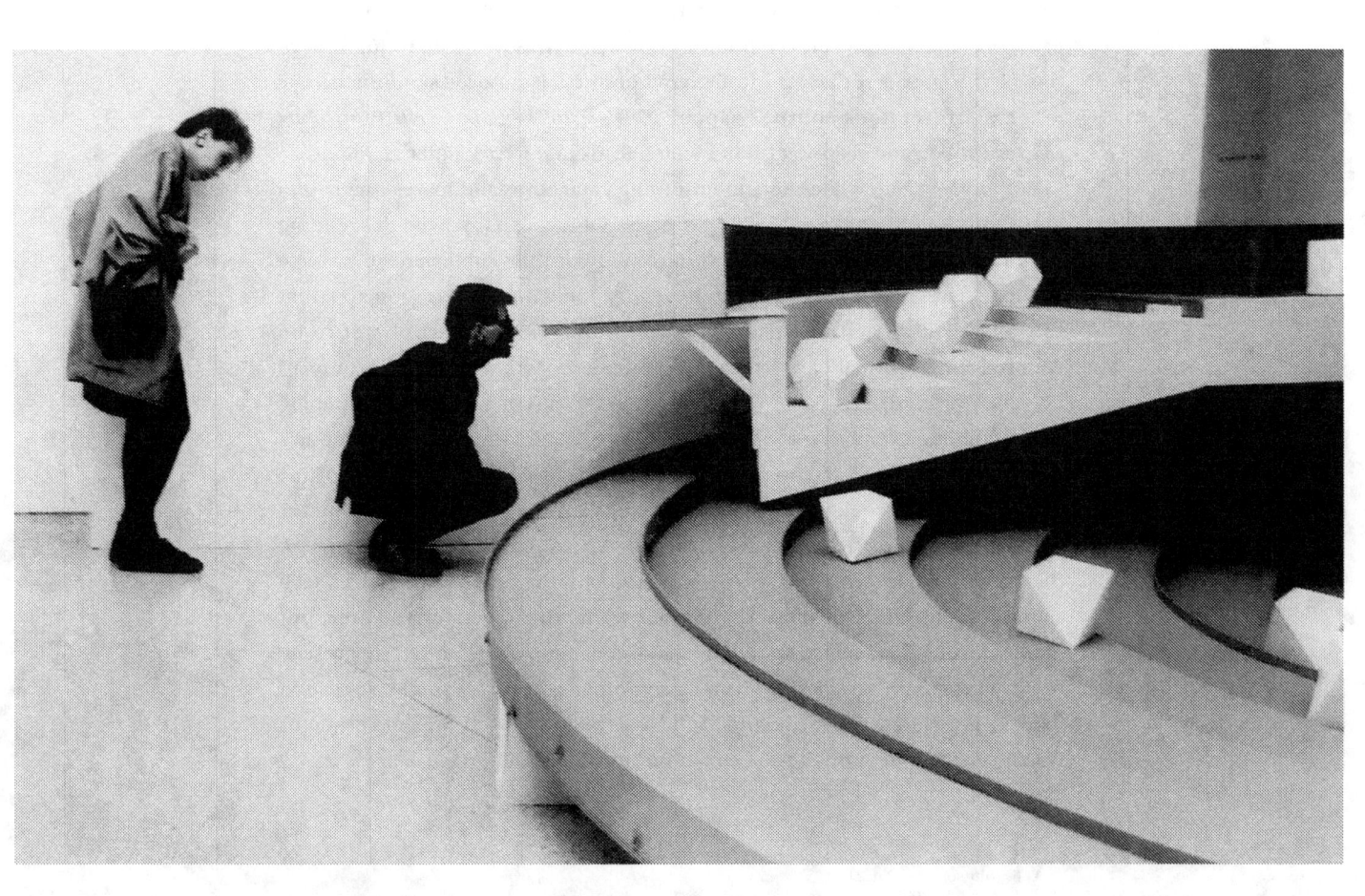

ALICE AYCOCK: *WALLED TRENCH/ EARTH PLATFORM/ CENTER PIT*

Alice Aycock's 1974's *Walled-Trench/ Earth Platform/ Center Pit* was a series of three concentric walls made from concrete blocks. A platform of earth was made between the inner two walls: it was possible to jump onto this platform over the outer pit. Only when the spectator is standing on the inner platform does another aspect of *Walled-Trench/ Earth Platform/ Center Pit* become visible: a tunnel which leads into a dark inner chamber.

With Aycock's bewildering and unsettling catacombs and mazes one had to move 'one's body through them', a process which also involved descending back through time and memory.[1] Confronted with the subterranean passage or the *Circular Building with Narrow Ledge for Walking* it is soon apparent to the spectator that one is not dealing simply with an art object to be admired for its formal characteristics alone. Aycock wants the spectator to become physically involved in the sculpture: the physical actions of climbing and scrabbling over and through the sculpture trigger an exploration of one's own psychology and memory.[2] The physicality of the body as a tool for exploration in Aycock's works soon becomes a pretext or an inspiration for an exploration of personal psychology. Spectators are invited to risk themselves in exploring her works. Her land/ site art offers seductive as well as potentially dangerous spaces. Aycock wants the spectator to enter, but then confronts her/ him with a door that opens onto a wall, or a tiny passage to crawl through, or a ledge over a precipice, or a pit to vault over. Such devices go straight back to childhood, to acts of dare and bravado (such as walking along a high brick wall, egged on by other children).

1. E. Johnson, 1982, 221.
2. A. Aycock, 1977.

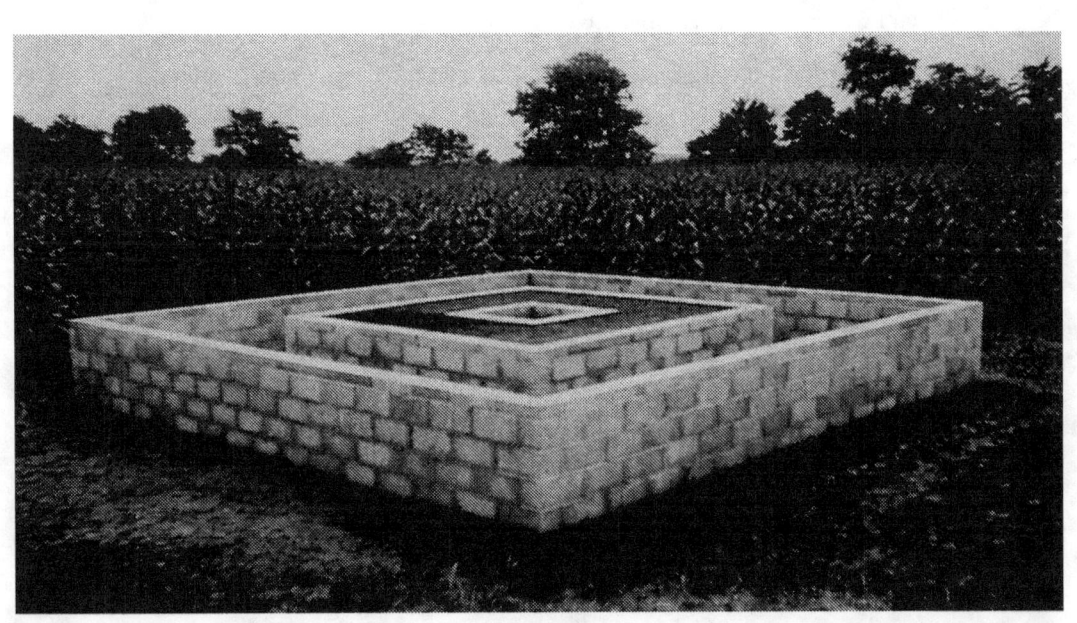

RICHARD SERRA: *SPLASHES*

In "Notes On Sculpture", Robert Morris quoted a famous Q & A session aimed at Tony Smith, *pace* his *Die* sculpture:

> Q: Why didn't you make it larger so that it would loom over the observer?
> A: I was not making a monument.
> Q: Then why didn't you make it smaller so that the observer could see over the top?
> A: I was not making an object.[1]

A good example of the new sense of the sculpted object was Richard Serra's *Splashes* (1968, destroyed), installed at Leo Castelli's New York gallery. With its emphasis on process and 'anti\form', *Splashes* was more Postminimal or Process sculpture, than Minimal art. A sense of the random and immediate was central to *Splashes*, which comprised some lead that Serra splashed and poured along the join of a wall and floor. *Splashes* evoked spontaneity, waste, ephemerality and 'organic' form. It was also a work which couldn't be bought (or sold) or transported, or hung on a wall, or exhibited elsewhere.[2] *Splashes* was distinctly a new kind of sculpture – it was *new* 'new sculpture', and a significant departure from the 'new sculpture' that had been heralded by Anthony Caro and David Smith. It didn't look like traditional sculpture, or previous sculpture (it was a splash mark on the wall and floor); it wasn't welded and constructed Cor-Ten steel or cast in bronze or chiselled marble; it wasn't based on a clay model; it didn't arise from sketches or plans; it wasn't figurative; it didn't conform to traditional notions in sculpture of 'beauty', volume, form, illusion and allusion; the form it took was partly haphazard, and not wholly dictated by the artist; it wasn't placed on a pedestal; it could only be experienced in that particular context (it was site-specific); it didn't draw attention to itself (it could easily be overlooked, or mistaken for dirt); it wasn't permanent; and it could be not become another commodity in the exchange of objects in the commercial art world.

1. T. Smith, quoted in G. Battock, 1995, 228-230.
2. R. Williams, 2000, 10.

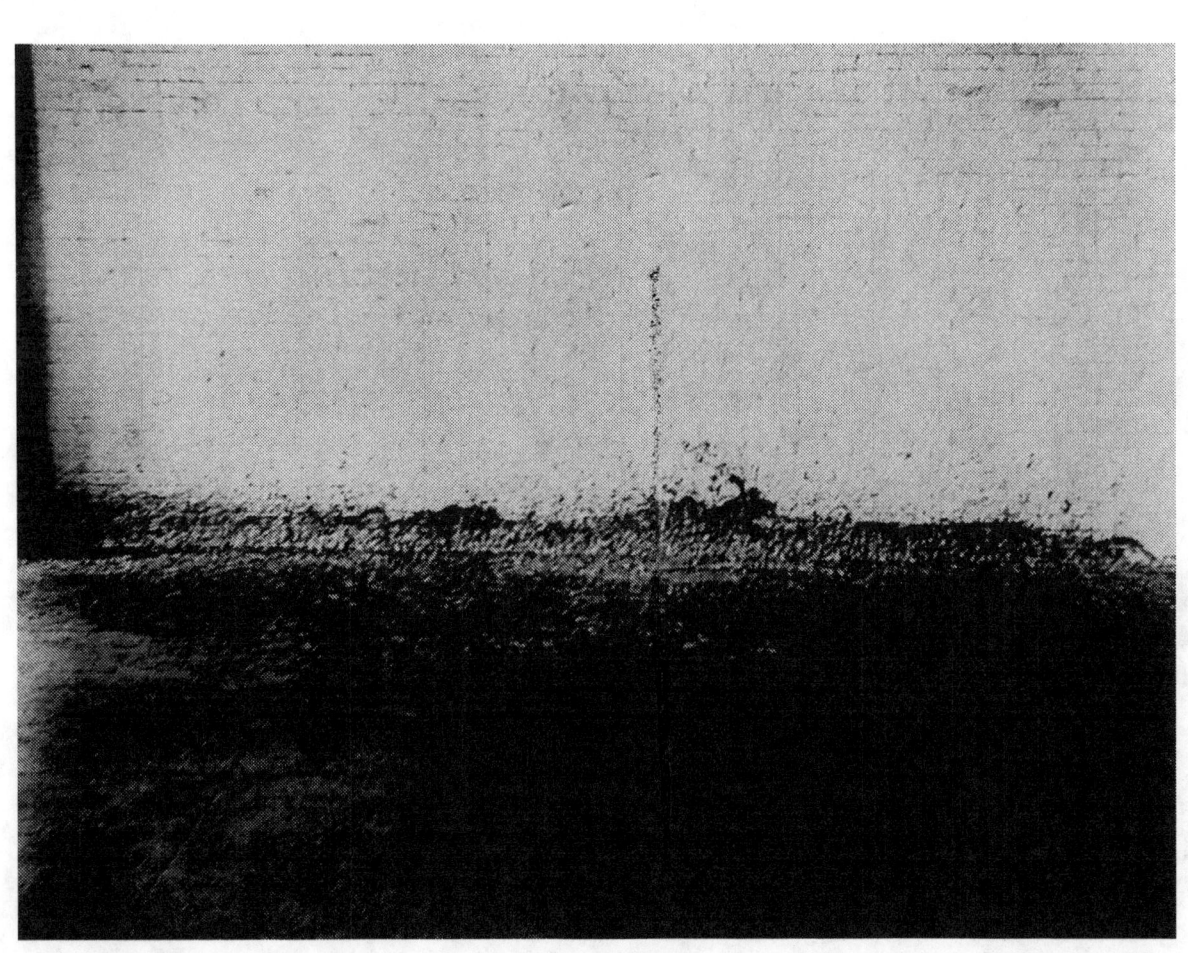

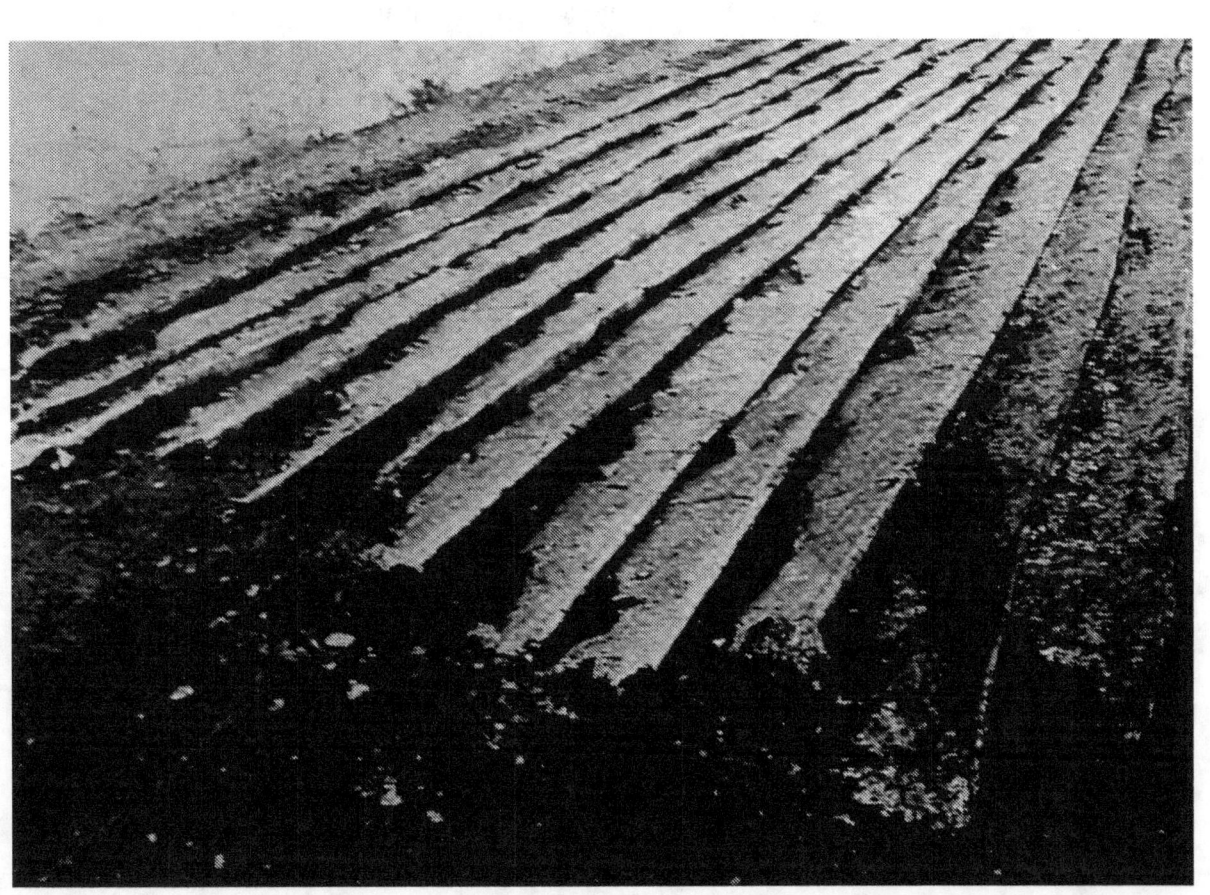

ANDY GOLDSWORTHY: *TIME MACHINE*

Andy Goldsworthy, like Michael Heizer, Waler de Maria and Robert Smithson, has made some huge pieces, such as the long 'snake' and the 'pool' or maze, in Country Durham, large works which take up a lot of space, and certainly dominate the surrounding landscape. Goldsworthy's large-scale outdoor works often use the serpent coil as a fundamental form. Goldsworthy maintains, however, that his 'snake-like' or serpent-shaped sculptures do not refer directly to snakes.[1] Whatever the artistic intention, however, it is impossible to limit readings of sculptures such as *Sidewinder, Lambton Earthwork* or the serpentine shapes in the British Museum's Egyptian Hall to responses to the environment.

The serpent connotes time, change, seasons, birth-and-death-and-rebirth, eternity, sexuality, evil, the cosmos, and so on. Goldsworthy might wish to determine how viewers read his serpent-shaped forms, and emphasize the response he makes to the natural environment, but consumers of art will make any interpretation they like, and some they might wish to suppress (snakes also connote dirt – they slide on the dust; and excrement; the alimentary canal; eating and defecating; poison; reptile life, and so on).

The theme of the winding serpent was especially pertinent to Goldsworthy's installations in the Ancient Egyptian galleries of the British Museum and the Museo Egizo in Turin. Goldsworthy's large sculpture was made with local sand on the floors of the museums, snaking in between the exhibits of Egyptian artefacts. It was there for one day then dismantled (after being photographed, of course – the photographic record incorporated the themes of time and death just as piquantly as the sculpture itself). Even if not explicitly like 'snakes', these sculptures evoked the Ancient Egyptian preoccupation with time, death, eternity and immortality. Goldsworthy spoke of the sand snake flowing 'through the room – touching the sculptures and incorporating them into its form to give a feeling of the underlying geological and cultural energies that flow through the sculptures' (*Time Machine*). The sweet chestnut leafworks which accompanied the sand serpent also evoked time – they were spiral shapes, set in an Egyptian sarcophagus and a libation bowl.[2]

1. 'Some works have qualities of snaking but are not snakes. The form is shaped through a similar response to environment' (*Andy Goldsworthy,* 1990).

2. Goldsworthy wrote that a 'work made with leaves is a celebration of growth, yet cannot work without expressing some anticipation of death, in a way that understands that death is a part of growth. The sarcophagi are not just containers of death, they are containers of life, in that out of death comes life' (*Time Machine*, British Museum, 1995).

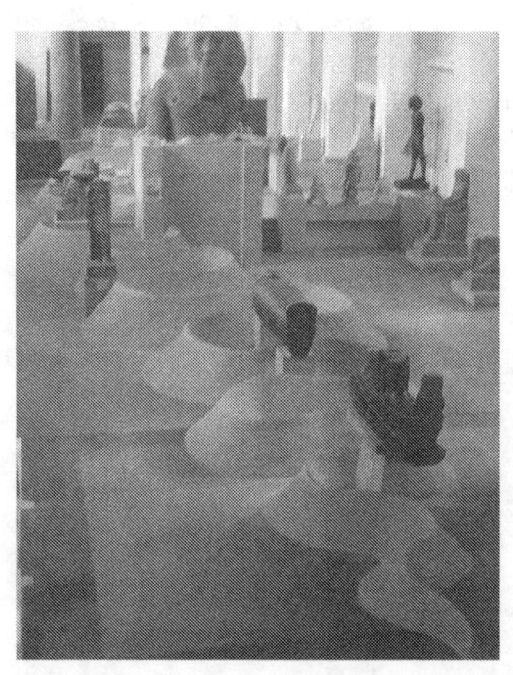

ANDY GOLDSWORTHY: *SCREENS AND DRAWINGS*

Andy Goldsworthy has made more 'traditional' forms of art in galleries: his bracken, fern and horse chestnut stalk works, for instance, were made by pinning the materials onto white gallery walls. These works – *Bracken fronds* (Ecology Centre, London, 1985), *Reeds, bracken and horse chestnut stalks* (Centre d'Art Contemporain, Castres, and Galerie Aline Vidal, Paris, 1989) and *Reed line drawing* (Paris, 1990) – were essentially free, open wall drawings, often employing basic motifs such as the circle and open curve. Screens of plants that Goldsworthy made in galleries include the *Susuki grass* and *Horse chestnut leaf stalks* (both made in Japan in 1993), and *Rushes thorns* (1992, San Francisco).

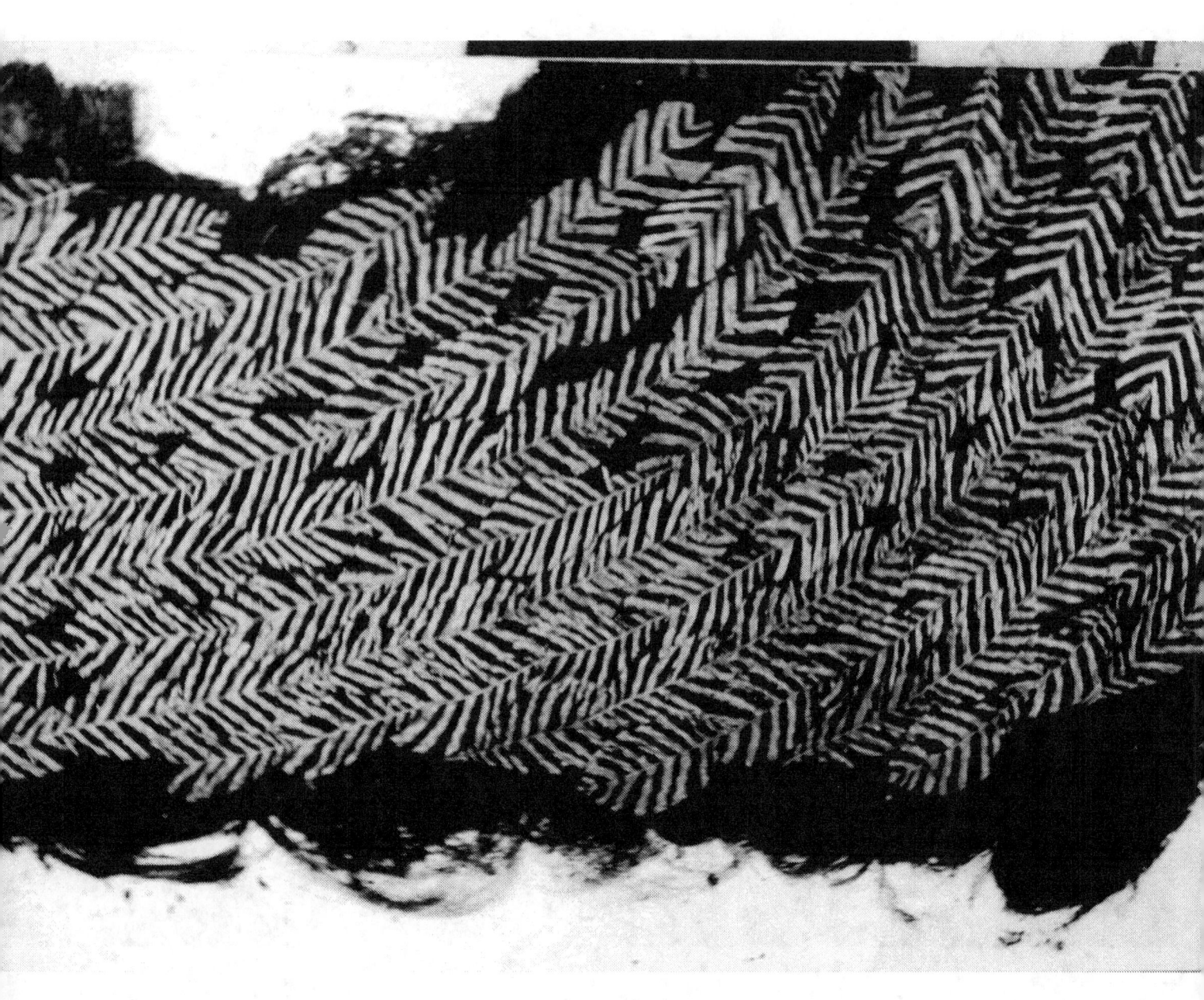

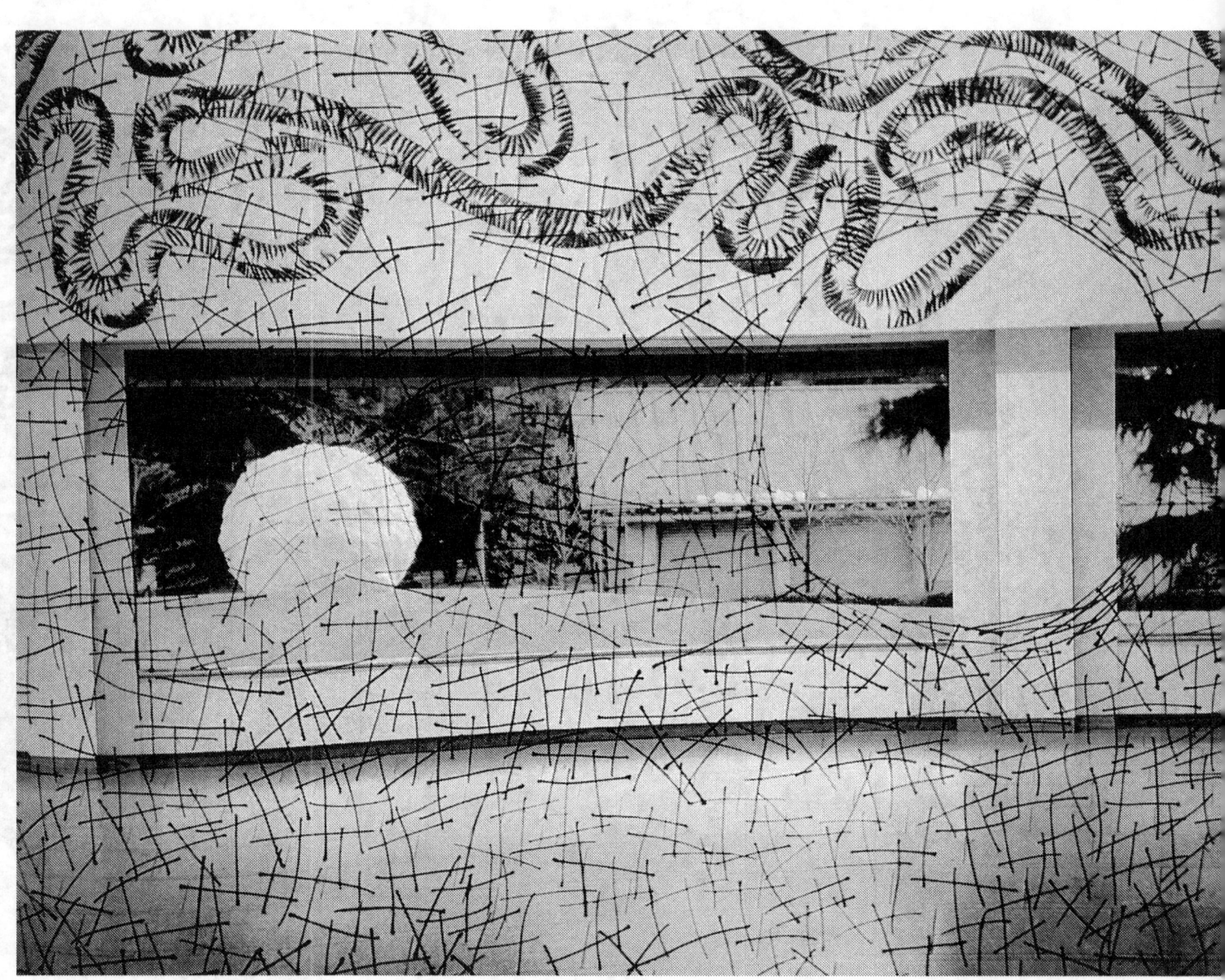

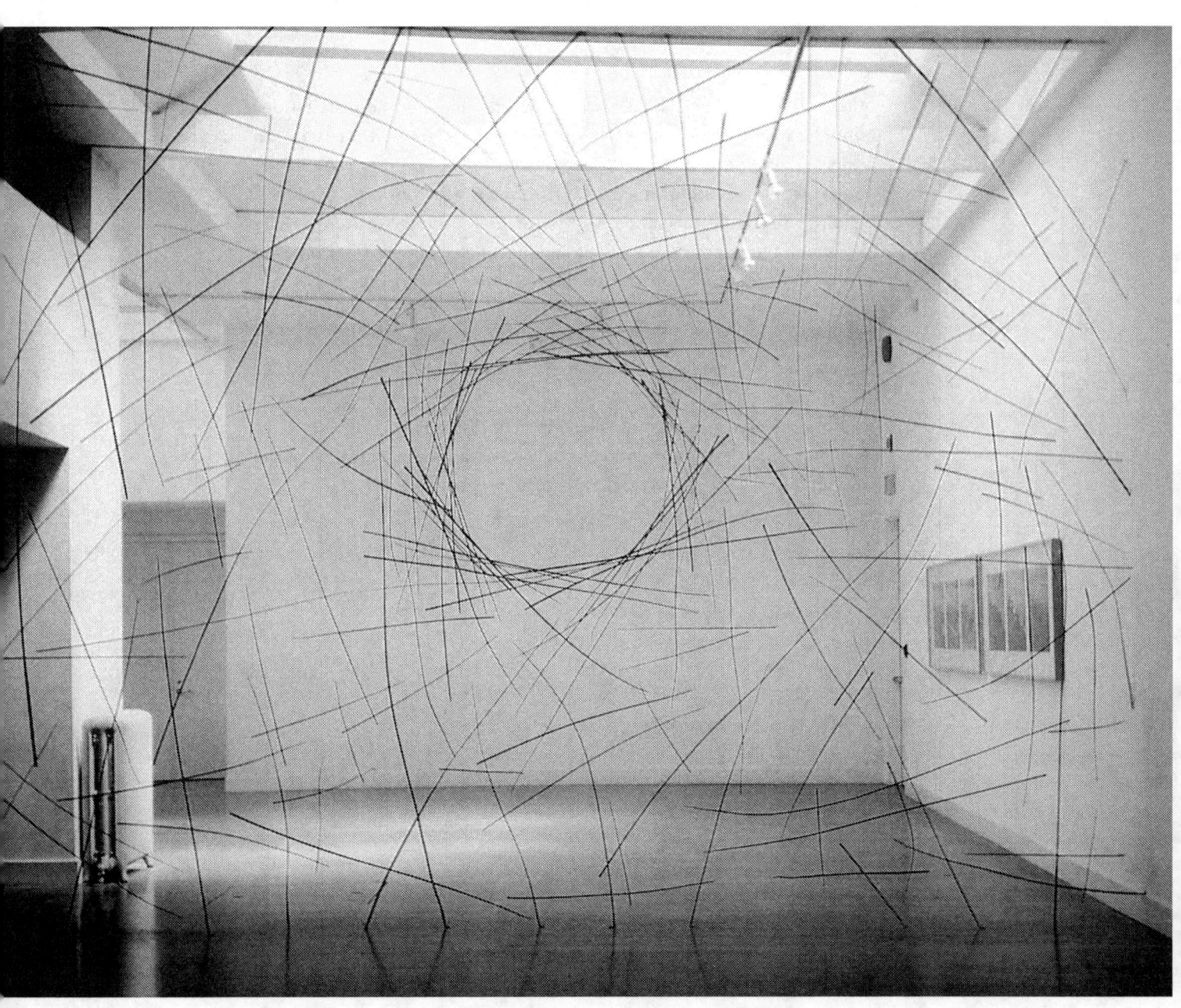

ANDY GOLDSWORTHY: *CLAY WALL*

Other large-scale works by Andy Goldsworthy include the installations *Slate Wall* and *Clay Wall* (1998, Edinburgh), *Clay Wall* (1996, San Francisco) and *Clay Wall* (2000, London). For his dance collaboration, Goldsworthy had one of his clay walls filmed over ten days to form a backdrop to the performance. Goldsworthy found he was not wholly happy with the filmed *Clay Wall*: 'I found the flicker and movement of the image as it goes through the projector more disturbing than I had anticipated'. It was the unstable, flickering quality of the footage that unsettled Goldsworthy, the changes in colour and light: 'the physical nature of the film and its projection makes the medium more present that I would like it to be'. That's an interesting remark that suggests that Goldsworthy prefers recording media to be transparent. He doesn't want his photographs drawing attention to themselves as photographs; he wants the viewer to look through them to the sculptures and places he's photographing.

1. A. Goldsworthy, *Time*, 84.

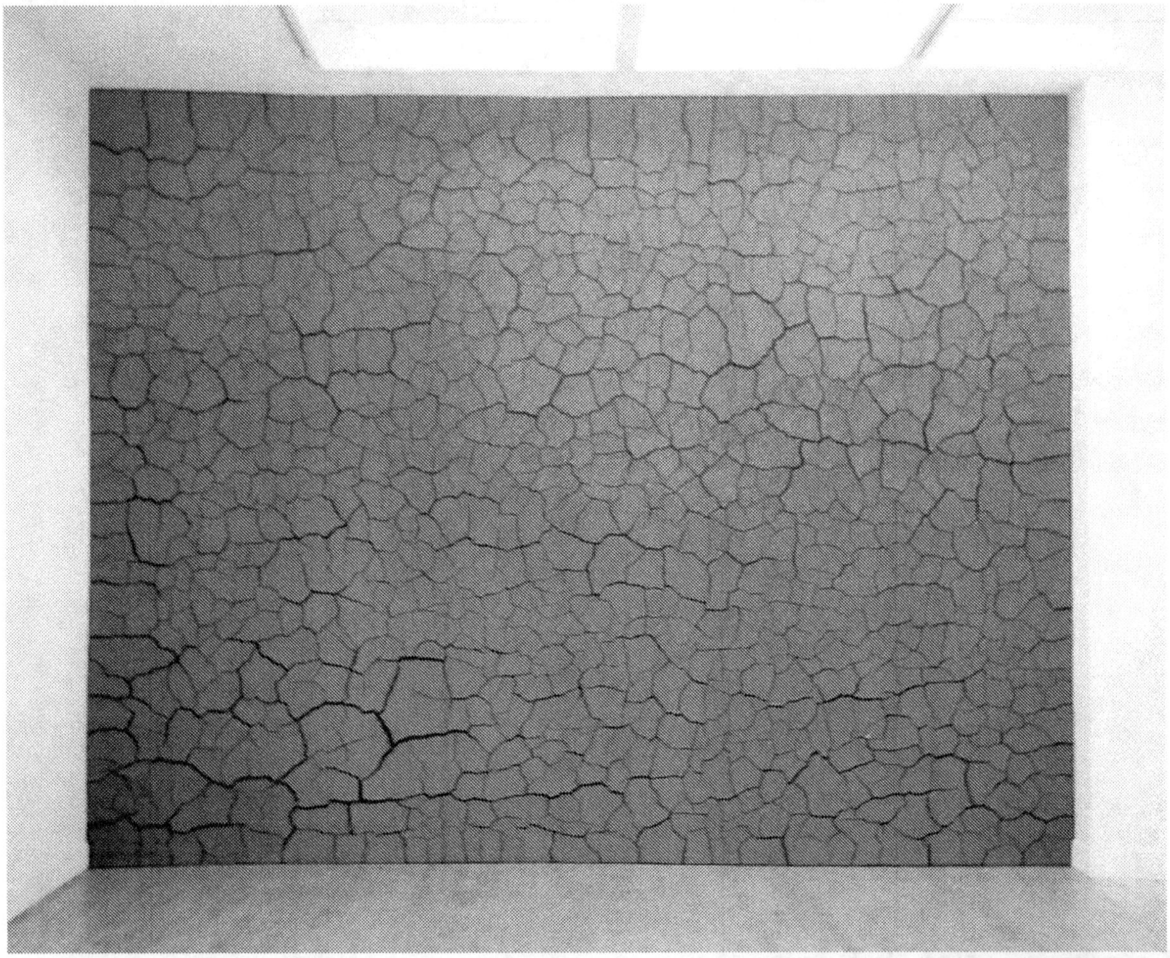

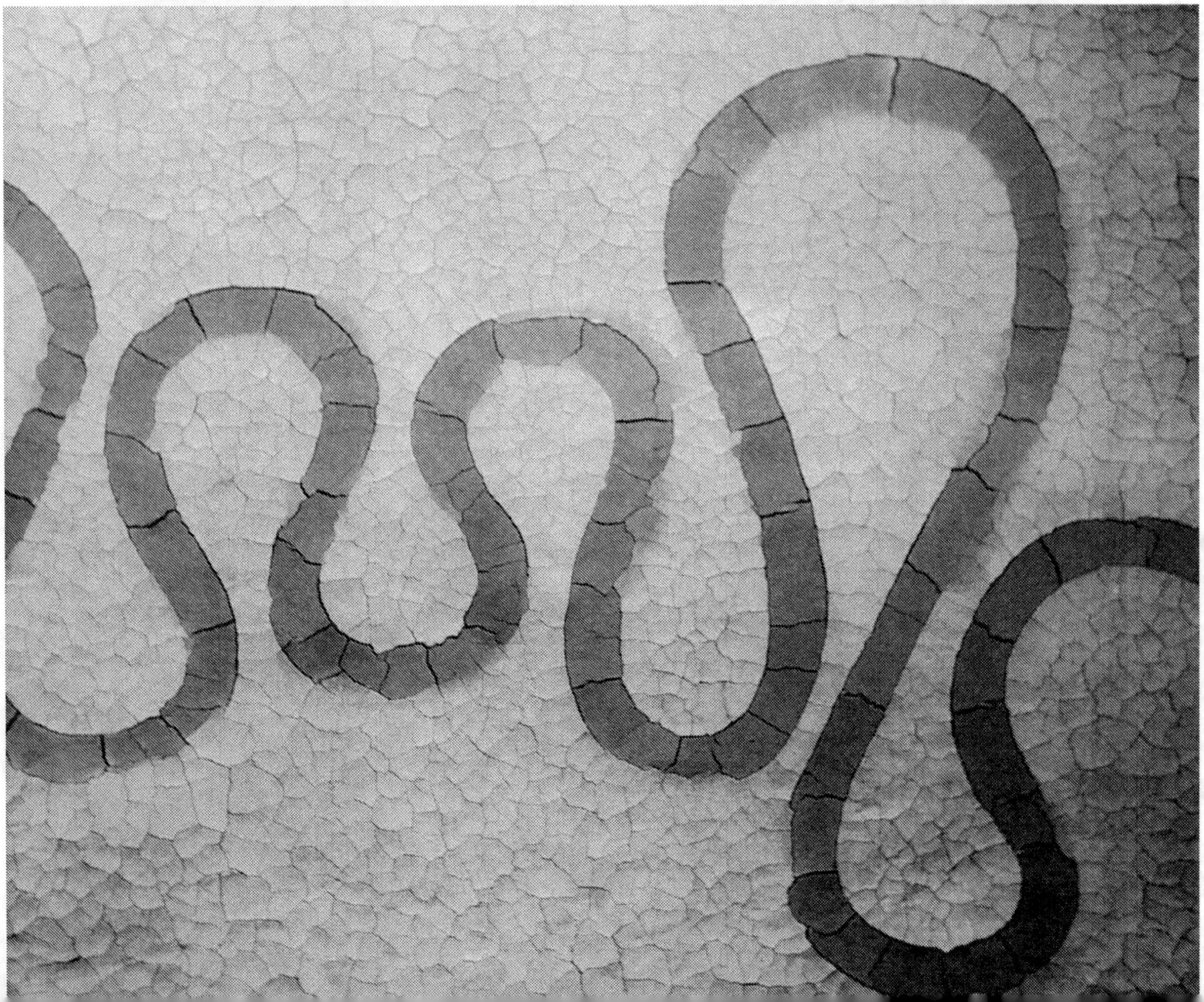

ANDY GOLDSWORTHY: *STONE HOUSES*

Stone Houses was a prestigious commission from the Metropolitan Museum of Art in Gotham, for its roof garden. The rocks were taken from Glenluce Bay in Scotland and transported to the US, but the wood (white cedar) for the *Stone Houses* was from New England. The roof garden overlooked Central Park and the formidable skyline of Manhattan, so the sculptures had plenty to contend with visually. This setting certainly wasn't the undulating hills around Penpont or the windswept beaches of Scotland or California, but one of the most famous cityscapes in the world.

The two columns of granite stones were about thirteen feet high. They were fashioned in the familiar Goldsworthy form of a tapering column, decreasing in size so that the topmost stone was a pebble. Around the columns of stones Goldsworthy constructed an octagonal 'house' – basically a domed-shaped shelter structure which enclosed the columns (they were eighteen feet tall). The cedar wood had been split into rails, with each end overlapping.

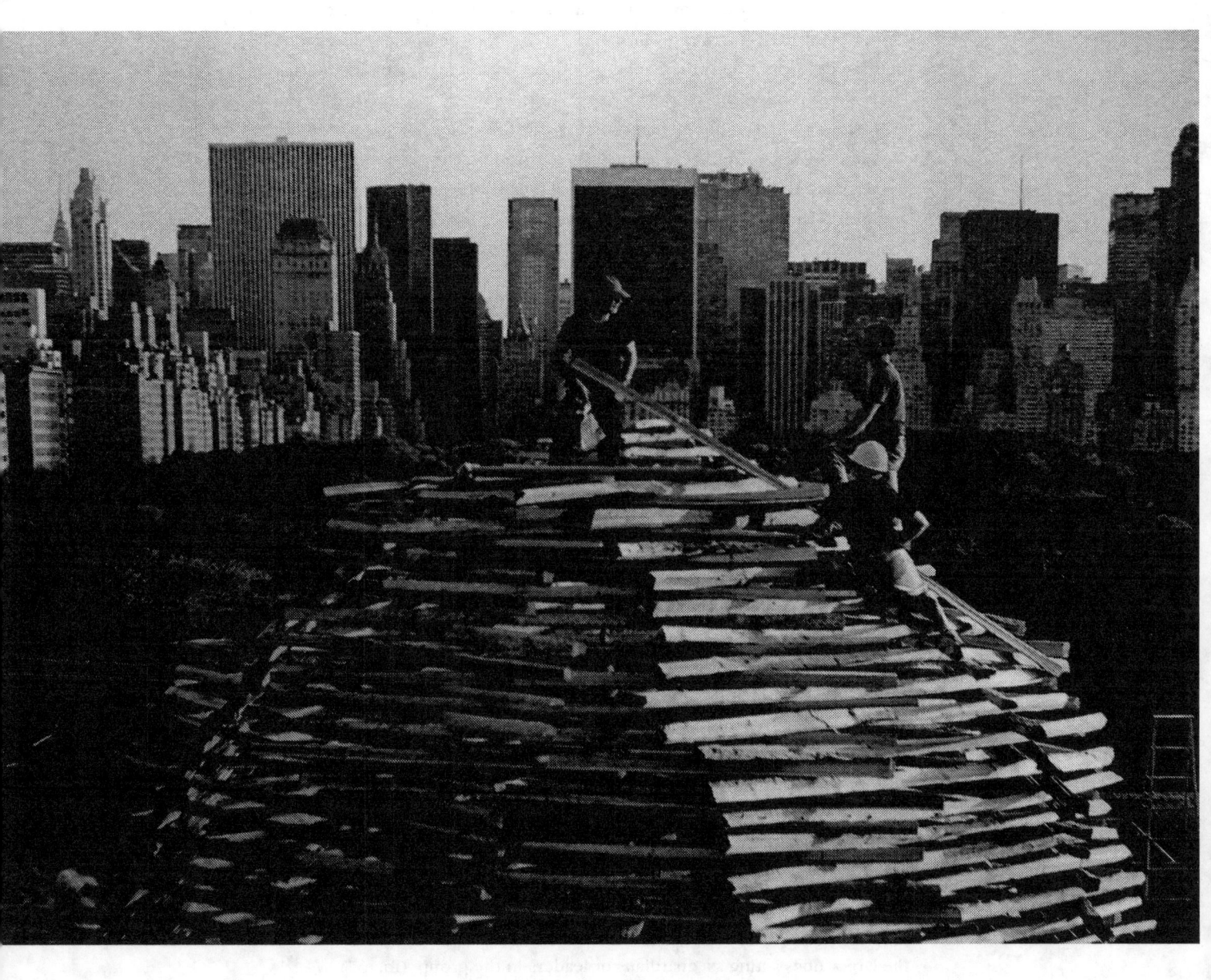

ANDY GOLDSWORTHY: *GARDEN OF STONE*

One of the most important of Andy Goldsworthy's later commissions was the installation *Garden of Stone* (2003) at the Museum of Jewish Heritage in Lower Manhattan. *Garden of Stone: A Living Memorial* was a group of 18 hollowed Vermont granite glacial boulders, with an oak tree inside (dwarf oaks, which only grow very slowly). The trees were planted at the top of each stone, with the hollow space below for the roots. The largest boulders weighed 13 tons. *Garden of Stone* was situated on the second floor garden, overlooking the river, with socio-political icons such as the Statue of Liberty and Ellis Island easily visible beyond. *Garden of Stone* cost a million dollars (the Public Art fund collaborated with the museum), making it easily Goldsworthy's most expensive commission to date. Jacob Ehrenberg was project manager.

The glacial granite boulders were taken from Vermont (near Barre). They were then transported to a Connecticut quarry (Stony Creek) where Ed Monti, a guy in his seventies, hollowed them using a cutting torch. The bases were flattened so that the rocks would sit properly on the ground (Goldsworthy said that in trimming the stones, he aimed to retain as much height to each stone as possible). Goldsworthy allowed the marks made on the boulders by their journeys and hollowing to remain. That was part of his preference for retaining evidence of the transformations materials under-go. It was part of the social project of Goldsworthy's art: it was important for the artist where the stones came from; the source was part of the overall sculpture. Hence the boulders were collected from fields and the landscape, rather than quarries (the more obvious place to shop for stones): 'how the sculpture is made and the journey of both the ideas and material are also important' (*Passage*, 65).

Goldsworthy also wanted to maintain the integrity of his garden of trees and stones, and was concerned about the planting the Jewish Museum planned for the borders of the site. Goldsworthy said he hoped to retain the 'sense of barrenness' of just the stones and the trees, and the introduction of other plants would compromise his sculpture, as well as the look of the building (ib., 69). Originally, Goldsworthy planned to have all of the stones roughly the same size, but the idea developed to having a range of sizes, with the larger ones acting as 'guardians or leaders in the group' (ib., 67).

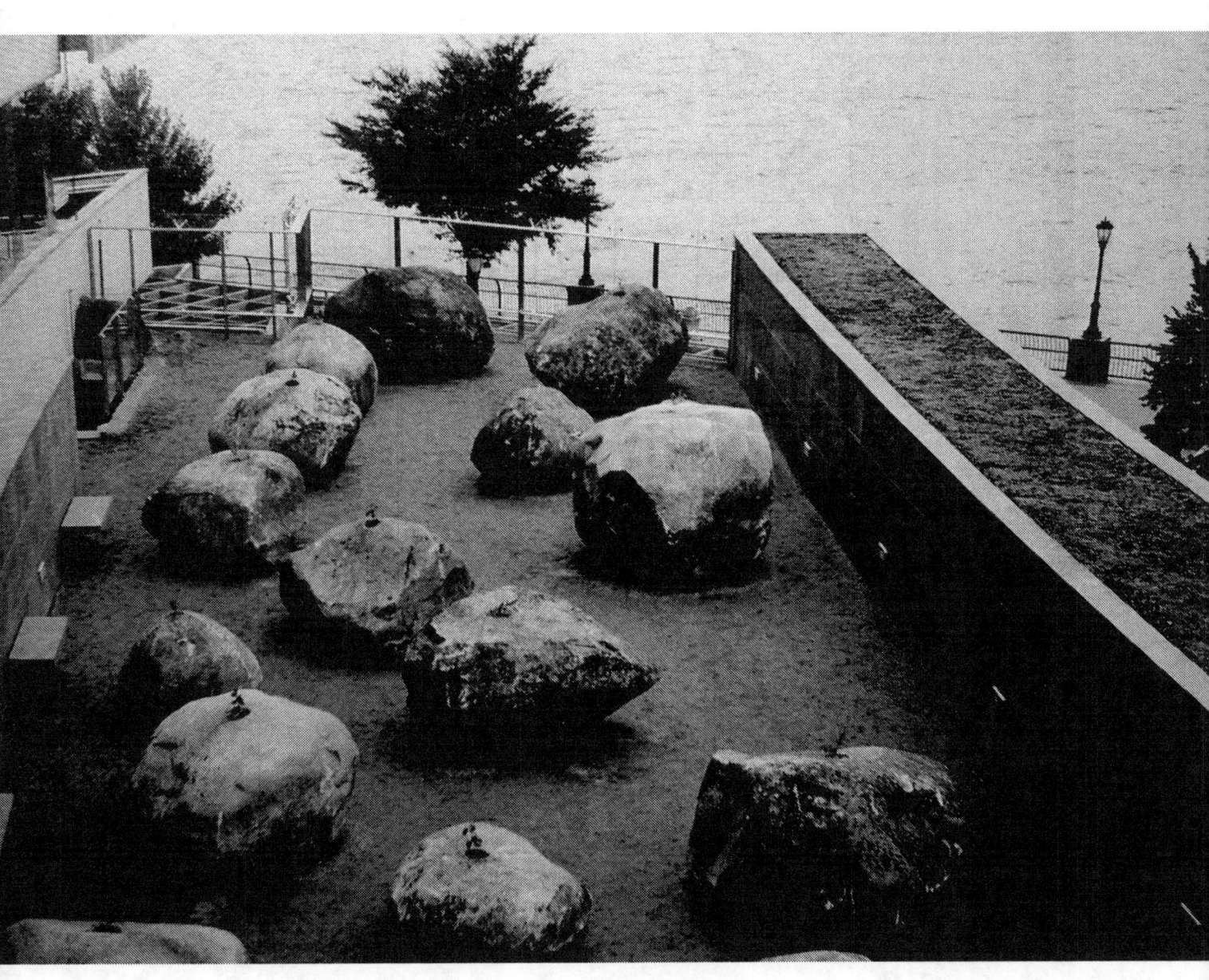

ANDY GOLDSWORTHY: *SNOWBALLS IN SUMMER*

Snow melts, and Andy Goldsworthy's sculptures exploit the precariousness and impermanence of snow as a material. He speaks of being frustrated in making snow sculptures, of snow crumbling before he could complete the piece. Yet his snow works are some of his most exciting pieces: a snowball, for instance, caught in the branches of a tree. It looks impressive in the photographs, the ball of snow, so heavy and cold, floating, it seems, in the black, leafless branches of a tree. Goldsworthy has brought snow into the studio, most impressively in the series of large snowballs he brought from Craighall near Blairgowrie to Glasgow. Goldsworthy waited and waited for snow to fall during 1988-89. When it did, eventually, he made a series of snowballs which were exhibited in the Old Museum of Transport in Glasgow during the summer of 1989.

In 2000, for the major London exhibition at the Barbican, Goldsworthy recreated the *Snowballs in Summer* event, this time located in various sites around the City of London. A video, *Midsummer Snowballs* (produced by University of Hertfordshire students) was shown at the Barbican.

The lines of snowballs, in rows in the museum space, recall directly the Minimal exhibitions of the 1960s. Each snowball was roughly the same size, but, like Minimal artists such as Donald Judd, Goldsworthy made each one slightly different. Within each snowball, Goldsworthy rolled in different elements, most of which are favourite Goldsworthy materials: willowherb stalks, pine needles, pebbles, reeds, oak sticks, and so on. Each snowball, then, was not just a sphere of ice melting slowly in summer, it was a container of natural materials, each with their own properties, which affected the melting of the snow. The melting of the snowballs itself was a natural process which the environment of a museum made highly visible. Each snowball melted in a different way. The inner stalks and pebbles became gradually more and more apparent, appearing on the outside of the snowball as it decreased in size. A pool of water formed around the snowball. Slowly, webs of stalks appeared, or a covering of old orange pine needles, looking like a cake decoration.

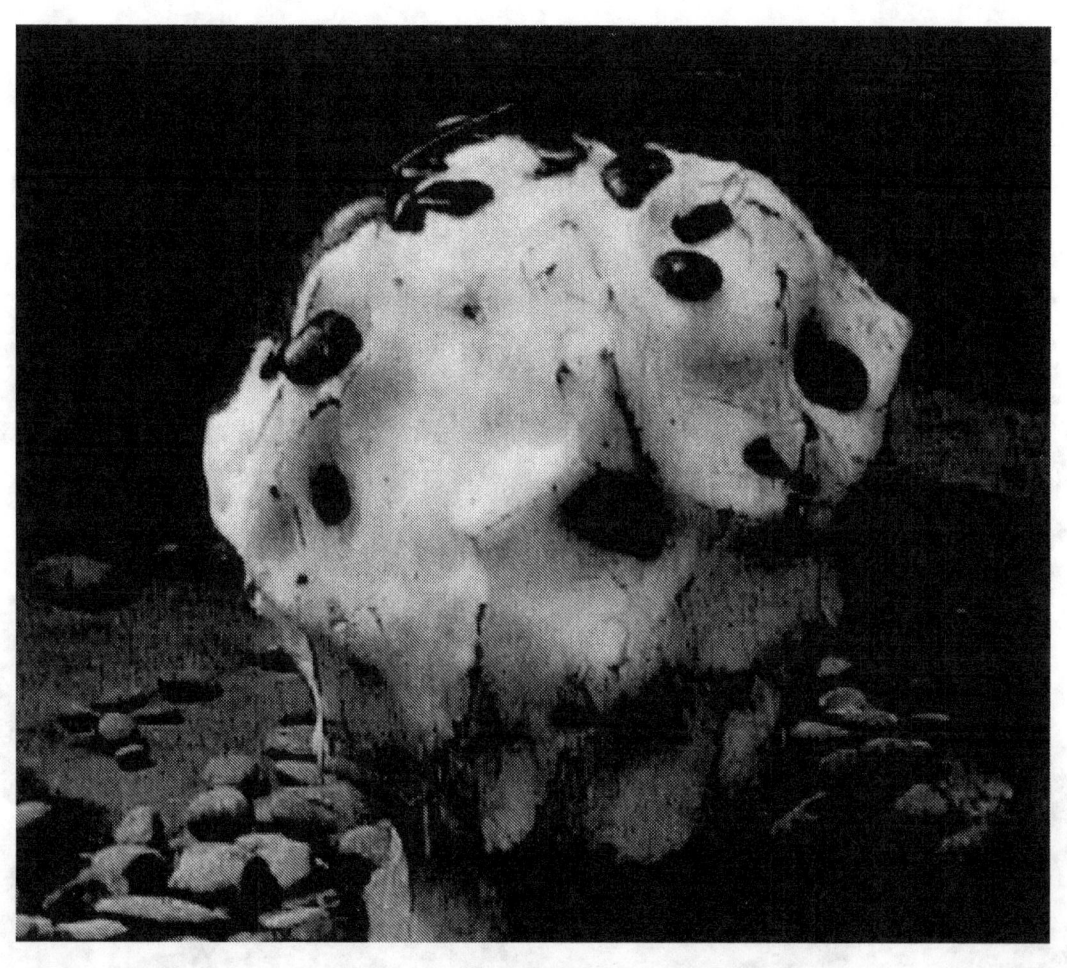

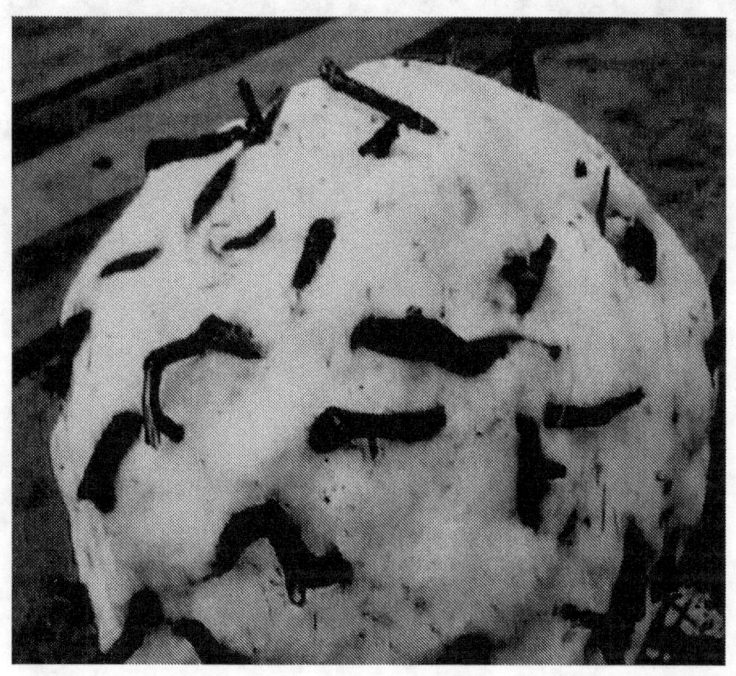

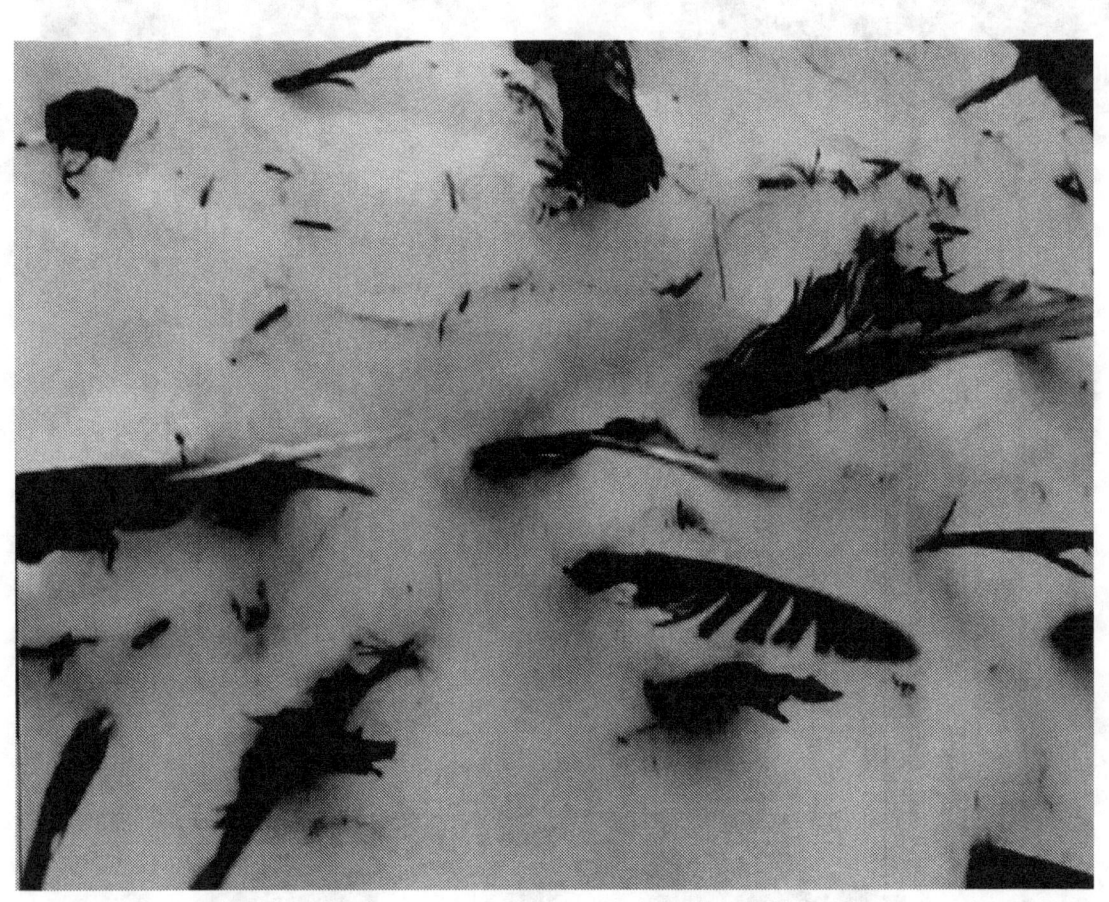

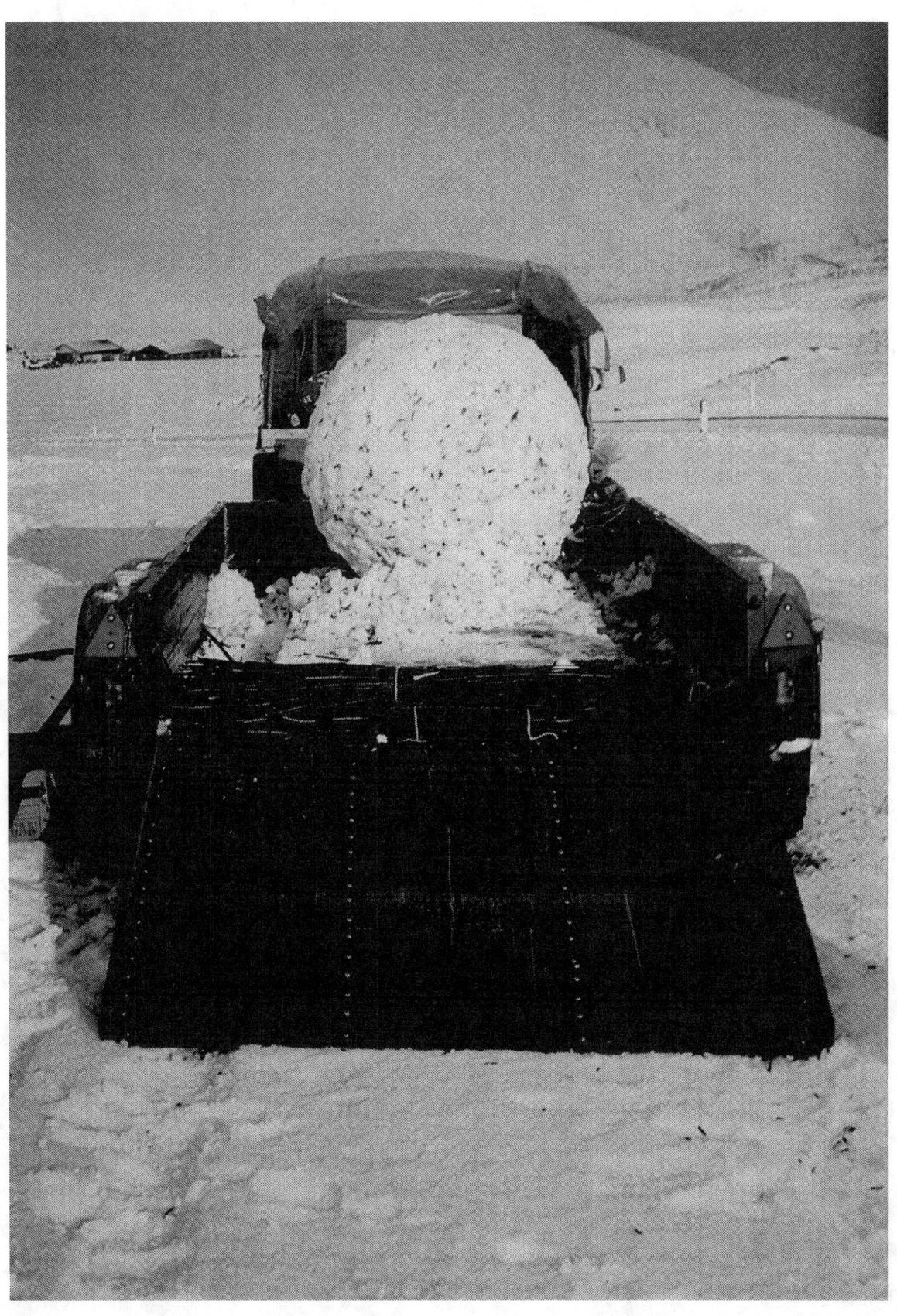

CONSTANTIN BRANCUSI: *ENDLESS COLUMN*

The influence of Brancusi is apparent in Minimal and Arte Povera, and contemporary sculpture – including installation art. Robert Morris, Donald Judd, Carl Andre and Dan Flavin acknowledged Brancusi's art, in particular his *Endless Column*. Andre's early work *Last Ladder* is something like Brancusi's *Endless Column*. Andre said: '[a]ll I am doing is putting Brancusi's *Endless Column* on the ground instead of in the air… The engaged position is to run along the earth'.[1]

The Brancusi ethics, of simplicity, purity, smoothness, interiority and organic form are found in the Minimal sculptors, as well as the Constructivist notion of working with materials in a 'natural' way, so that the material dictates the form you create with it. Barry Flanagan has commented that sculpture works directly with materials: '[t]he convention of painting has always bothered me. There always seemed to be a *way* of painting. With sculpture, you seemed to be working directly, with materials and with the physical world inventing your own organisations'.[2]

Quite a few artists (not all of them sculptors) have expressed admiration for Brancusi's photographs, and the way he would set up his sculptures in his studio and photograph them at particular times of day, when the lighting was just right. They are early examples of installation art (and some of the best, too). Andy Goldsworthy said he admired how Brancusi created the conditions in his studio so that his work 'comes alive at a particular time of day as the light momentarily touches it'.[3] For Goldsworthy, Brancusi's works were at their best when they were arranged by the sculptor in his studio and photographed.[4] Somehow, it wasn't quite the same when they were displayed in modern art museums (such as the Pompidou Centre in Paris or the Museum of Modern Art in Gotham, which have important Brancusi pieces).

1. In D. Waldman, 1970, 19.
2. B. Flanagan, quoted in the catalogue of *Entre el Objeto y la Imagen: Escultura britanica contemporanea*, Palacio de Velasquez, Madrid, 1986, 233.
3. A. Goldsworthy, *Réfuges d'Art*, 85.
4. A. Goldsworthy, *Sheepfolds*, 22-23.

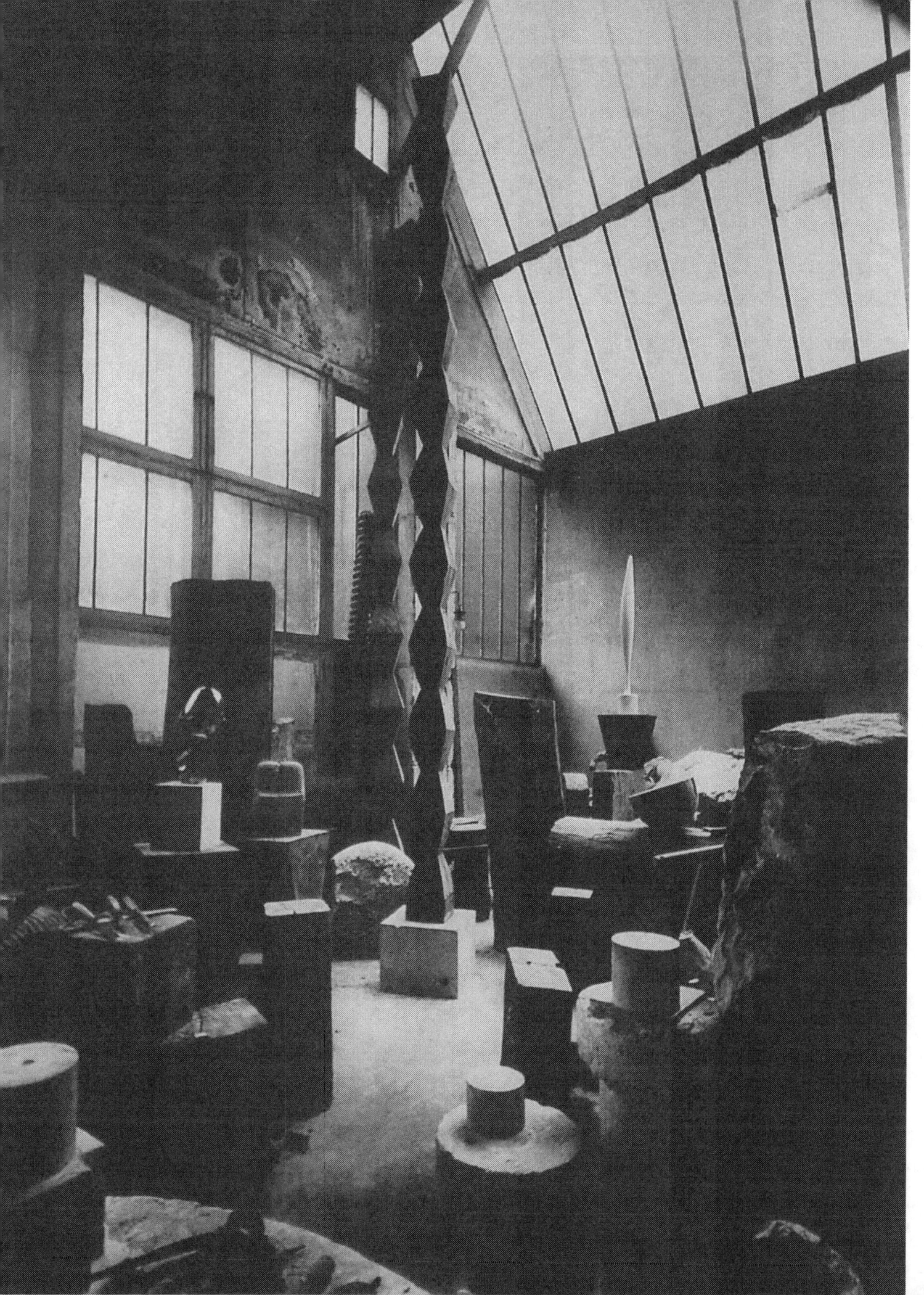

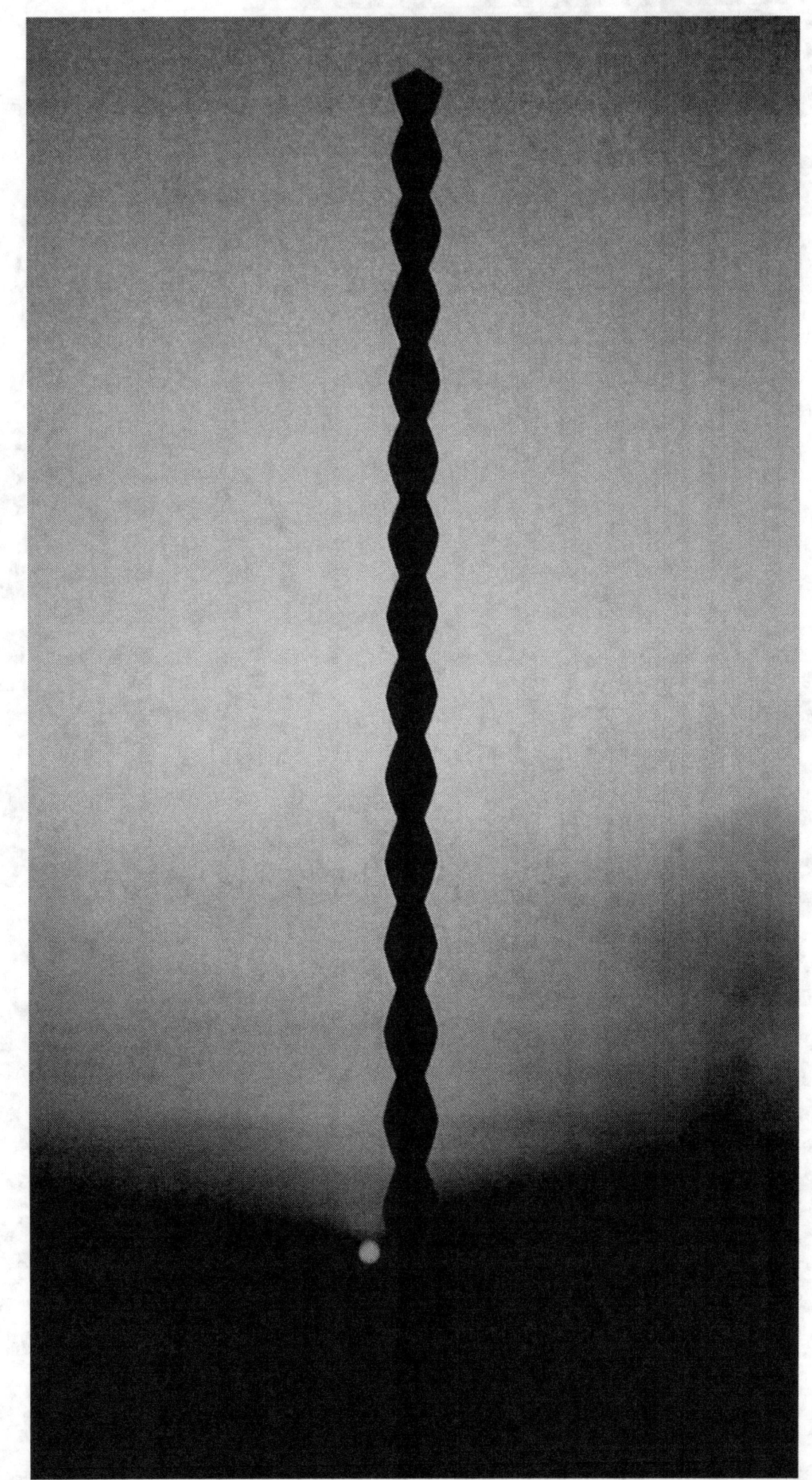

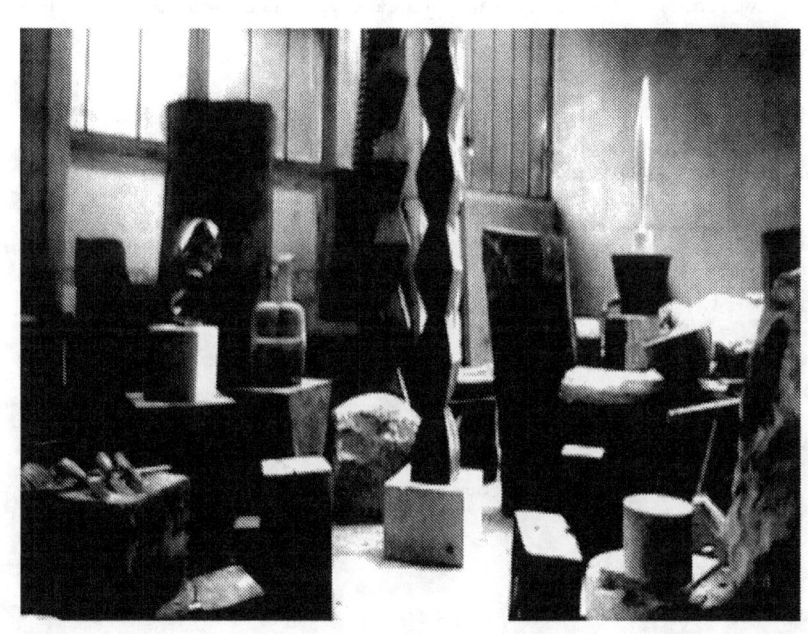

JANNIS KOUNELLIS: *HORSES*

Jannis Kounellis was associated with European Arte Povera and Minimal/ Conceptual artists (Lucio Fontana, Alberto Burri, Piero Manzoni, Daniel Buren, Giovanni Anselmo, Mario Merz, Hans Haacke and Christo). Of his Italian horse piece, made in 1969, Jannis Kounellis said the aim was to increase awareness of the 'basic nature of a gallery, of its bourgeois origin', its economic and ideological aspects.[1]

1. J. Kounellis, in W. Sharp: "Structure and Sensibility", *Avalanche*, 5, Summer, 1972.

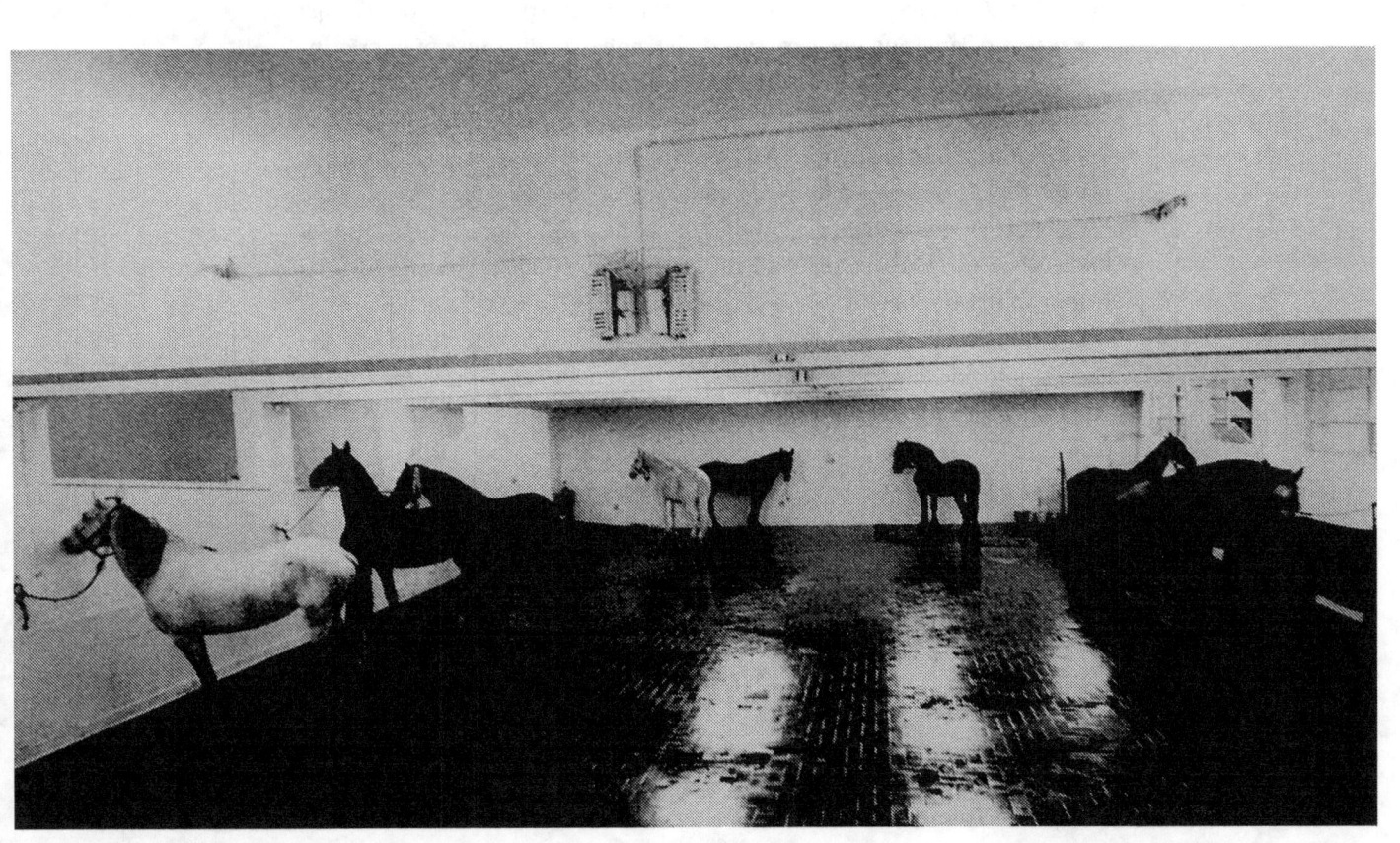

ALISON WILDING: *PULSE*

In 1991 at Dean Clough (Halifax), Alison Wilding created a site specific sculpture, *Pulse*, for the Henry Moore Sculpture Trust. *Pulse* was a large walk-through installation of white polypropylene. *Pulse* and the tiny meteorite (*Iron Meteorite*) were seen as symbiotic structures, even though one was very large and one very small. To emphasize the sense of interiority, Wilding had the windows of the gallery varnished over and stippled with sponges. She explored similar notions of opacity in works such as *Veiled no 2* in Cornwall. As a structure, with its hard white edges and large planes of plastic, *Pulse* owes much to the Minimalists, to artists such as Donald Judd and Robert Morris. Wilding had produced installations before 1991 – much of her work in the 1970s, after she had left the Royal College, was installation work.[1] In Halifax there was an opportunity to go to town on a gallery space. Developing her sculpture in the space at Dean Clough created many logistic and æsthetic challenges, and at times Wilding found she was losing overall control of the work. The two spaces were light and dark, and Wilding responded directly to the sense of illumination. *Pulse* is thus a light work, which explores the relation to light, while sculptures such as *Assembly* and *Stain* deal with darkness. *Pulse* was the result of many compromises, and Wilding was adamant that the staircase piece would stick to her original conception. In the end, she had to change many aspects of it, which proved disheartening. *Pulse* was intended to be about entering a different kind of interiority, separate from the surrounding gallery space, but also complementing it. Like so many of Wilding's sculptures, it was meant to isolate a space of its own while at the same time reacting to the space around itself. Wilding was also conscious of trying to manipulate the viewer's sense of space, so that one moved through a series of different spaces. There was a movement from familiar spaces to unfamiliar ones, from spaces that were 'conventional' to spaces that disrupted convention. At Dean Clough, Wilding aimed to provide a different sense of time, space and matter from the usual gallery or museum experience.

1. A. Wilding, 1991, 62.

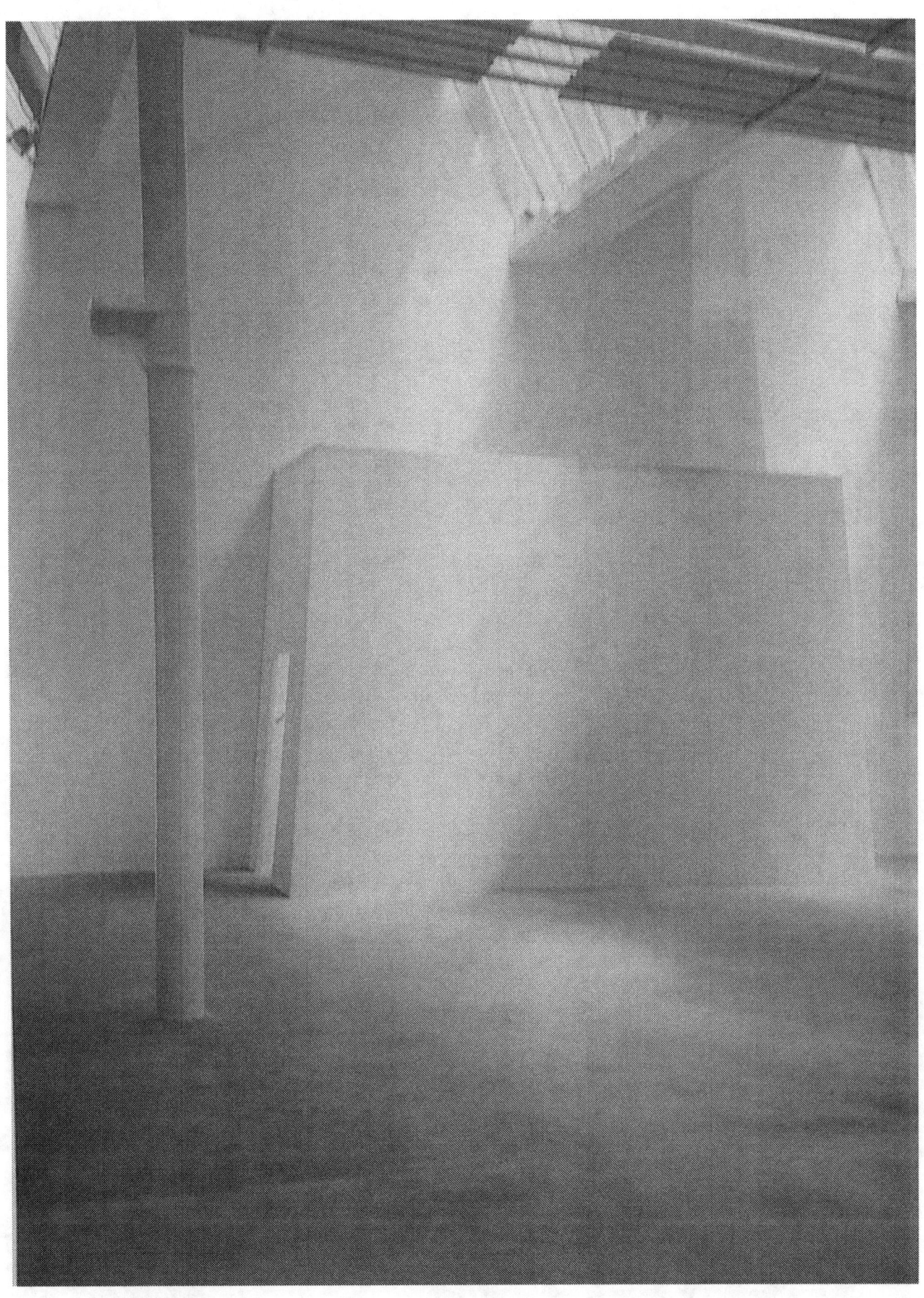

ALISON WILDING: *IRON METEORITE*

Alison Wilding is one of the very few contemporary women sculptors in Britain who are spoken of highly, and is regarded by some as approaching the status of such luminaries of the sculpture world as Barry Flanagan, Richard Long, Anish Kapoor, Tony Cragg, David Nash and Bill Woodrow. But Wilding's sculpture stands alone. No one else is making work like hers, as Fenella Crichton writes:

> Her work is impossible to categorise because she has created her own sculptural language, which is special to her, and which does separate her from the new wave of British sculpture... Like Eva Hesse, Wilding's language is in large part the result of her passionate involvement with the materials she uses. Whether brass, silk, copper, or wax, she works with their pliability and texture in order to bring out the most secretive and sensuous aspects of their nature.[1]

Alison Wilding's use of meteoritic material (the tektites), as here, automatically gives the works a cosmic and cosmological dimension (even though Wilding plays down such starry connotations, and does not refer to the origin of these chunks of material). Wilding admits to being fascinated by meteorites. 'I find the whole galaxy difficult to comprehend' she says.[2] Wilding was awed by outer space; she explores some this strangeness with her tektite sculptures. Meteorites are rare – and expensive – you can buy little fragments of tektite, but not large pieces. Meteorites chime alchemically: like the Philosopher's Stone, they are distinctly other-worldly, made of a material not of this Earth. Meteorites are quite different from most other materials, being formed from the inter-planetary media of the universe. Indeed, in one sense, meteoritic material is rarer than gold. One of Wilding's most intriguing sculptures is a real iron meteorite mounted in plexiglass and set up high in a slanted window. The meteorite is framed against the sky. Clouds are seen moving behind it. It looks as if it's fallen and landed on the gallery window.

1. F. Crichton, "When Form Engenders Attitude", in P. de Monchaux, 1983, 57.
2. A. Wilding, 1991, 63.

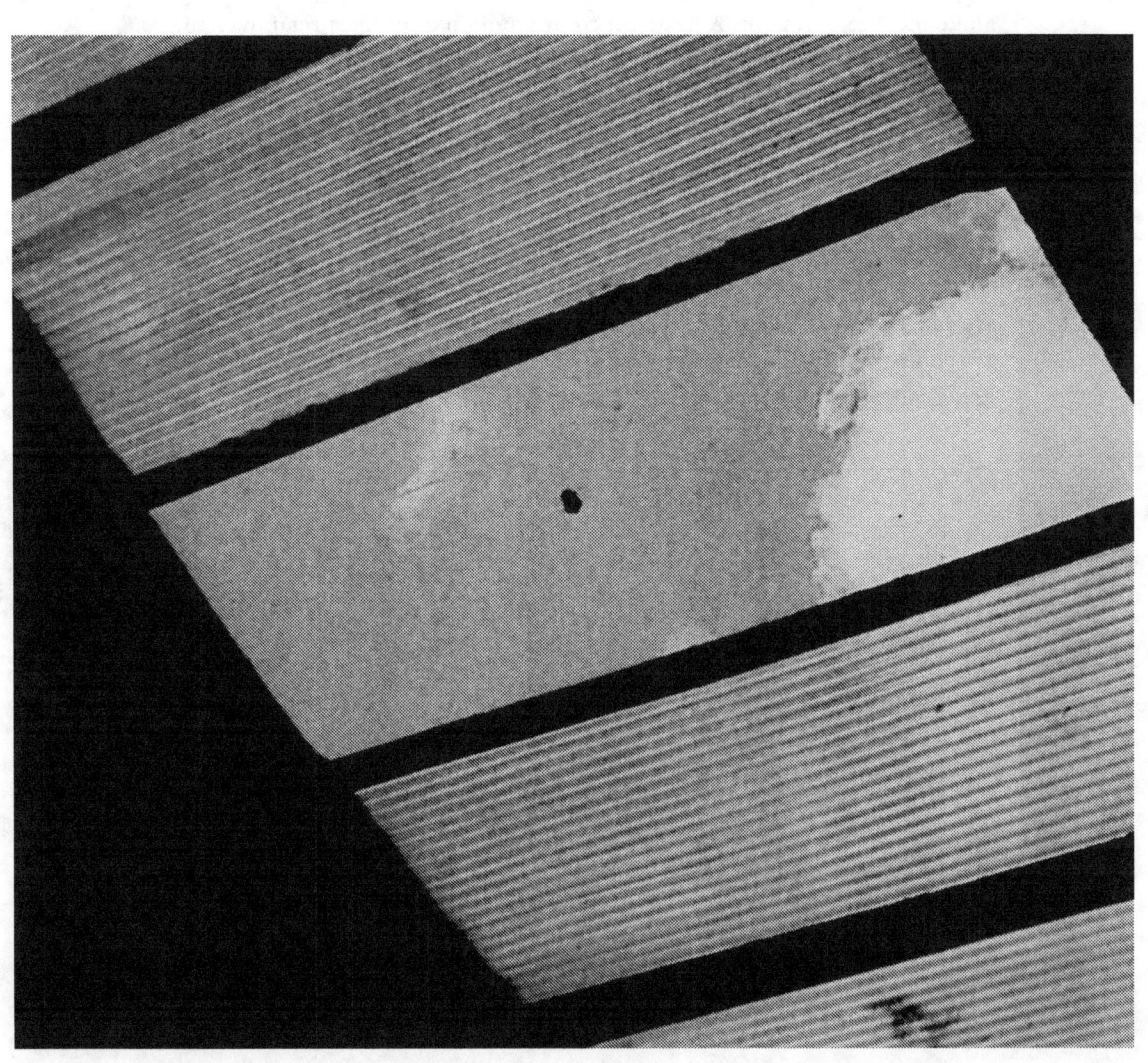

ALISON WILDING: *STAIN*

In Alison Wilding's large piece *Stain* (1991) we seem to be in the midst of an alchemical experiment. A large piece of woollen cloth is spread over the floor, perhaps to represent staining liquid. The cloth spreads out from a tall structure which stands in what looks like a large upturned tin bath. The anthropological reading of *Stain* might be that it depicts someone standing up in a bath and the liquid pours out from underneath the bath. Like a strange flood, the cloth seeps out from underneath the bath-like structure. While many works suggest liquid and the qualities of liquids (movement, transparency, viscosity), Wilding has not yet used liquids in her work. There are materials such as beeswax, and lead, which appear as semi-viscous elements. Wilding does not move into kinetic sculpture, though, like, say, Rebecca Horn with her rivers of bubbling, dripping mercury.

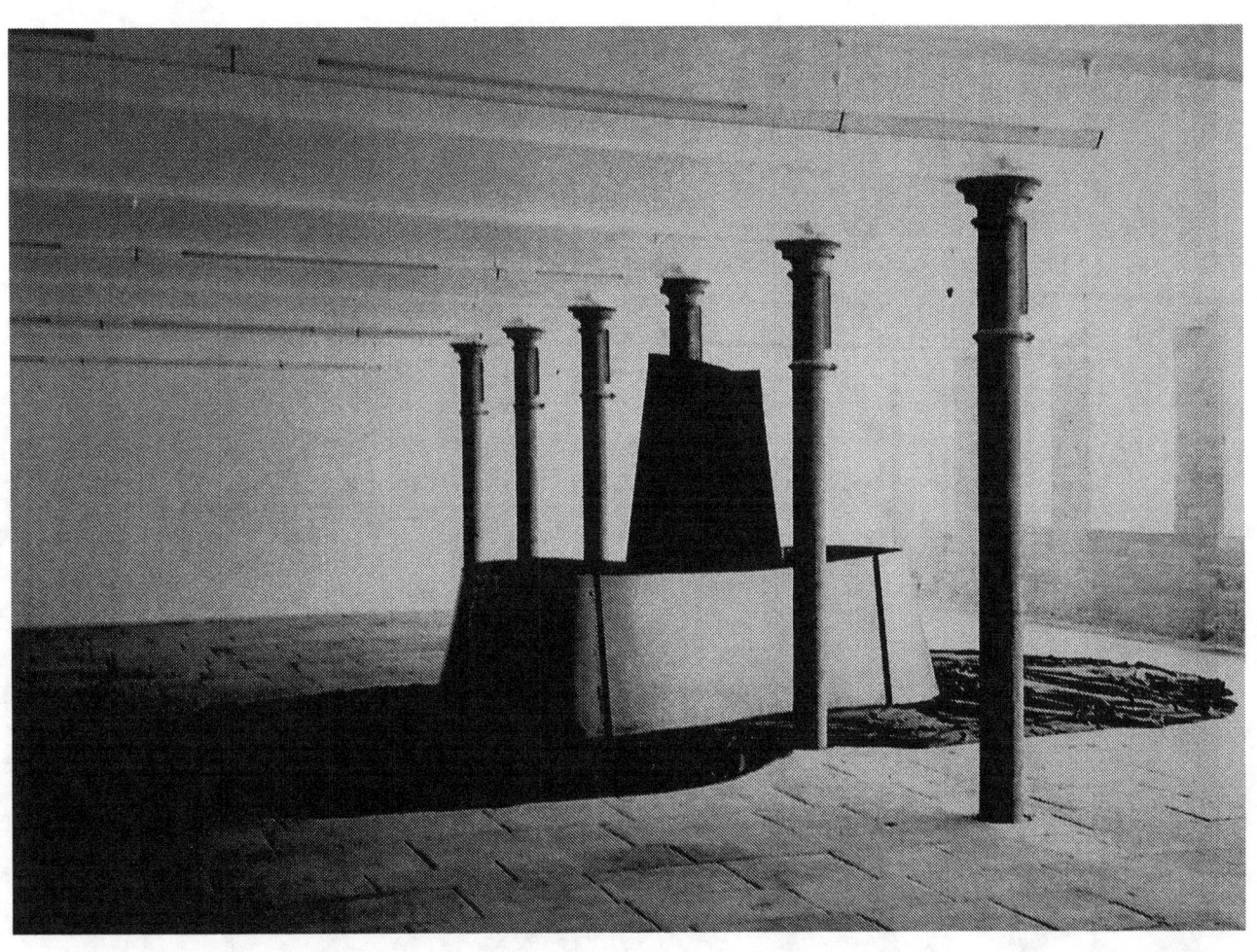

BRUCE NAUMAN: *NEON TEMPLATES OF THE LEFT HALF OF MY BODY TAKEN AT TEN-INCH INTERVALS*

Bruce Nauman is associated with Minimal art (though, like most good artists, he defies categorization: there's performance art, body art, Conceptual art, Process art, Arte Povera, assemblage and installation art in his output, among other art movements). Nauman became a deity among modern artists, often cited by younger artists as an inspiration (like Joseph Beuys or Salvador Dali). Nauman's also one of those artists, like Andy Warhol or Yves Klein, whose works have been prototypes or influences on a range of art movements. One can see how a variety of art movements seem to develop from Nauman's *œuvre*.

   In *Neon Templates of the Left Half of My Body Taken At Ten-inch Intervals* (1966, New York), green neon tubes were mounted on the wall in a vertical series relating to the artist's body. (Nauman was very fond of neon: the typical Nauman neon piece comprised short ironic phrases in different coloured neon: 'desire', 'hope', as in *Human/ Need/ Desire* [1983, MOMA, New York]).

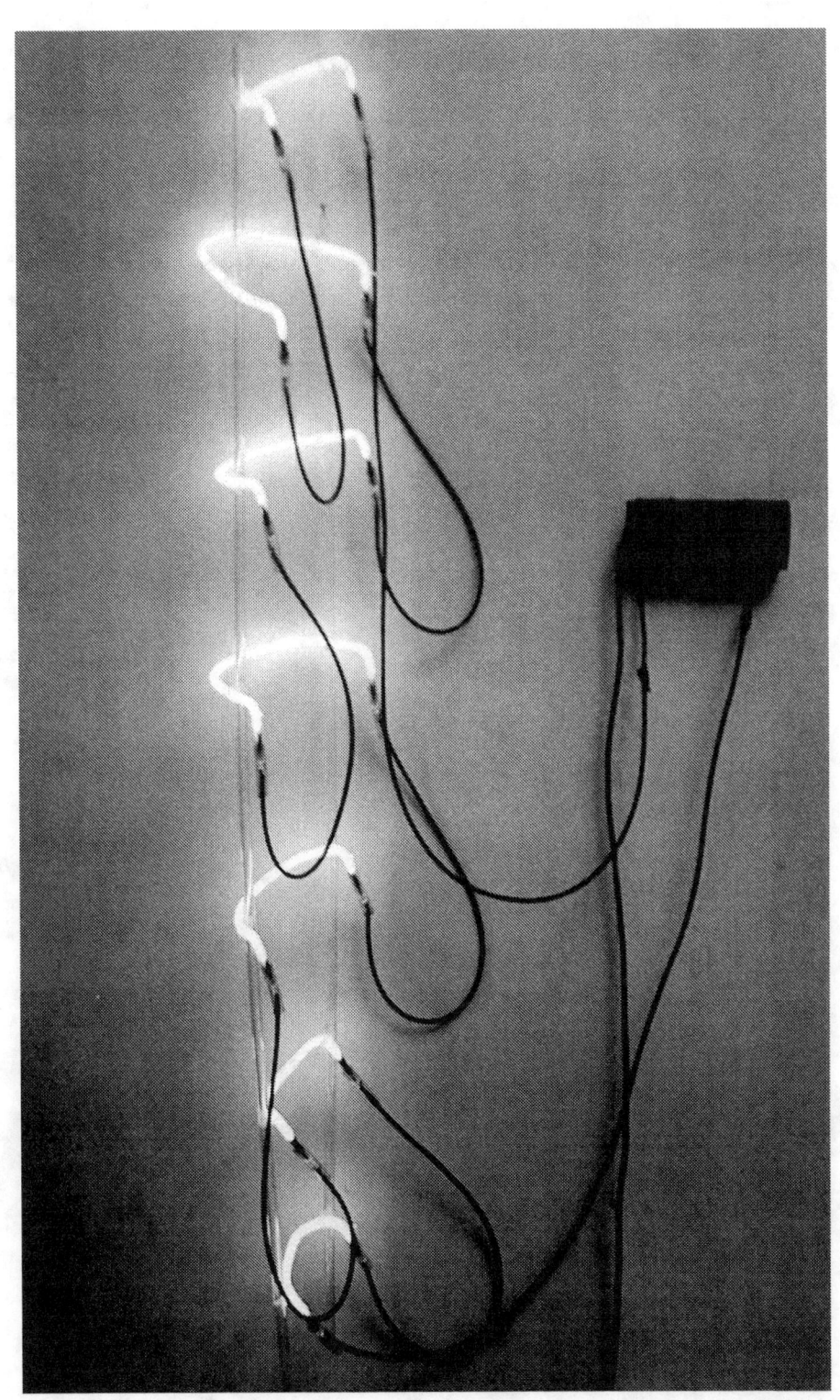

BRUCE NAUMAN: *GREEN LIGHT CORRIDOR*

Green Light Corridor (1970, Guggenheim, New York) is a typical Nauman lightwork: a narrow 12-metre corridor is created between tall two flats (higher than average human height), and lit by white fluorescent tubes above (inside the corridor) in a room suffused with green lamps. The idea was to enclose the visitor in a narrow, claustrophobic space and limit their perception.[1]

1. I. Sandler, 1996, 32.

CHRISTO: *WRAPPED COAST*

Christo makes huge gestures everyone can see, with his plastic-covered buildings, his wrapped Pont Neuf or curtains hanging across valleys. His art is not 'invisible' like de Maria's kilometre-long brass rod which only reveals a brass disc on the ground, or Long's walks, which are only memories or text pieces. Born in 1935, in Bulgaria, Christo (Christo Javacheff) attended the Fine Arts Academy in Sofia. One of his early activities as a student involved tidying up the Orient Express route through Bulgaria by covering old farm machinery and haystacks with tarpaulin. At Prague Christo studied set design, and one of his mid-1960s works in New York involved making replicas of shopfronts, like a stage set, but the windows were covered with cloth or paper. In his early works, Christo wrapped up items such as books, bottles, tins and boxes. Other Assemblages or *empaquetages* (Assemblages as packages) included nude models, cars, chairs and motorbikes.

In 1969 Christo wrapped a mile-long section of the Australian coastline. The use of open weave cloth (1 million ft²) meant that wildlife would not be affected. *Wrapped Coast*, at Little Bay near Sydney, stayed for 4 weeks. It was a dramatic land art gesture, difficult to ignore.

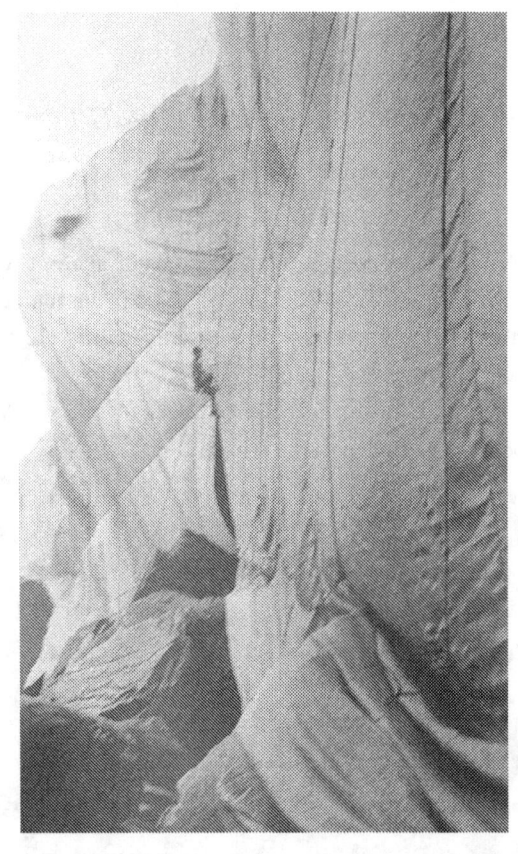

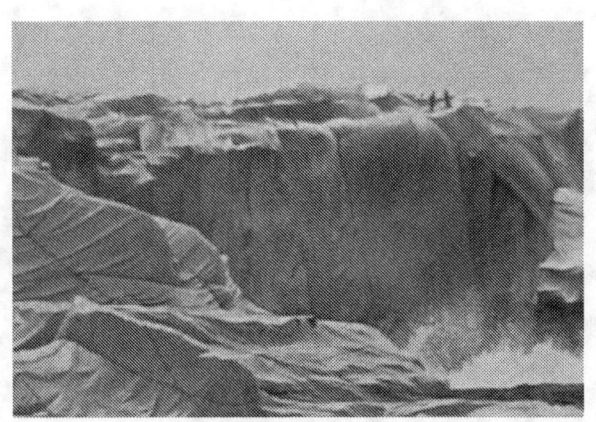

CHRISTO: *WALL OF OIL BARRELS – IRON CURTAIN*

Christo's most famous Assemblage was on a larger scale, the *Wall of Oil Barrels – Iron Curtain* (1962). This was a pile of barrels stacked across and blocking one of Paris's oldest streets, Rue Visconti. *Wall of Oil Barrels – Iron Curtain* parodied the Berlin Wall, which had recently been constructed. The sculpture annoyed the locals, and Christo's large-scale works have been upsetting neighbours ever since.

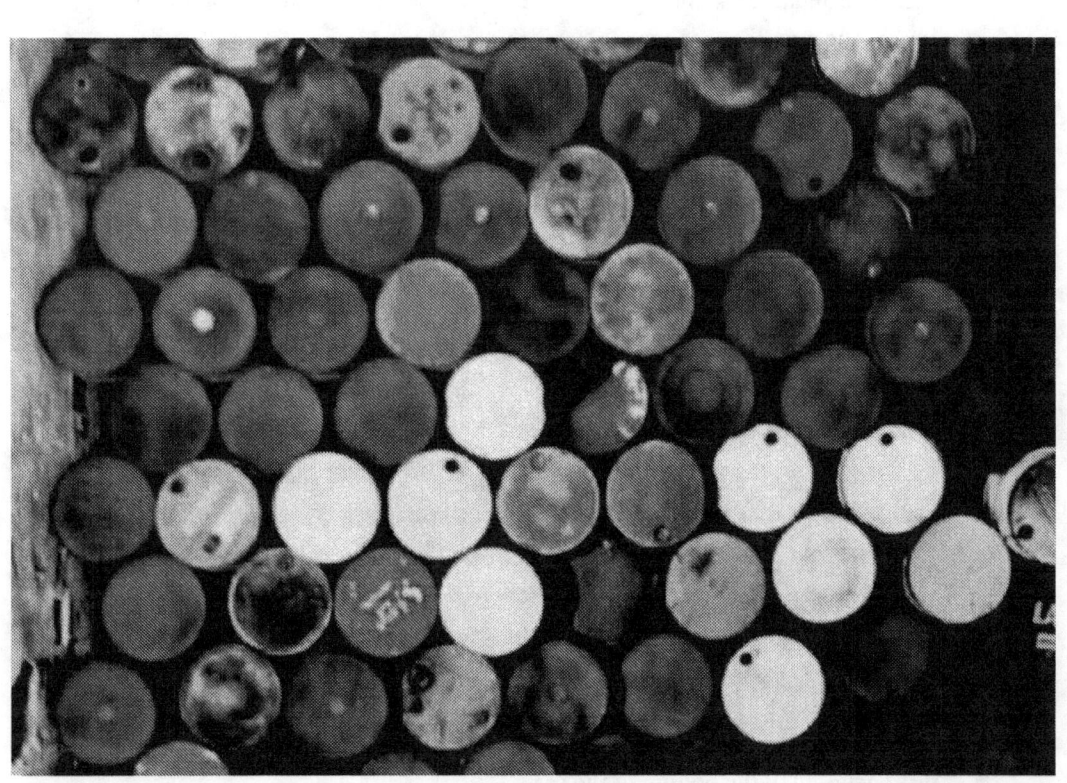

CHRISTO: *RUNNING FENCE*

Running Fence (1972-76) consisted 2,050 18 foot panels of white nylon attached to steel poles, running across Marin and Sonoma counties and 12 roads in California. As with Christo's other mammoth projects, there was much opposition to *Running Fence*. A committee designed to 'stop Running Fence' brought the subject to the Superior Court of the State of California 3 times. The subsequent report on the environmental impact of the *Running Fence* project found that there were no endangered species in the region, except for the Brown Pelican, and virtually no wildlife would be affected by it. *Running Fence* went ahead, and stayed up for two weeks in September 1976.[1] When it was taken down, nothing remained of it in the area: the holes were filled in, and bare parts of soil were reseeded. As with other Christo projects, when it was taken away some locals were dismayed, the work had helped them realize the beauty of the area. Christo says his art is

> about displacement. Basically even today I am a displaced person. And this is why I make art that does not last. Of course, it will stay for ever in the minds of people.[2]

Christo here espouses the fundamental Romanticism in land art: that it will live on in the memories of people. Christo's large-scale projects – *Running Fence, Surrounded Islands, Wrapped Coast* – are spectacular works, part of the land art tradition which moves towards the sublime in landscape art (which resurfaced in the Abstract Expressionism of Rothko, Newman and Motherwell). The ocean end of *Running Fence* is particularly impressive: at Bodega Bay the *Fence* extended gracefully into the Pacific, 558 feet, descending from a height of 18 feet on land to 2 feet at the section which was anchored to the bottom of the sea.

1. See Werner Spies, *The Running Fence Project, Christo*, Abrams, New York, NY, 1977.
2. In A. Haden-Guest, 40.

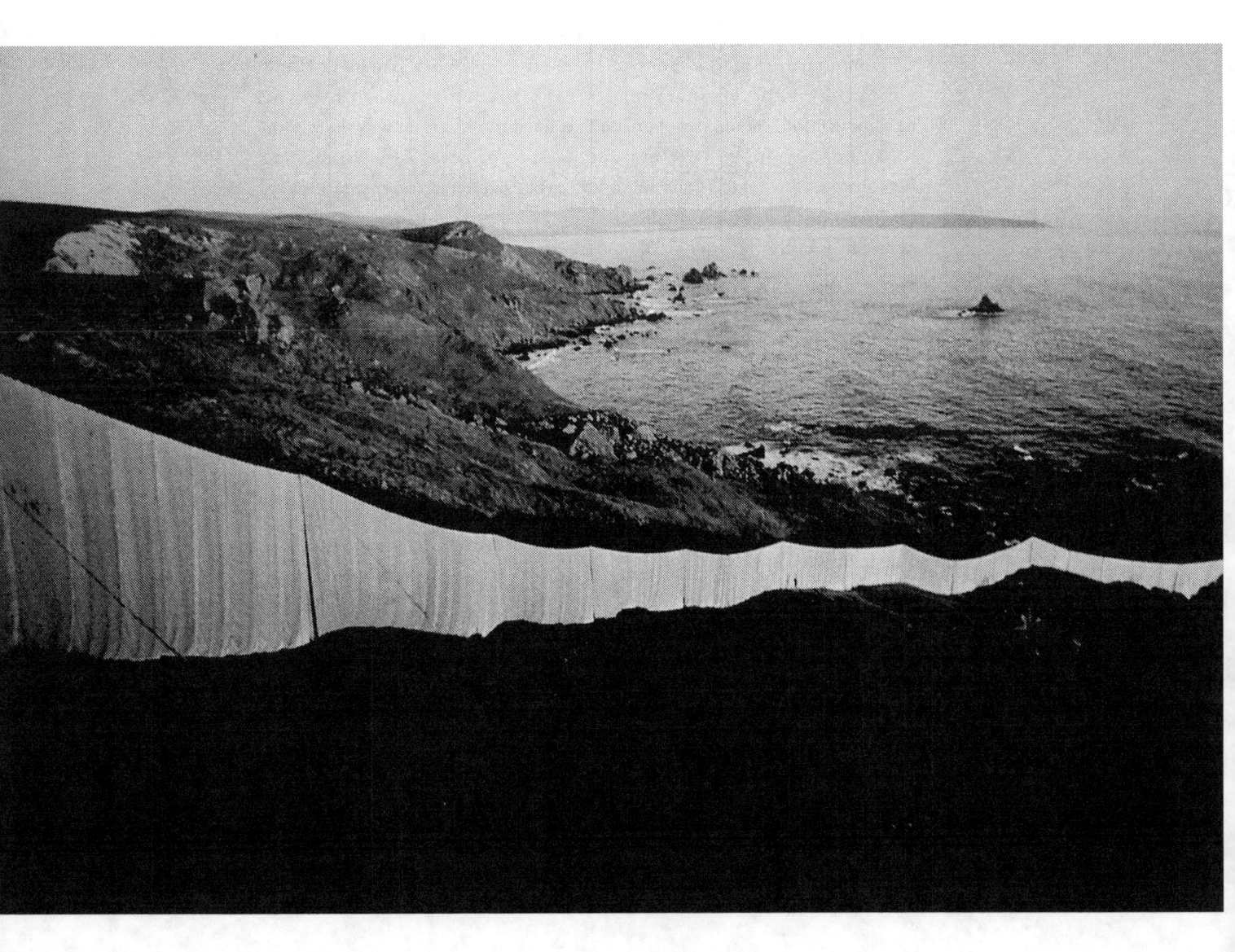

CHRISTO: *WRAPPED MUSEUM OF CONTEMPORARY ART, CHICAGO*

Christo's first large-scale wrapping was to cover the Museum of Contemporary Art in Chicago with 10,000 ft² of brown tarpaulin. Christo's wrapping of the museum made it the focus of attention in the neighbourhood – some people hadn't realized the museum was there until it had been wrapped. The museum's director reckoned Christo had parodied 'all the associations a museum evokes: a mausoleum, a repository for precious contents, an intent to wrap up all of art history'.[1] Inside the museum was the *Wrapped Floor*, consisting of 2,000 ft² of rented drop cloths.

1. Jan van der Marck, *Wrapped Museum*, Museum of Contemporary Art, Chicago, 1969.

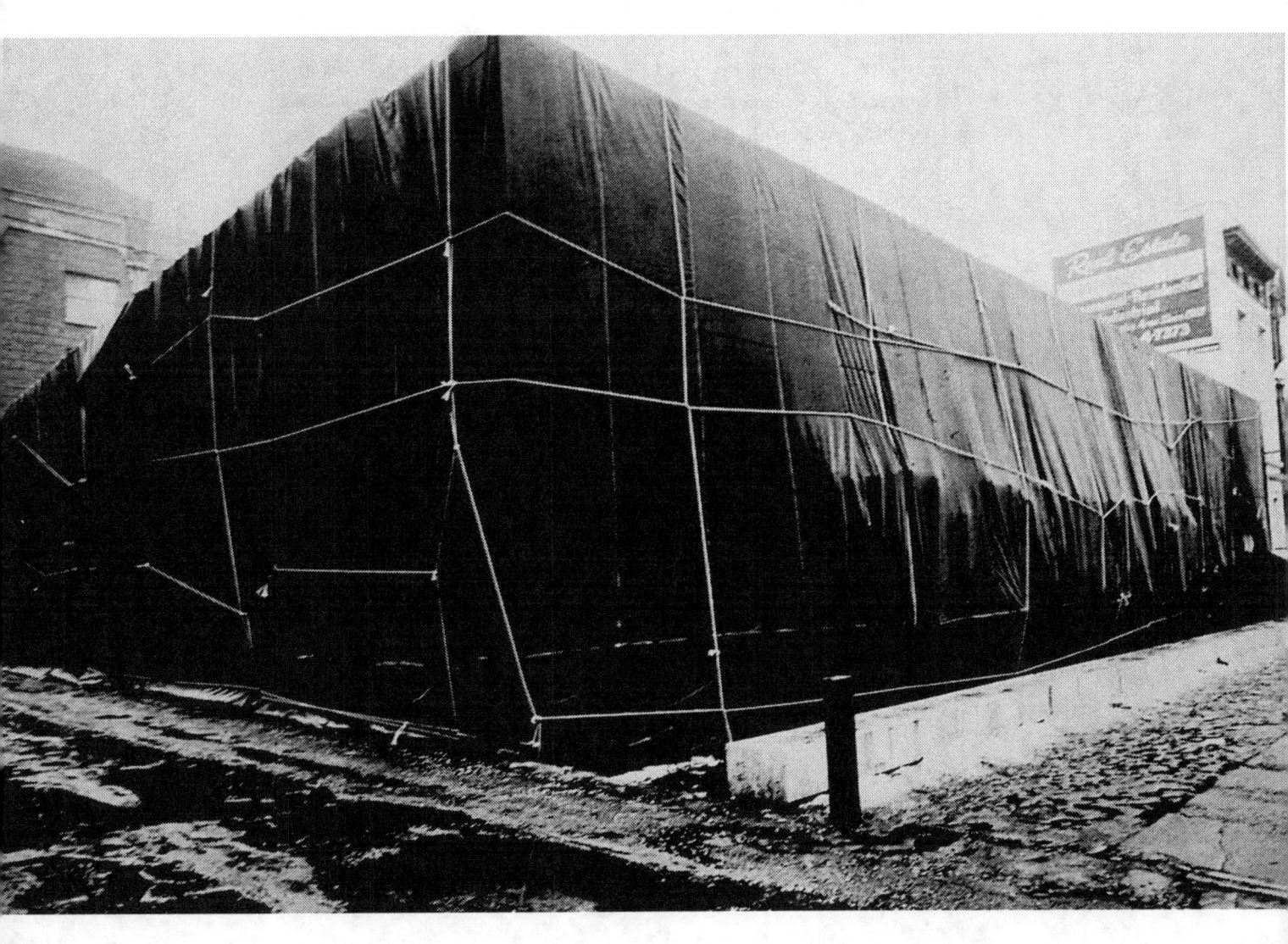

CHRISTO: *THE UMBRELLAS*

Christo's large-scale works are expensive: *Running Fence* cost over $3 million, *Surrounded Islands* cost $3.5 million, and *The Umbrellas* in Japan and California cost $26,000,000. Denigrators of Christo's work have noted the expense of the projects, but Christo pays for them himself, by selling photos, drawings, collages, models, lithographs and plans and other works, and by collaborating with industry.

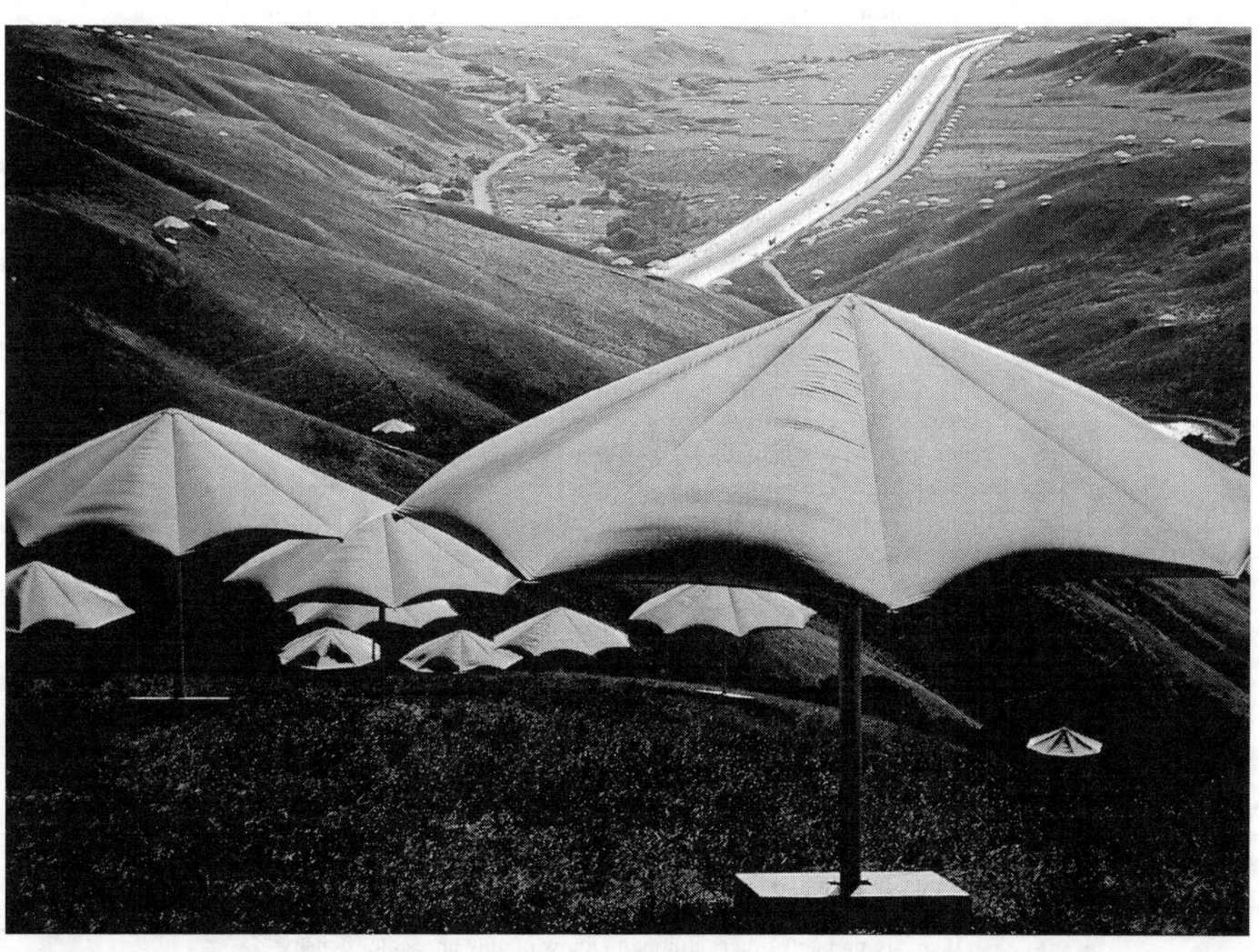

FRANK STELLA

Frank Stella has carved out a niche in the art world for himself. There are no works quite like Stella's around. There are similar pieces, but Stella's works remain instantly recognisable as Stella's own. The same cannot be said for any number of other artists.

Frank Stella moved into three dimensions in the 1970s (although his paintings had always been 3-D, as all paintings are), seeming to depart from his radical Minimal origins, building his paintings out from the wall, with work such as *Warka III* (1973) and *Leblon II* (1975). There are many other contemporary artists who have developed out of Jasper Johns' and Frank Stella's post-Abstract Expressionist painting: among the more successful were (are) painters such as Christopher Le Brun, Thérèse Oulton, Lance Smith, Hughie O'Donoghue, R. B. Kitaj, Jim Dine, Richard Diebenkorn and Anselm Keifer. (Keifer's *Wayland's Song* [1982], for instance, uses oil, emulsion, straw on photo, on canvas with lead). Painters who seem to have a direct Stellan component include Brice Marden, Sean Scully, Howard Hodgkin and Gerard Richter. Minimal sculptors – Donald Judd, Robert Morris, Carl Andre – have acknowledged Stella's importance.

Frank Stella employed hard-edged, angular motifs, shapes such as Vs, Zs, Xs, Hs, Ls, Ts, Us, 'notched Vs', polygons, squares and rectangles. He also utilized symmetry, an exact symmetry made explicit and bold by his stripes and the shaped stretchers, so that the stripe pattern, wrote John Coplans, 'begins at the center and spreads outward by his use of various kinds of symmetry'.[1] For Frank Stella, the new sense of symmetry was not sited within an illustionistic space; rather, the use of hard edges, symmetry and the monochrome bands helped to push away illustionistic space:

> A symmetrical image or configuration placed on an open ground is not balanced out in the illustionistic space. The solution I arrived at – and there are probably others although I know of only one, color density – forces illusionistic space out of the painting at a constant rate by using a regulated pattern.[2]

1. J. Coplans, "Serial Imagery", 37.
2. B. Rose, "ABC Art", 59.

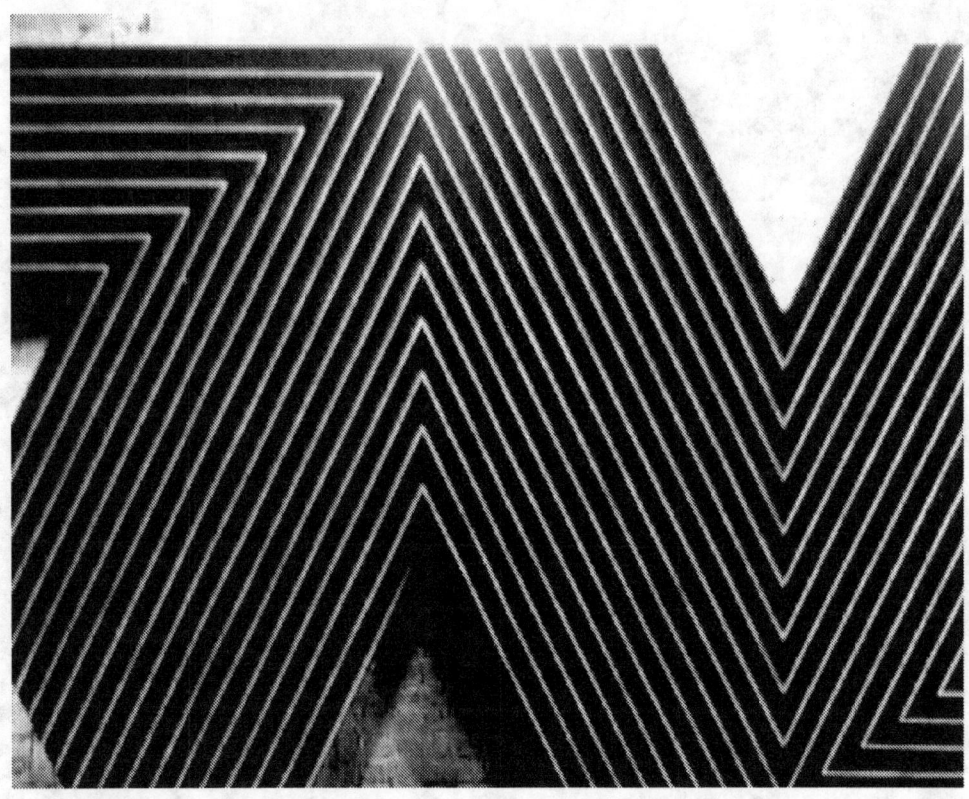

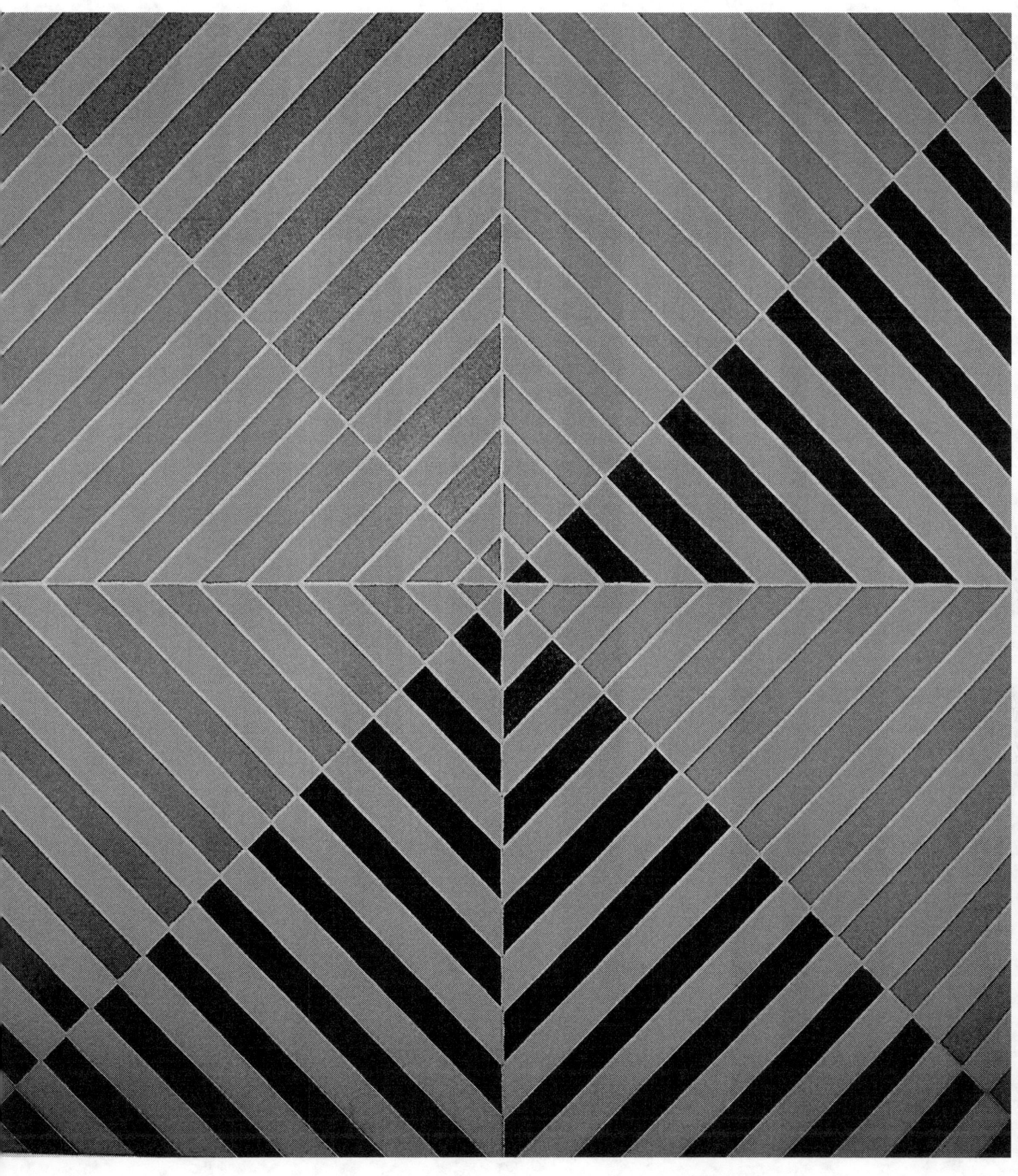

FRANK STELLA: *LA VECCHIA DELL'ORTO*

In Frank Stella's post-1970s paintings, there is no attempt to smooth over the edges, or to provide a smooth surface to the paint, as with the Sixties *Protractor* paintings or the metallic paintings. Rather, Stella draws attention to the expressive qualities of his brushwork, as with William de Kooning or Julian Schnabel, and seemed to reject Minimal æsthetics. The expressiveness of Stella's gestures becomes an important element in the painting. The brushstrokes are not hidden as in Barnett Newman's art, who painted with a small brush in small strokes, building up his layers of paint carefully, so that no brushstrokes showed. Stella, rather, constantly draws attention to his brushstrokes, to the very manufacture of his paintings. Works such as *La Vecchia dell'orto* (1986), *Shards II* (1982), *Steller's Albatross* (1976) and *Shama* (1979), open out to reveal their manufacture. In the 1960s, Frank Stella used bright colours, like Morris Louis, but kept them neatly bounded within their stripe patterns. The late maximalist works continually refer to the making of paintings. Stella would not return to the austerity of his early Minimal paintings, but his later work retained many formal links with Minimalism (in a way it could be termed Postminimal).

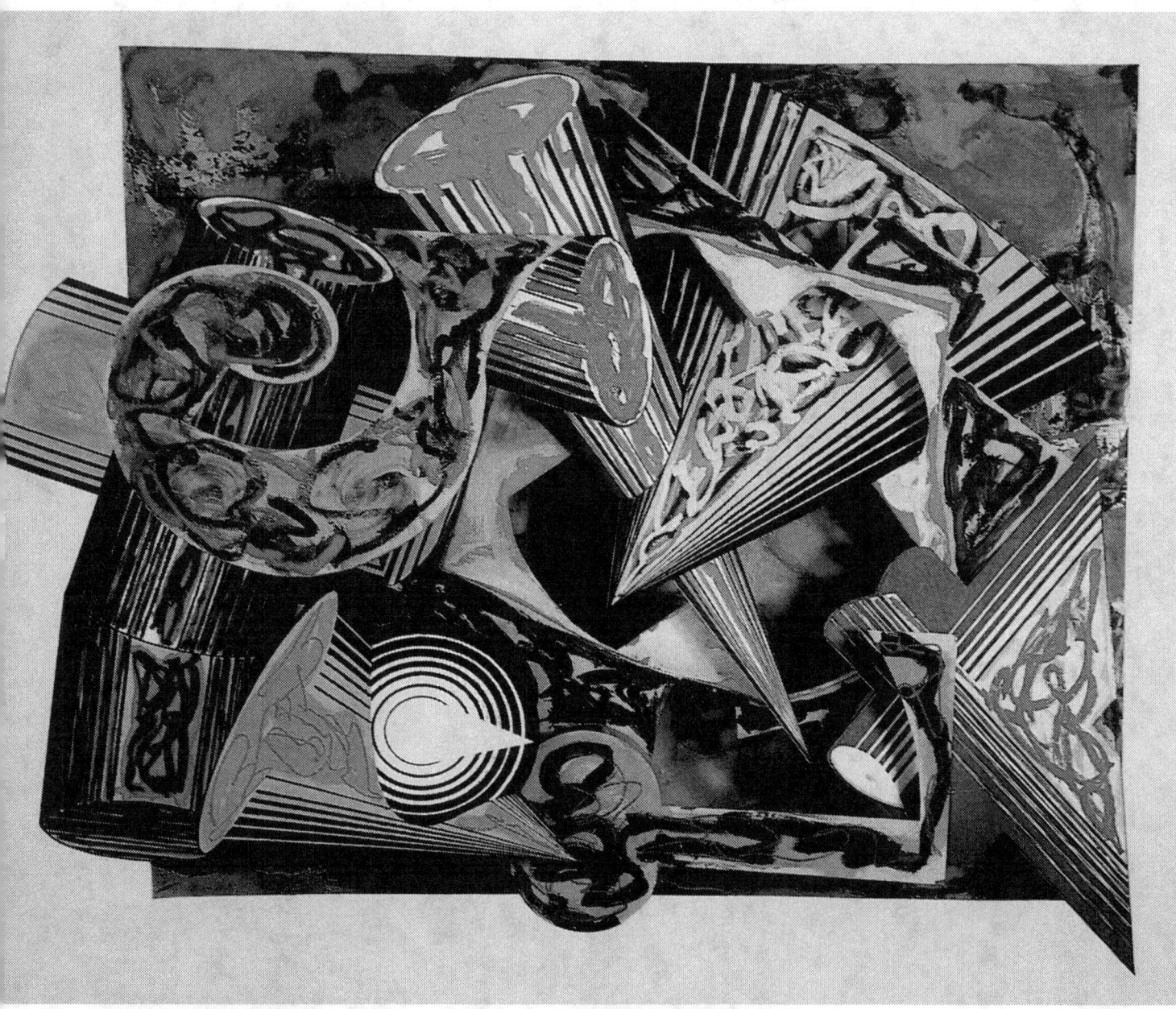

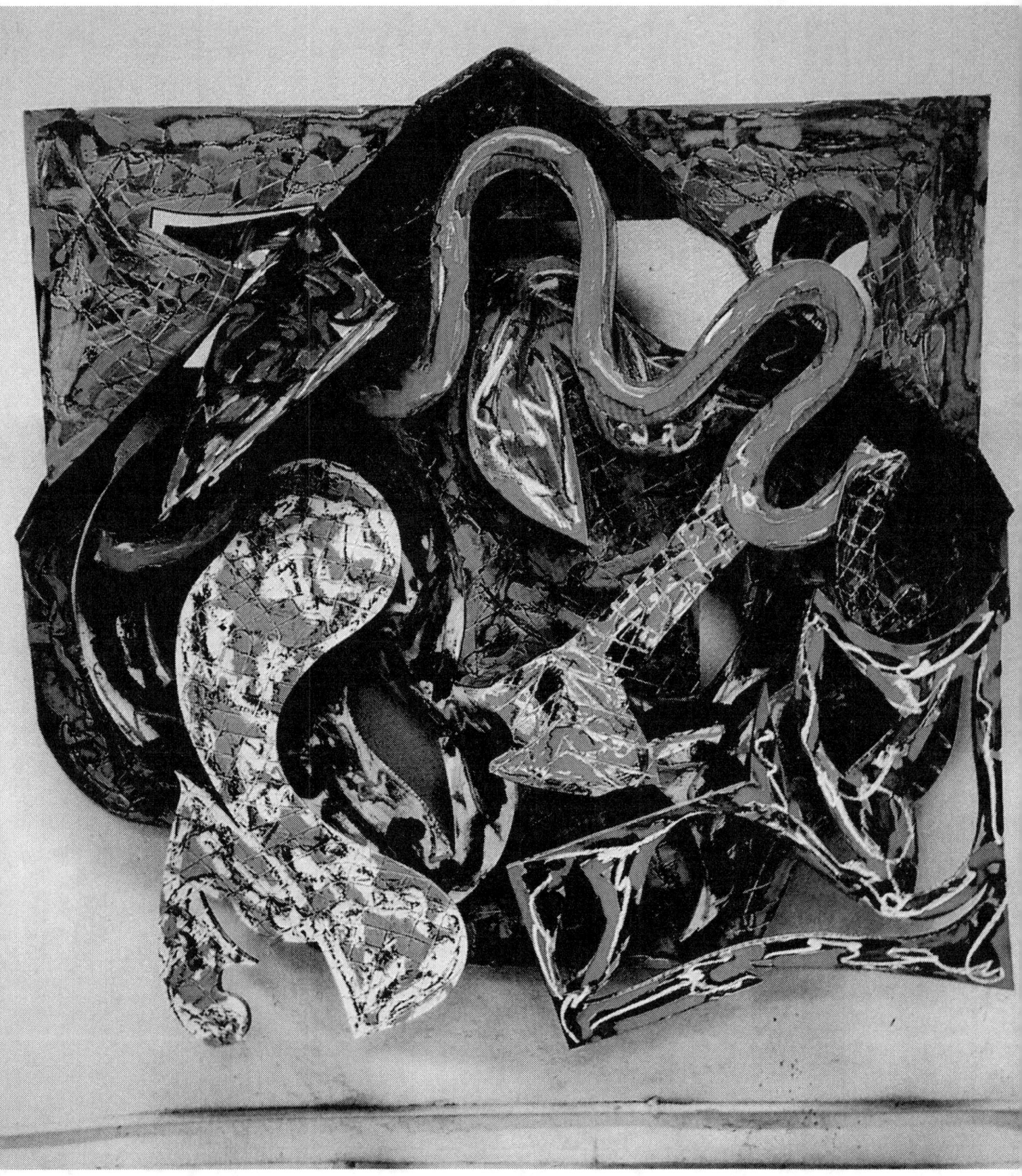

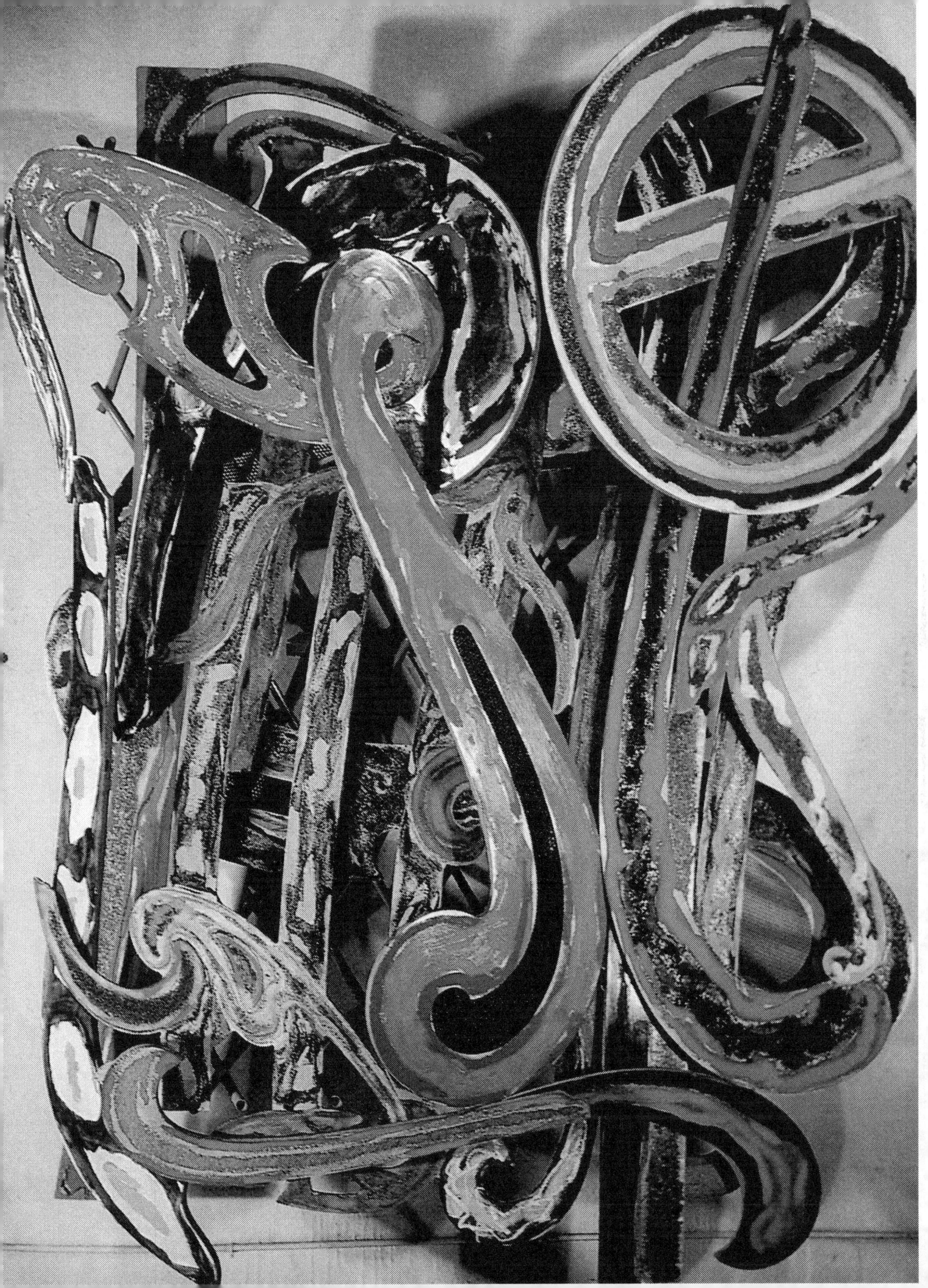

ANA MENDIETA

Ana Mendieta covered herself in mud (while nude, of course) and stood against a tree (for *The Tree of Life* series, 1977, made in Old Man's Creek, Iowa), a combination of Goddess art, performance art and environmental art. In *The Tree of Life* series, Mendieta left the outline of her body in leaves on a tree trunk. In the *Silueta* series (1979), Mendieta imprinted her body in the snow in Amana, Iowa, and in mud on a river-bank, or set the form on fire in the earth, or made a silhouette from flowers. These pieces echo Andy Goldsworthy's rain and snow 'body prints' (however, Mendieta's art has an undisguised ideological, spiritual and ecological agenda; some of Mendieta's works are explicit performance explorations of rapes, and Mendieta was also exploring her Cuban and Latin American heritage).

In some pieces Mendieta remodelled the entrance of a cave and a ravine into her Goddess shape. She also buried herself under turf – a literal Earth-Goddess mound, and had herself photographed in an ancient Mexican stone grave. Mendieta also lit fires in sculptures (such as *Volcano*, 1979), like Chris Drury and David Nash, and lit candles and fireworks in the shape of a woman.

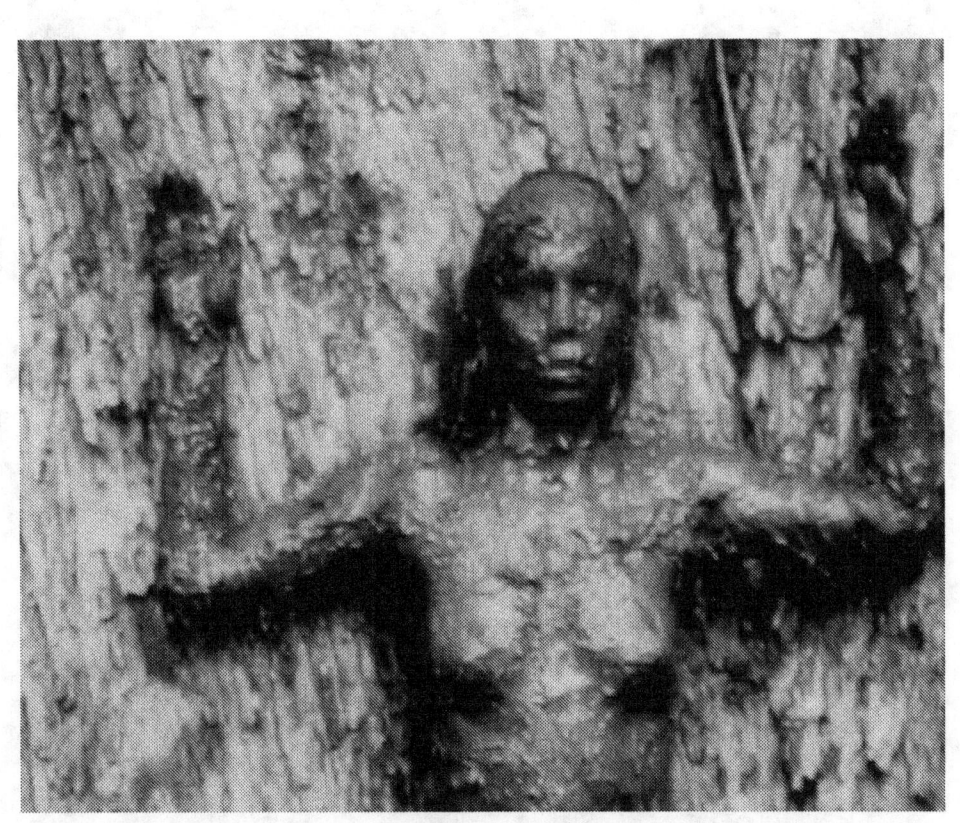

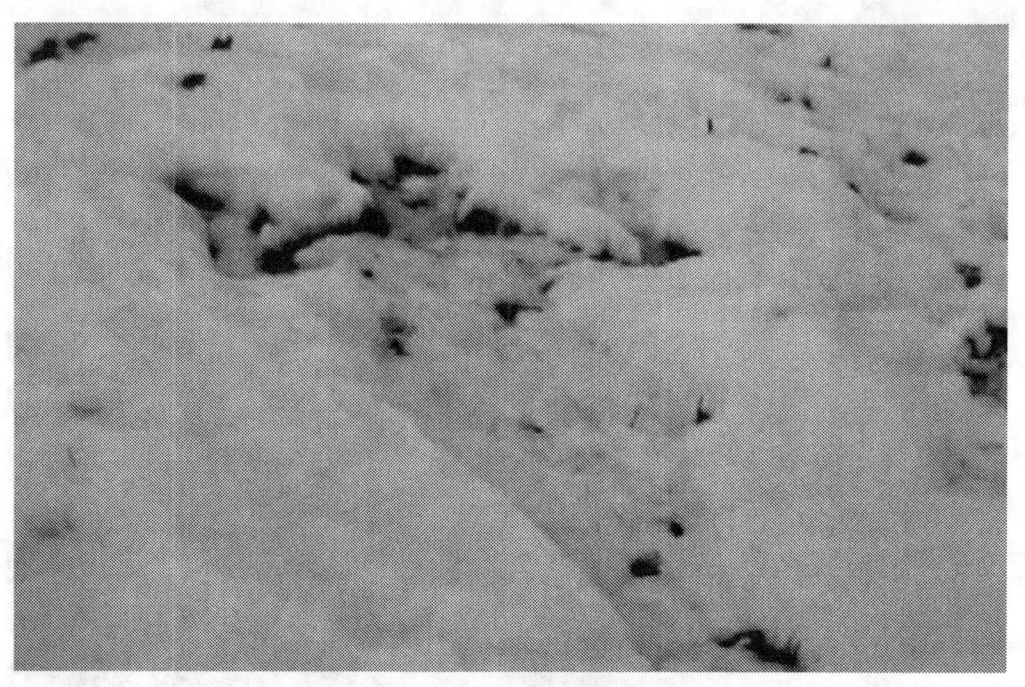

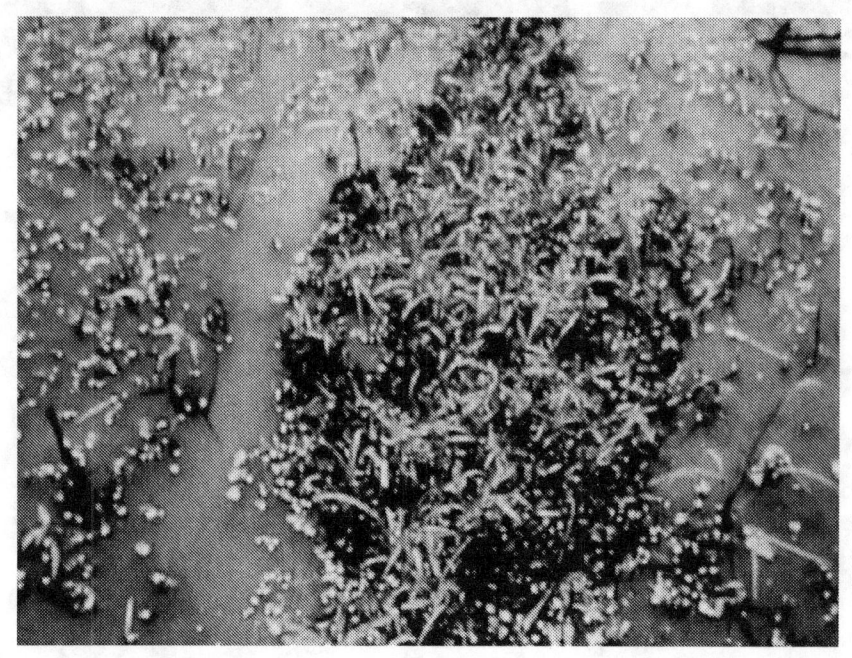

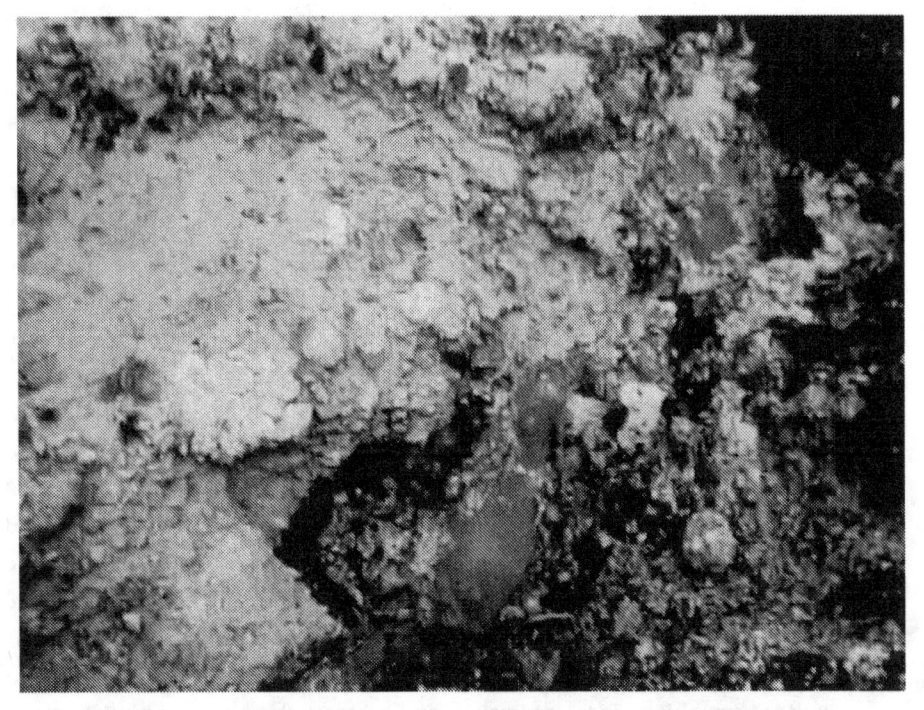

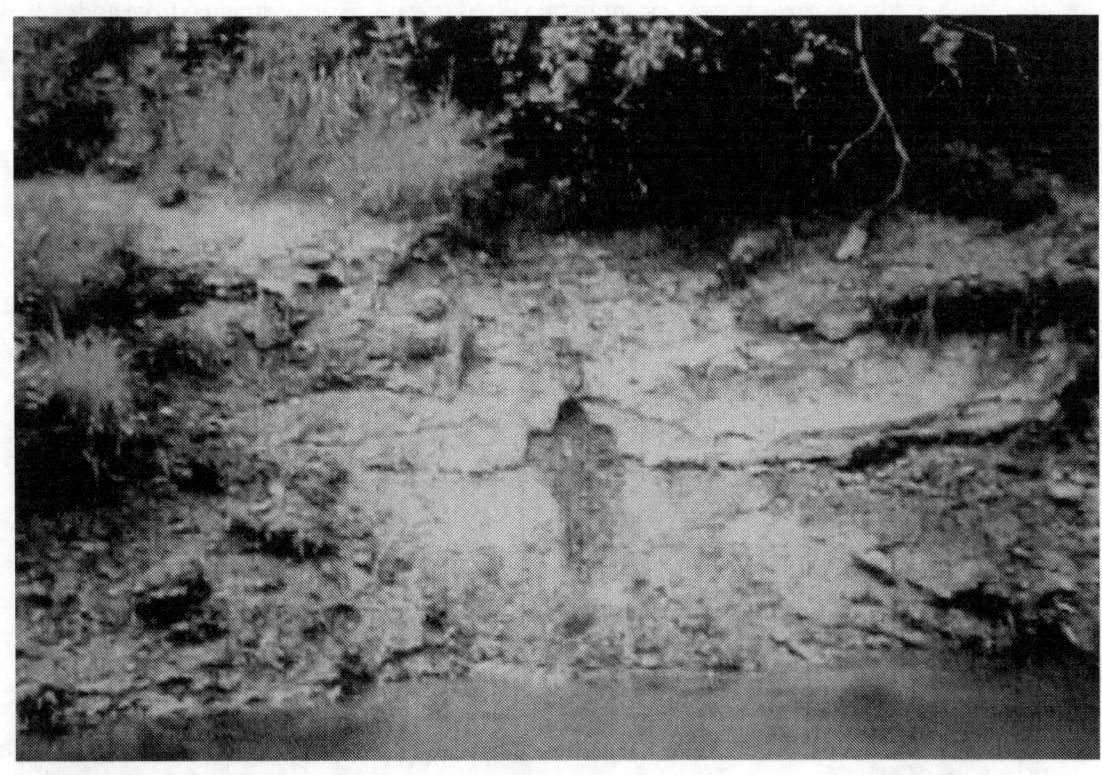

DENNIS OPPENHEIM: *ANNUAL RINGS*

Many of Dennis Oppenheim's artworks are conceptual pieces in the tradition of Sixties Conceptualism. That is, many are works made to be exhibited in galleries, on walls. They comprise photographs, drawings and maps, with Oppenheim's typewritten captions and explanations: *Three Downward Blows* (1977), *Salt Flat* (1969), *Boundary Split* (1968), and *Negative Board* (1968) (maps were central to Oppenheim's art). Many of Oppenheim's land artworks also existed as these framed photo-text-sketch-map works. One of Oppenheim's specialities was to impose humanmade geometries, symbols and ideas onto the landscape: to transpose map contours, for instance, or the rings of a tree trunk onto snow (in *Annual Rings*), or the International Date Line in snow (*Time Pocket*). Robert Smithson remarked that Oppenheim was 'transforming a terrestrial site into a map'.[1] Generally, Oppenheim tended to enlarge symbols or ideas or images, and recreate them on a colossal scale in the landscape.

Speaking in 1970, Dennis Oppenheim opined that art was now 'more concerned with the location of material and with speculation' (i.e., locations or ideas). Now, art was meant to be visited (location) or 'abstracted from a photograph' (conceptualized).[2] Oppenheim moved towards a kind of art that would be discovered or visited by the spectator, rather than 'made' in the old, traditional manner (this was part of the 'dematerialization' of the art object in Sixties art). Oppenheim moved away from the idea of the special, unique art object, towards found objects, and utilizing existing sites. Oppenheim was replacing objects with locations. The *Site Markers* series (1967) comprised posts in locations which were documented with texts, maps and photos. The maps and photos explained where the posts were situated, so that the location, rather than the object, became the centre of the piece. As Oppenheim pointed out, the *Site Markers* works were intended to be about the sites themselves, rather than the manipulation of replication of an object: 'beginning with the site-markers started in a sense a journey: art is travel'.[3]

1. In M. Heizer, 1970.
2. D. Oppenheim, in M. Heizer, 1970.
3. In D. Oppenheim, 1978.

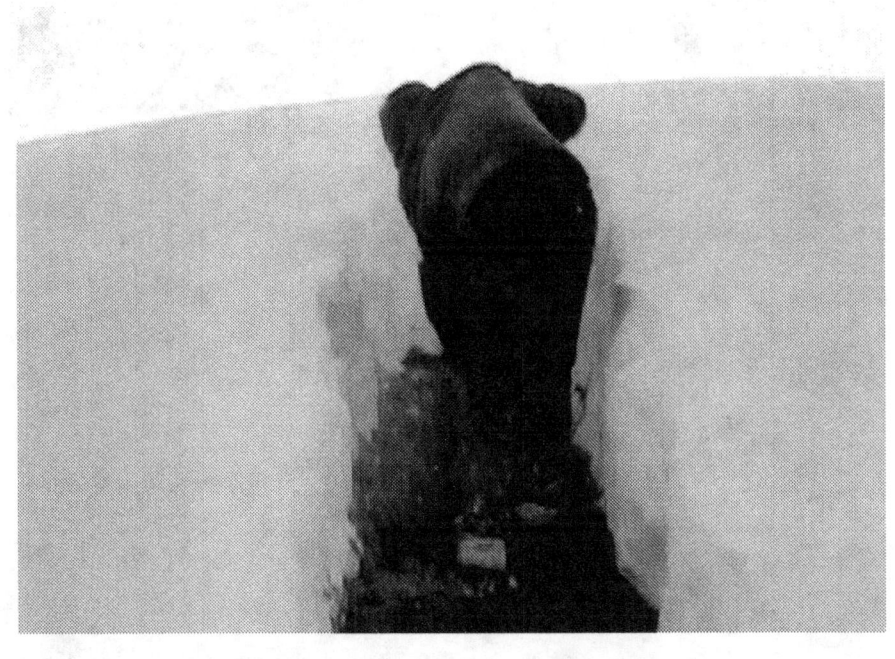

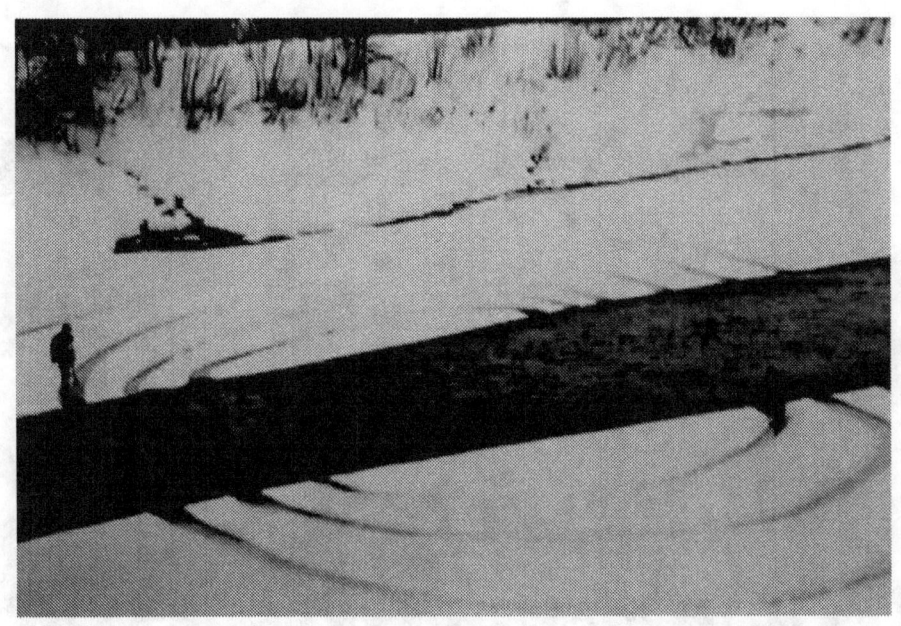

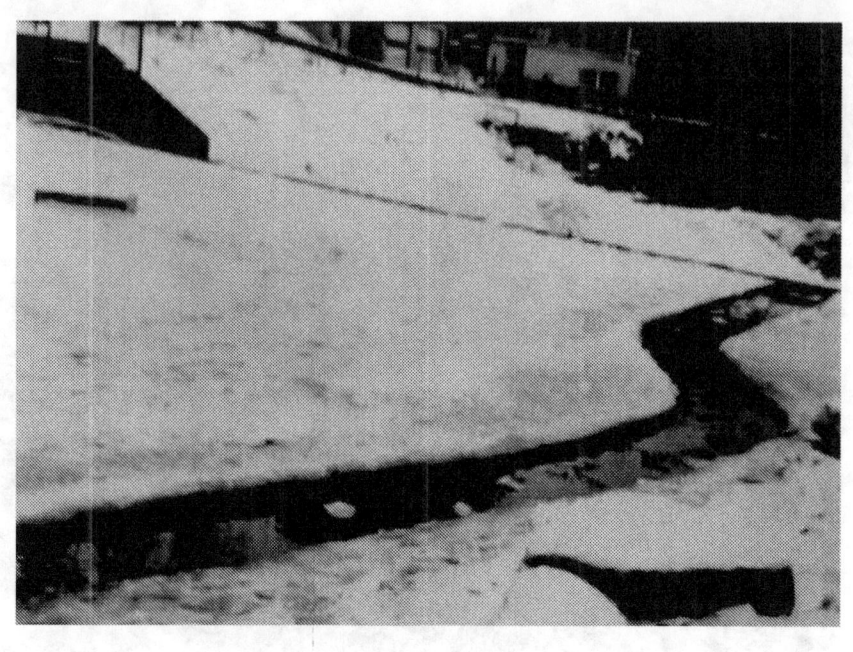

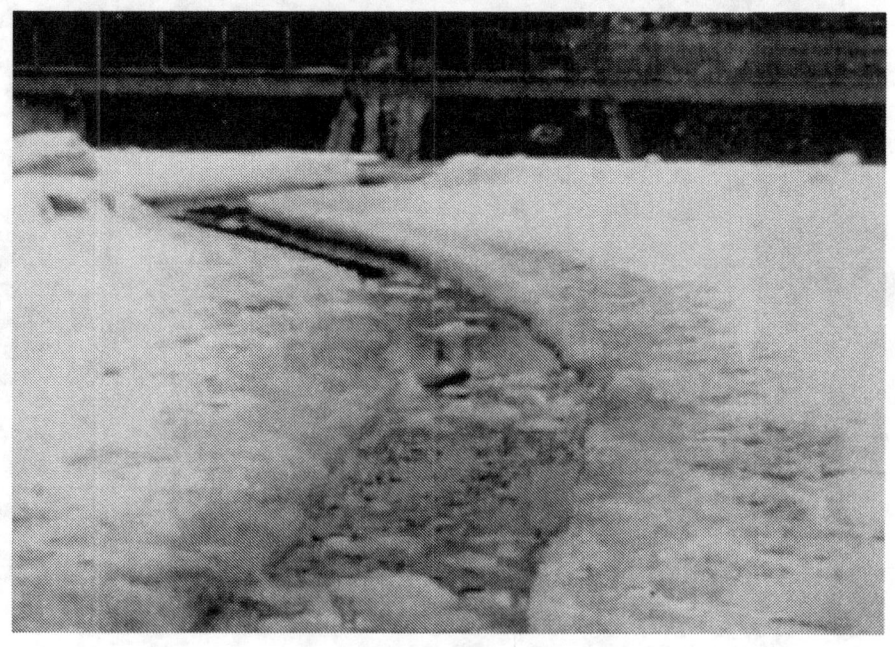

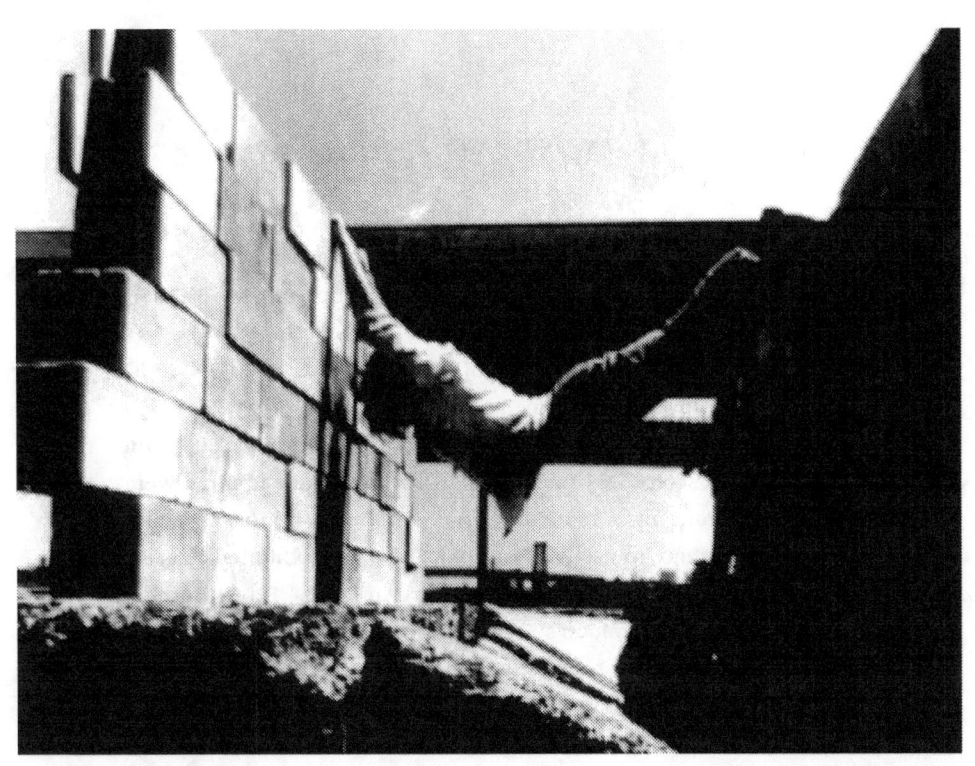

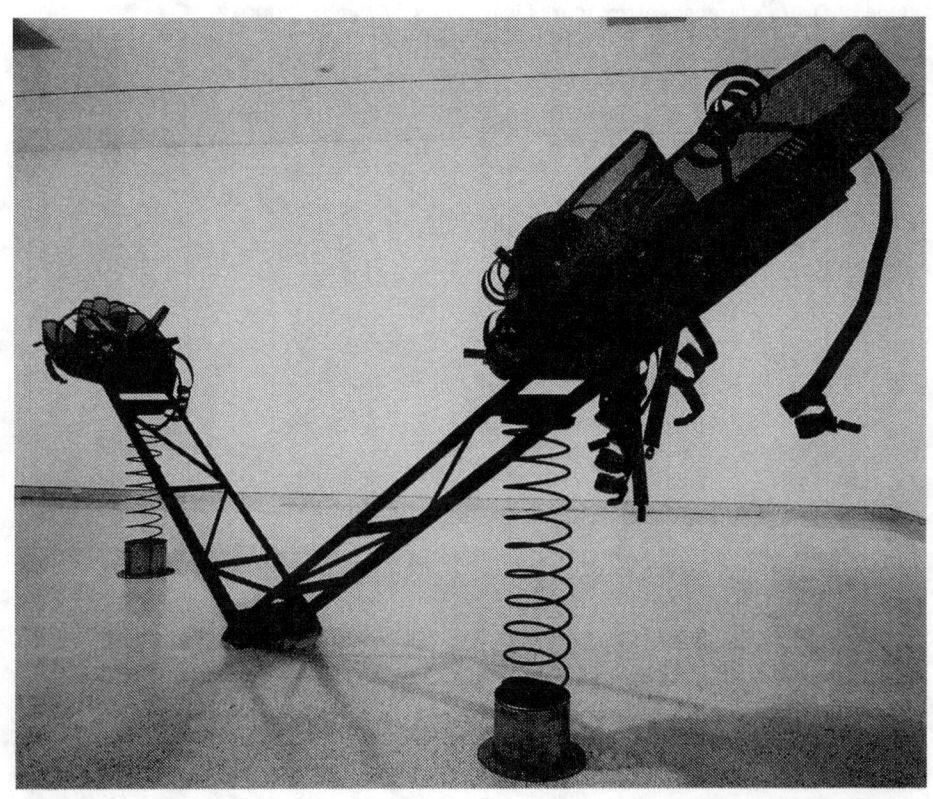

CHRIS DRURY: *STONE WHIRLPOOL*

Chris Drury, one of the key British land artists, was born in 1948 (in Sri Lanka), and educated at Camberwell School of Art in London in the late Sixties. Drury belongs to the generation of Alan Sonfist, Charles Simonds, Michael Heizer, William Furlong, Alice Aycock, Mary Miss, David Nash and Richard Long (all born between 1944 and 1946). Drury had started out in the field of figurative sculpture. Among the artists that Drury admired were Roger Ackling and Constantin Brancusi (Drury said he found Joseph Beuys 'immensely irritating' and 'too self-obsessed').[1] Drury has exhibited in many solo shows, including the Henry Moore Centre in Leeds, Royal Botanic Gardens in Edinburgh, and London's Serpentine Gallery.

One of Chris Drury's most striking sculptures was *Stone Whirlpool* (1996), built from river stones arranged into a spiral in a Japanese river (in Okawa-mura), near a waterfall. It was one of a number of Drury's works which explored vortexes and spirals. An associated work which took on currents of energy was *Edge of Chaos* (2000), a large paper work covered with handwritten texts describing the world's ocean currents and winds. One of Drury's largest vortex works was *Heart of Reeds* (2000).

1. C. Drury, M. Gooding & W. Furlong. *Song of the Earth*, Thames and Hudson, London, 2002, 91.

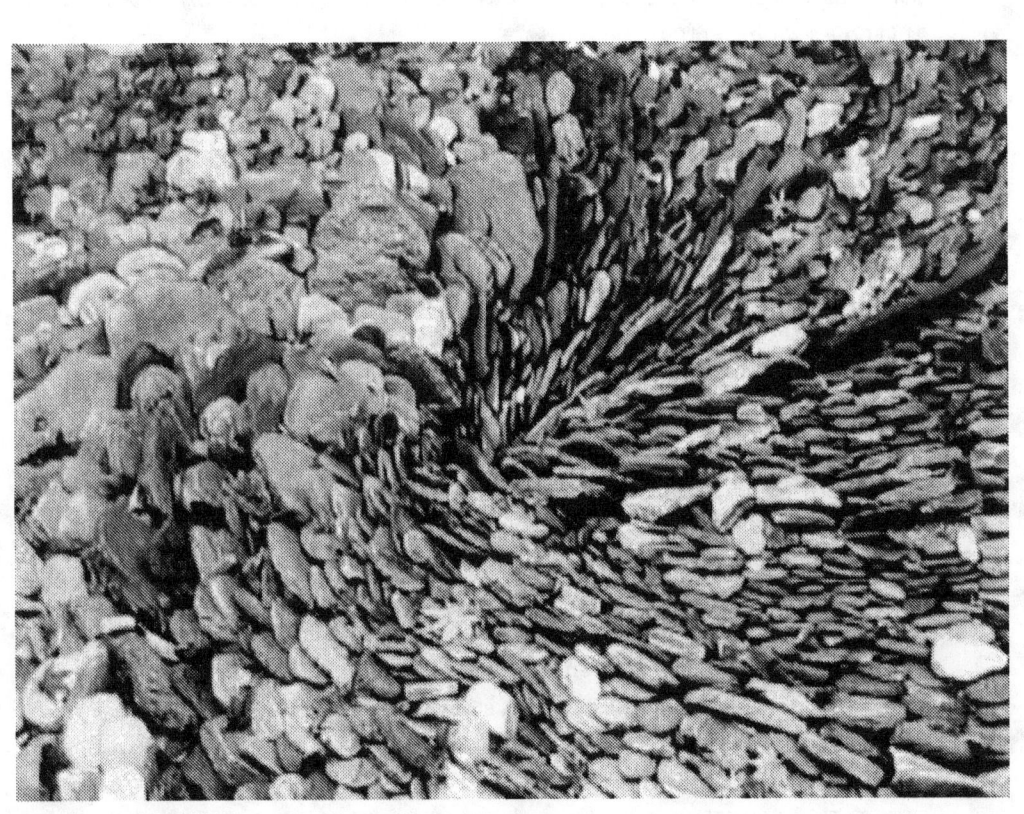

CHRIS DRURY: *CAIRNS*

Chris Drury has treated his cairns in different ways: many of the stone cairns have had fires lit inside them, such as *Midsummer Fire Cairn* (1989), *Falling Water Fire Cairn* (1997, Norway), *Fire Cairn* (1993, Ireland), *Fire Mountain Cairn* (1996, Japan), and *Fire Cairn* (1989, Colorado). Some cairns have been enclosed with basket weaving (such as *Basket Cairn*, 1991) and *Covered Cairn* (1993, Denmark).

Like Long's stone rows or Goldsworthy's cairns, Drury's stone cairns are usually erected in wilderness or spectacular scenery: Norway (1988), New Mexico (1993), De Lank River, Cornwall (1990), Lappland (1988), Webster Ross, Scotland (1992), Kintail, Scotland (1994), Ladakh (1997) and Colorado (1989). For Drury, the cairns are about commemorating a particular moment in a special place: 'they're just saying, 'this is an extraordinary place. Grab a few rocks, put them up before the moment's gone and photograph it" (2002, 79). If the shelters were the stopping-places on a journey, the cairns were the 'markers of highpoints/ moments of exhilaration along the way' (1998, 58).

Another favourite Drury motif is the shelter: low, squat structures, sometimes like teepees or witches' hats, some like prehistoric beehive huts. The shelters were often made from stone (but also in chalk, turf, ice, wood, plants and coal. Some of these materials, such as turf, coal and chalk, are unexpected, and give Drury's shelters a very particular quality). The shelters are usually (but not always) constructed at human scale. That is, in the correct scale for someone to enter them bodily. *Beara Shelter* (1995), in West Cork, Ireland, was a squat, square, stone structure, with views of the sea and Bulls Rock. 'The intention was to provide a space for being and contemplation' (1998, 20). Some of the shelters, such as *Shelter For the Winds That Blow From Siberia*, made near Drury's home in Lewes in 1986, have a distinctly Goldsworthyan flavour: blocks of ice mounted on a hazel frame, looking like an igloo. *Shelter For the Northern Glaciers* (1988) was constructed in the spectacular coastal setting of Seiland island, in Norway, surrounded by snow-capped mountains. Geoffrey Harris has also constructed wooden shelters in forests (*Hollow Spruce*, 1988).

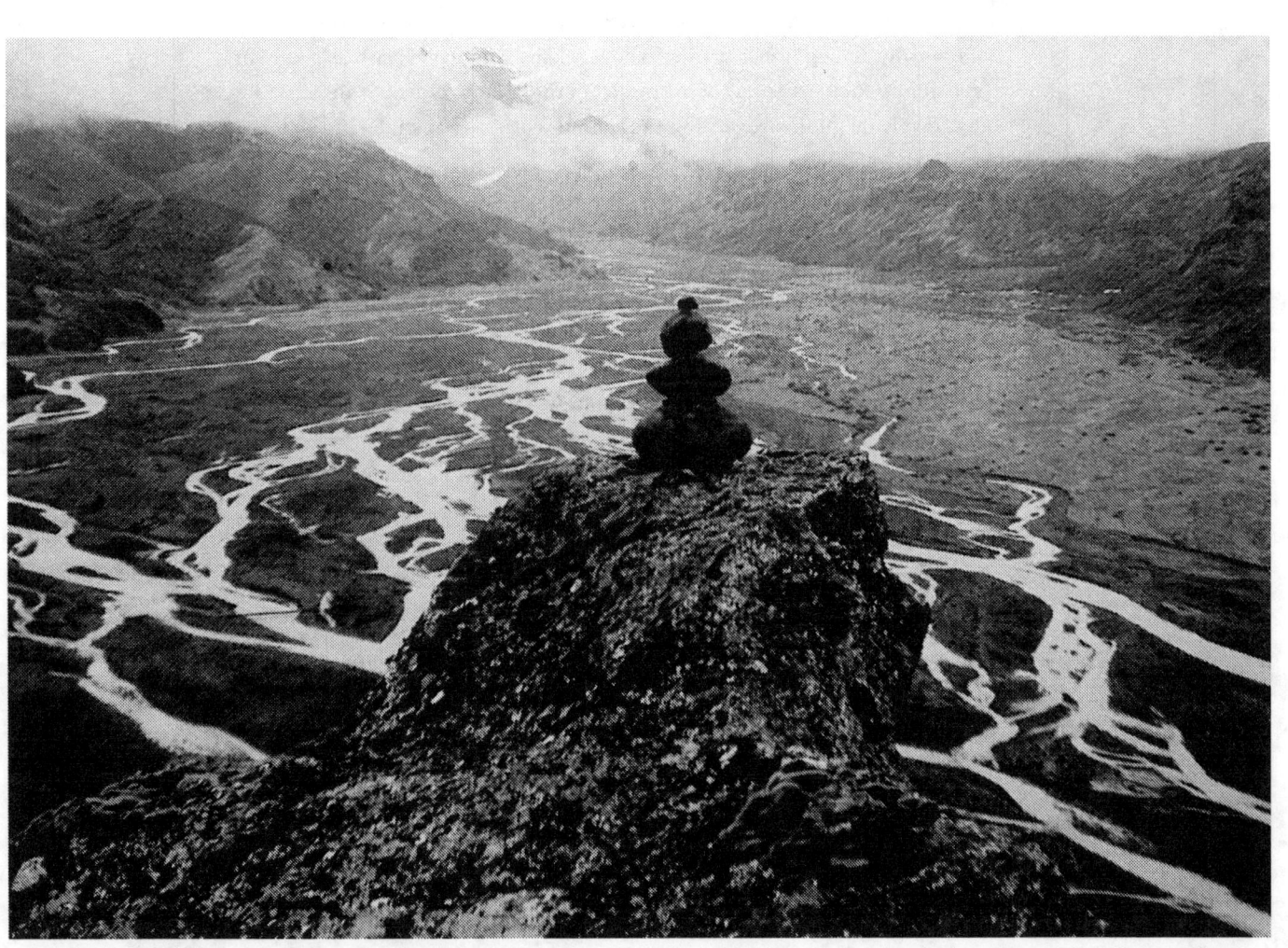

DAVID NASH: *SLATE STOVE*

One of the most intriguing and sensual of land artists is David Nash (born in the same year as Richard Long, 1945), with whom Andy Goldsworthy worked. Nash's æsthetics chime with those of Richard Long and Andy Goldsworthy among British artists.[1] Hugh Adams sees David Nash as a kind of 'fixed abode Richard Long', working from one place (North Wales), while Long travels the globe, regarding the whole world as his studio, as material for making art.

David Nash has built a number of 'stoves' and 'hearths', out of natural materials – snow, slate, wood. These structures burn away – fire as 'living' sculpture. *Snow Stove,* made in Japan in 1982, burns beautifully – a snow pyramid, fusing those two eternal mysteries – fire and snow, fire and ice. Nash has also made a *Wood Stove* (1979), a *Slate Stove* (1981) and also a *Sea Hearth.* Anyone who's lit a fire right next to the ocean will know what a magical experience it can be, and Nash's *Sea Hearth* is certainly rich in magic. Nash set his fire built of large stones inches from the waves, to accentuate the contrast between the two elements. Nash's stoves and hearths are rich in alchemical and elemental allusions: they are a poetry of elements, the basic elements out of which everything is made.

1. See A. McPherson, 1978; H. Adams, 1979; D. Nash, 1980.

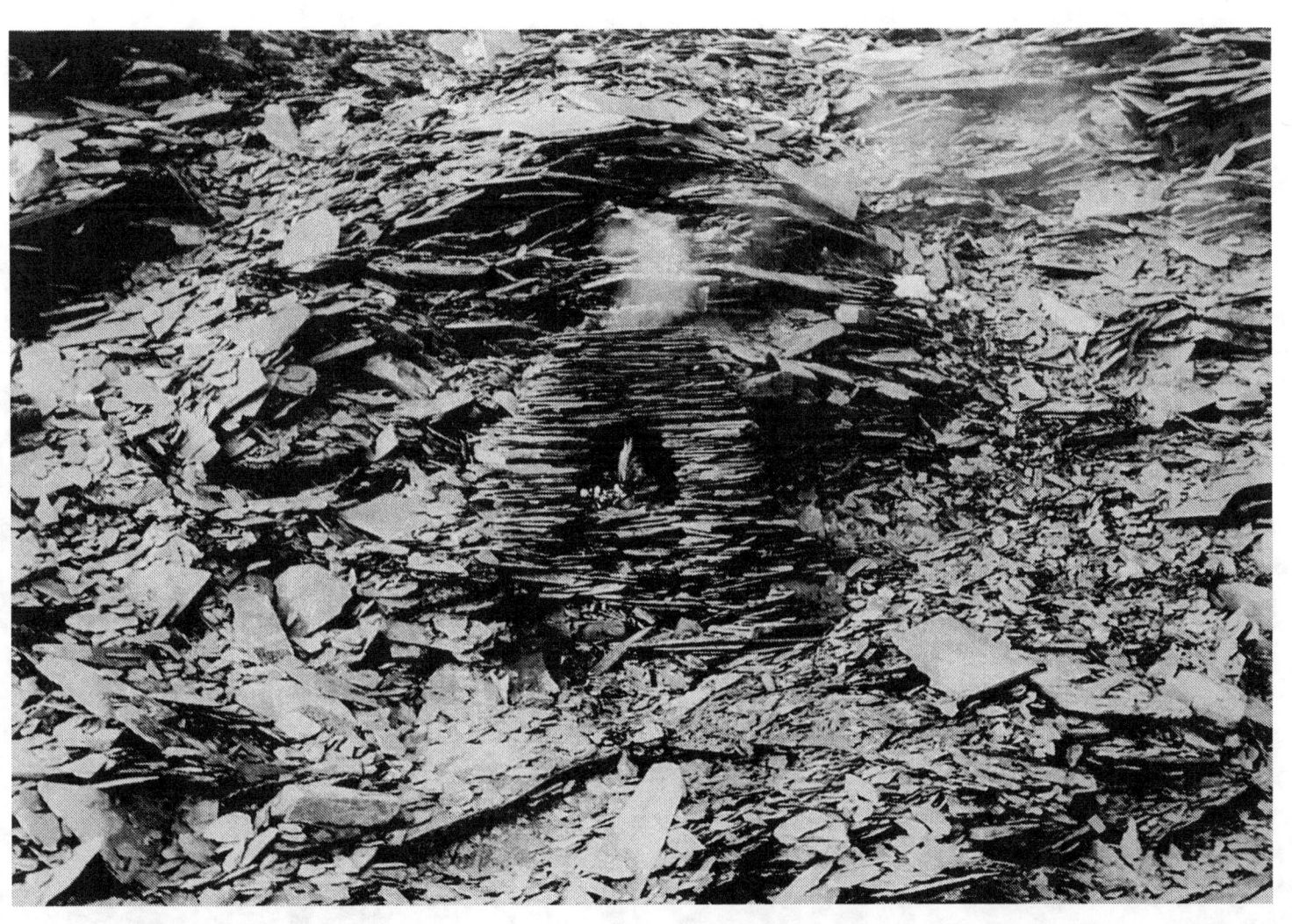

DAVID NASH: *FLETCHED OVER ASH DOME*

David Nash makes fascinating pieces, works which are instantly appealing, partly because of the materials, the natural materials which urban-based cultures are so thirsty for: wood, stone, water, fire. These are the elements not found in cities. Well, one sees trees, stones, skies and wood in cities, but it's not the same: land artists make the spectator aware, again, of nature, of natural materials. How refreshing it is, after being encased in grey concrete and a maze of straight lines in the city to imbibe these works of Long, Nash, Goldsworthy and Pope. What a wonder, really, is David Nash's marvellous *Fletched Over Ash Dome*. This is a circular group of trees in Wales which Nash planted in 1977: it is a 'living' sculpture, which, over thirty years, will be trained into a dome. It will be not only a circle of trees, but a dome of trees. Nash explains:

> A circle of young ash trees fletched and woven into a thirty foot dome fletched three times at ten year intervals then left alone. A silver sculpture in winter, a green canopy space in summer, a volcano of growing energy. (1978)

While Robert Morris uses steam, and Nancy Holt uses stone, Nash's use of living trees (such as in his *Fire Engine Sweep*, planted in 1980) creates a new form of sculpture, a sculpture which is alive, which changes over decades, rather than seconds. Morris's steam works last mere moments, while Nash's fires last a few hours. *Fletched Over Ash Trees*, though, is a sculpture that lasts decades, and changes year in year out. Nash's trees will grow and develop for a long time before they decay, which will make them a particularly exciting type of sculpture.

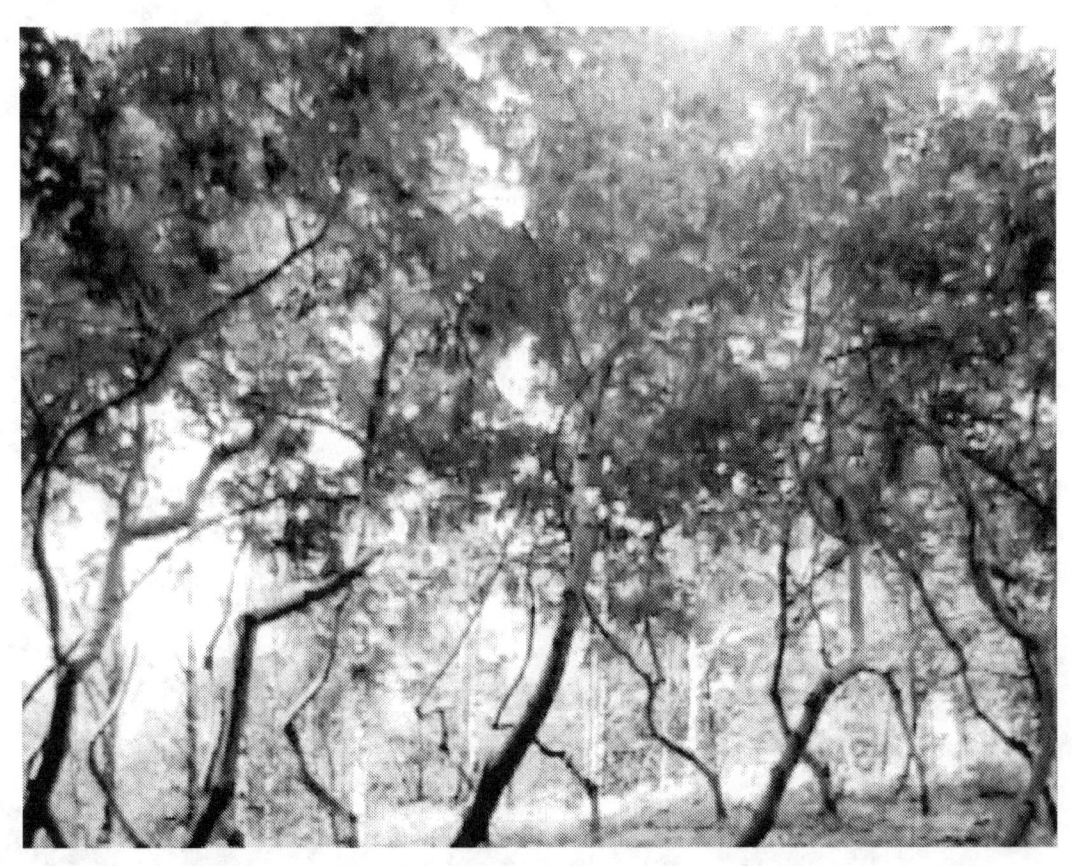

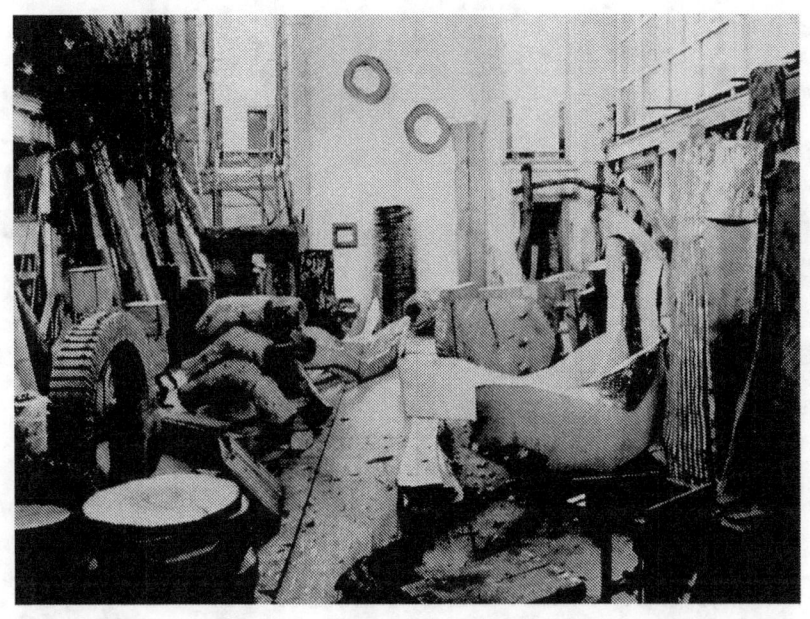

JEAN TINGULEY

The master of kinetic sculpture must be the rebellious Jean Tinguely, whose motorized sculptures mischievously create chaos. Tinguely's sculptures don't just move – in all directions – they are very noisy, with clatterings, bangs, pants, grinds and wheezes. The most famous, *Hommage à New York* of 1960, was a sculpture 'created for self-destruction'. The sculpture was intended to perform many bizarre actions. Daniel Wheeler describes Tinguely's monster machine:

> Few of these particular 'events' ever took place, owing to immediate and chronic breakdown, which almost invariably happened in Tinguely's Metamatic performances, but all kinds of other wonders did come to pass, which, being, unexpected, struck Tinguely as far superior to anything he had programed. (1991, 239-240)

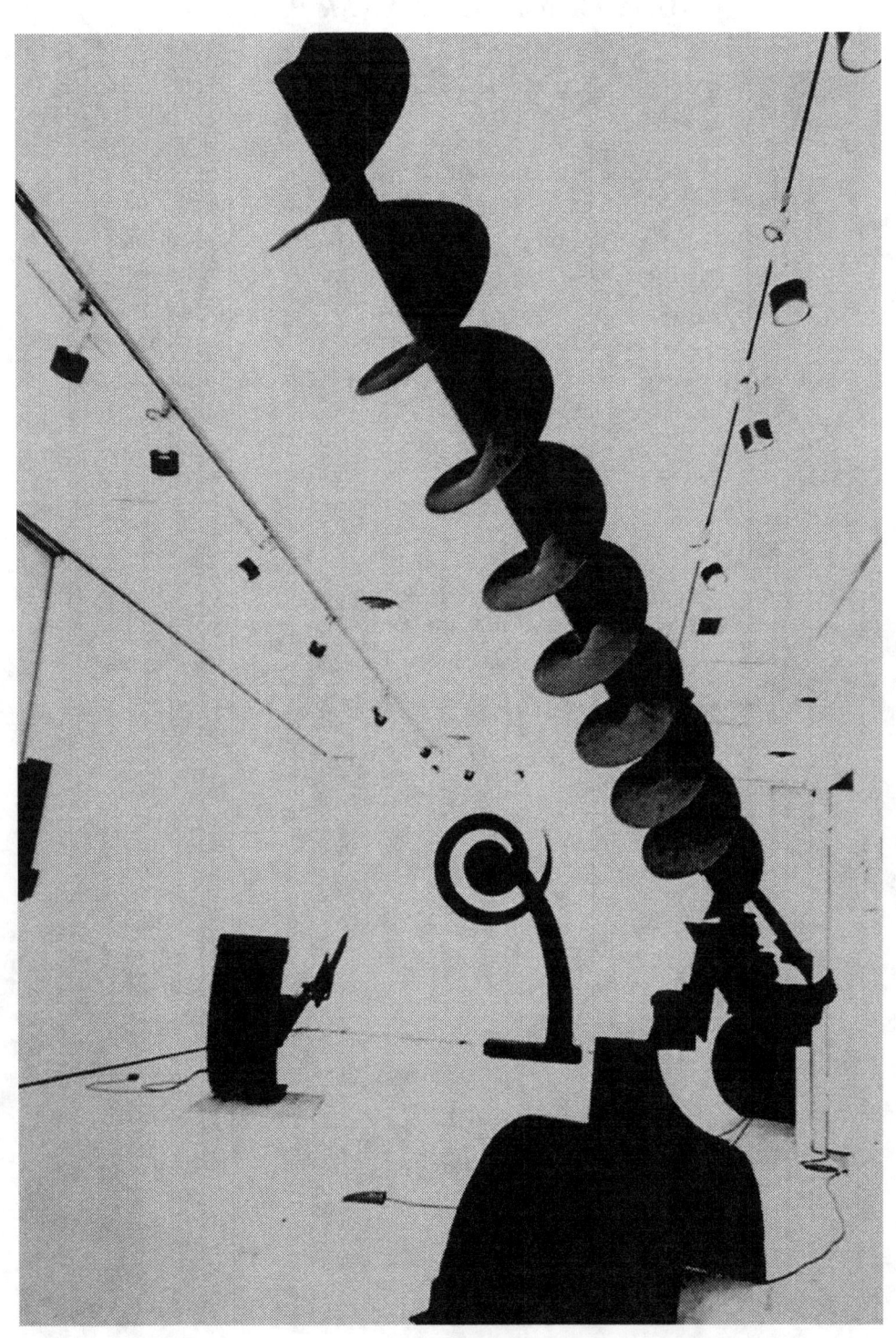

JUDY CHICAGO: *DINNER PARTY*

So much art has to be censored, edited, screened, so that nothing offends anybody. The list of television shows that have not been broadcast because of their political or sexual content is enormous. Huge numbers of TV programmes and documentaries have simply been ditched, often banned by governments.[1] The feminist Judy Chicago's *The Dinner Party* was reviled by critics because it focused on the vulva, what the art critic Robert Hughes called 'Chicago's relentless concentration on the pudenda'.[2] It's OK for male artists to paint the female genitals over and over (Picasso, for instance, or Hans Bellmer, or Egon Schiele), but not for female artists. For Hilton Kramer, *The Dinner Party* was 'vulgar',[3] while Robert K. Dornan called it 'ceramic 3-D pornography'.[4]

1. See J. Pilger: "Silence of the Lambs", *The New Statesman and Society*, August 20, 1993, 14.
2. R. Hughes: "An Obsessive Feminist Pantheon", *Time*, December 15, 1980, 85-86.
3. H. Kramer: "Art: Judy Chicago's *Dinner Party*, Comes to Brooklyn Museum", *New York Times,* October 17, 1980. And see C. Rickey: "Judy Chicago, *The Dinner Party*, The Brooklyn Museum", *Artforum*, January, 1981.
4. *Congressional Record*, 101st Session, volume 136, no.98, July 26, 1990.

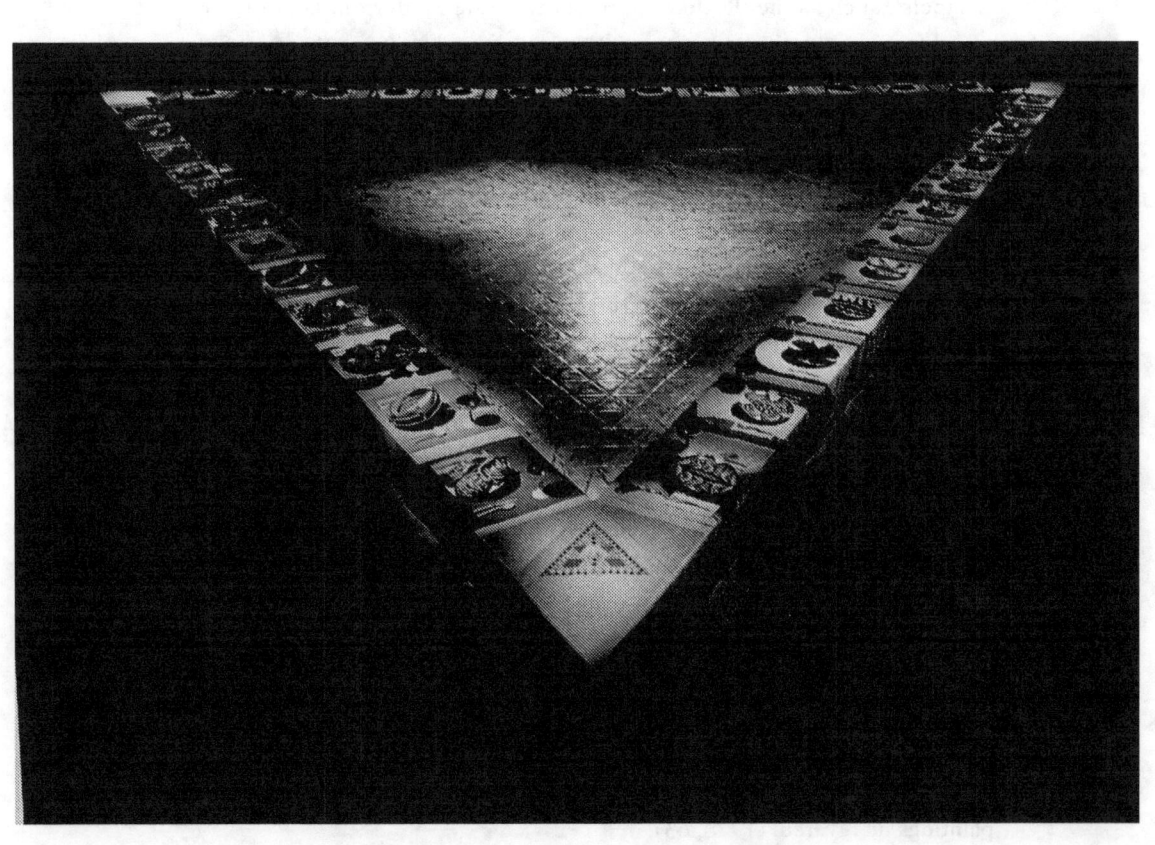

MARK ROTHKO: *HOUSTON CHAPEL MURALS*

It was inevitable that Mark Rothko should produce paintings to decorate a chapel. Indeed, the Rothko's paintings have become the focal point of the Rothko Chapel in Houston, Texas. This Chapel, and other Rothko 'chapels', such as the 'Rothko Room' at the Tate Modern in London, are seen by some as Rothko's greatest achievements.[1] The effects that Rothko's paintings seem to aim for – quietness, authority, humility, tragedy, spirituality – are also the qualities treasured in religion, and in particular in Judæo-Christianity. These are the emotional qualities one associates with being in a church or monastery: spacious interiors, lit with a soft, diffuse light, smooth stone floors, whitewashed walls, a dim sense of the outside world, a feeling of sanctity. These are the spaces – in the cathedral, the chapel, the monk's cell – that are intended to induce contemplation, interiority, self-enclosure, holiness. For Robert Rosenblum, the Rothko Chapel 'summed up countless Romantic problems and ambitions, all responses to the crisis of faith in organized religion that launched the 19th century' (1988, 118).

In taking on the commissions, Rothko approached them in the thoughtful, considerate manner of the Renaissance painter. He knew well and loved the Early Renaissance artists, in particular Fra Angelico. It is no accident that Rothko's Chapel and the mural series recall the chapels and monasteries decorated by painters such as Giotto, Masaccio, Duccio, Cimbaue and Angelico. With the Houston commission, Rothko stated his intention was to 'make East and West merge in an octagonal chapel'.[2] 'In these transcendental works,' Diane Waldman wrote of the mature works, 'Rothko creates the contemporary equivalent of the great Renaissance paintings he revered' (1978, 63).

Mark Rothko began work on the Houston Chapel murals in Winter, 1964-65. They were completed by the end of 1967, though Rothko continued to alter them slightly. The octagonal plan of the chapel was designed by Philip Johnson, the building work being supervised by Howard Barnstone and Eugene Aubrey. The Houston commission came from John and Dominique de Menil. The chapel was going to be Roman Catholic, part of the University of St Thomas, but it was ultimately an interdenominational chapel affiliated to the Rice University's Institute of Religion and Human Development.

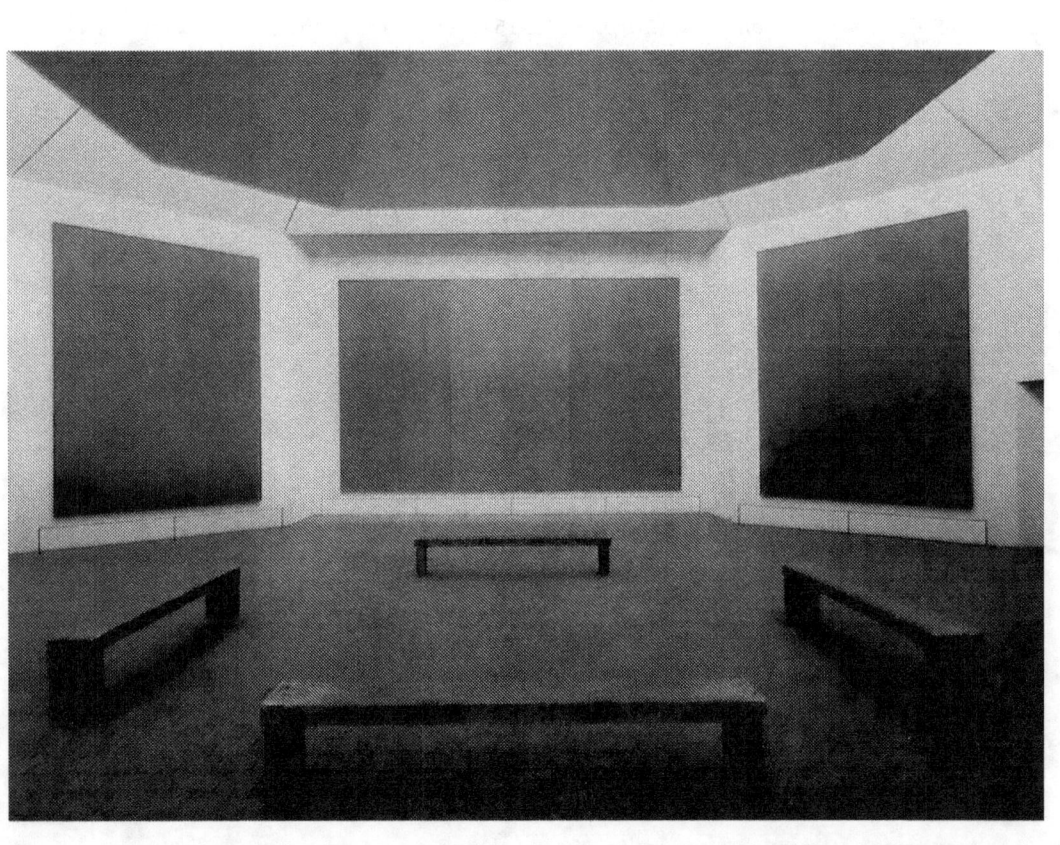

The Houston Chapel murals are the tightest and most carefully controlled of the murals series. The colours are extremely close. One of the triptychs, with its dark monochrome panels, shows the influence of the Colourfield and the Post-Painterly Abstractionists, as well as Motherwell and Newman. Another element of the Houston murals is intriguing: the triptych between the two doors has the central panel raised, which makes the triptych appear even more like a Renaissance altarpiece, in which the central panel is typically larger than the wings, which would fold over (as in Matthias Grünewald's *Isenheim Altarpiece* [*c*. 1510-15, Colmar] and Robert Campin's *Mérode Altarpiece* [*c*. 1425-30, Metropolitan Museum]). Rothko meticulously controlled the amount of light the murals emitted, and the amount of light they would absorb.

It is easy to understand how viewers speak of the 'subliminal' or 'transcendent' qualities of the Houston Chapel murals. There seems to be hardly anything in them, to grasp onto. At least in Monet's *Waterlilies* the viewer can always return to natural forms, to the painted shapes of the lilies and the reflections on the water. In Monet, one can find the way back to nature and the world. Rothko's Houston Chapel paintings invite a different sort of participation. His murals invite the viewer to lose themselves in the paintings, thereby losing themselves to themselves, in themselves. That is, the paintings are not the final stage in the participants' (religious) project. They can't be. Art in churches, religious art in general, is not the endpoint. One must not get stuck on the art object, but on what the art object is trying to evoke, or point towards. In the case of Rothko's murals, which is church art like Renaissance altarpieces were church art, the viewer is invited to go beyond the paintings and ponder on holiness within and without the self (in a similar way, Rothko encouraged spectators not to get stuck on contemplating the colours in his works).

One of the key reference points for the Rothko chapels is Fra Angelico's beautiful series of frescoes at San Marco monastery in Florence.3 Rothko was aware of creating a series of paintings which would have a common theme, as with Angelico's frescoes. Created in a profoundly secular world, where the sense of the holy is lost amidst the conspicuous consumption of late capitalism, Rothko's Houston paintings are a version of the Passion. San Marco is the primary place for an Angelico pilgrimage. For Leonardo da Vinci fans, the Louvre is high up on the lists of targets; for Van Gogh lovers, there is Amsterdam and Arles; for Turner followers, the Clore Gallery in London, for Gustave Moreau *aficionados*, the Moreau Museum in Paris, and for Rothko fans, Houston Chapel, the Rothko Room in the Tate Modern, as well as major museums such as the Museum of Modern Art,

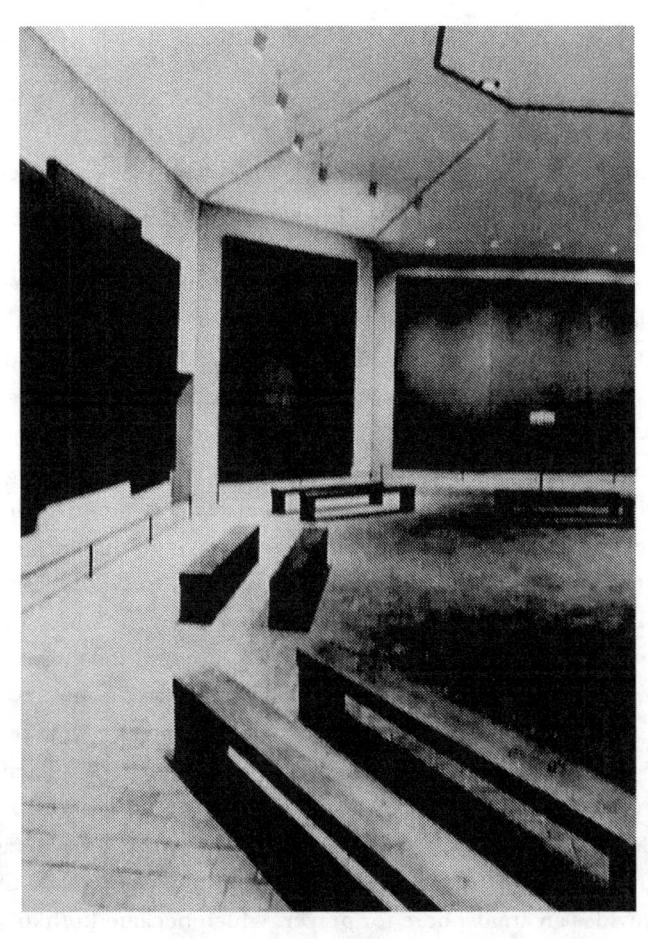

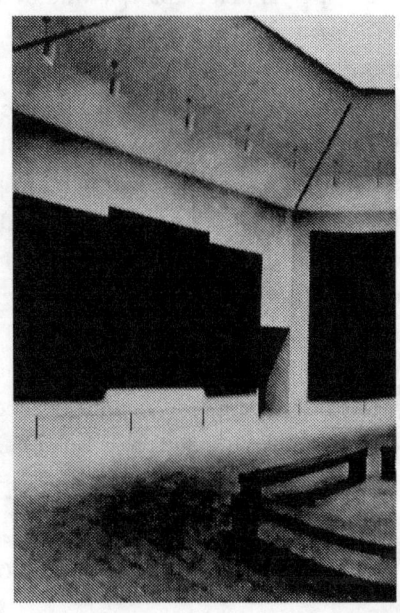

New York, are important centres. To find such a concentration of one artist's works in one place is rare. There is the Gustav Moreau Museum and Rodin Museum in Paris, for instance, which are wonderful.

To make sure viewers, positioned psychologically by the church context as pilgrims or initiates, would not get stuck on the paintings themselves, Rothko made them his most abstract and reduced images. There are no easy to identify architectural forms, as in the Harvard murals, or even vaguely discernible gateways, as in the Seagram murals. Instead, the Houston murals consist of coloured panels, of dark red and red-black. The Houston paintings consist of three triptychs and single panels. The use of the triptychs adds to the religious allusion, as does Rothko's idea of putting fourteen numbers on the building outside, to correlate to the Stations of the Cross and the paintings inside. Black predominates in two of the triptychs, with a layer of plum over the top. Emptied of recognizable imagery, the Houston murals become an ambience or context in which the visitor can meditate, pray, dream, whatever. It is the *context* of the chapel that is important, just as much if not more than the 'content' of the paintings themselves. Religious art works very much in terms of context, on the building and its significance. Wandering into S. Agostino church in the back streets of Rome one can just about perceive the dark forms of a Caravaggio painting in the dim candleshine. The context of being in the shadowy, incense-rich interior of the church does much of the work in encouraging a religious response to the artwork. Similarly with Rothko's Houston Chapel, which provides an atmosphere for prayer, which became Rothko's goal. Rather than physical colour, wrote Diane Waldman, the Houston murals exist as 'tranquil, tragic, twilit dreams of color' (1978, 68). Peter Selz spoke of Rothko's paintings as 'special place apart, a kind of sanctuary, where they perform what is essentially a sacramental function'.[4]

Rothko's Houston murals evoke certain proportions and rhythms, an atmosphere of ambiguous colour, which eschews theological dogma. Rothko is not making a particular ecumenical/ theological point with these murals. Instead, he evokes, in non-representational but powerful ways, a religious atmosphere, which one can associate with Byzantine icons, incense-filled Greek Orthodox churches, the Catholic fervour of churches in Brazil or Spain, or the synagogues of Rothko's motherland, Russia. Or going back further, in certain cloudy illumination on dull days, the Rothko Rooms may evoke those palæolithic caves and underground vaults which pre-date Christianity, Hebraic religion, and ancient Greece. The intangible, abstract spaces of Rothko's Houston murals have an aura about them (in

them) of primal religion, the animism which predates organized or mono-
theic religion (animism is the origin of all religion).[5] This interpretation is
possible because Rothko leaves the paintings open: one can read anything
one likes into them. They are mirrors, just like the face of God is a mirror.
'Every face that looks into God's sees nothing but its own truth' wrote
Weston La Barre (7).

1 There has been much critical attention focussed on the Houston Chapel. For example, J.-P.
Marandel, "Une chapelle oecuménique au Texas", *L'Oeil*, 197, May, 1971; D. Menil, "The
Rothko Chapel", *Art Journal*, 30, 3, Spring, 1971; D. Ashton, "The Rothko Chapel in Houston",
Studio, 181, 934, June, 1971; B. O'Doherty, "The Rothko Chapel", *Art in America*, 61, 1, Jan,
1973; A. Holmes, "The Rothko Chapel Six Years Later", *Art News*, 73, 10, Dec, 1976; C.R.
Cernuschi, "Mark Rothko's mature paintings", *Arts Magazine*, May, 1986; Rothko, 1978; R.
Hughes' *Shock of the New*, BBC, London, 1981; S. Barnes, "The Making of the Chapel: *Broken
Obelisk*", in *The Rothko Chapel*, 1989.

2. D. Ashton, 1983, 169.

3. On Fra Angelico and San Marco, see: W. Hood, "Fra Angelico at San Marco: Art and the
Liturgy of Cloistered Life", in T. Verdon & J. Henderson, eds., *Christianity and the
Renaissance*, Syracuse University Press, Syracuse, 1990, 108-131; "St Dominic's Manners of
Praying: Gestures in Fra Angelico's Frescoes at S. Marco", *Art Bulletin*, LXVIII, 1986, 195-206;
L. Berti *et al*, *Angelico at San Marco*, Sansoni, Florence, 1965; P. Cardile, "Fra Angelico's Shop
at San Domenico in Fiesole", Ph. D thesis, Yale University 1974; A. Francini Ciaranfi, *Beato
Angelico: Gli affreschi di San Marco*, Amilcare Pizzi S. p. A, Milan 1940; S. Madigan, "A New
Interpretation of the Iconography of Fra Angelico: Rosarian Organization in the Frescoed Cells
of San Marco", MACAA paper, Hamlite University, St Paul, 1977; P. Sheaffer, "White Light and
Meditation at San Marco", *Memorte Domenicane*, XIV, 1983, 329-334.

4. In H. Rosenberg, 1972.

5. W. La Barre, 1972.

MARK ROTHKO: *THE HARVARD MURALS*

The accounts of Mark Rothko's creation of the Harvard mural series record how much time he spent just sitting in front of his paintings and musing. Often he would sit and contemplate the stretchers, even before the canvas had been stretched on them. There are published photographs of Rothko, often with his back to the camera, sitting down, quietly smoking, looking at his paintings leaning against the walls of his studio. Observers of Leonardo da Vinci at work in Milan described how the Italian Renaissance master would sit and stare at his *Last Supper* for hours on end, sometimes leaving it for a few days, then returning to dab at it for a moment, then leaving again. In the traditional manner, Rothko used rabbit skin glue to size the canvas, mixing in dry pigment, with oil and turpentine. The grounds were mixed with alizarin crimson and black. Then Rothko began to arrange the doorway shapes. At times, he would alter the composition by a quarter of an inch: this shows how crucial the placement of the forms were, for a quarter of an inch on a fifteen foot canvas is a tiny proportion. The proportions had to be exactly right: the murals are a complex interrelation of sizes, edges and interior forms. According to Robert Motherwell, Rothko was very secretive about his working methods. Apparently, he used to work from dawn (5 am) until 10 am (this was partly because he found it difficult to sleep). Rothko put a parachute over the skylight of his studio – an effect which was reproduced in subsequent Rothko 'chapels', such as at the Tate Modern in London (but he also admitted to using high intensity lights which were arranged like stage lights in a theatre).[1] The bright lighting was probably necessary to create the subtle differences in tone and hue of Rothko's canvases, which would then be viewed by the public in dim conditions.

The Harvard murals are easily the most 'expressive', gesturally, of the three mural series (the Harvard, Seagram/ Tate and Houston Chapel murals). The 1961 commission for the Harvard murals came from Professor Wassily Loentief, Chairman of the Society of Fellows and Henry Lee Professor of Economics at Harvard University and John Coolidge, Director of the Fogg Art Museum in Cambridge, Massachussetts. They were due to be put in the Holyoke Center penthouse, which was designed by José Luis Sert. The murals were eventually sited in the faculty dining room, after being shown at the Guggenheim in 1963. There are five panels, three of which Rothko hung as a triptych for the exhibition.

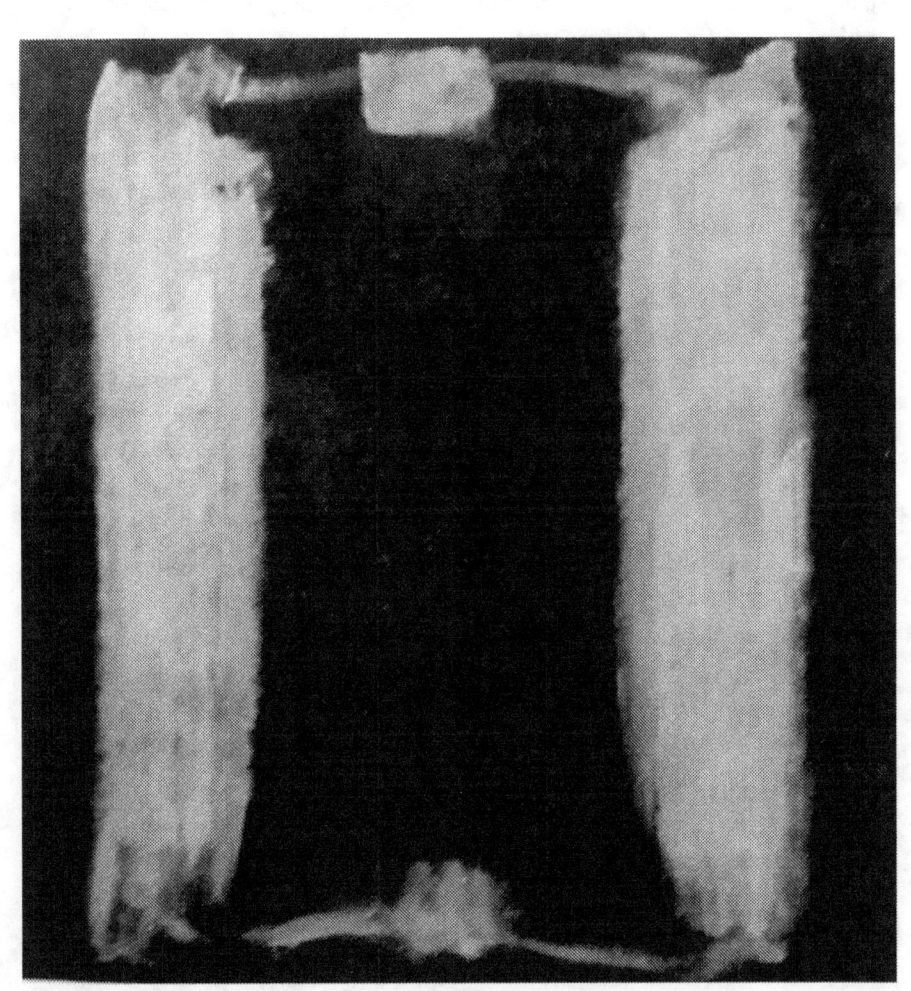

The Harvard murals (1962) are large, as in the grand Abstract Express-ionist tradition (104.8 inches inches high by widths such as 96, 180.5 and 117 inches). The post-and-lintel forms are much clearer than in the Seagram paintings: these paintings more directly recall, in their inner architectural forms, the blank windows of Michelangelo's Medici Library in Florence. The prominent pillar-forms recall doorways or windows. The colour and tonal values of the Harvard murals are the widest of the three mural series. They are the loosest and most 'open' of the murals, made with vigorous brushstrokes. The basic colour of the Harvard murals is a mix of crimson, black and maroon.

Some critics have seen the murals as the apotheosis of Rothko's art; for others, they are a failure. When Rothko dropped his luminous colour and concentrated on the two colours, black and red, some critics felt he had jettisoned what made his art so effective. Instead of an intensification, there is a lessening of power. There are no colours against which the black-reds can work, and harmonize. The lack of secondary colours means the main colours have to do all the work themselves. Without the dark blue or purple or orange backgrounds, the 'things' of the murals have nowhere else to go but to refer to themselves. The negation/ deletion/ reduction of colour is also a limitation of the artist's tools of expression. In limiting his colours the artist may be plunging himself into a self-negation. For some critics, the dark reds 'do not permit very much resonance at all' (M. Kozloff, 1961). In 1964, David Hockney said that 'Rothko's a painter whose subject matter is very small – tiny – and he obviously thinks he can do everything he wants within his range and I suppose it's O.K. But I, for one, couldn't work with a range that tiny'.[2] The technical reductionism may force Rothko into a corner out of which he cannot manœuvre himself. Instead of extending colour, there may be a chromatic dead-end: painting as a kind of invisibility. What this results in is the paintings become opaque, do not allow the viewer to enter them and move around. Instead of a welcoming glow they offer a wall of solid, impenetrable oil paint. Emptiness becomes a barrier. This is where Rothko's murals become forbidding and tragic, because they oppress or prevent transcendence. This relates to Rothko's impression of the Michelangelo Laurentian Library in Florence. Michelangelo, Rothko said

makes the viewers feel that they are trapped in a room where all the doors and windows are bricked up, so that all they can do is butt their heads forever against the wall.[3]

Here Rothko's scenario becomes a horror story scene, with the viewers of his murals feeling bricked up with no way out. Of course, Rothko's reading of Michelangelo's architecture says much about his state of mind, but it also adds a flavour of the macabre to his project with his murals. One can interpret Rothko's many commands for the exhibition of his pictures, his demands for lighting and having his large paintings shown in small rooms, as an authoritarian attempt to produce a claustrophobic environment, in which the viewer is not allowed any let-up from being immersed in the paintings. It is as if Rothko wants the viewer to experience something of the same suffering that he himself underwent in making the pictures. It's as if he's saying, 'I've suffered – now it's your turn!' And galleries follow this project with sanctimonious diligence, taking care not to hang Rothko's works too near other artists' works. At times, Rothko's paintings are approached with the servile unctuousness of over-zealous acolytes.

1. R. Motherwell in R. Hobbs, 1978; O'Doherty, 1973.
2. D. Hockney, in *Art & Literature*, 2, Summer, 1964.
3. In Fischer, 16.

BARNETT NEWMAN:
STATIONS OF THE CROSS

Not a few critics have seen correspondences between Mark Rothko's mural rooms and Barnett Newman's *Stations of the Cross* series of paintings: both were New York School abstract meditations on emotions and themes some of which corresponded or alluded to the Christian Passion. Newman's *Stations of the Cross* paintings are different in some key formal respects from Rothko's Houston Chapel and mural series: the reference to the Christian Stations, for example, was only one of many allusions Newman wanted to make (he also used the Old Testament, Greek mythology, the Qabbalah and Jewish religion). Each of Newman's *Stations of the Cross* uses the same format (6.5 by 5 foot canvases, with the bands and 'zips' in the same place, painted mainly in black, with some white paint), while Rothko's are determinedly grave and dark, without any lighter tones, and in a variety of sizes and proportions. Even within his tight set of formal components, Newman works out many variants: in *The First Station*, a black stripe on the left is disturbed by a roughly daubed stripe on the right. The loose brushmarks of the right-hand 'zip' upset the steady equilibrium of the area of black and white paint on the left-hand side of the painting. In subsequent *Stations of the Cross* this right-hand 'zip' settles down somewhat, to become a very narrow black stripe in *The Fifth Station*. At this point, though, the left-hand black stripe, which has been in a state of passivity up 'til now, suddenly deliquesces, its edge becoming fractured. By *The Twelfth* and *Thirteenth Stations*, the black has enveloped most of the canvas, so that, in the penultimate *Station*, the configuration of white and black of the first *Stations of the Cross* has been reversed.

Although Newman employed the potent phrase *lema sabachthani*, the allusions to the Christian Passion are much stronger in Rothko's mural series and 'chapels' than in Newman's *Stations of the Cross*. Both Rothko's and Newman's series of paintings, though, were about the importance of (religious) faith, of the subjectivity and intensity of being a pilgrim, someone on a quest for something transcendent, something beyond, timeless, unknown, eternal. The cry *lema sabachthani* was the 'question that has no answer' said Newman, a cry of despair (and also exaltation) that is uttered outwards, into the darkness (of ignorance, alienation, Godlessness) that surrounds the modern soul.

AD REINHARDT: *ABSTRACT PAINTINGS BLACK*

Ad Reinhardt was an Abstract Expressionist artist who made a lengthy series of five foot square black canvases, featuring dim cruciform shapes, in the 1960s. Reinhardt's project had a mythic, 'religious' flavour; he wrote at length of Zen, Taoism, Buddhism, the dark night of the soul of Christianity, the dark-on-dark of Meister Eckhart, *The Cloud of Unknowing*, St John of the Cross, Mother Night, and so on. Reinhardt's square black paintings can be seen as equivalents for this kind of religious darkness, which was defined by Reinhardt in countless notes and essays in the terms of Buddhism – 'not this, not that'. 'I'm just making the last paintings anyone can make' said Ad Reinhardt.[1] This extract from Reinhardt's unpublished notes is typical, and defines not only his own form of painting, but also that of other 'Northern' painters such as Rothko, Barnett Newman, Christopher Le Brun, Thérèse Oulton, Brice Marden and Anselm Keifer:

> "Northern" preferences for black medium
> "Black," medium of the mind
> Puritan, self-righteous, self-criticism
> Conscience of a bad conscience
> Luminous darkness, true light, evanescence
> "Him that has made the dark his hiding place"
> "Flight of the lone to the alone"
> Perfection, central, cohesive, purifying principle
> Polemic, dogmatic, scriptural (1991, 90)

Reinhardt's writings are sometimes pretentious and portentous, quite different from Barnett Newman's matter-of-fact statements, or Joseph Cornell's wistful, dreamy diaries. Reinhardt, for example, discarded the 'religious' monicker, and disliked the allusions viewers made to Islam, Christianity, Buddhism and Hinduism when discussing his paintings (even though he wrote about religion more than almost any other postwar painter). Reinhardt even stated that 'painting really has no relation to any of the religions nor ever has' (1991, 14). This is an extraordinary statement from a well-read artist, for art since earliest times has been associated deeply with religion, and much of the greatest art made in the last hundred thousand years has been made in the service of religion.

1. A. Reinhardt, interview, *Art International*, Dec, 1966, 18f.

ROBERT IRWIN: *INSTALLATION*

Robert Irwin's installations include: *Fractured Light – Partial Scrim Ceiling – Eye-level Wire* (1971), *Eye-level Room Division* (1973), *Soft Wall* (1973), *Scrim Veil* (1975), *Window Room* (1973), *Black-Line Volume* (1976), *Scrim Veil – Black Rectangle – Natural Light* (1977) and *Untitled (Three Triangul-ated Light Planes)* (1979).

One of Irwin's favourite devices is to re-structure a museum interior with large semi-transparent scrims and veils, so that visitors aren't sure which is the wall, or the ceiling, or the door, or where the light is coming from (Irwin controls lighting carefully as well as spaces). At first it can seem as if the artist hasn't done much to alter the environment; the visitor isn't sure where the existing room ends and Irwin's art begins; only on closer inspection does the extent of Irwin's interventions in the gallery space become apparent.

REBECCA HORN

Rebecca Horn's sculptures are based, like land art, on natural forms, but also on movement, dance, time and environments. Horn's wonderful *Peacock Machine* is an exuberant activator of space, one of those pieces that aims for the essence of a natural form and captures it: a peacock's magnificent tail.[1] In *The Hydra Forest/ Performing: Oscar Wilde*, Horn included electrical sparks flying across a gap in a chandelier comprised of wires.

It was Constantin Brancusi's task to strip away the detritus that had accumulated around sculpture, Henry Moore said, and to give the viewer the pure, simple shape. What Brancusi did was 'to concentrate on very simple shapes, to keep his sculpture, as it were, one-cylindered, to refine and polish a single shape to a degree almost too precious.'[2] This is what many contemporary sculptors have done, keeping their shapes simple and purified: David Nash, Richard Serra, Donald Judd and Robert Smithson.

1. See M. Roustayi, "Getting Under the Skin: Rebecca Horn's Sensibility Machines", *Arts*, May, 1989, 58-68; M. Kimmelman, "A Sculptural Circus of Whips and Suspense", *New York Times*, 23 Sept, 1988, C29.
2. H. Moore, in *The Listener*, 1937, quoted in H. Chipp, 595.

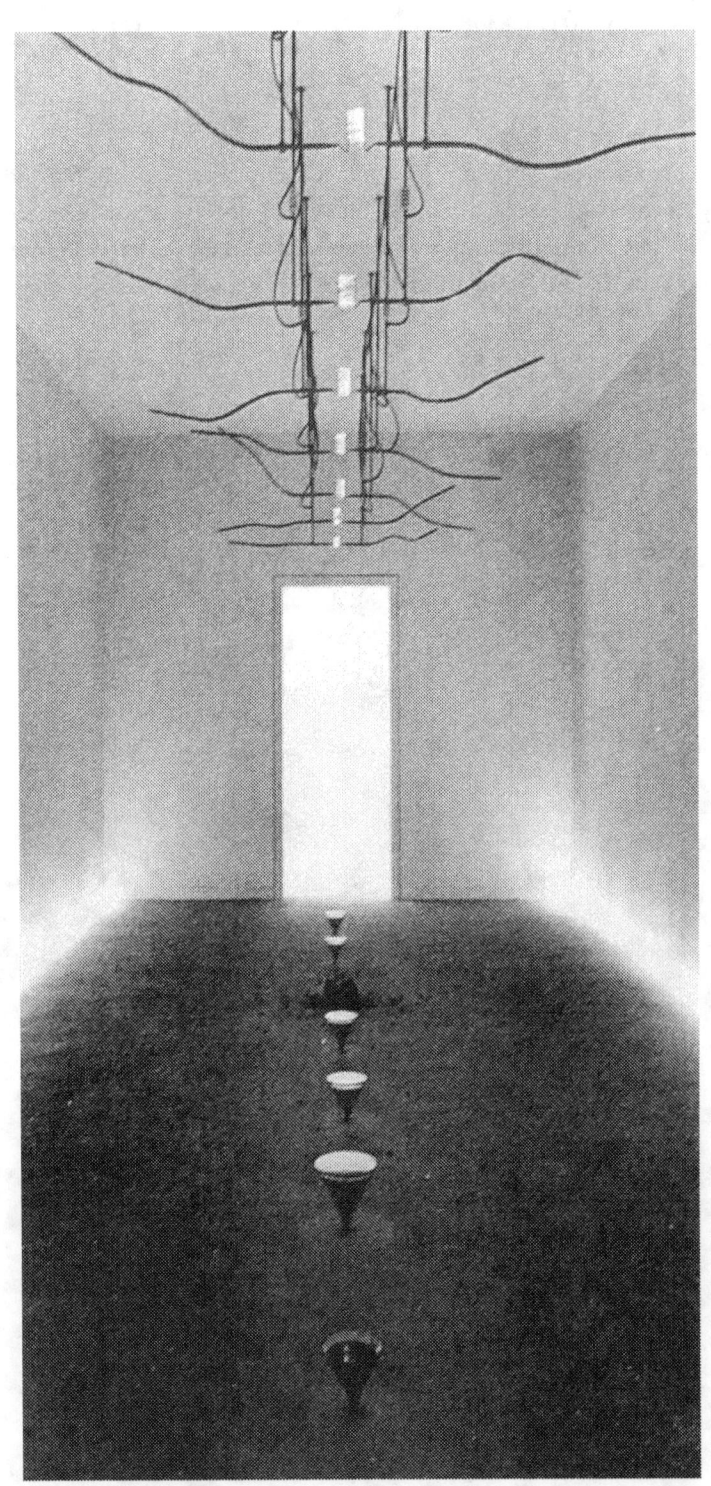

DAVID MACH: *FULLY FURNISHED*

David Mach, a Scottish sculptor of the same generation as Bill Woodrow, Tony Cragg and Barry Flanagan, is known for his ironic commentaries on late capitalist consumerist society, expressed in giant sculptures made from car tyres or, as here, in *Fully Furnished* (1994), from newspapers.

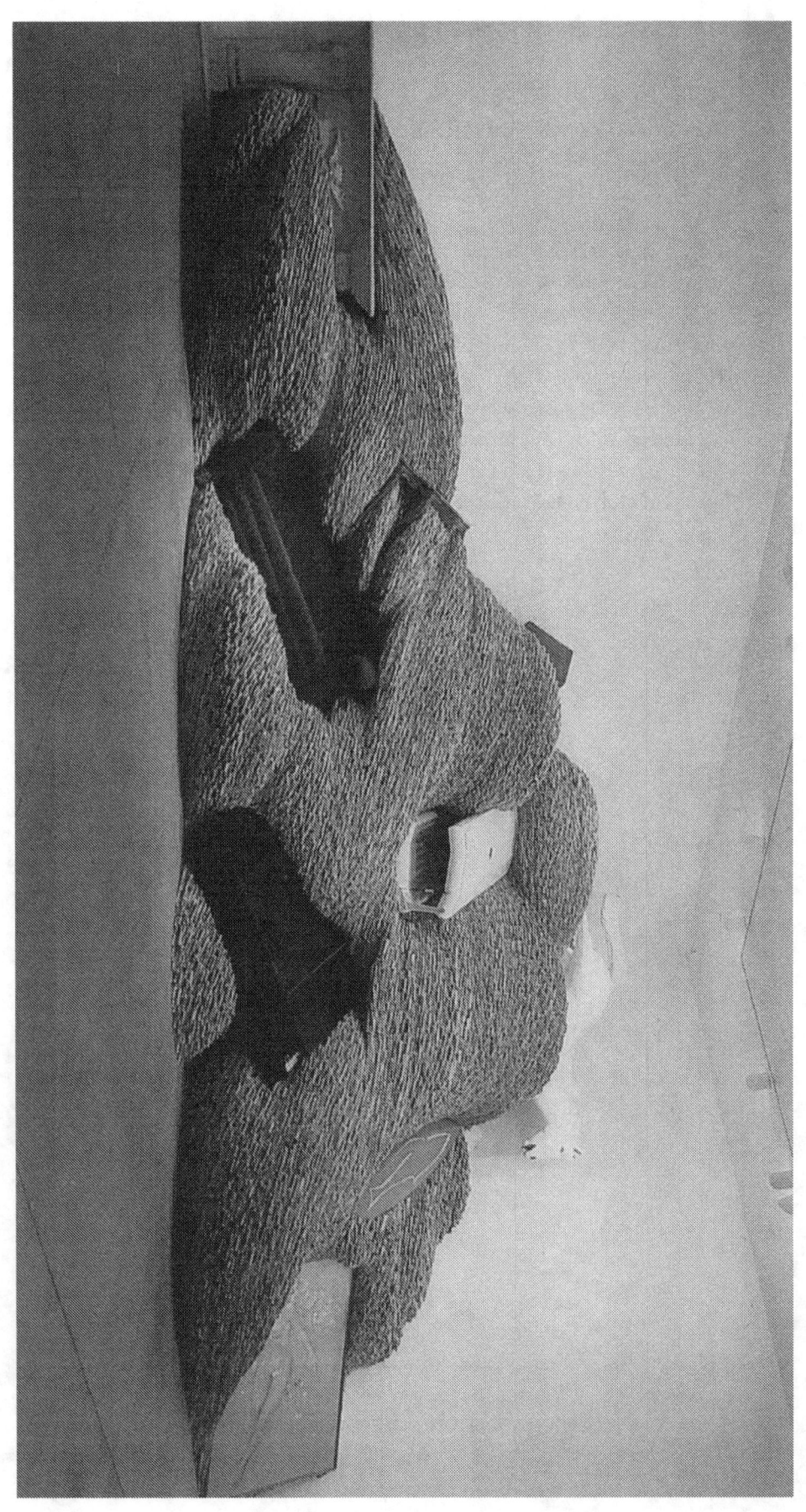

DAMIEN HIRST: *WHEN LOGICS DIE*

Friend of stars (David Bowie, Damon Albarn of Blur, Keith Allen and other Britpop and 'Cool Britannia' wannabes), chief mouthpiece of 'young British artists', the ex-Goldsmiths College and *Sensation* crowd who gained fame in the mid-1990s (Tracey Emin, Sarah Lucas, Gavin Turk, the Chapman brothers), spouter of art bollocks in a Mockney accent, Damien Hirst was renowned for his dead sharks, cows and sheep which he cut up and stuck in glass boxes filled with formaldehyde, apparently outraging Middle England. *When Logics Die* (1991) is a typical Hirst installation, comprising photographs of dead bodies, medical implements and supplies, and a table.

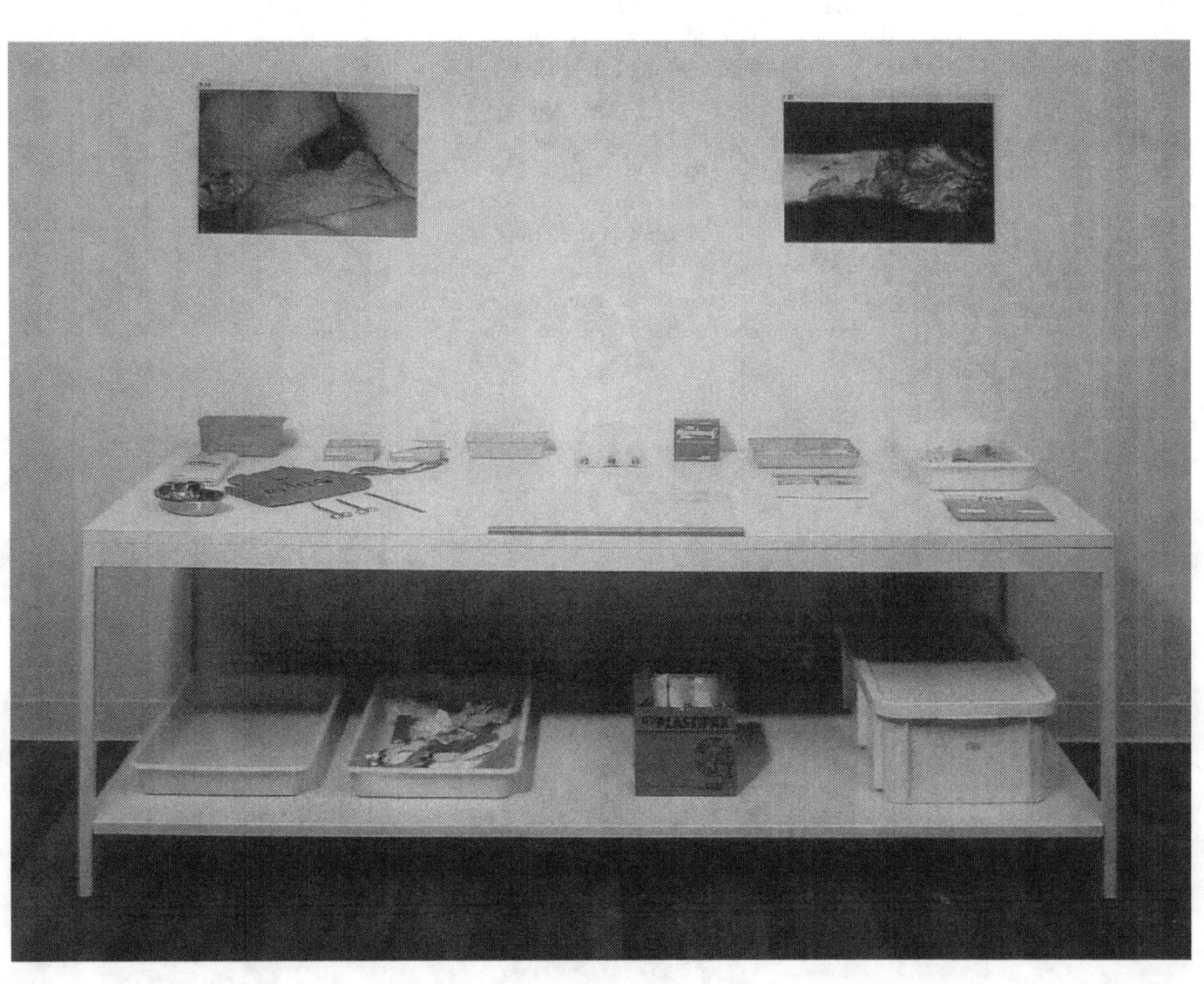

ANTHONY GORMLEY: *FIELD*

Anthony Gormley (b. 1950) covered the entire area of a gallery floor in his *Field* installation (1991) with over 35,00 small humanoid figures made from clay, which appear to be staring at the viewer. For the British public, Gormley attained notoriety (and fame) in the late 1990s for his giant *Angel of the North* sculpture, near a motorway in t' North of England.

Gormley also made more 'conventional' sculptures, such as his emulations of a large granite glacial boulder in 1981. Each of Gormley's *Two Stones* is nine feet high, one made of granite, the other of bronze. Set beside an artificial lake in Kent, the 'natural' granite stone is already contextualized as a work of art by its placement in such a setting, just as Carl Andre's boulders on the city street are made into art by their context (ditto with Andre's infamous bricks).

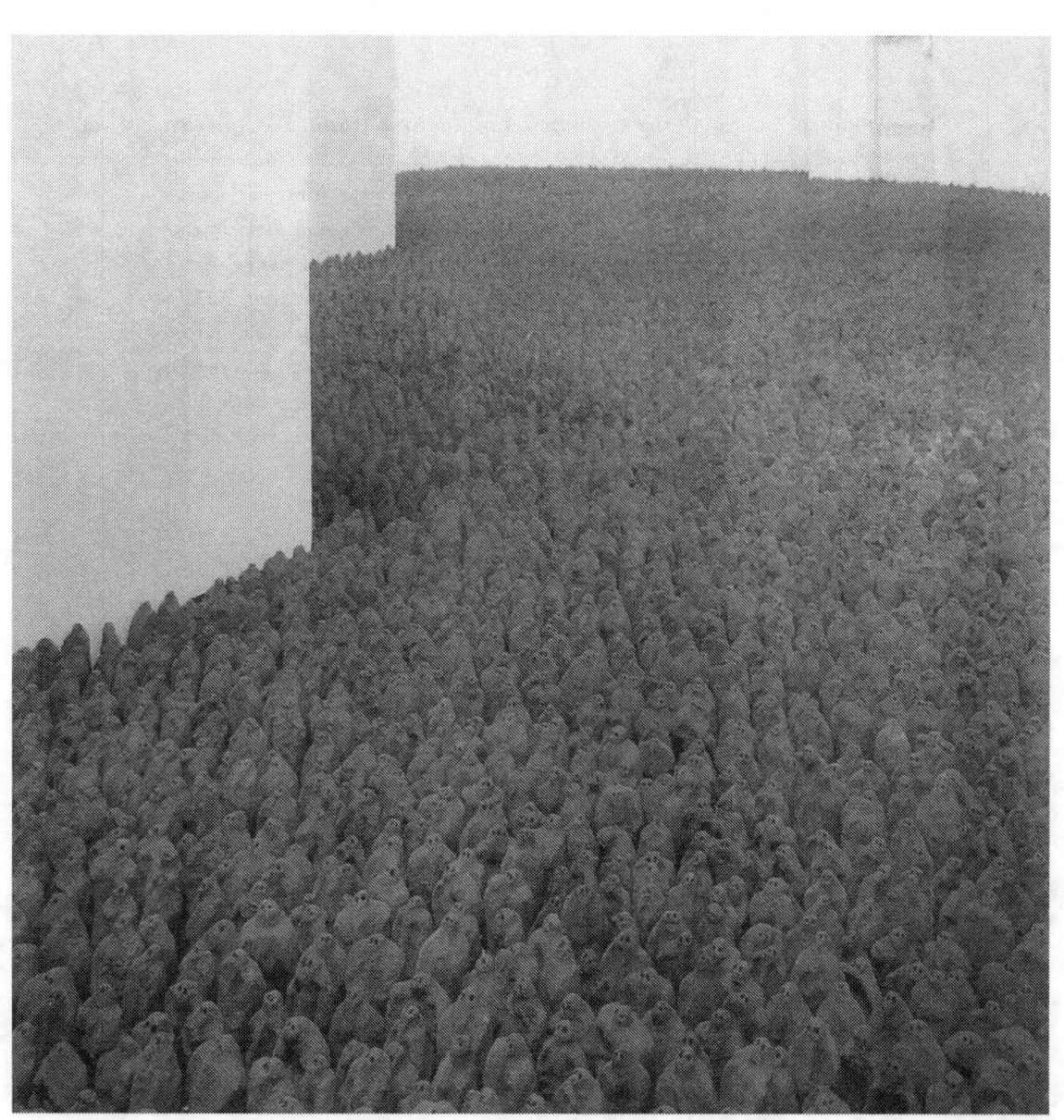

CHRIS BURDEN: *ALL OF THE SUBMARINES OF THE UNITED STATES OF AMERICA*

Chris Burden's satiric *All the Submarines of the United States of America* (1987) consisted of 625 cardboard subs hanging from the ceiling (at Newport Harbor Art Museum in CA). It was one of many contemporary artworks which took on political issues of the 1980s, such as the massive arms expenditure of the superpowers, Cold War stand-offs, and the ever-present threat of nuclear war. Another of Burden's ideological installations, 1979's *The Reason For the Neutron Bomb,* comprised 50,000 nickels spread across the gallery floor, each with a match glued to them (each nickel and match represented a Soviet tank). Prior to his political work, Burden was known for his dangerous performances (which included, in 1971's *Shooting Piece,* having a friend fire a gun at his arm).

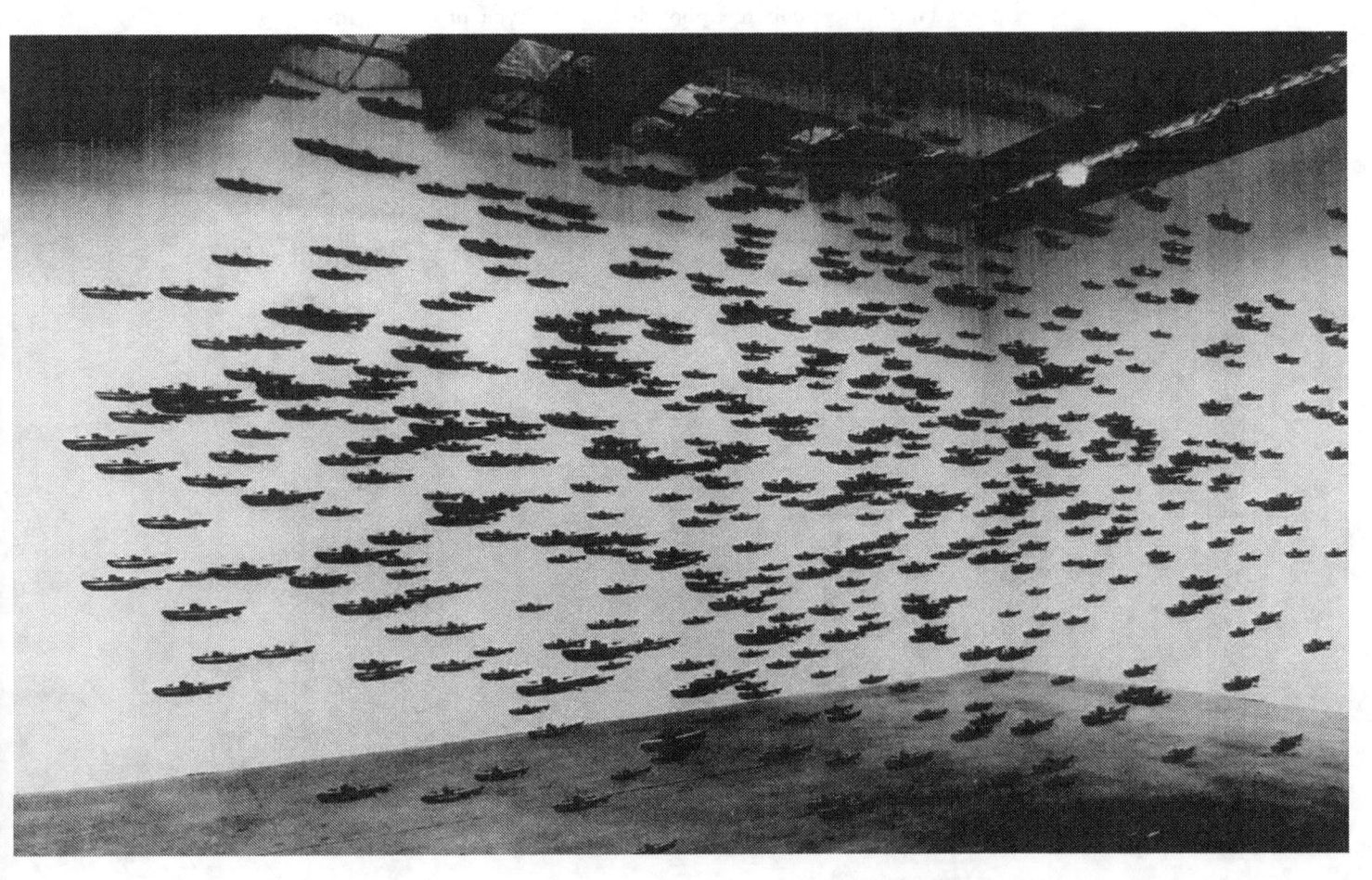

GLEN ONWIN: *AS ABOVE, SO BELOW*

In Glen Onwin's installations in Halifax (1991), water, wax and black brine were poured into a large concrete pool, as part of a cycle of works with an alchemical basis. Other works included *The One To the One – Organic/ Inorganic*, two pools, one with black brine and white gypsum in it, the other one with white brine and black coal.

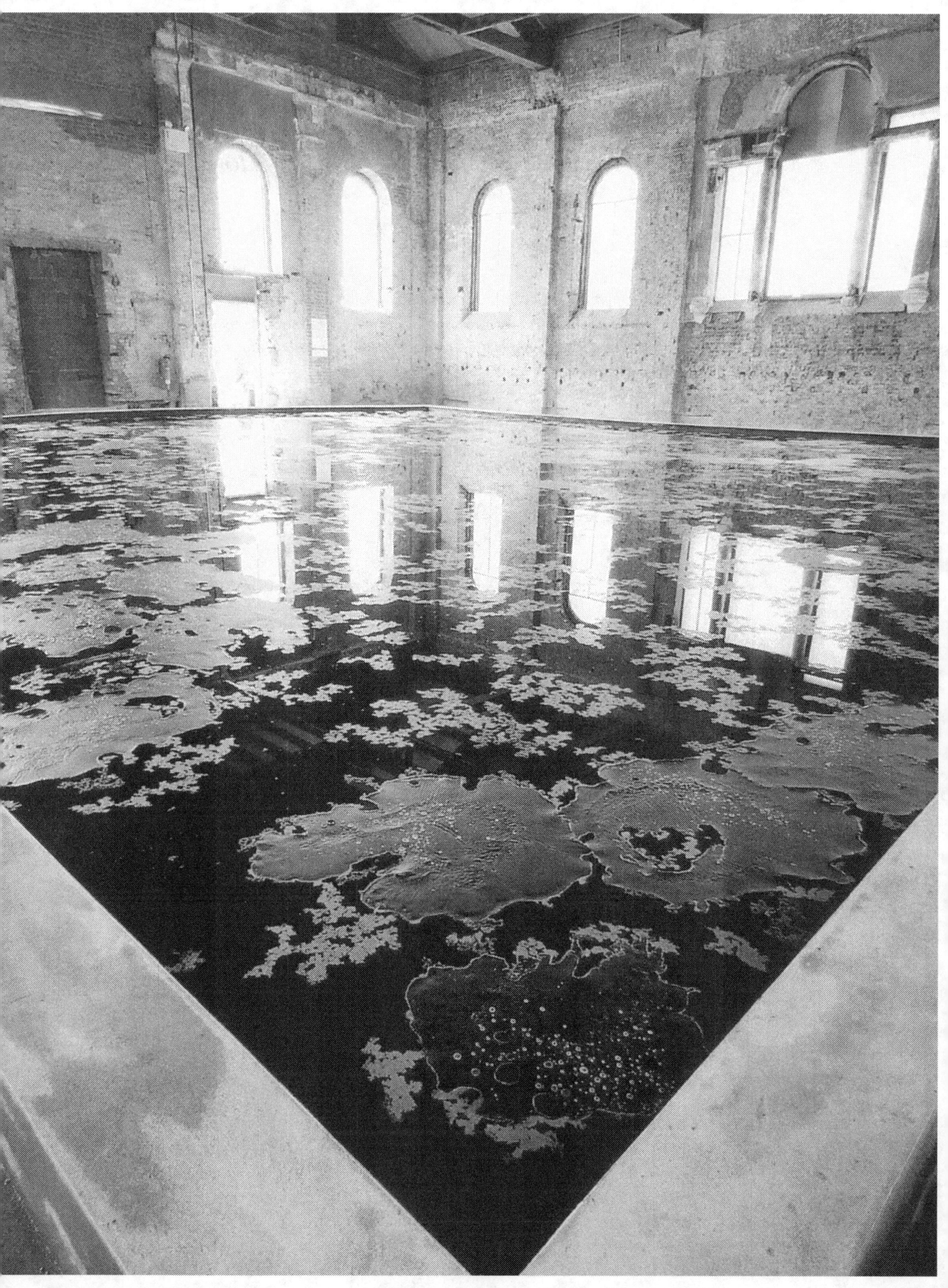

JOSEPH KOSUTH: *EX LIBRIS – J.F. CHAMPOLLION (FIGEAC)*

Ex-Libris – J.F. Champollion (Figeac) was made by Joseph Kosuth in 1991 for the French Ministry of Culture (Champollion was the main decoder of Egyptian hieroglyphics). Kosuth, whose art grew out of Sixties Conceptualism, constructed a hundred metre square version of the *Rosetta Stone* out of black granite.

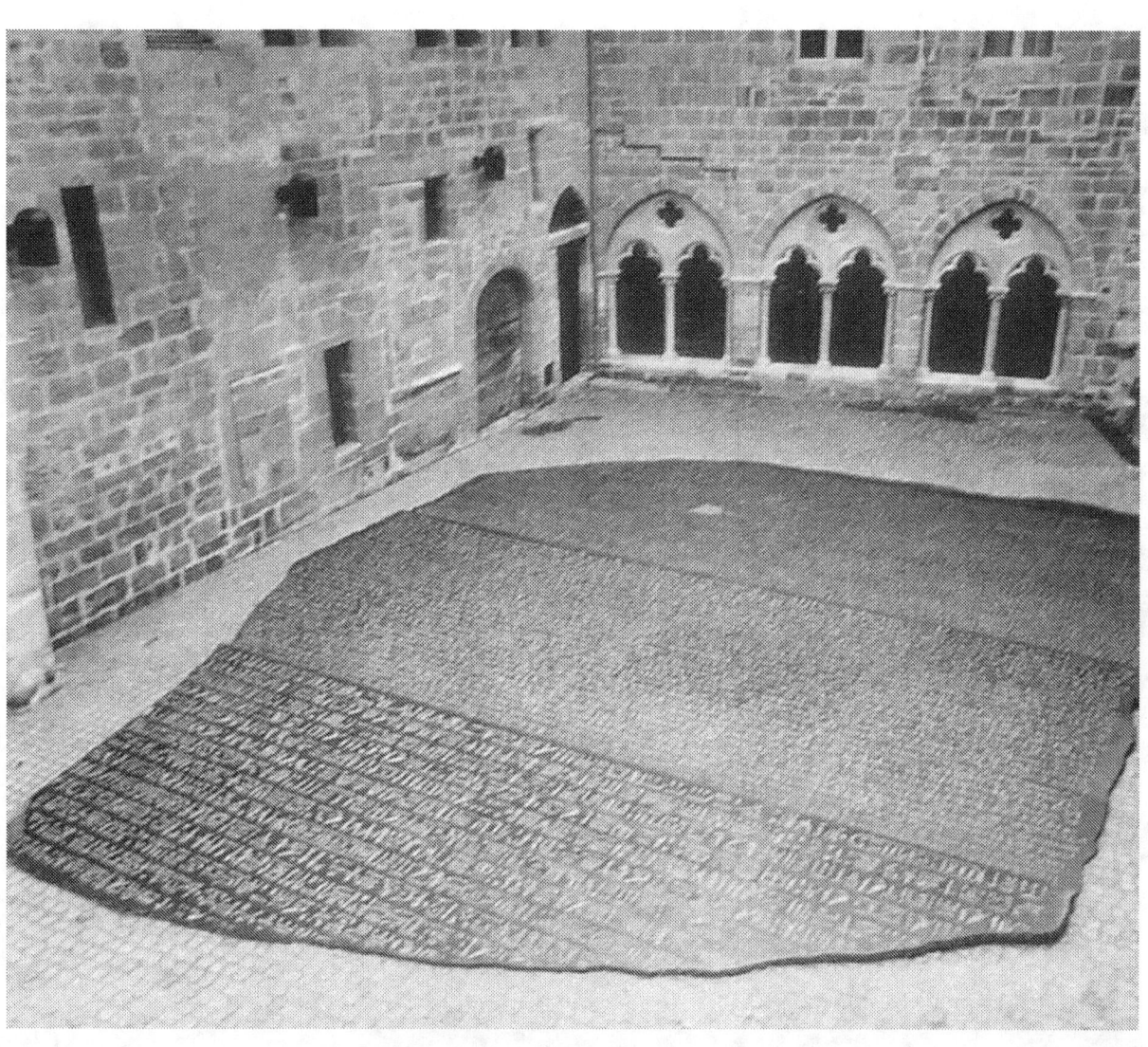

BARBARA KRUGER: *UNTITLED* (INSTALLATION)

Barbara Kruger covered the floor, walls and ceilings with giant slogans in her customary black, red and white colours and extra bold headline typeface in her 1991 installation in New York. Kruger's known for her photographic, collaged deconstructions of global media and society, its slogans. advertizing, and superabundant imagery. One of Kruger's tactics is the simple one of 'second wave' feminism: to put an object, image or word in a different context, to highlight its latent ideological content.

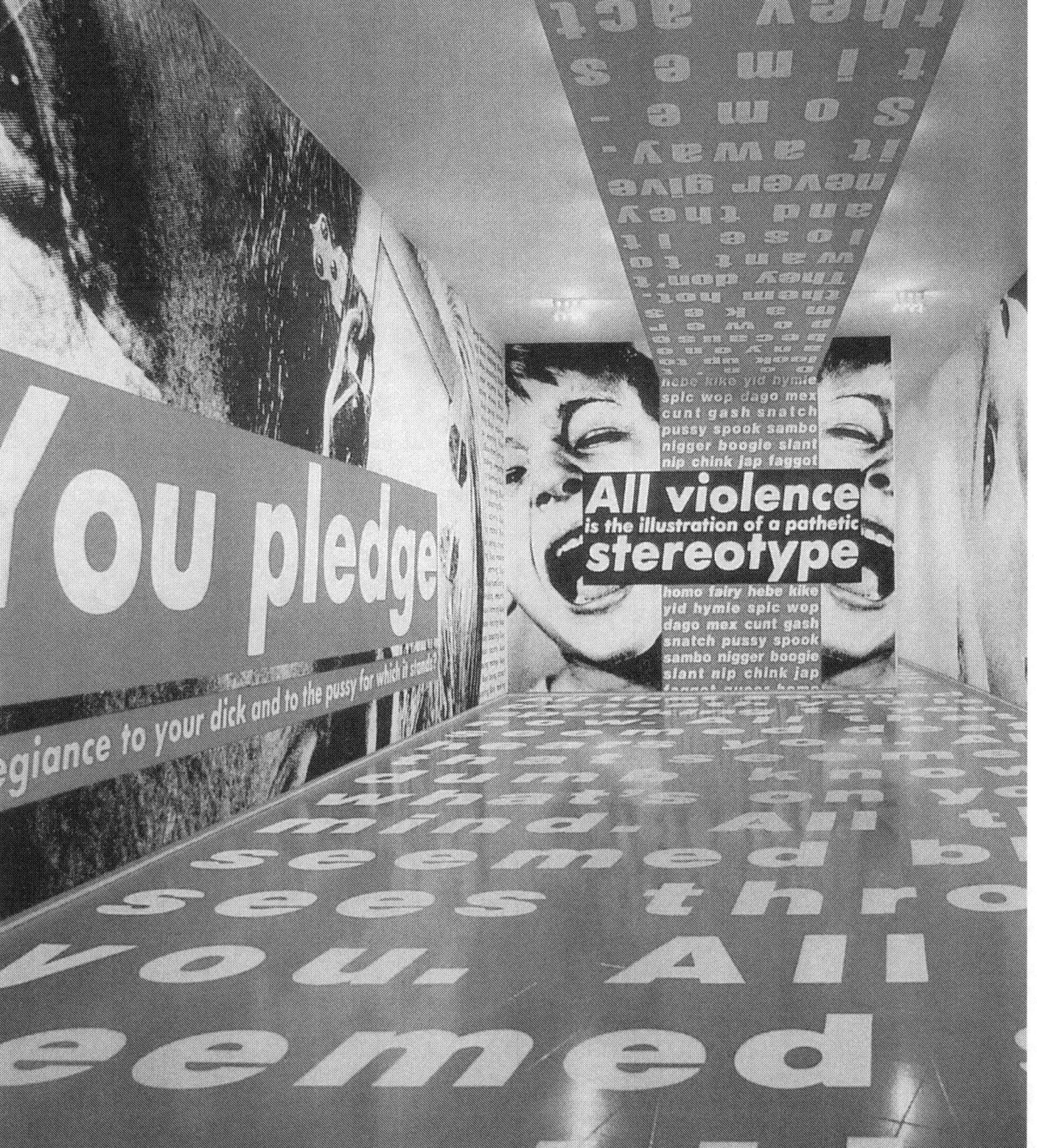

RICHARD WILSON: *20/50*

Richard Wilson's *20/50* (1987) was a steel pool of sump oil with a walkway into the middle of it, so the visitor could walk into the midst of the black liquid. The oil reflected the rest of the gallery. It was one of many installations which brought liquids into the art gallery.

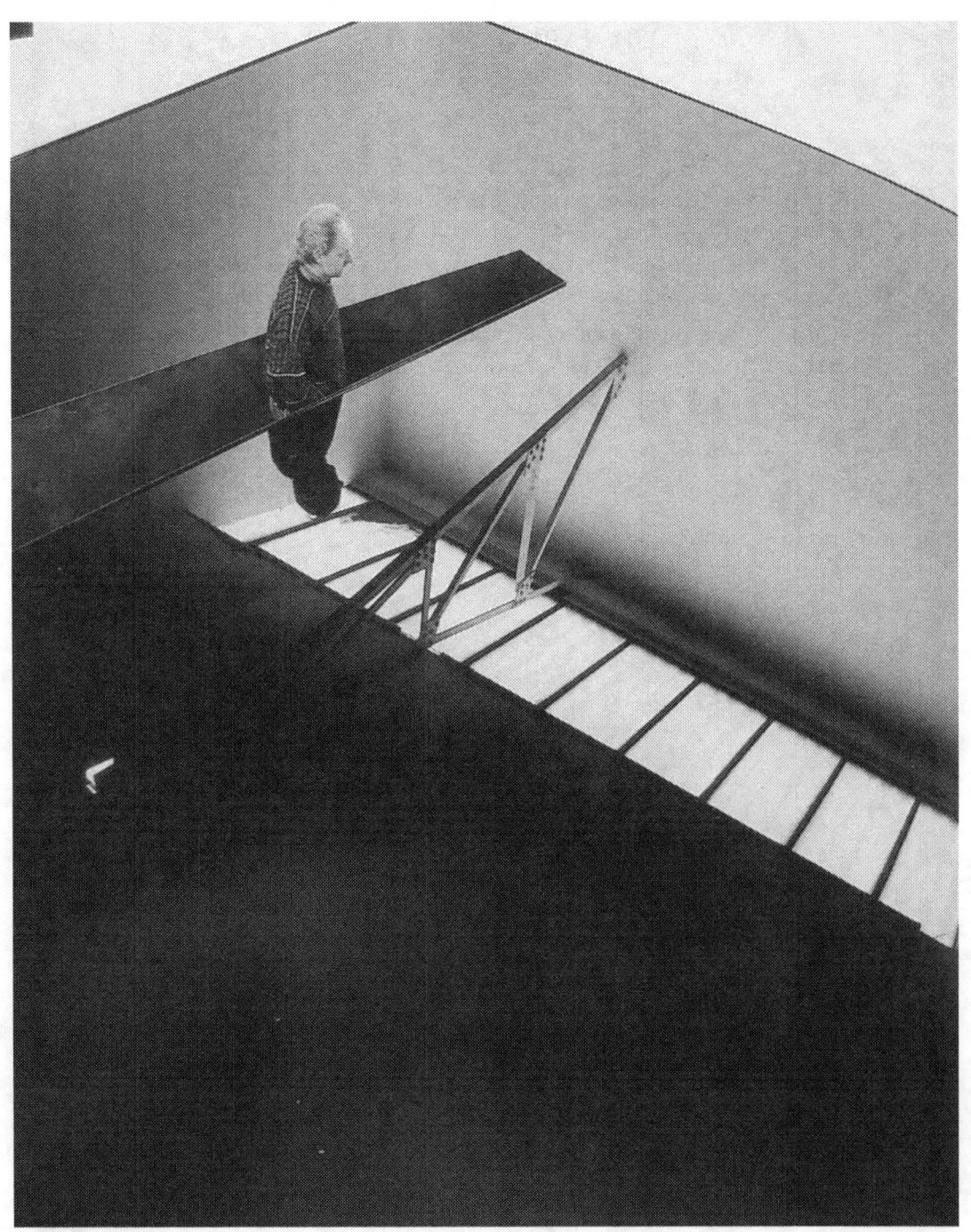

ANISH KAPOOR: *UNTITLED*

Anish Kapoor's erotic, mysterious painted objects, such as *Untitled* (1990), are bizarre yet wholly believable departures from natural forms – three hemispherical forms, a pitted surface like that of a blackcurrant, interfolding petals like those of a rose, multi-part spirals, cones made of shapes like the folds in robes – but the most startling thing about Kapoor's forms are their colours, powdery blues, lemon yellow and scarlet, at once seductive and unreal, simultaneously, like all sculpture, inviting touch and repelling it, perhaps by being indifferent to it.

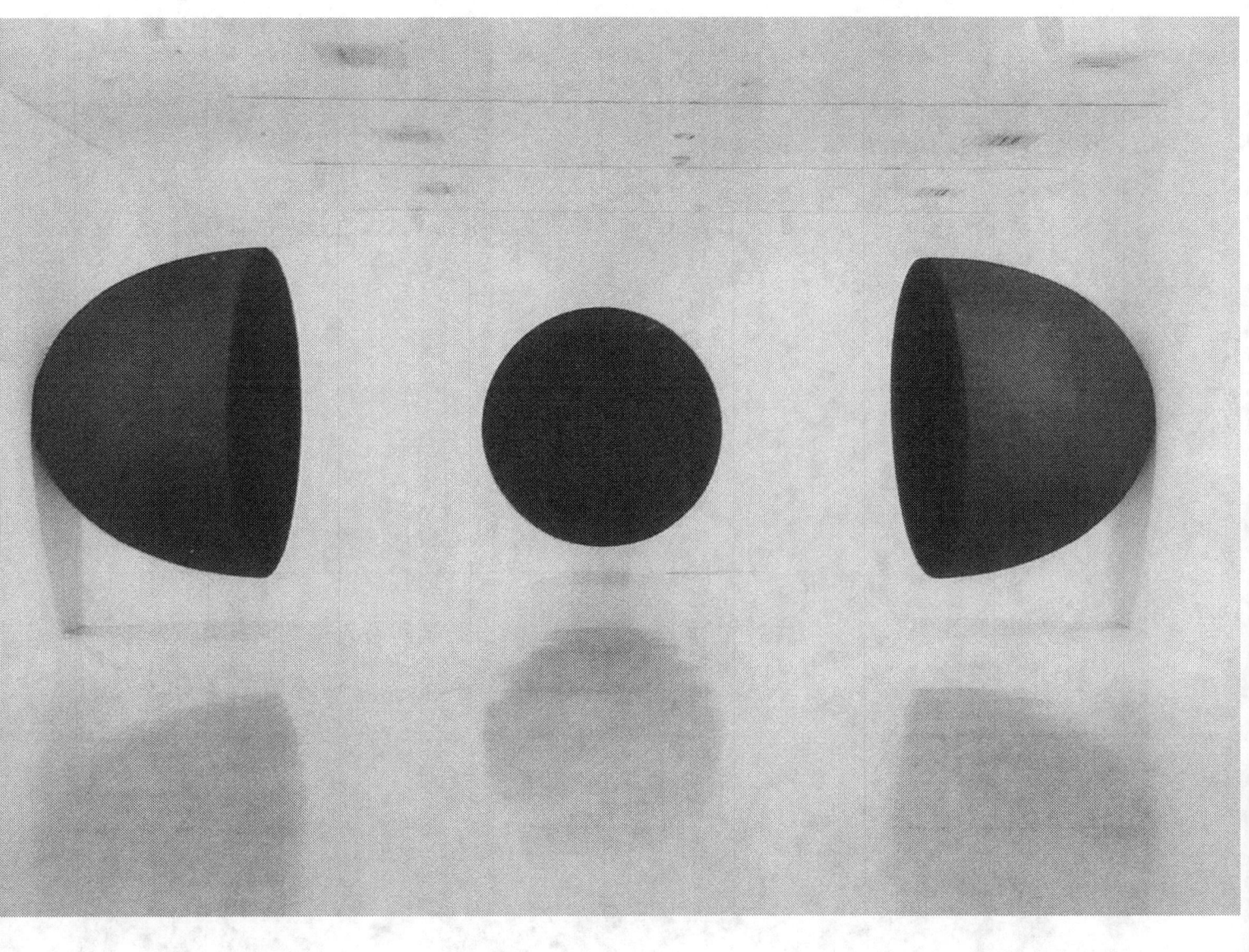

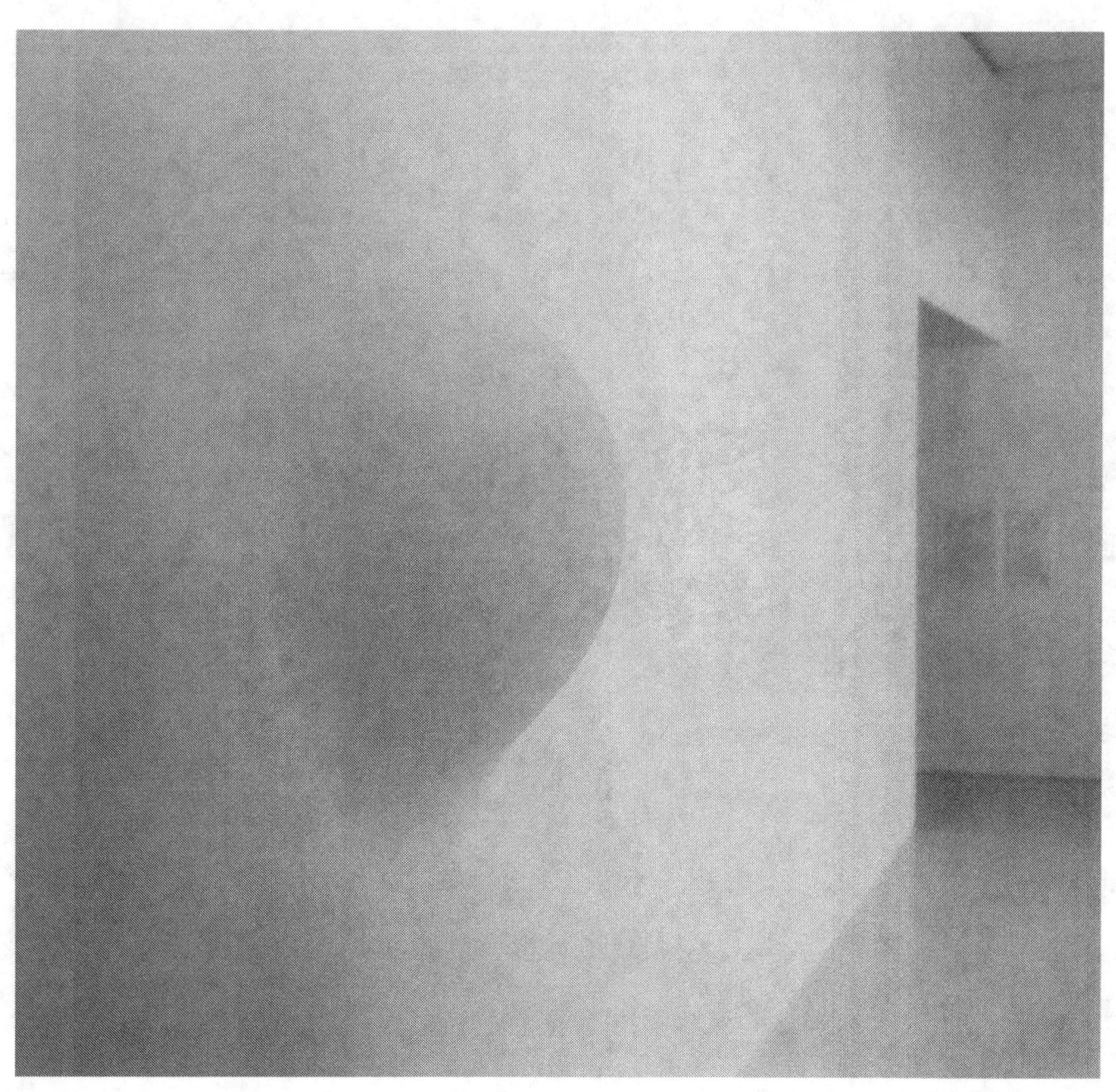

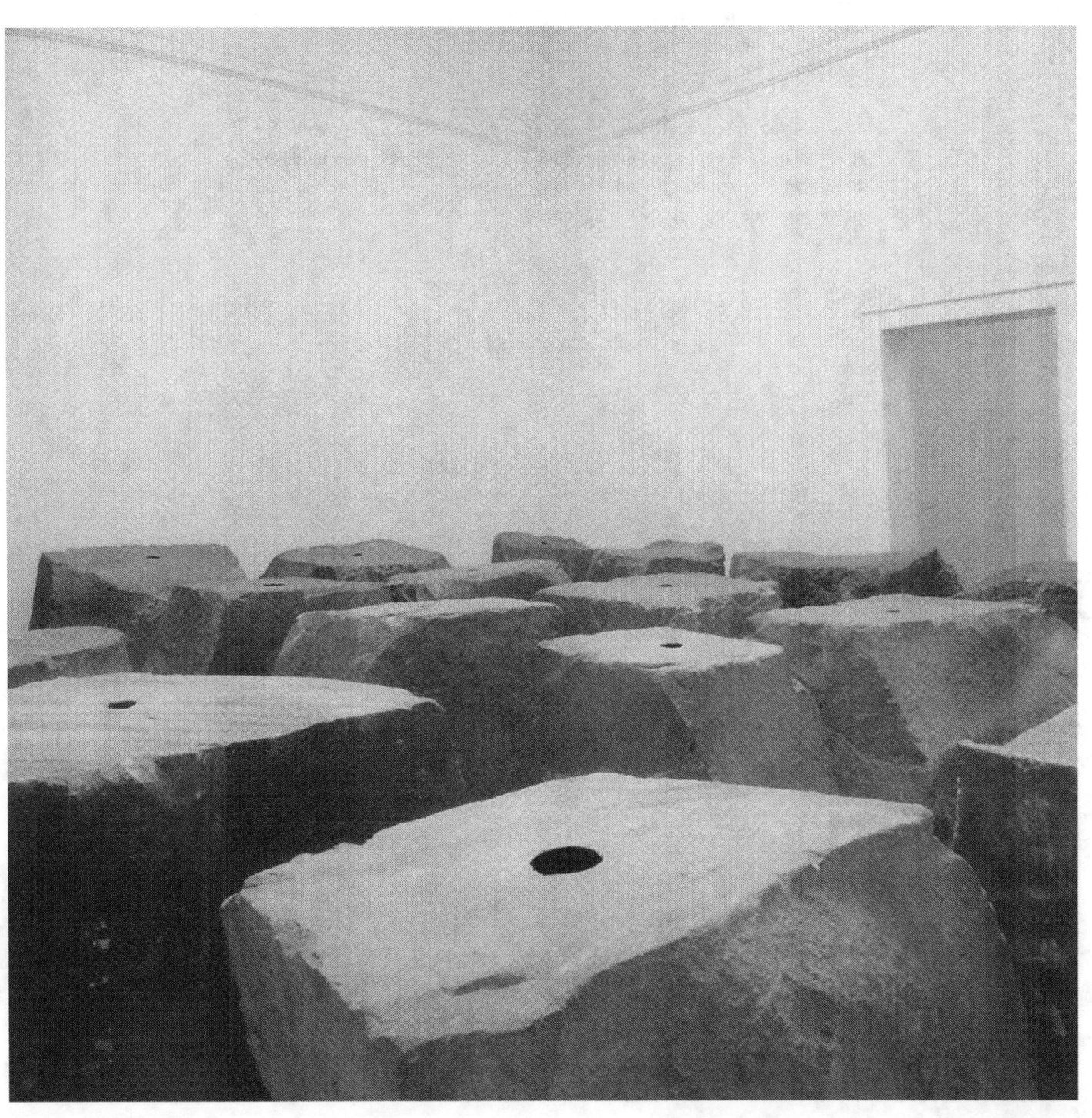

ROSE FINN-KELCEY: *UNTITLED*

British artist Rose Finn-Kelcey produced a steam work: her *Untitled* (1992, Chisenhalle Gallery, London) comprised of water placed on a sheet metal base, with an extractor hood hung above it. In between the two was a cloud of steam, made dramatic by the lighting.

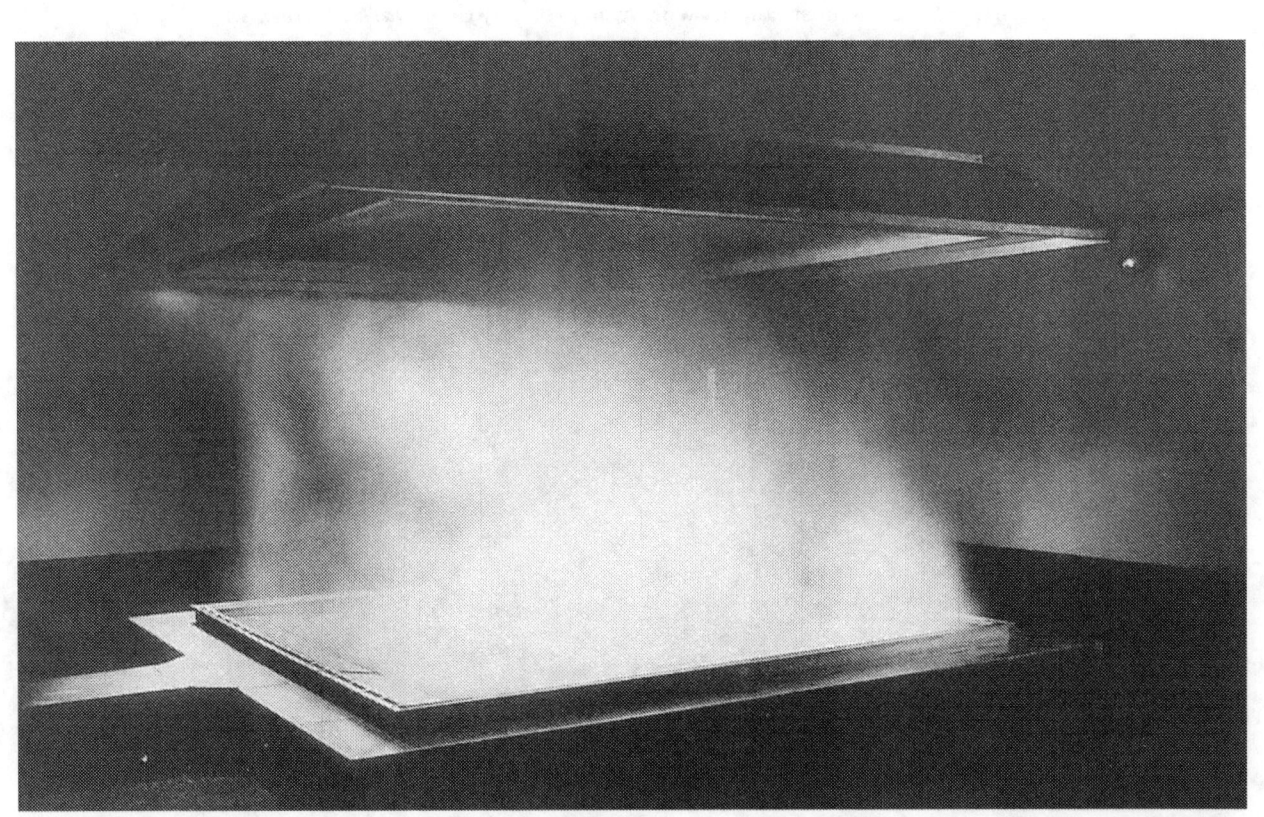

CORNELIA PARKER: *COLD DARK MATTER: AN EXPLODED VIEW*

Cornelia Parker's most famous work was probably *Cold Dark Matter: An Exploded View* (1991), an installation of a garden shed that Parker had blown up by army experts, exhibiting the debris hung from wires in the gallery. It looked like a 3-D version of a movie still of an explosion (like the endlessly exploding house at the end of Michelangelo Antonioni's *Zabriskie Point*). Parker's installation concerned cosmological themes of opposites, inhaling and exhaling, centripetal and centrifugal motion.

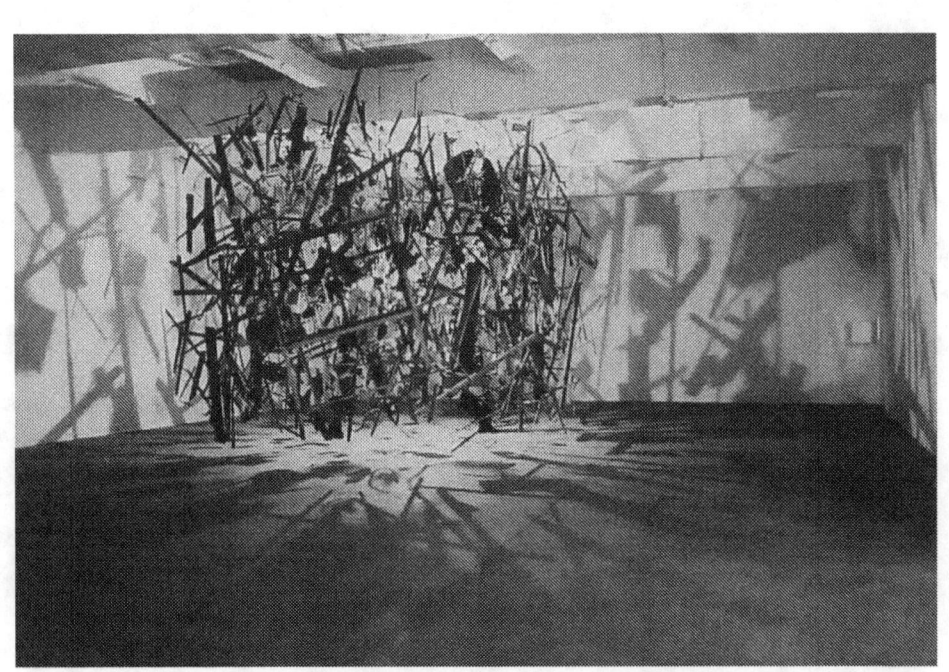

Some more recent examples of installation art:

1. Patrick Tuttofuoco, *Walkaround*, 2002.
2. Terry Smith, *Marking Time*, 1999, typical installation video art.
3. Vanessa Beecroft, *VB46.026.ali*, 2001.
4. Hans Weigand, *Cotton*, 2001.
5. Jason Rhoades, *The Great Sea Battles of Wilhelm*, 1994-95.
6. Renato Niemis, 1994.
7. Aernout Mik, *Piñata*, 1999.
8. Atelier van Lieshout, *Compostopia*, 2002.
9. Christoph Draeger, *Apocalypso Place*, 2000.
10. Alicia Framis, *Blood Sushi Bank*, 2000.
11. Diller & Scofidio, *Blur Building*, 2002.
12. Børre Sæthre, *My Private Sky, unit 1/ trauma white*, 2001.
13. Barbara Bloom, *Pictures From the Floating World*, 1995.
14. Yayoi Kusama, *Dots Obsession*, 2000.
15. Elmgreen & Dragset, *Powerless Structures*, 2001.
16. Olafur Eliasson, *Die Dinge die due nicht siehst*, 2001.
17. Bill Woodrow, *Ship of Fools, Captain's Table*, 1985.
18. Lawrence Weiner, installation.
19. James Turrell, *Milk Run III*, 2002.
20. Mary Miss, *Perimeters/ Pavilions/ Decoys*, 1977-78.
21. Richard Serra, *Equal and Diagonally Opposite Corners: For Samuel Beckett*, 1990.
22. Robert Smithson, *Mono Lake, Non-site*.
23. Joseph Beuys, *Plight*, 1985.
24. Dan Flavin, *Untitled*, 1976.
25. Joseph Kosuth, *Zero & Not*.
26. Eva Hesse, installation, 1970.
27. Tony Cragg, *Untitled*, 1975.

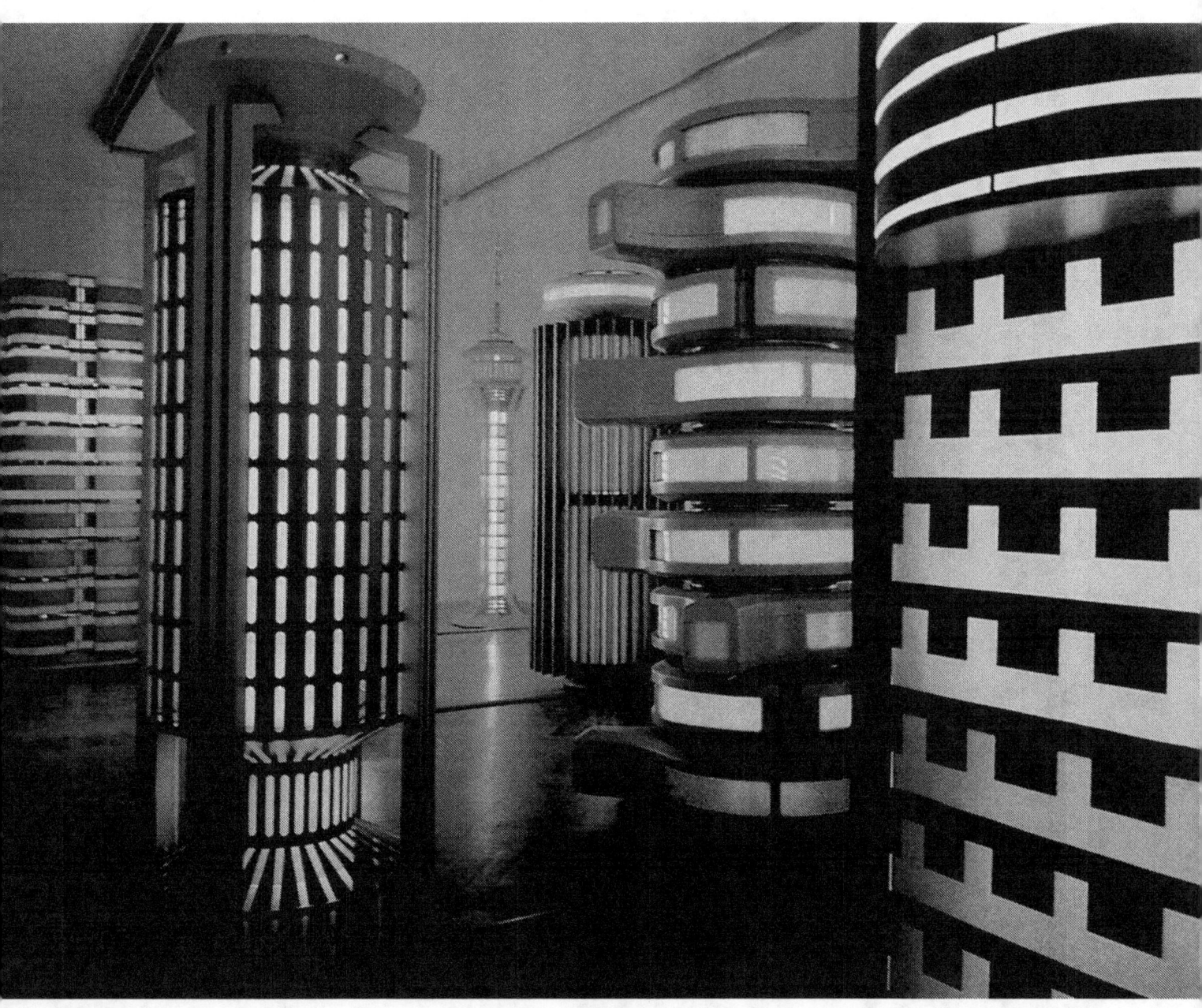

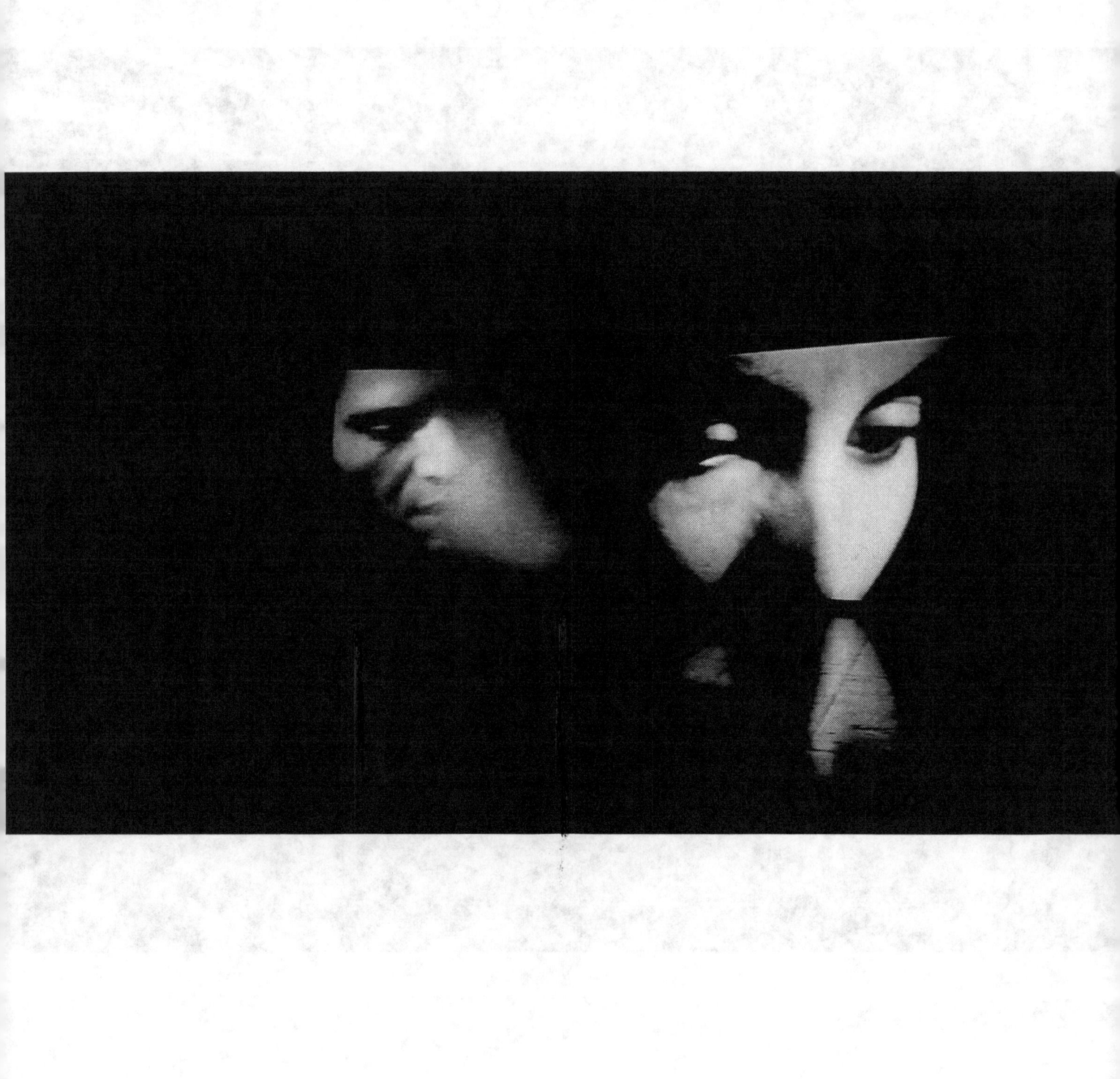

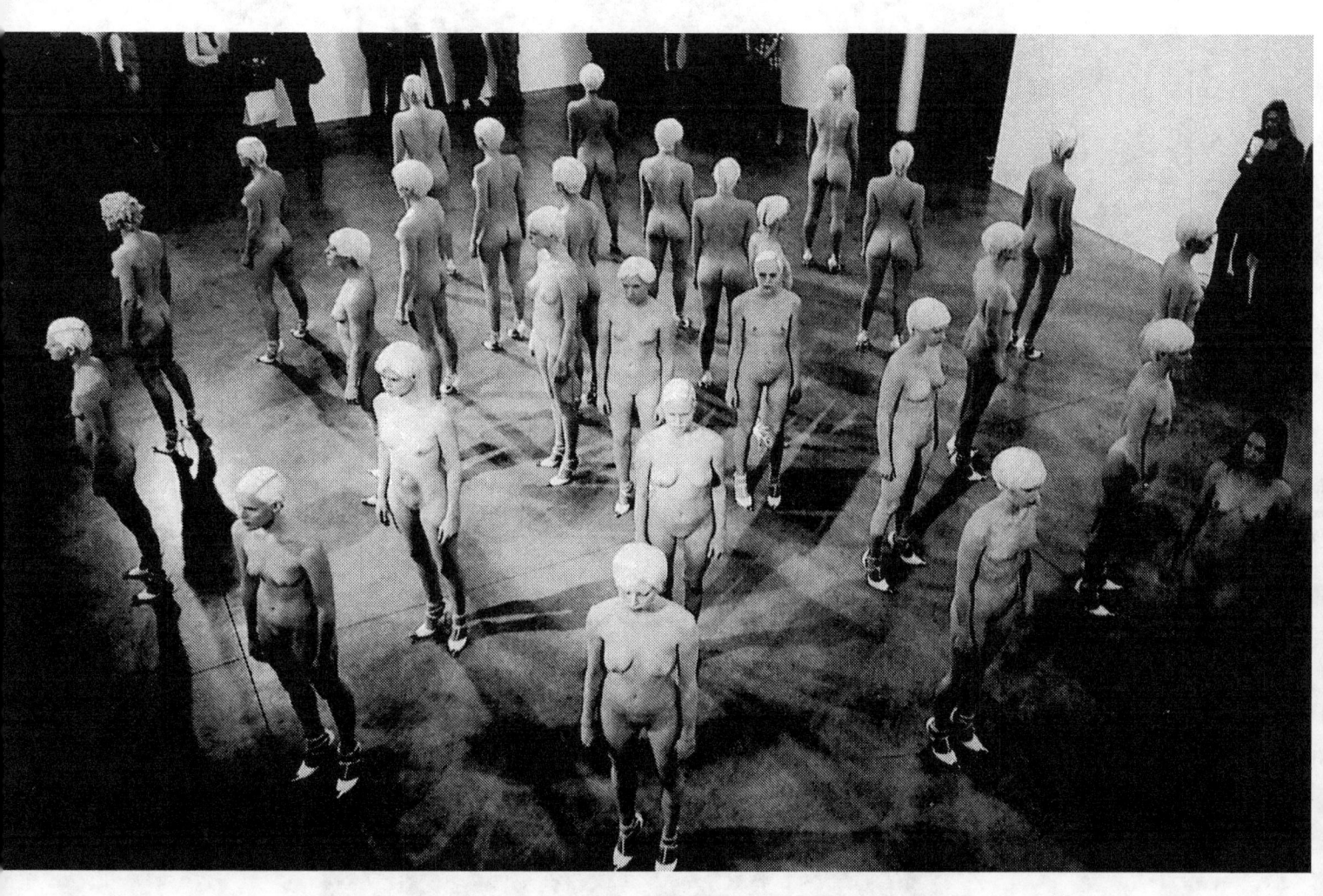

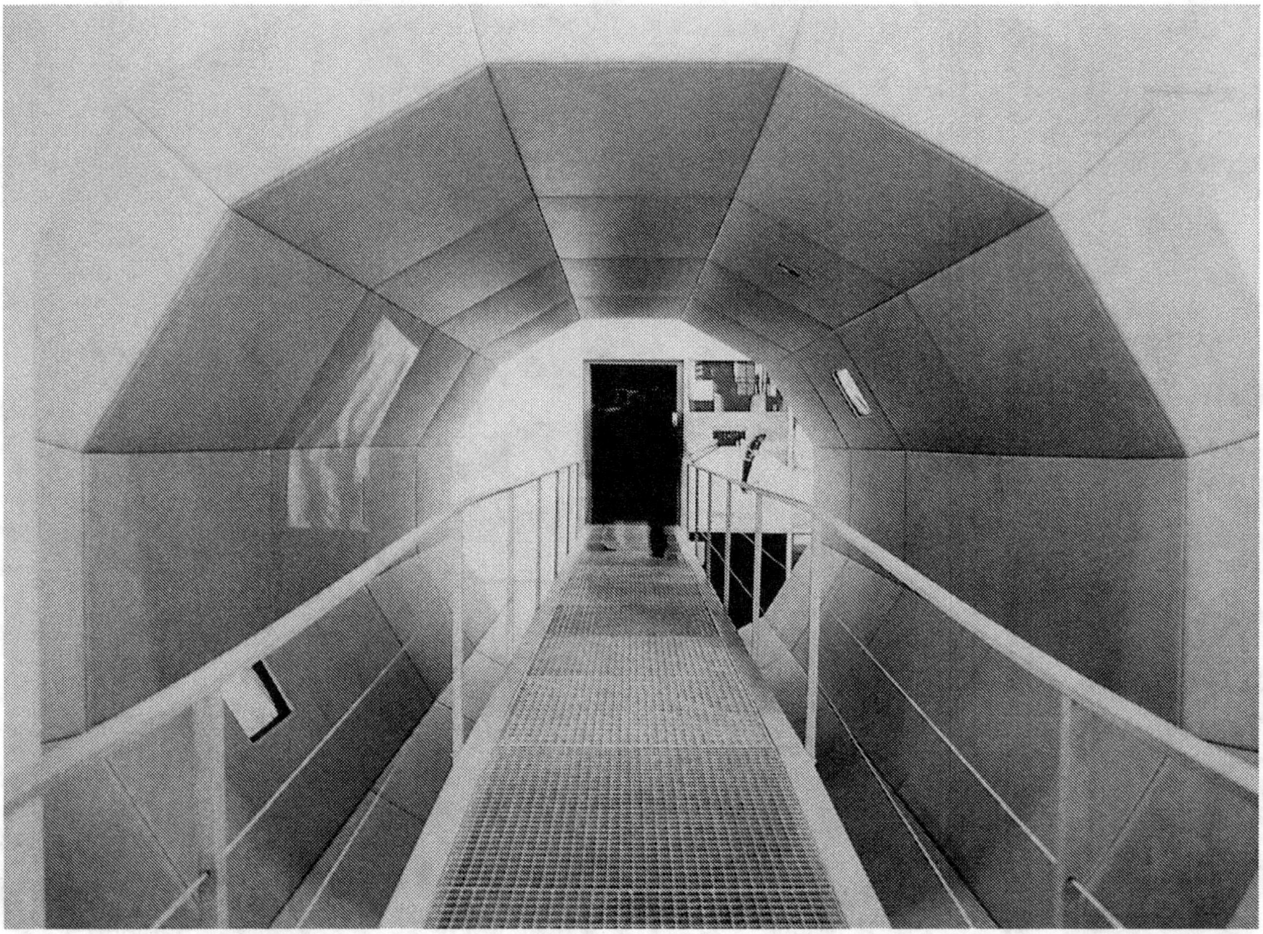

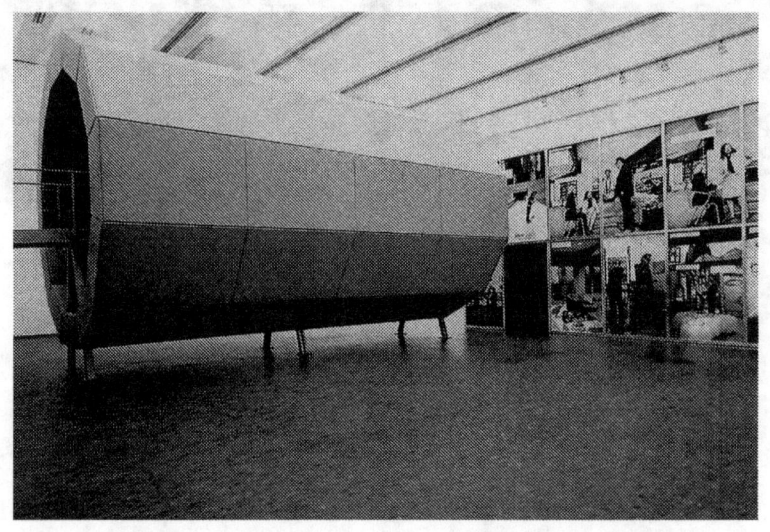

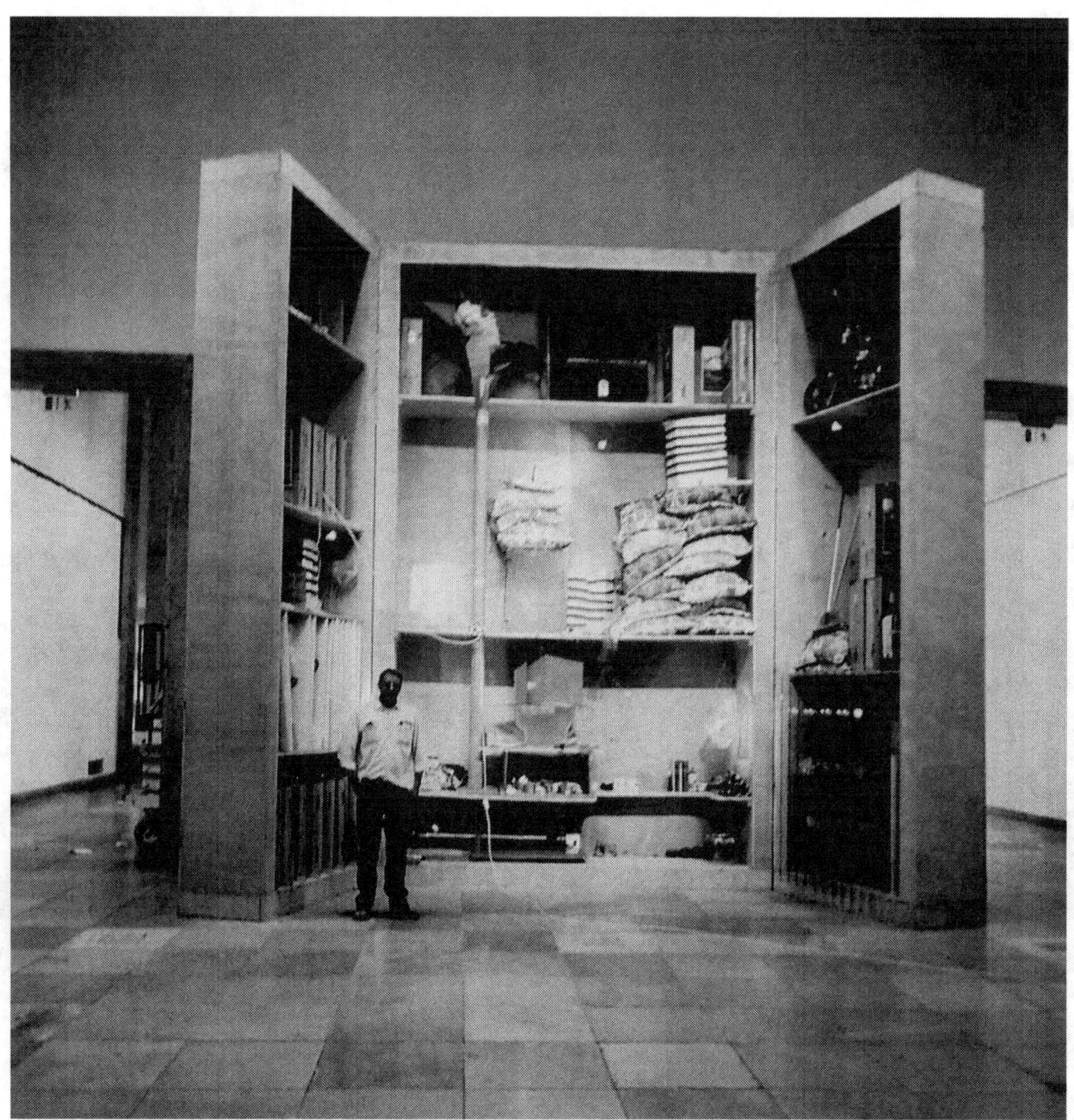

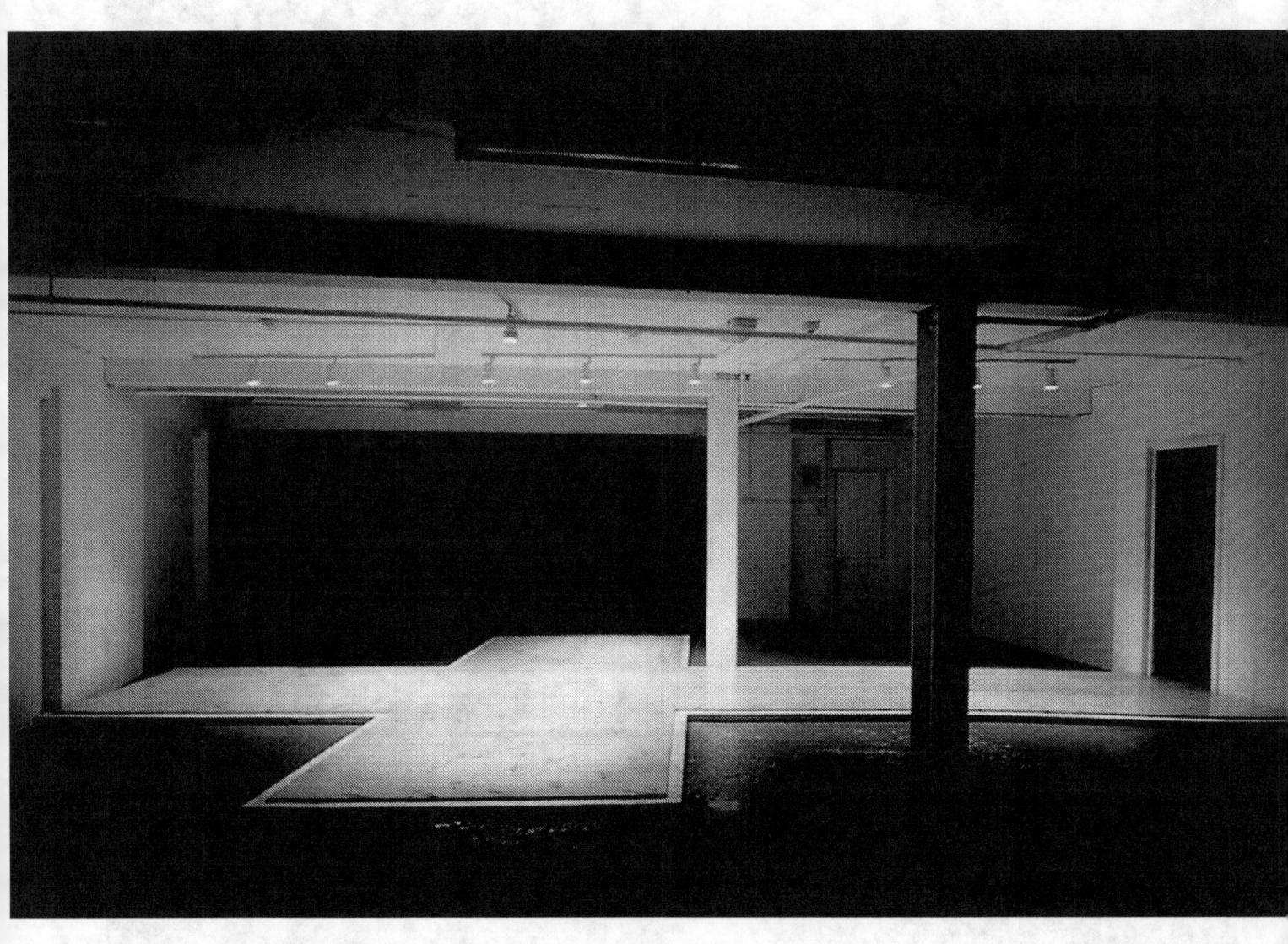

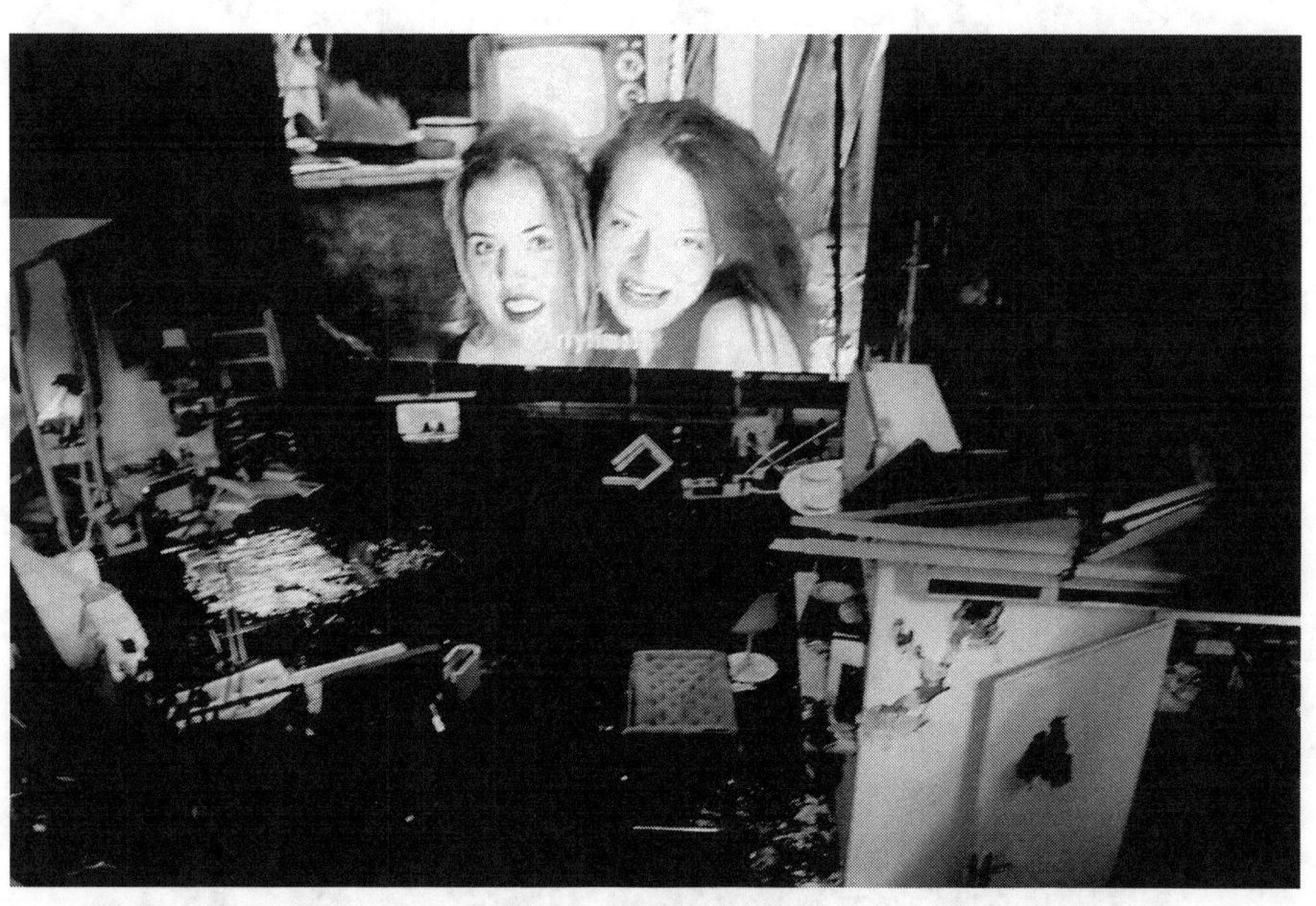

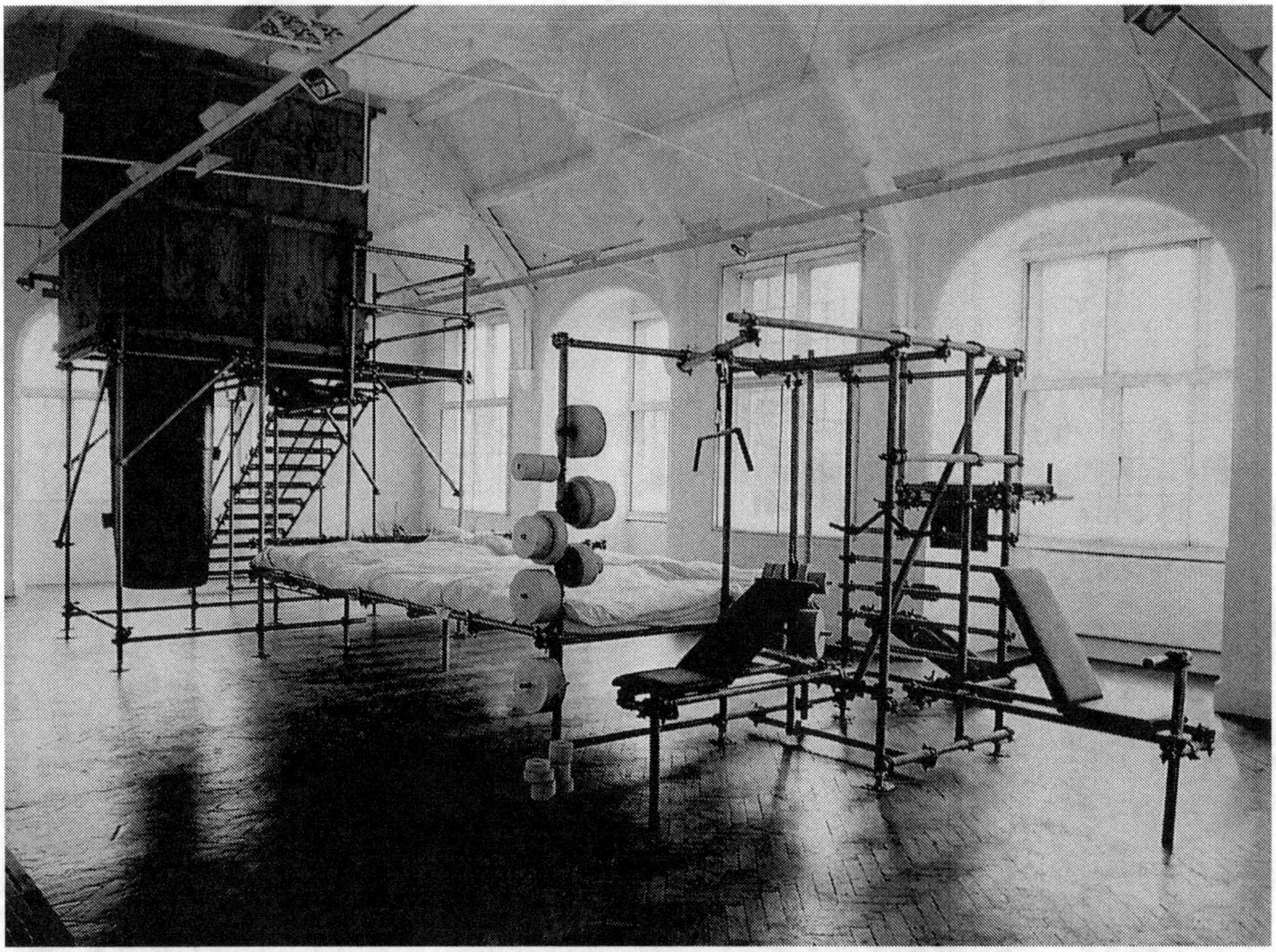

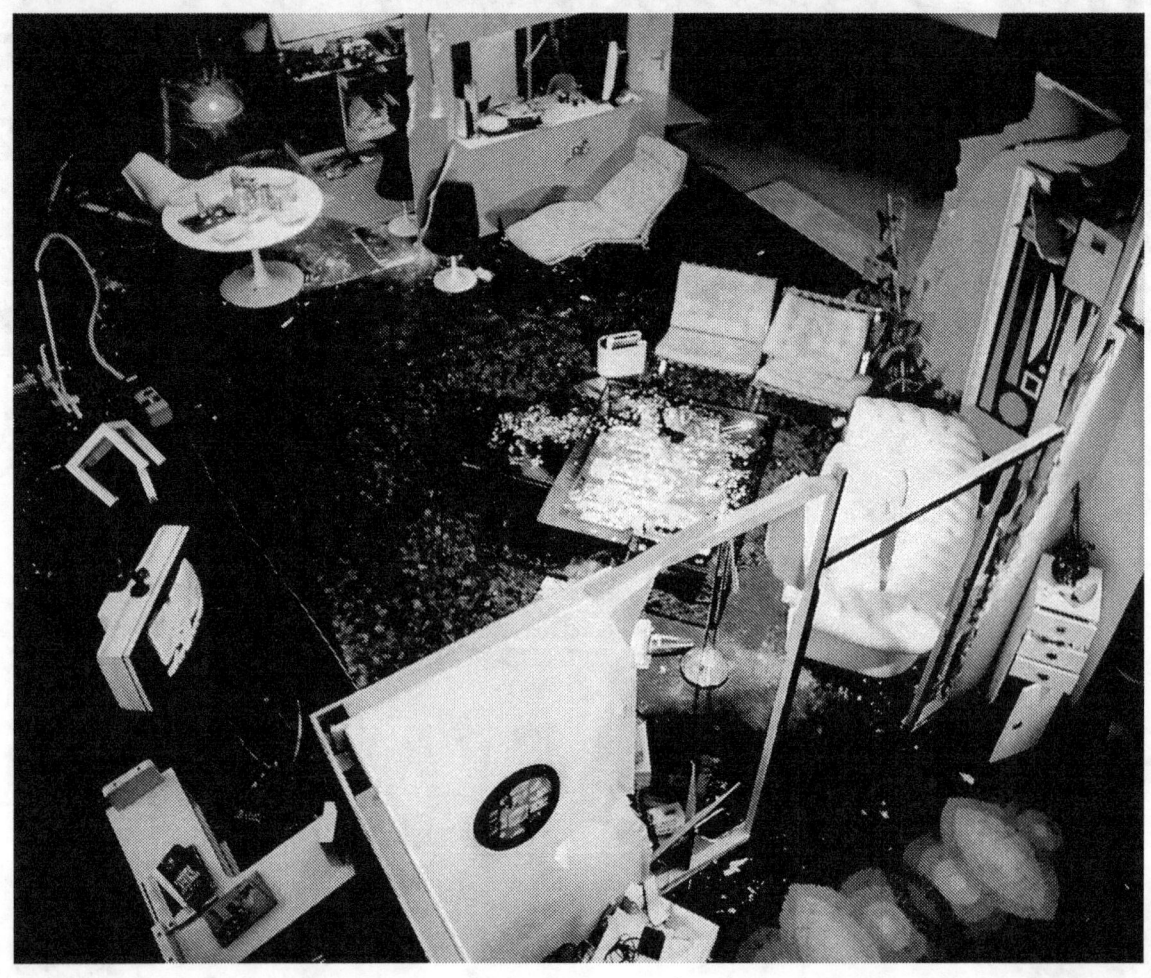

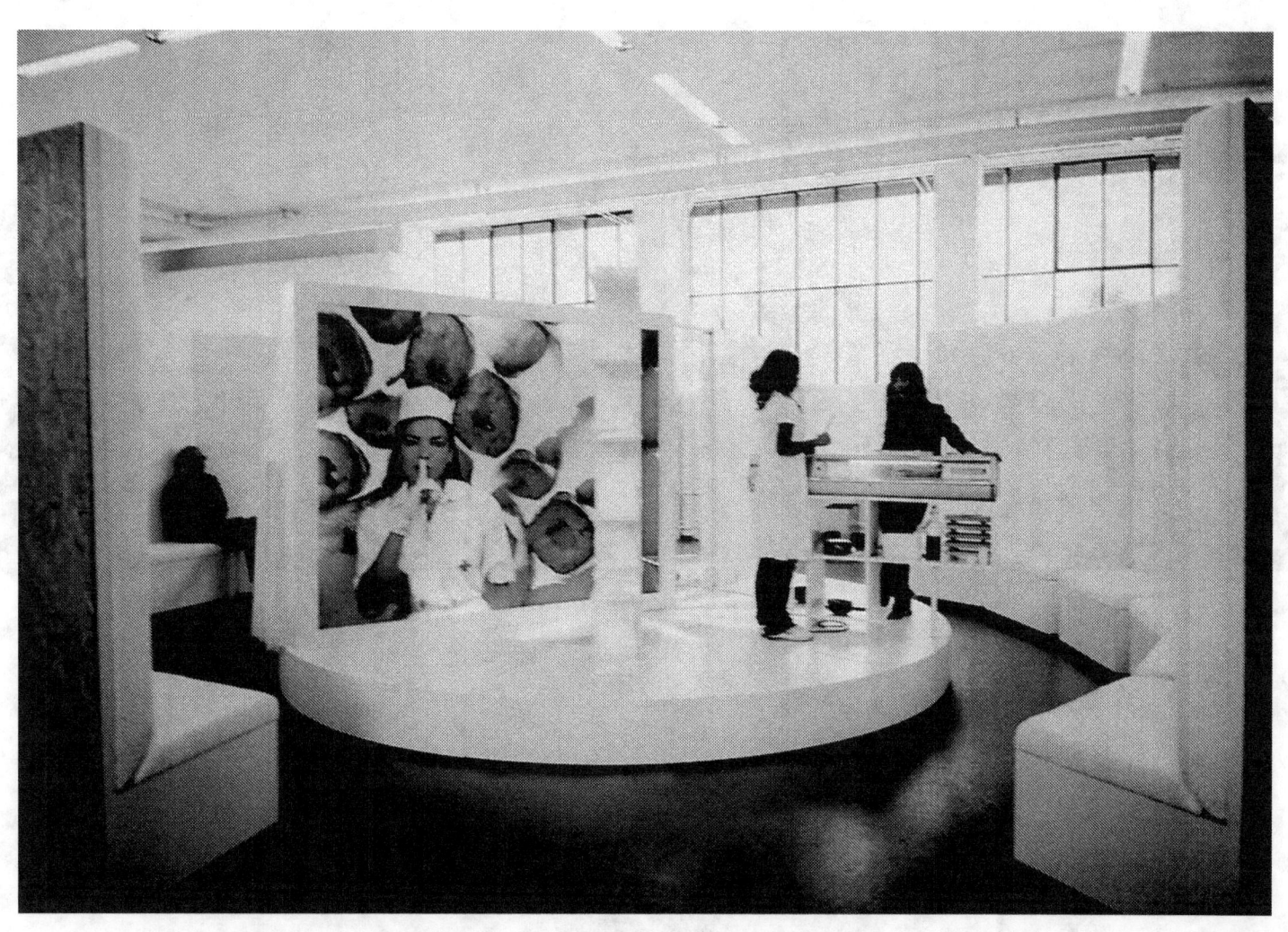

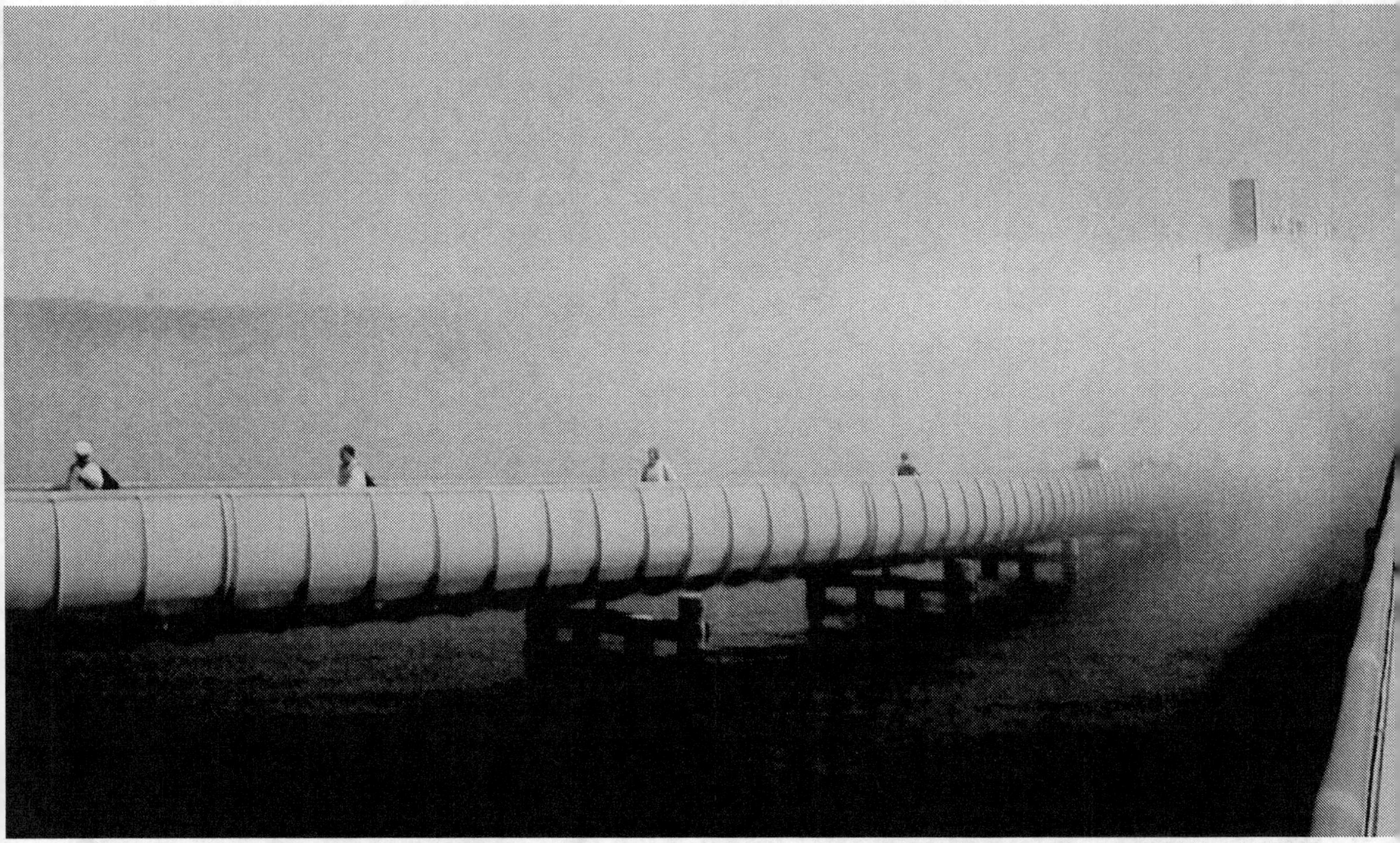

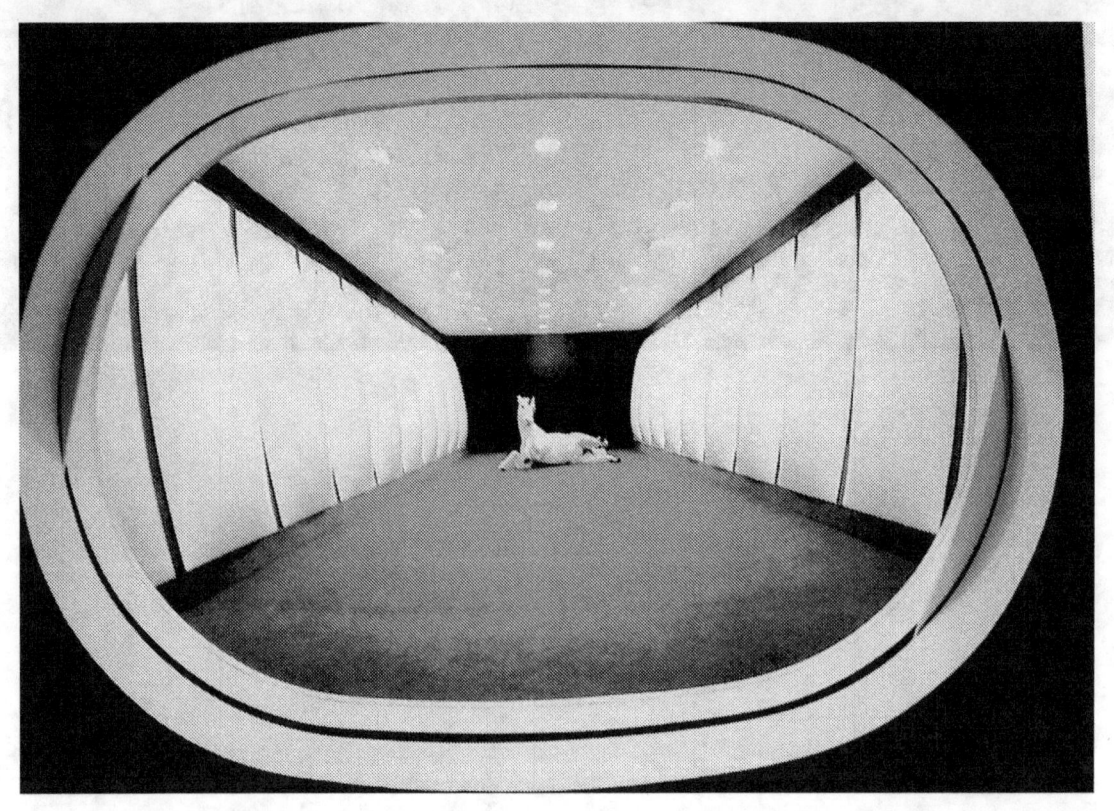

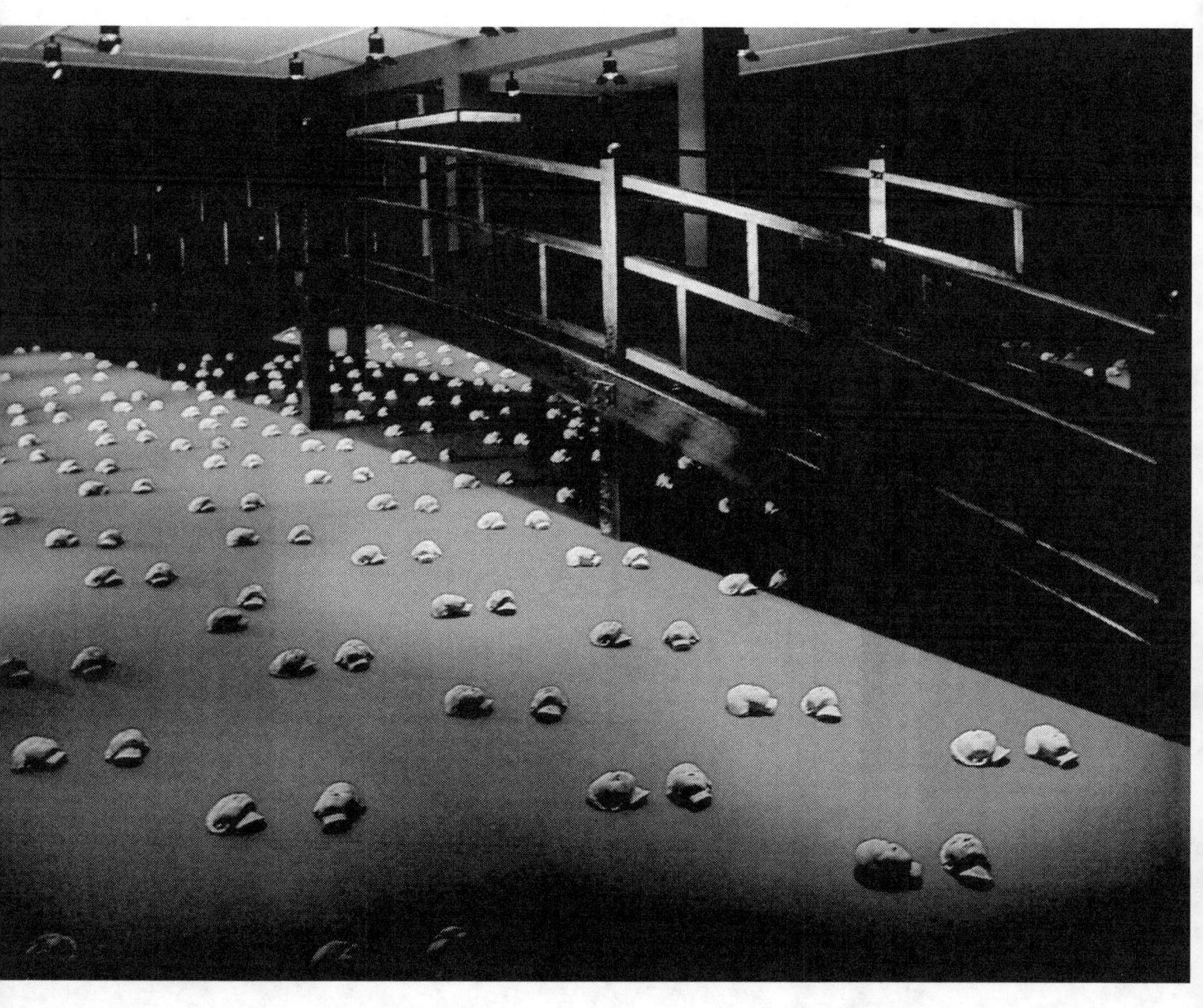

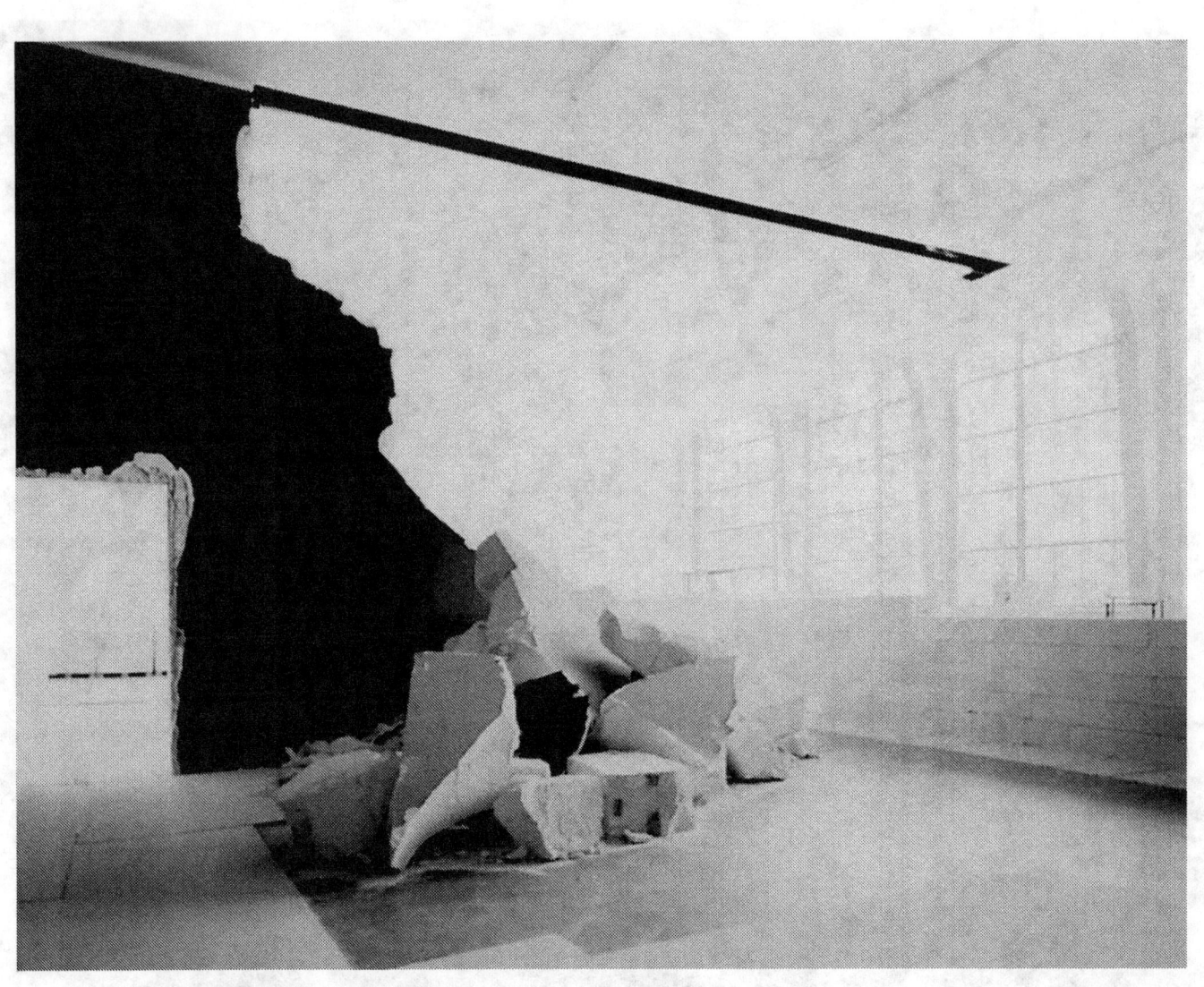

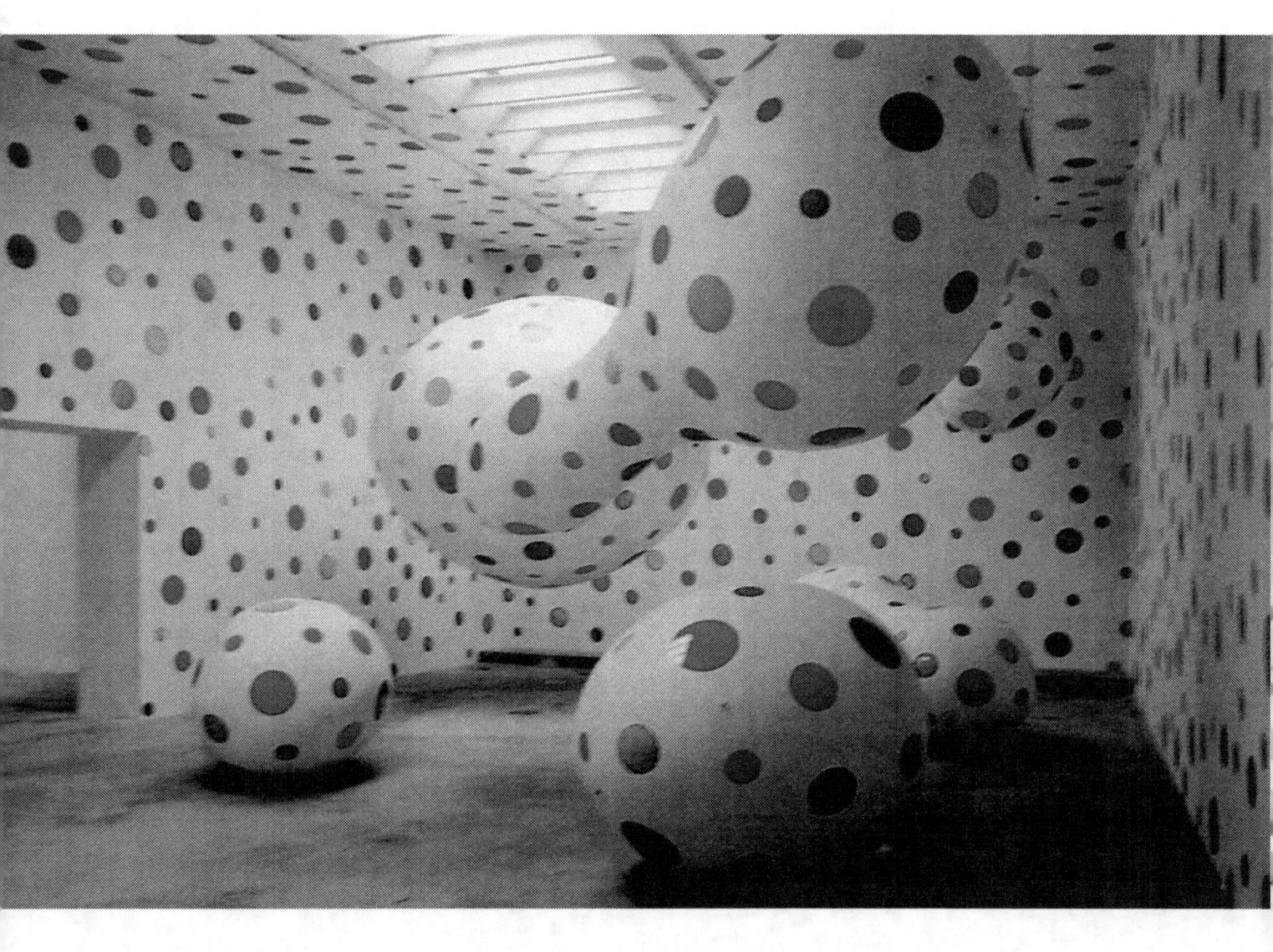

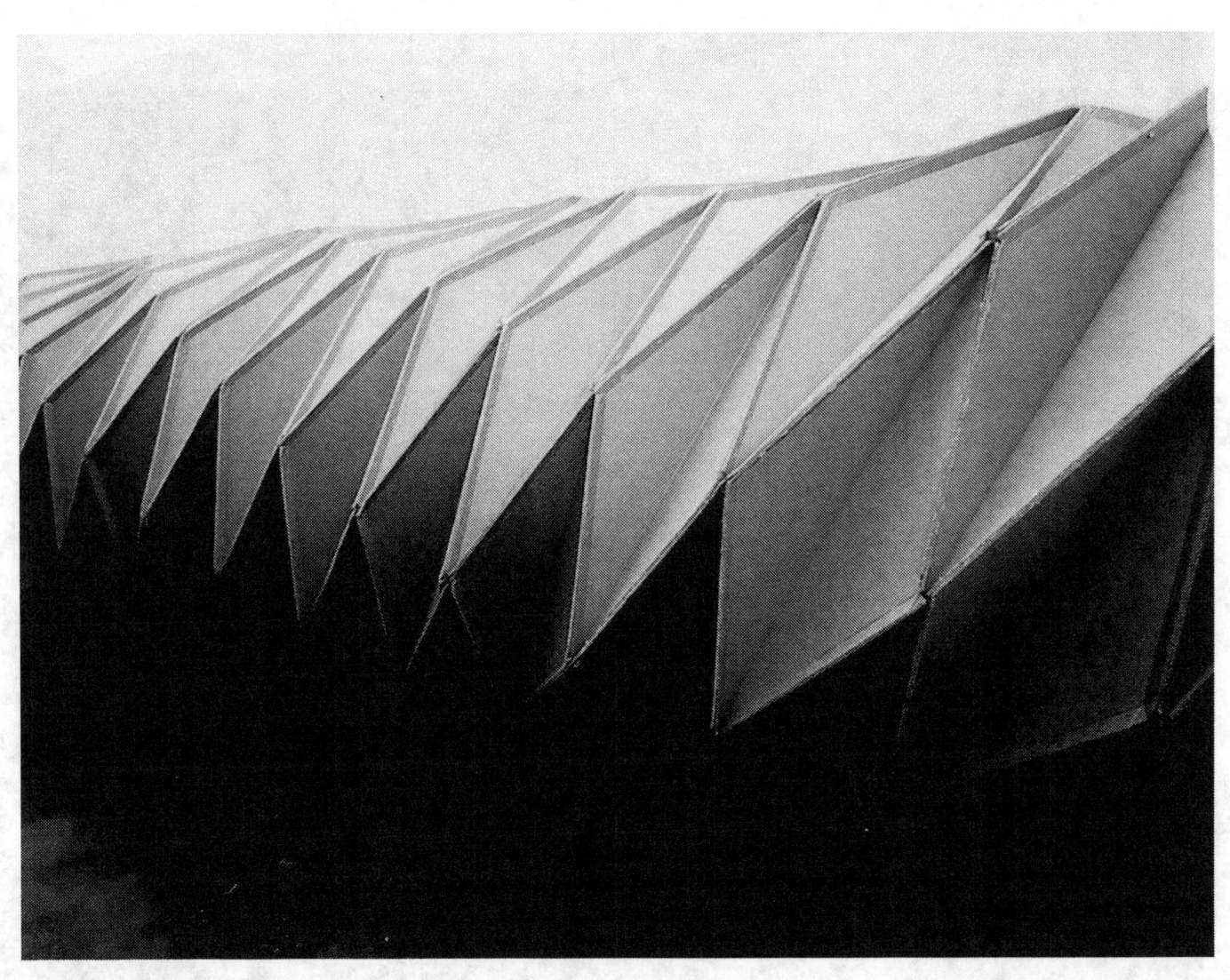

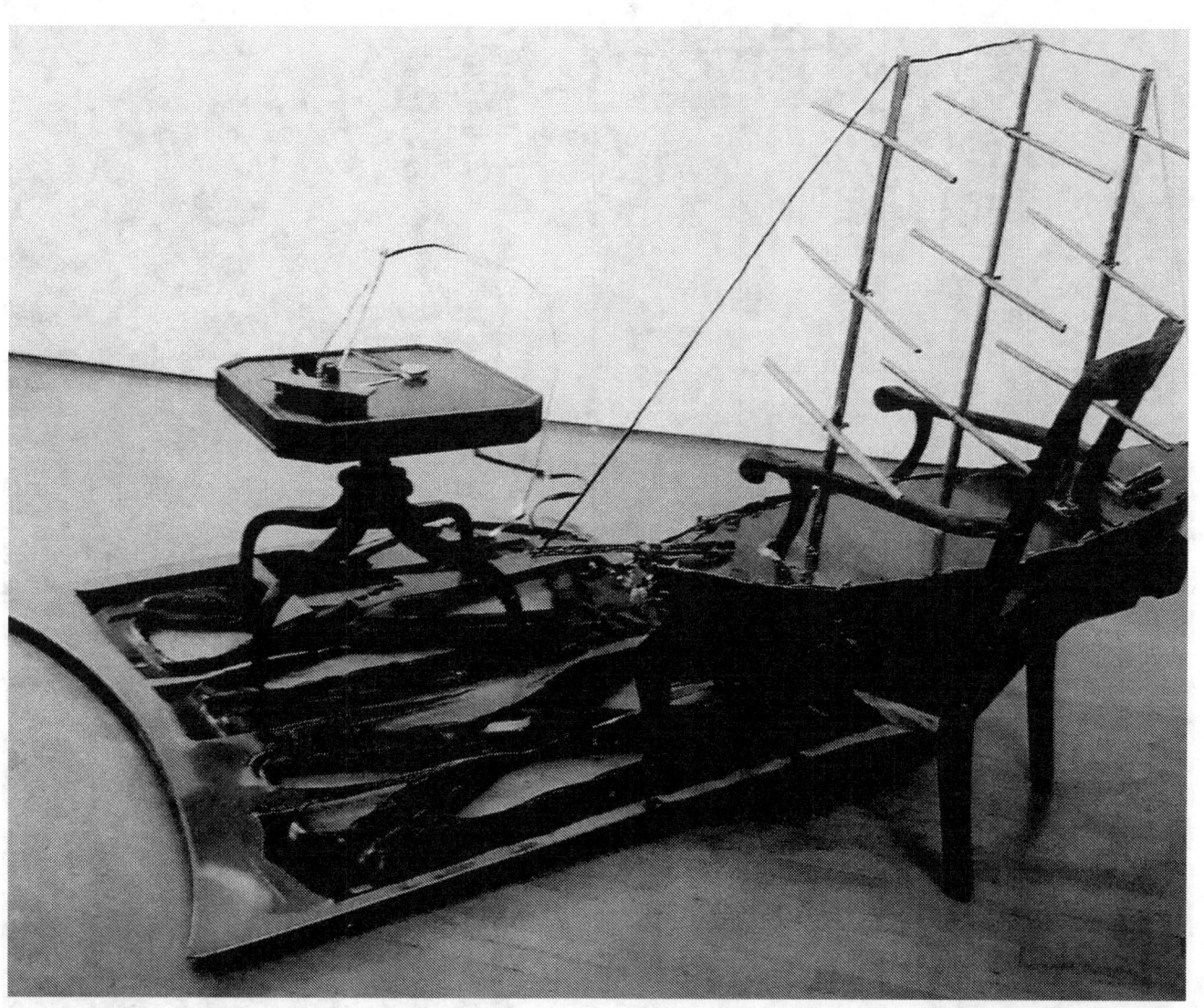

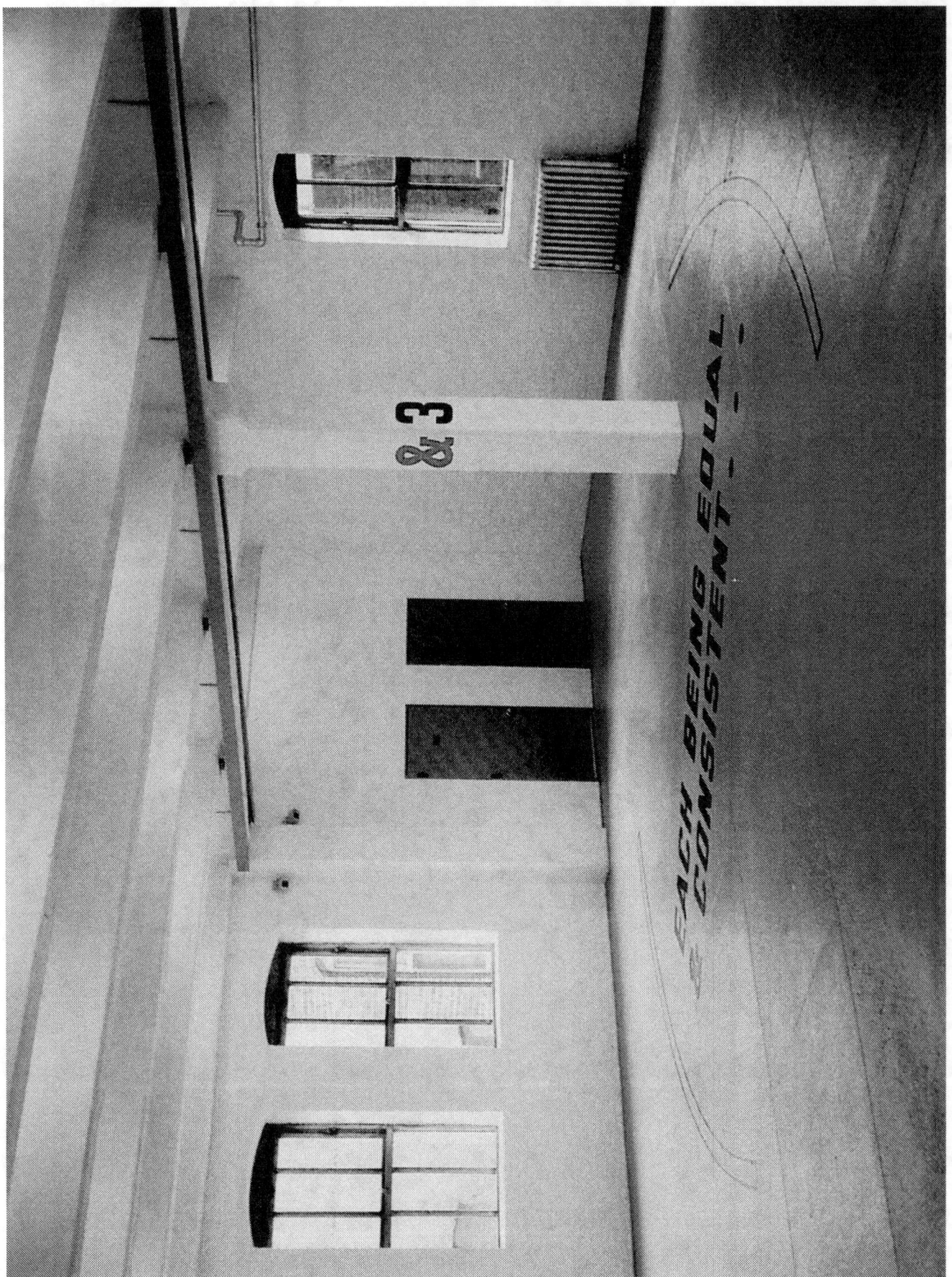

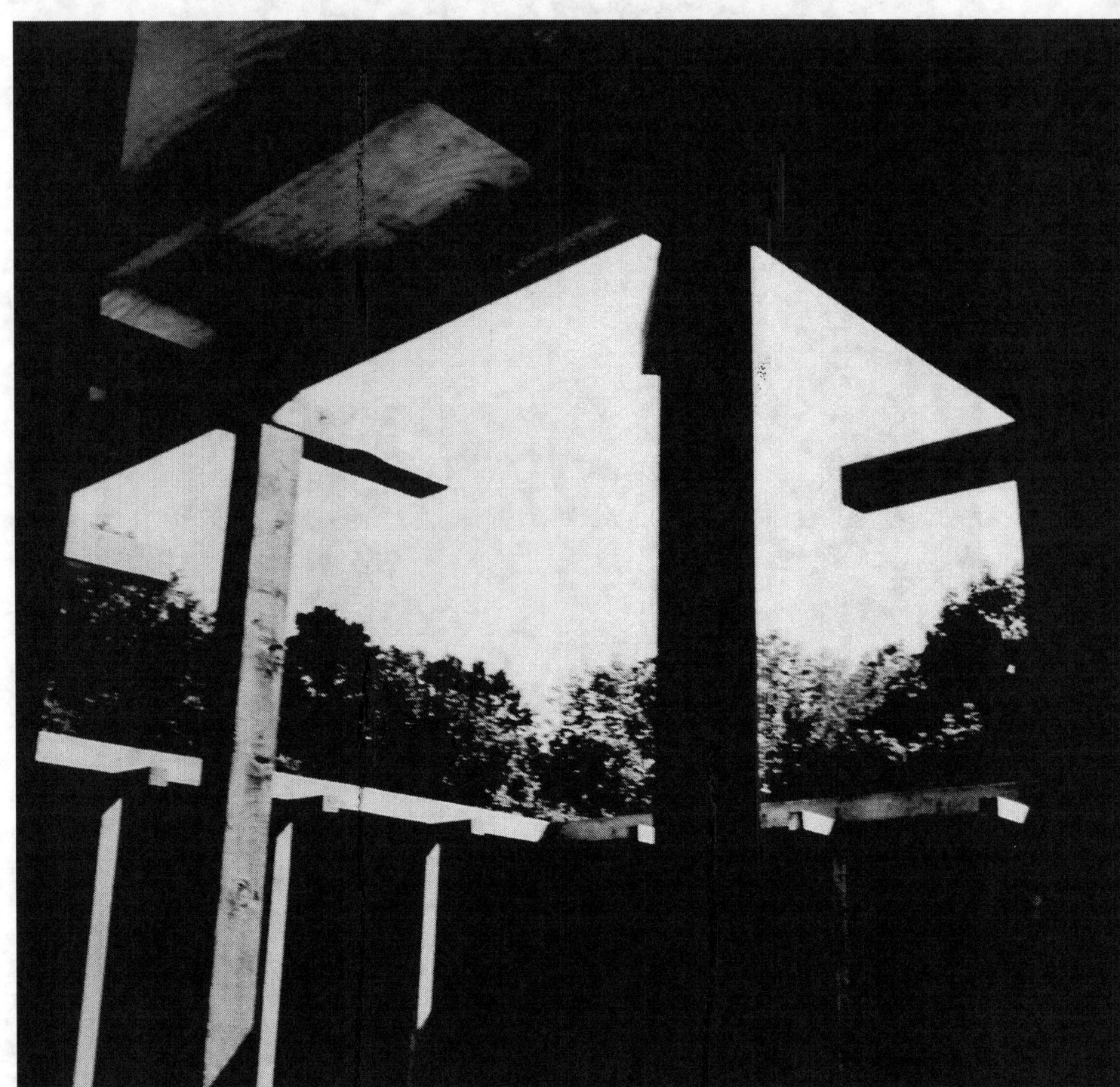

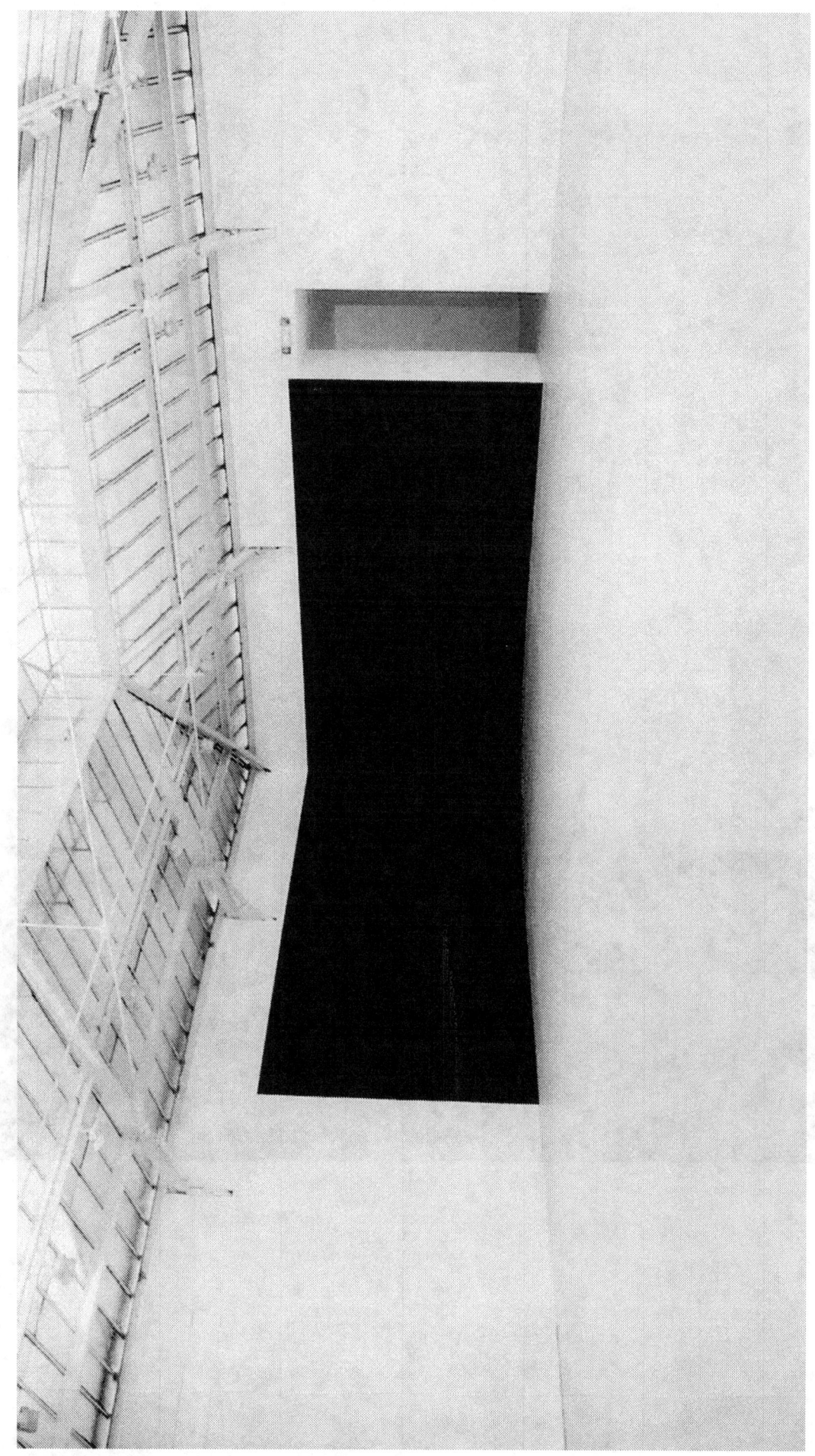

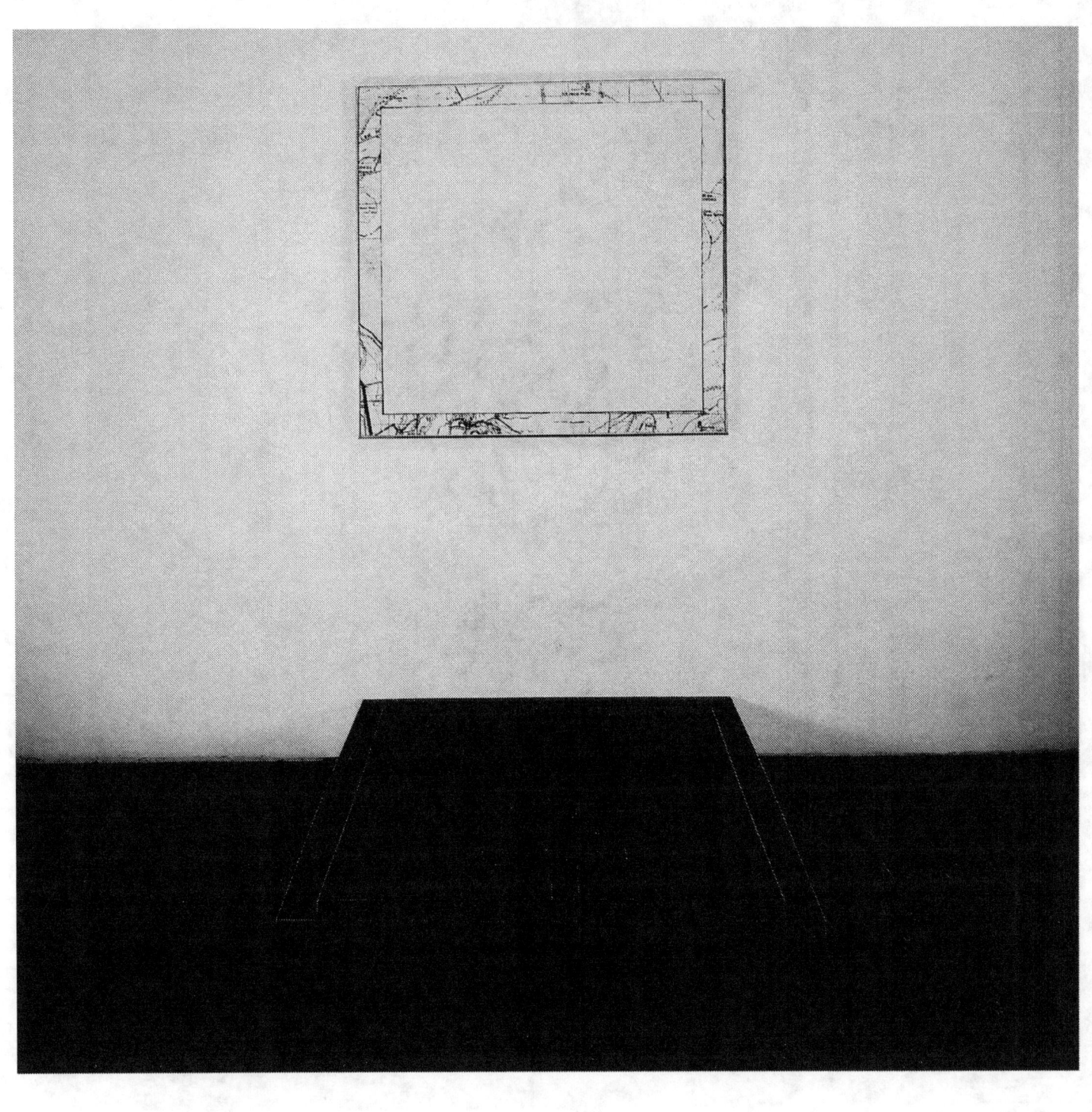

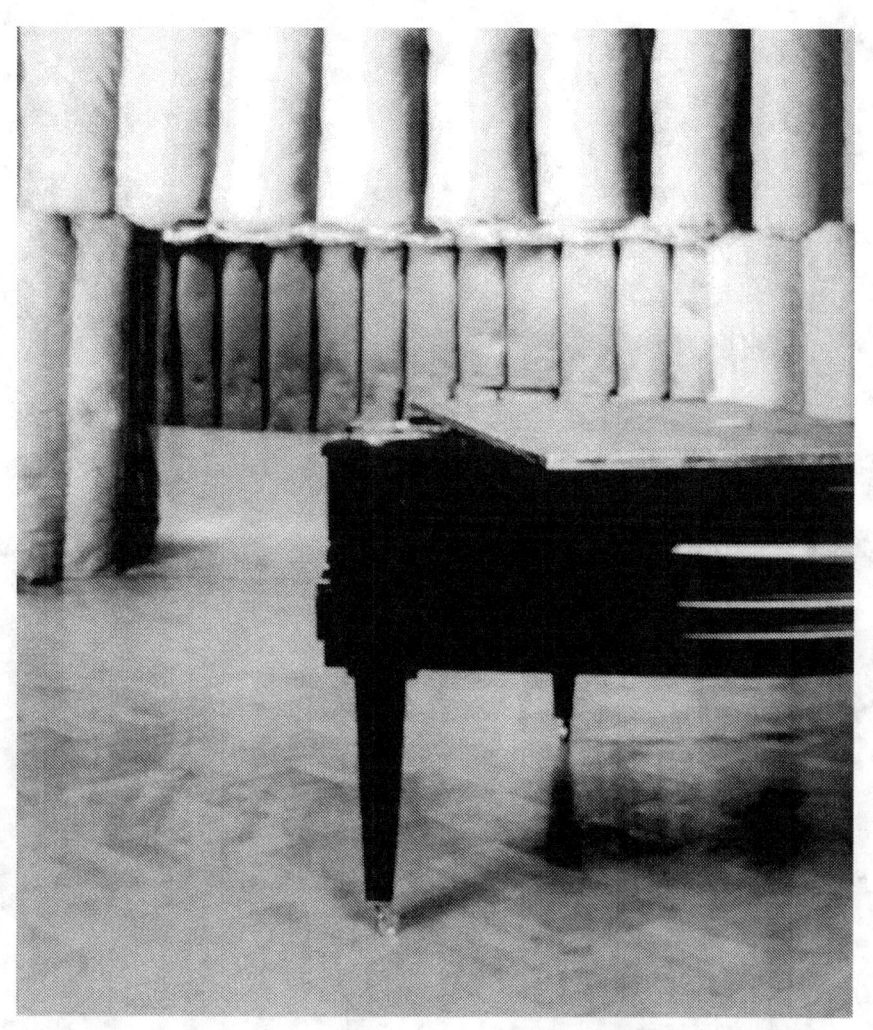

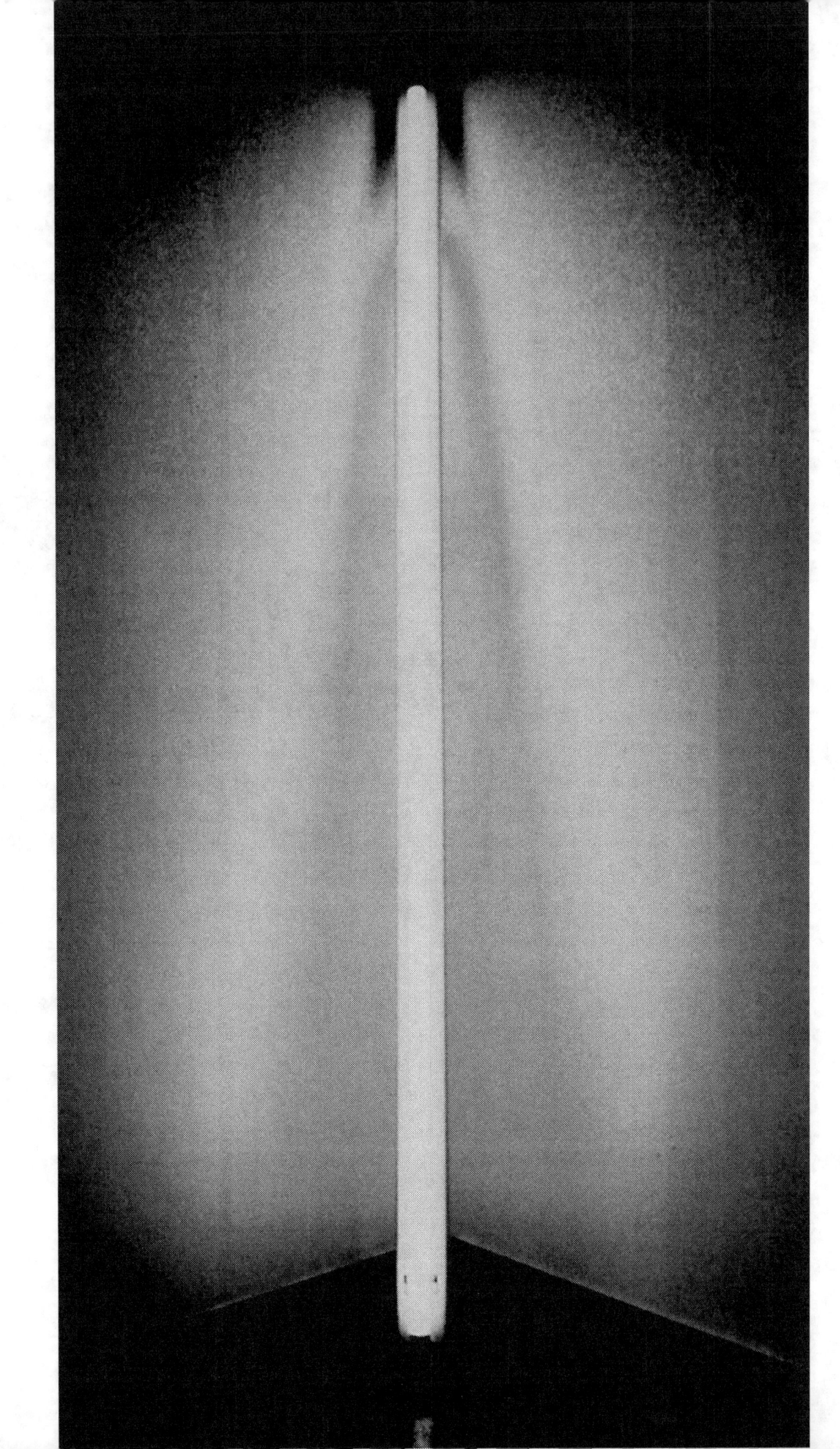

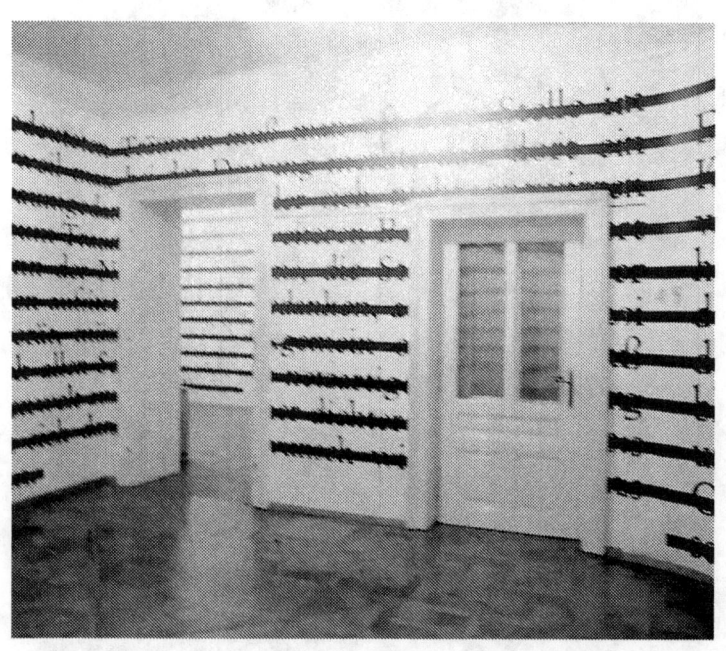

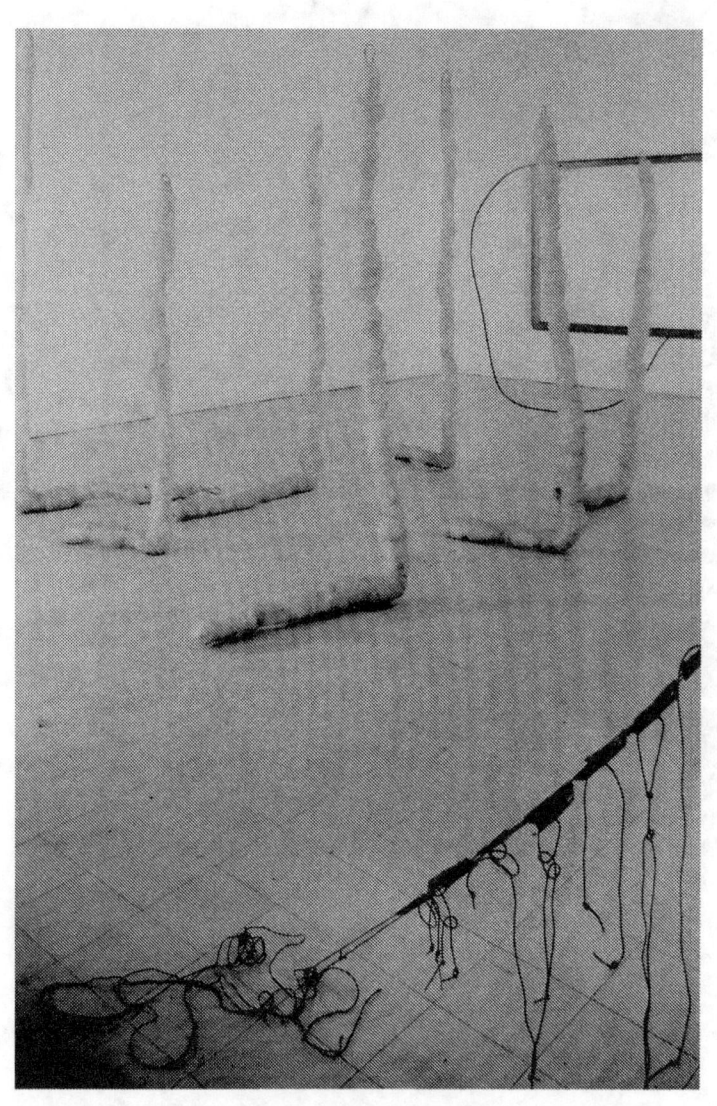

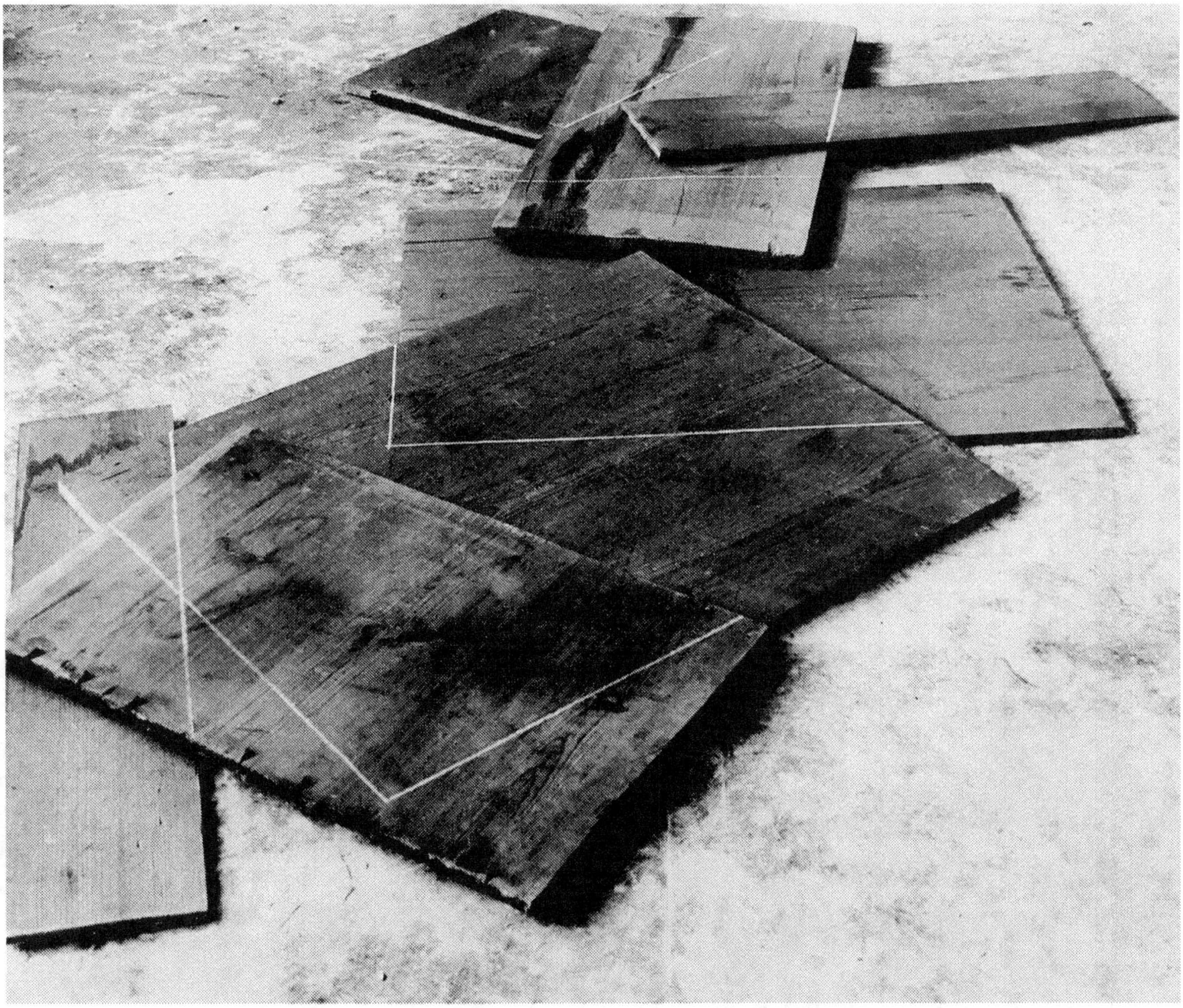

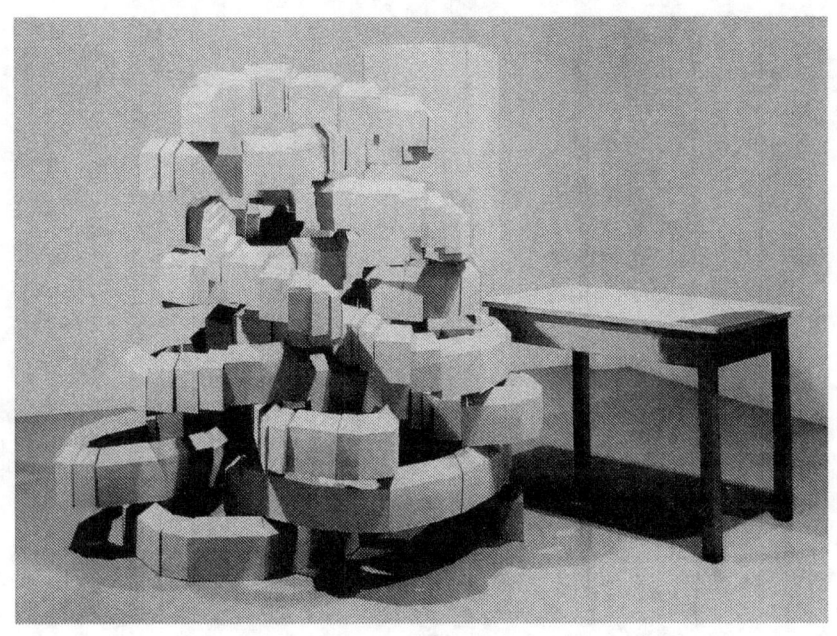

BIBLIOGRAPHY

H. Adams. "The Woodman", *Art and Artists*, 13, Apl, 1979

—. "Fabian Carlsson Gallery: London: Exhibit", *New Art Examiner*, 15, May, 1988

W.C. Agee. *Don Judd*, Whitney Museum of American Art, New York, NY, 1968

—. "Unit, Series, Site: A Judd Lexicon", *Art in America*, May, 1975

—. *The Sculpture of Donald Judd*, Art Museum of South Texas, Corpus Christi, TX, 1977

L. Aldrich. *Cool Art: 1967*, Museum of Contemporary Art, 1968

L. Alloway. "Site Inspection", *Artforum*, Oct, 1976

W. Andersen. *American Sculpture in Process, 1930/ 1970*, New York Graphics Society, Boston, MA, 1975

L. Anderson. "Mary Miss", *Artforum*, Nov, 1973

C. Andre. "Object v Phenomenon", *Sculpture Today*, The International Sculpture Center, Toronto, 1978

—. "An Interview with Carl Andre", Phyllis Tuchman, *Artforum*, 8, 10, June, 1970

M. Archer. *Art Since 1960*, Thames & Hudson, London, 1997

C. Arscott, ed. *On Installation*, Oxford, 2002

D. Ashton. *American Art Since 1945*, Thames & Hudson, London, 1982

—. *Modern American Sculpture*, Abrams, New York, NY, 1968

—. *About Rothko*, Oxford University Press, New York, NY, 1983

A. Aycock. "Work", "Maze", 1975, in Sondheim, 1977

K. Baker. "Andre in Retrospect", *Art in America*, Apl, 1980a

—. "Reckoning with Notation: The Drawings of Pollock, Newman, and Louis", *Artforum*, 18, 10, Summer, 1980b

—. *Minimalism: Art of Circumstance*, Abbeville, New York, NY, 1988

S. Bann & W. Allen, eds. *Interpreting Contemporary Art*, Reaktion Books, London, 1991

—. "Shrines, Gardens, Utopias", *New Literary History*, 24, 4, Autumn, 1994a

—. "The Map As Index of the Real: Land Art and the Authentication of Travel", *Imago Mundi*, 46, British Library, London, 1994b

S. Bann & W. Allen, eds. *Interpreting Contemporary Art*, Reaktion Books, London, 1991

—. "Shrines, Gardens, Utopias", *New Literary History*, 24, 4, Autumn, 1994

G. Baro. "Toward Speculation in Pure Form", *Art International*, Summer, 1967

—. "American Sculpture", *Studio International*, 172, 896, 1968

G. Battock, ed. *Idea Art*, Dutton, New York, NY, 1973

—. ed. *Minimal Art: A Critical Anthology*, Dutton, New York, NY, 1968

J. Beardsley. *Probing the Earth: Contemporary Land Projects*, Smithsonian Press, Washington, 1977

—. *Art in Public Spaces*, Partners For Liveable Places, Washington DC, 1981

—. *Earthworks and Beyond: Contemporary Art in the Landscape*, Abbeville Press, New York, NY, 1984/ 1998

M.R. Beaumont. "Romantic Sculpture", in Papadakis, 1988

A. Benjamin, ed. *Installation Art, Art & Design*, 30, 1993

M. Berger. *Labyrinths: Robert Morris, Minimalism, and the 1960s*, Harper & Row, New York, NY, 1989

K.C. Bloomert & C. Moore. *Body, Memory and Architecture*, New Haven, CT, 1977

M. Bochner. "Art in Process – Structures", *Arts Magazine*, 40, 9, 1966

—. "Primary Structures", *Arts*, June, 1966

—. "Systematic", *Arts Magazine*, 41, 1, Nov, 1966

—. "Serial Art Systems: Solipsism", *Arts Magazine*, 41, 8, Summer, 1967

D. Bourdon. "The Razed Sites of Carl Andre", *Artforum*, 5, 2, Oct, 1966

—. "Walter de Maria: The Singular Experience", *Art International*, Dec 20, 1968

—"The Mini-Conceptual Age", *Village Voice*, Oct 17, 1974

—. "You Can't Tell a Painter By His Colors", *Village Voice*, Mch 24, 1975

—. *Carl Andre: Sculpture, 1959-1977*, Jaap Rietman, New York, NY, 1978

J. Bradley. *Richard Long*, National Gallery of Canada, Ottawa, 1982

J. Brown *et al. Michael Heizer: Sculpture in Reverse*, see Heizer

J. Burnham. *Beyond Modern Sculpture*, Braziller, New York, NY, 1968

J. Butterfield. *The Art of Light and Space*, Abbeville Press, New York, NY, 1993

N. & E. Calas. *Icons and Image of the Sixties*, Dutton, New York, NY, 1971

J. Campbell. *The Power of Myth*, with B. Moyers, ed. B. Flowers, Doubleday, New York, NY, 1988

T. Castle. "Nancy Holt, Siteseer", *Art in America*, Mch, 1982

A. Causey. *Nature as Material: An Exhibition of Sculpture and Photographs Purchased For the Arts Council Collection,* Arts Council, 1980

—. "Space and Time in British Land Art", *Studio International*, 193, 98, Feb, 1977

—. "Environmental Sculptures", in Goldsworthy, *Hand to Earth*, 1990

G. Celant. "Introduction", *Arte Povera*, Praeger, New York, NY, 1969

—. *Conceptual Art, Arte Povera, Land Art*, Galeria Civica d'Arte Moderna, Turin, 1970

—. "Tony Cragg and Industrial Platonism", *Artforum*, 20, 3, Nov, 1981

—. *Dennis Oppenheim*, Edizioni Charta Srl, 1997

A. Chave: "Minimalism and the Rhetoric of Power", *Arts*, Jan, 1990

H.B. Chipp, ed. *Theories of Modern Art,* University Press of California, LA, CA, 1968

F. Colpitt. *Minimal Art: The Critical Perspective,* University of Washington Press, Seattle, WA, 1990

M. Compton & D. Sylvester. *Robert Morris*, Tate Gallery, London, 1971

L. Cooke. "Between Image and Object: The "New British Sculpture"", in Neff, 1987

H. Cooper, ed. *Eva Hesse*, Yale University Press, New Haven, CT, 1992

J. Coplans. "Serial Imagery", *Artforum*, 7, 2, Oct, 1968

—. *Donald Judd*, Pasadena Art Museum, CA, 1971

—. "Robert Smiithson", *Artforum,* Apl, 1974

P. Crowther. "Barnett Newman and the Sublime", *Oxford Art Journal*, 7, 2, 1984

—. ed. *The Contemporary Sublime, Art & Design,* 40, 1995

H. Davies *et al. Blurring the Boundaries: Installation Art 1969-1996*, Museum of Contemporary Art, San Diego, CA, 1997

R. Davies & T. Knipe, eds. *A Sense of Place: Sculpture in Landscape*, London, 1984

W. de Maria. "The Lightning Field", *Artforum,* 18, 8, April, 1980

P. de Monchaux *et al*, eds. *The Sculpture Show*, Arts Council of Great Britain, London, 1983

A. Dempsey. *Styles, Schools Movements*, Thames & Hudson, London, 2002

N. de Oliveira *et al. Installation Art*, Thames & Hudson, London, 1994

—. *et al. Installation Art in the New Millennium*, Thames & Hudson, London,

2003

E. Develing. *Carl Andre*, Gemeentenmeuseum, The Hague, 1969

—. & L. Lippard. *Minimal Art*, Stadtische Kunsthalle, Dusseldorf, 1969

P. Downes & T. Knipe, eds. *A Sense of Place*, Coelfrith Gallery, 1984

I. Dunlop. "Edvard Munch, Barnett Newman and Mark Rothko. The Search For the Sublime", *Arts Magazine*, 53, 6, Feb, 1979

G. Evans. "Sculpture and Reality", *Studio International*, 177, 908, February, 1969

D. Factor. "Los Angeles", *Artforum*, 4, 9, May, 1966

J. Fineberg: "Robert Morris Looking Back", *Arts Magazine*, 55, 1, 1980

A. Fisher & G. Gerster. *The Art of the Maze*, Weidenfeld & Nicholson, London, 1990

S. Foley. *Unitary Forms: Minimal Structures by Carl Andre, Donald Judd, John McCracken, Tony Smith*, Museum of Modern Art, San Francisco, CA, 1970

M. Fried. "New York Letter", *Art International*, 8, 3, Apl, 1964

—. *Three American Painters: Kenneth Noland, Jules Olitski, Frank Stella*, Fogg Art Museum, Harvard University, Cambridge, MA, 1965

—. "Shape as Form: Frank Stella's New Paintings", *Artforum*, 5, 3, Nov, 1966

—. "Art and Objecthood", *Artforum*, 5, Summer, 1967

—. *Morris Louis*, Abrams, New York, NY, 1970

M. Friedman. "Robert Morris: Polemics and Cubes", *Art International*, 10, 10, Dec, 1966

—. *14 Sculptors*, Walker Art Center, Minneapolis, MN, 1969

E. Fry. *Alice Aycock*, University of South Florida Art Galleries, Tampa, FL, 1981

—. *et al. Robert Morris*, Museum of Contemporary Art, Chicago, IL, 1986

H. Fulton. *Hamish Fulton: Selected Walks, 1969-89*, Albright-Knox Art Gallery, Buffalo, New York, NY, 1990

E. Gillen, ed. *German Art From Beckmann To Richter*, Dumont Buchverlag, Cologne, 1997

J. Giovannini. *Mary Miss*, Architectural Association, London, 1987

T. Godfrey. *Conceptual Art*, Phaidon, London, 1998

R. Goldberg. *Performance: Live Art Since the 60s*, Thames & Hudson, London, 1998

A. Goldsworthy. *Andy Goldsworthy*, Viking, London, 1990

—. *Hand to Earth: Andy Goldsworthy, Sculpture, 1976-1990*, Henry Moore Centre for Sculpture, Leeds, Yorkshire, 1990

—. *Stone*, Viking, London, 1994

—. *Wood*, Viking, London, 1996

—. *Sheepfolds*, Michael Hue-Williams Gallery, London, 1996

—. *Andy Goldsworthy: A Collaboration With Nature*, Abrams, New York, NY, 1996

—. *Arch*, with D. Craig, Thames & Hudson, London, 1999

—. *Wall*, intr. K. Baker, Thames & Hudson, London, 2000

—. *Time*, Thames & Hudson, London, 2000

—. *Passage*, Thames & Hudson, London, 2004

—. *Encosure*, Thames & Hudson, London, 2007

M. Gooding & W. Furlong. *Song of the Earth*, Thames and Hudson, London, 2002

C. Greenberg. *Art and Culture*, Beacon Press, Boston, MA, 1961

H. Gresty & D. Reason. *Bare: Alison Wilding: Sculptures, 1982-1993*, Newlyn Art Gallery, Cornwall, 1993

A. Haden-Guest. "The King of Wrap", *The Sunday Times Magazine*, January, 1994

A.M. Hammacher. *The Evolution of Modern Sculpture: Tradition and Innovation*, Abrams, New York, NY, 1969

C. Harrison. "Sculpture's Recent Past", in Neff, 1987

B. Haskell. *Donald Judd*, Whitney Museum of American Art, New York, NY, 1988

M. Heizer *et al*. "Discussion", *Avalanche*, 1, Autumn, 1970

—. *Sculpture in Reverse*, Museum of Contemporary Art, LA, CA, 1984

A. Henri. *Environments and Happenings*, Thames & Hudson, London, 1974

—. *Total Art*, Praeger, New York, NY, 1974

C. Henry. "Lumps of the Landscape", *The World of Interiors*, Oct, 1987

A. Hess. "Technology Exposed", *Landscape Architecture*, May, 1992

Galerie Max Hetzler. *Carl Andre, Gunther Forg, Hubert Kiecol, Richard Long, Meuser, Reinhard Mucha, Bruce Nauman and Ulrich Ruckreim*, Cologne, 1985

G. Hilty. *Recent British Sculpture*, Arts Council, London, 1993

R. Hobbs. *Robert Smithson: Sculpture,* Cornell University Press, Ithaca, NY, 1981

N. Hodges ed. *Art and the Natural Environment, Art & Design,* 36, 1994

—. ed. *The Contemporary Sublime, Art & Design,* 40, 1995

N. Holt. "Amarillo Ramp", *Avalanche*, Fall, 1973

—. "Hydra's Head", *Arts Magazine,* Jan, 1975

—. "Sun Tunnels", *Artforum*, April, 1977

K. Honnef. *Concept Art*, Phaidon, Oxford, 1971

S. Hubbard, intr. *Sculpture At Goodwood: A Vision For 21st Century British Sculpture*, Sculpture At Goodwood, Sussex, 2002

R. Hughes. *The Shock of the New*, Thames & Hudson, London, 1991

—. *Nothing If Not Critical: Selected Essays on Art and Artists*, Collins Harvill, London, 1990

—. *American Visions: The Epic History of Art In America*, Knopf, New York, NY, 1997

E.H. Johnson, *Modern Art and the Object*, Harper & Row, New York, NY, 1976

—. ed. *American Artist on Art*, Harper & Row, New York, NY, 1982

B. Jones. "A New Wave in Sculpture: A survey of recent work by ten younger sculptors", *Artscribe*, 8, Sept, 1977

D. Judd. "Specific Objects", *Arts Yearbook*, 8, Art Digest, New York, NY, 1965

—. *Complete Writings, 1959-1975*, Nova Scotia College of Art and Design, Halifax, Canada, 1975

—. *Complete Writings, 1975-1986*, Van Abbemuseum, Netherlands, 1987

J. Kastner, ed. *Land and Environmental Art,* Phaidon, London, 1998

N. Kaye, ed. *Site-Specific Art, Performance, Place and Documentation*, London, 2000

S. Kemal & I. Gaskell, eds. *Landscape, natural beauty and the arts,* Cambridge University Press, Cambridge, 1993

Z. Kraus, ed. *From Nature to Art, From Art to Nature*, Venice Biennale, Milan, 1978

R. Krauss. *Passages in Modern Sculpture,* Thames & Hudson, London, 1977

—. "Sculpture in the Expanded Field", *October*, 8, Spring 1978

—. *et al. Robert Morris*, Abrams, New York, NY, 1994

D. Kuspit. "Sol LeWitt", *Art in America*, 63, 5, 1975

—. "Authoritarian Abstraction", *Journal of Aesthetics and Art Criticism*, 36, 1, Autumn, 1977

—. "Robert Smithson's Drunken Boat", *Arts Magazine*, Oct, 1981

—. "Aycock's Dream Houses", *Art in America*, Sept, 1985

—. "Donald Judd", *Artforum*, 23, 5, Feb, 1985

W. La Barre. *The Ghost Dance*, Allen & Unwin, London, 1972

I. Lamaitre. "Interview with Tony Cragg", *Artefactum*, 2, Dec, 1985

B. Laws. "Where Art and Nature Meet", *The Telegraph Weekly*, 12 Nov, 1988

D. Lee. "Opinion: Richard Long and Hamish Fulton", *Arts Review*, 26 July, 1991

—. "Serial Rights", *Art News*, 66, 8, Dec, 1967

A. Legg, ed. *Sol LeWitt*, Museum of Modern Art, New York, NY, 1978

P. Leider. "Literalism and Abstraction: Frank Stella's Retrospective at the Modern", *Artforum*, 8, Apl, 1970

—. "For Robert Smithson", *Art in America*, Nov, 1973

—. *Stella Since 1970*, Fort Worth Art Museum, Texas, TX, 1978

S. LeWitt. "Paragraphs on Conceptual Art", *Art Language*, May, 1969

—. *Sol LeWitt*, Gemeentemuseum, The Hague, 1970

L. Lippard. "New York Letter: April-June, 1965", *Art International*, 9, 6, 1965

—. "New York Letter: Recent Sculpture as Escape", *Art International*, Feb, 1966

—. *Ad Reinhardt*, Jewish Museum, New York, NY, 1966

—. "An Impure Situation", *Art International*, 20 May, 1966

—. "The Silent Art", *Art in America*, 55, 1, Jan-Feb, 1967

—. "Sol LeWitt: Non-Visual Structures", *Artforum*, Apl, 1967

—. "Tony Smith", *Art International*, Summer, 1967

— "Rebelliously Romantic?", *New York Times*, 4 June, 1967

—. "Escalataion in Washington", *Art International*, 12, 1, Jan, 1968

—. ed. *Surrealists on Art*, Prentice-Hall, Englewood Cliffs, NJ, 1970

—. *Tony Smith*, Thames & Hudson, London, 1972

—. *Grids*, Philadelphia Institute of Contemporary Art, PA, 1972

—. *Six Years: The Dematerialization of the Art Object from 1966 to 1972*, Praeger, New York, NY, 1973

—. *From the Center: feminist essays on women's art*, Dutton, New York, NY, 1976

—. *Eva Hesse*, New York University Press, New York, NY, 1976

—. "Complexities: Architectural Sculpture in Nature", *Art in America*, Feb, 1979

—. *Ad Reinhardt*, Abrams, New York, NY, 1981

C. Loeffler, ed. *Performance Anthology*, Contemporary Art Press, San Francisco, 1979

R. Long. *Richard Long: In Conversation*, Parts 1 & 2, MW Press, Noordwijk, Holland, 1985-86

—. *Richard Long: Walking in Circles*, Hayward Gallery/ Thames & Hudson, London, 1992

E. Lucie-Smith. *Art of the Seventies*, Phaidon, London, 1980

—. *Sculpture Since 1945*, Phaidon, London, 1987

—. *Art Today*, Phaidon, London, 1989

—. *Movements In Art Since 1945*, Thames & Hudson, London, 1995

N. Lynton. *David Nash: Sculpture, 1971-90*, Serpentine Gallery, 1990

J. van der Marck. *Wrapped Museum*, Museum of Contemporary Art, Chicago, IL, 1969

R. Martin. *The Sculpted Forest: Sculpture in the Forest of Dean*, Redcliff, Bristol, 1990

D. Mayall. *The Minimal Tradition*, Aldrich Museum of Contemporary Art, Ridgefield, CT, 1979

A. McPherson, "David Nash: interviewed by Allan McPherson", *Artscribe*, 12, June, 1978

K. McShine. *Primary Structures*, Jewish Museum, New York, NY, 1966

U. Meyer. *Conceptual Art*, Dutton, New York, NY, 1972

M. Miss. *Mary Miss: Interior Works*, Bell Gallery, University of Rhode Island, Autumn, 1981

J. Morland. *New Milestones: Sculpture, Community and the Land*, Common Ground, London, 1988

R. Morris. "Notes on Sculpture", *Artforum,* Feb, 1966, Oct, 1966, June, 1967, April, 1969

—. "Aligned with Nazca", *Artforum*, Oct, 1975

—. *Robert Morris: Mirror Works, 1961-1978*, Leo Castelli Gallery, New York, NY, 1979

—. *Continuous Project Altered Daily*, MIT Press, Cambridge, MA, 1993

S. Morris. "A Rhetoric of Silence: Redefinitions of Sculpture in the 1960s and 1970s", in S. Nairne, 1981

J. Morland. *New Milestones: Sculpture, Community and the Land*, Common Ground, London, 1988

G. Muller. "Michael Heizer", *Arts Magazine*, Dec, 1969

S. Nairne & N. Serota. *British Sculpture in the Twentieth Century*, Whitechapel Art Gallery, London, 1981

—. *State of the Art: Ideas & Images in the 1980s*, Chatto, London, 1987

D. Nash. *Fletched Over Ash*, AIR Gallery, 1978

—. "David Nash", *Aspects*, 10, Spring, 1980

—. *Stoves and Hearths*, Duke Street Gallery, London, 1982

T.A. Neff, ed. *A Quiet Revolution: British Sculpture Since 1965*, Thames & Hudson, London, 1987

B. Nemitz. *Trans Plant: Living Vegetation in Contemporary Art*, Hatje Cantz, 2000

C. Nemser. "An interview with Eva Hesse", *Artforum*, May, 1970

—. "My Memories of Eva Hesse", *Feminist Art Journal*, Winter, 1973

M. Newman. "New Sculpture in Britain", *Art in America*, September, 1982

R. Onoratio. *Mary Miss - Perimeters/ Pavilions/ Decoys*, Nassau County Museum, 1979

P. Osborne, ed. *Conceptual Art*, Phaidon, London, 2002

A.C. Papadakis, ed. *The New Romantics, Art & Design,* 4, 11/12, Academy Group, London, 1988

P. Patton. "Robert Morris and the Fire Next Time", *Art News,* 82, 10, Dec, 1983

J. Perreault. "A Minimal Future? Union-Made: Report on a Phenomenon", *Arts Magazine,* 41, March, 1967

J. Perrone. "Seeing Through Boxes", *Artforum*, 15, November, 1976

R. Pincus-Witten. "Sol LeWitt", *Artforum*, 11, 6, Feb, 1973

—. *Postminimalism*, Out of London, New York, NY, 1977

C. Ratcliff. "Robert Ryman's Double Positive", *Art News*, Mch, 1971

—. "Once More With Feeling", *Art News*, 71, 4, Summer, 1972

—. "Abstract Painting, Specific Spaces: Novros and Marden in Houston", *Art in America*, 63, 5, Nov, 1975

—. *In the Realm of the Monochrome*, Renaissance Society, University of Chicago, Chicago, IL, 1979

—. "The Compleat Smithson", *Art in America*, Jan, 1980

—. "Mostly Monochrome", *Art in America*, 69, 4, Apl, 1981

—. "Robert Ryman Making Distinctions", *Art in America*, June, 1986

B. Redhead. *The Inspiration of Landscape: Artists in National Parks*, Phaidon, Oxford, 1989

A. Reinhardt. *Art as Art: The Selected Writings of Ad Reinhardt*, University of California Press, Berkeley, CA, 1991

J. Reiss. *From Margin To Center: The Space of Installation*, Cambridge, MA, 2000

H. Risatti. "The Sculpture of Alice Aycock", *Woman's Art Journal*, Summer, 1985

J. Roberts. *Postmodernism, Politics and Art,* Manchester University Press, Manchester, 1990

C. Robins. "Object, Structure or Sculpture: Where Are We?", *Arts Magazine*, 40, 9, 1966

—. *The Pluralist Era: American Art, 1968-1981*, Harper & Row, New York, NY, 1984

P Rodaway. *Sensuous Geographies*, Routledge, London, 1994

A. Rorimer. *New Art in the 60s and 70s*, Thames & Hudson, London, 2001

B. Rose. "ABC Art", *Art in America*, 53, 5, Nov, 1965

—. *A New Aesthetic*, Washington Gallery of Modern Art, Washington, DC, 1967

—. *American Art Since 1900*, Thames & Hudson, London, 1967

—. *American Painting*, Skira/Rizzoli International, New York, NY, 1986

—. *Robert Morris*, Corcoran Gallery, Washington, DC, 1990

H. Rosenberg. *The De-Definition of Art*, Horizon Press, New York, NY, 1972

—. *Barnett Newman*, Abrams, New York, NY, 1978/1994

—. *The Tradition of the New*, Da Capo Press, New York, NY, 1994

R. Rosenblum. "Notes on Sol LeWitt", in Legg, 1978

—. *Modern Painting and the Northern Romantic Tradition*, Thames & Hudson, London, 1978

—. "Romanticism and Retrospective: An Interview with Robert Rosenblum", in A. Papadakis, 1988

S. Ross. "Gardens, earthworks, and environmental art", in Kemal, 1993

M. Roth. "Robert Smithson on Duchamp", *Artforum*, Oct, 1969

M. Rothko. *Mark Rothko, 1903-1970: A Retrospective*, Guggenheim, New York, NY, 1979

—. *Mark Rothko, 1903-1970*, Tate Gallery, London, 1987

M. Ryan, ed. *Gravity and Grace: The Changing Condition of Sculpture, 1965-1975*, Hayward Gallery, London, 1993

A. Saalfield. *Mary Miss*, Fogg Art Museum, 1980

I. Sandler. *American Art of the 1960s,* Harper & Row, New York, NY, 1988

—. *Art of the Postmodern Era: From the 1960s to the Early 1990s*, HarperCollins, London, 1997

D. Schaff. "British Art Now, at the Guggenheim and Beyond", *Art International*, March, 1980

P. Schjeldahl. *Art in Our Time: The Saatchi Collection*, Lund Humphries, London, 1984

E. Shanes. *Constantin Brancusi*, Abbeville, New York, NY, 1989

G. Shapiro. *Earthworks: Robert Smithson and After After Babel*, University of California Press, 1995

H. Smagula. *Currents: Contemporary Directions in the Visual Arts*, Prentice-Hall, Englewood Cliffs, NJ, 1983

B. Smith. *Donald Judd*, National Gallery of Canada, Ottawa, 1975

D. Smith. *Sculpture and Drawings*, ed. Jorn Merkert, Prestel-Verlag, Munich, 1986

R. Smith. "Sol LeWitt", *Artforum*, Jan, 1975

—. "Review", *Artforum*, Dec, 1975

—. "De Maria: Elements", *Art in America*, May, 1978

R. Smithson. "Entropy and the New Monuments", *Artforum*, 4, 10, June, 1966

—. "A Museum of Language in the Vicinity of Art", *Art International*, 12, 3, Mch, 1968

—. *The Writings of Robert Smithson*, ed. N. Holt, New York University Press, New York, NY, 1979

—. *Robert Smithson*, ed. J. Flam, University of California Press, Berkeley, CA, 1996

T. Sokolowski *et al. Robert Morris*, New York University, 1989

A, Sondheim, ed. *Post-Movement Art in America*, Dutton, New York, NY, 1977

A. Sonfist. *Alan Sonfist*, Neuberger Museum, New York, NY, 1978

—. ed. *Art in the Land: A Critical Anthology of Environmental Art*, Dutton, New York, NY, 1983

W. Spies. *The Running Fence Project, Christo*, Abrams, New York, NY, 1977

K. Stiles & P. Selz, eds. *Theories & Documents of Contemporary Art: A Sourcebook of Artists' Writings*, University of California Press, Berkeley, CA, 1996

W.J. Strachan. *Open Air Sculpture in Britain*, Zwemmer, London, 1984

A. Staniszewski. *The Power of Display: A History of Exhbitions At the Museum of Modern Art*, MIT Cambridge, MA, 1999

E. Suderburg, ed. *Space, Site, Intervention*, University of Minnesota Press, 2000

D. Sylvester. *About Modern Art*, Chatto & Windus, London, 1996

C. Tomkins. "Profiles", *New Yorker*, Sept, 1984

—. *Post- to Neo-: The Art World of the 1980s*, Penguin, London, 1989

E. Tsai. *Robert Smithson Unearthed*, Columbia University Press, New York, NY, 1991

M. Tuchman. *American Sculpture of the Sixties*, Los Angeles County Museum of Art, LA, CA, 1967

P. Tuchman. "Minimalism and Critical Response", *Artforum*, 15, 9, May, 1977

—. "Background of a Minimalist: Carl Andre", *Artforum*, Mch, 1978

M. Tucker. *Robert Morris*, New York, NY, 1970

J. Turrell. *Mapping Spaces*, Peter Blum, New York, NY, 1987.

—. interview, in B. Oakes, 1995

G. de Vries, ed. *On Art: Artists' Writings on the Changed Notion of Art After, 1965*, Cologne, 1974

A.M. Wagner. *Three Artists (Three Women): Modernism and the Art of Hesse, Krasner and O'Keeffe*, University of California Press, Berkeley, CA, 1996

D. Waldman. *Carl Andre*, Guggenheim, New York, NY, 1970

—. "Holding the Floor", *Art News*, Oct, 1970

—. *Mark Rothko*, Thames & Hudson, London, 1978

J. Walker. *Art and Artists on Screen*, Manchester University Press, Manchester, 1993

—. *Art & Outrage: Provocation, Controversy and the Visual Arts*, Pluto Press, London, 1999

—. *Art and Celebrity*, Pluto Press, London, 2003

L. Weiner. *Lawrence Weiner, Works,* Anatol AV und Filmproduktion Hamburg, 1977

L. Weintraub. *The Maximal Implications of the Minimalist Line*, Edith C. Blum Art Institute, New York, NY, 1985

Welsh Sculpture Trust. *Sculpture in a Country Park*, Welsh Sculpture Trust, 1983

D. Wheeler. *Art Since Mid-Century: 1945 to the Present*, Thames & Hudson, London, 1991

O. Wick *et al*. *James Turrell*, Turske & Turske Gallery, Zurich, 1990

A. Wilding. *Inmmersion/ Exposure,* Tate Gallery, Liverpool, 1991

—. *Alison Wilding*, with M. Tooby, Tate Gallery, St Ives, 1994

R. Williams. *After Modern Sculpture: Art in the United States and Europe 1965-70,* Mancheser University Press, 2000

M. Winton, "Sculptures That Blow Away", *Ark*, Spring, 1970

W. Wilson. "Dan Flavin: Fiat Lux", *Art News*, Jan, 1970

C. van Winkel. "The Crooked Path, Patterns of Kinetic Energy", *Parkett*, 33, 1992

R. Wittkower. *Sculpture: Process and Principles*, Harper & Row, New York, NY, 1977

G. Woods *et al*, eds. *Art Without Boundaries*, Thames & Hudson, London, 1972

A. Sargent Wooster. "Sol LeWitt's Expanding Grid", *Art in America*, 68, 5, May, 1980

THE ART OF ANDY GOLDSWORTHY

COMPLETE WORKS: SPECIAL EDITION
(PAPERBACK and HARDBACK)

by William Malpas

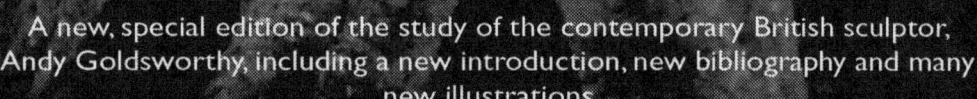

A new, special edition of the study of the contemporary British sculptor, Andy Goldsworthy, including a new introduction, new bibliography and many new illustrations.

This is the most comprehensive, up-to-date, well-researched and in-depth account of Goldsworthy's art available anywhere.

Andy Goldsworthy makes land art. His sculpture is a sensitive, intuitive response to nature, light, time, growth, the seasons and the earth. Goldsworthy's environmental art is becoming ever more popular: 1993's art book *Stone* was a bestseller; the press raved about Goldsworthy taking over a number of London West End art galleries in 1994; during 1995 Goldsworthy designed a set of Royal Mail stamps and had a show at the British Museum. Malpas surveys all of Goldsworthy's art, and analyzes his relation with other land artists such as Robert Smithson, Walter de Maria, Richard Long and David Nash, and his place in the contemporary British art scene.

The Art of Andy Goldsworthy discusses all of Goldsworthy's important and recent exhibitions and books, including the *Sheepfolds* project; the TV documentaries; *Wood* (1996); the New York Holocaust memorial (2003); and Goldsworthy's collaboration on a dance performance.

Illustrations: 70 b/w, I colour. 330 pages. New, special, 2nd edition.
Publisher: Crescent Moon Publishing. Distributor: Gardners Books.

ISBN 1-86171-059-3 (9781861710598) (Paperback) £25.00 / $44.00

ISBN 1-86171-080-1 (9781861710802) (Hardback) £60.00 / $105.00

ANDY GOLDSWORTHY IN CLOSE-UP

SPECIAL EDITION (HARDBACK and PAPERBACK)

by William Malpas

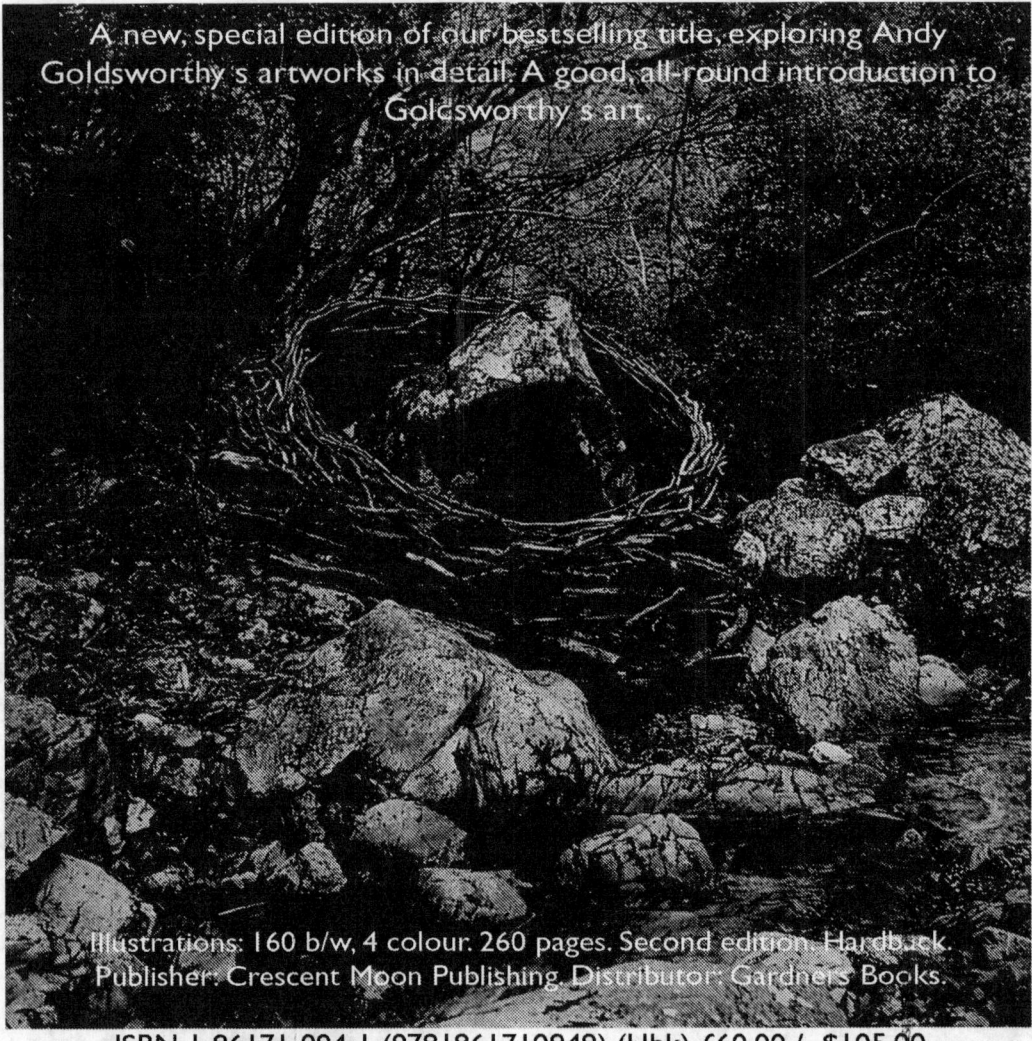

A new, special edition of our bestselling title, exploring Andy Goldsworthy's artworks in detail. A good, all-round introduction to Goldsworthy's art.

Illustrations: 160 b/w, 4 colour. 260 pages. Second edition. Hardback. Publisher: Crescent Moon Publishing. Distributor: Gardners Books.

ISBN 1-86171-094-1 (9781861710949) (Hbk) £60.00 / $105.00

ISBN 1-86171-091-7 (9781861710919) (Pbk) £25.00 / $44.00

Available from bookstores. amazon.com, play.com, tesco.com, and other websites.
In the United States from Baker & Taylor, (800) 7753760 or (800) 7751100 or (908) 5417062. electser@btol.com or btinfo@btol.com.

ANDY GOLDSWORTHY

TOUCHING NATURE:
SPECIAL EDITION

(PAPERBACK and HARDBACK)

by William Malpas

A new, special and updated edition of our bestselling title, providing
an excellent general introduction to the art of Andy Goldsworthy.

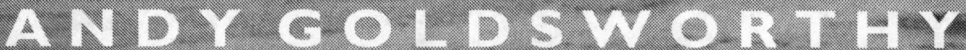

Illustrations: 75 b/w, 2 colour. 354 pages. Third edition. Paperback.

Publisher: Crescent Moon Publishing. Distributor: Gardners Books.

ISBN 1-86171-056-9 (9781861717) (Paperback) £25.00 / $44.00

ISBN 1-86171-087-9 (9781861710871) (Hardback) £60.00 / $105.00

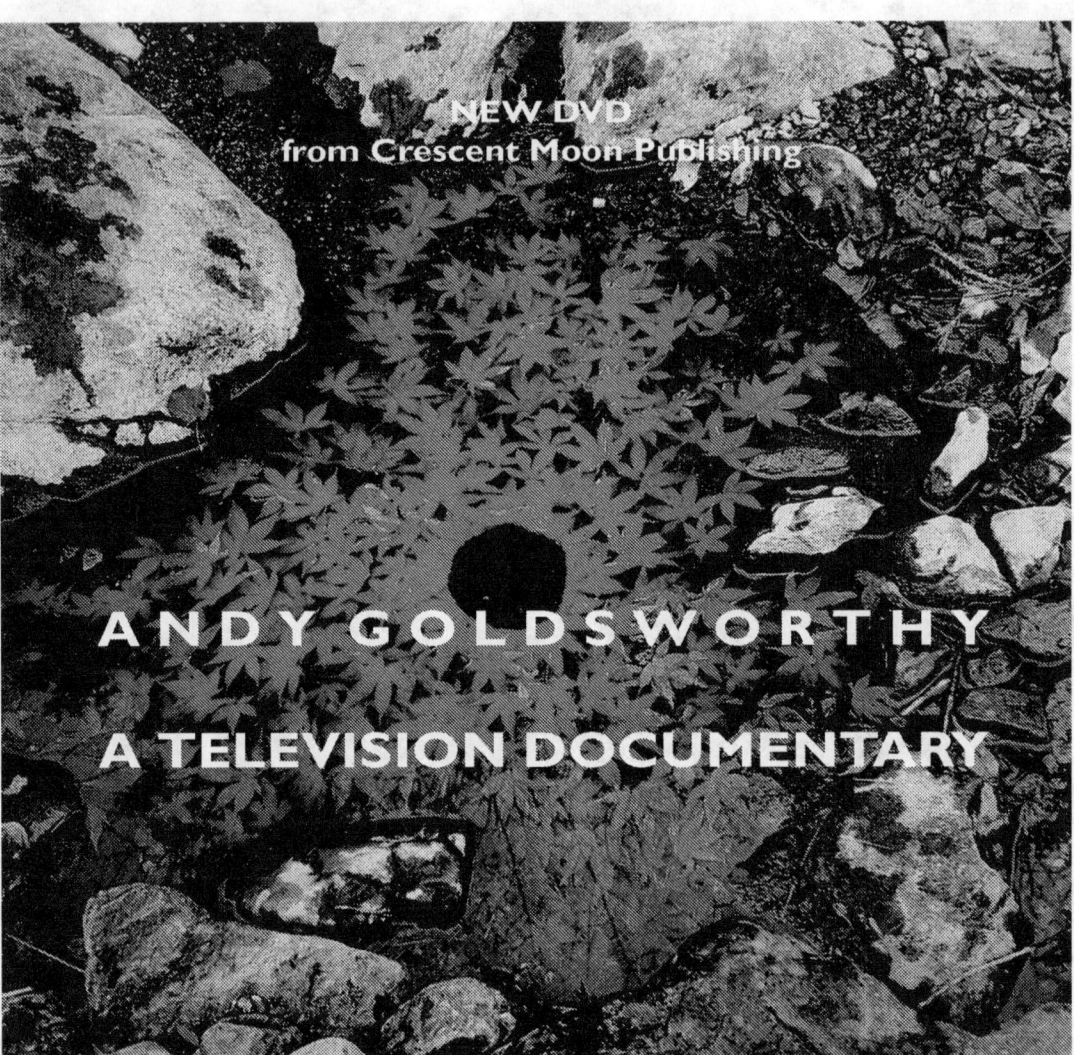

NEW DVD
from Crescent Moon Publishing

ANDY GOLDSWORTHY

A TELEVISION DOCUMENTARY

Andy Goldsworthy makes land art. His sculpture is a sensitive, intuitive response to nature, light, time, growth, the seasons and the earth. Goldsworthy's environmental art is becoming ever more popular: his art books are bestsellers; he has exhibited around the world; important and recent exhibitions include the Sheepfolds project; the Washington installation (2005); Passage (2004); the New York Holocaust memorial (2003); and a collaboration on a dance performance.

This video documentary surveys every aspect of Andy Goldsworthy's art, and all of his major works. It also discusses his relation with other land artists such as Robert Smithson, Walter de Maria, Richard Long and David Nash, and his place in the contemporary art scene in the UK.

This is the only TV documentary of its kind available on DVD and video.

EXTRAS

Resources: further reading; complete bibliography of Andy Goldsworthy, and life and work (on DVD-ROM); and weblinks.
Photo library of land artworks.
Extra footage.

55 minutes. PAL and NTSC. Colour. DVD. Multi-region. VHS video.
Stereo. E (Exempt from classification)

LAND ART

A COMPLETE GUIDE TO LANDSCAPE, ENVIRONMENTAL, EARTHWORKS, NATURE, SCULPTURE AND INSTALLATION ART

by William Malpas

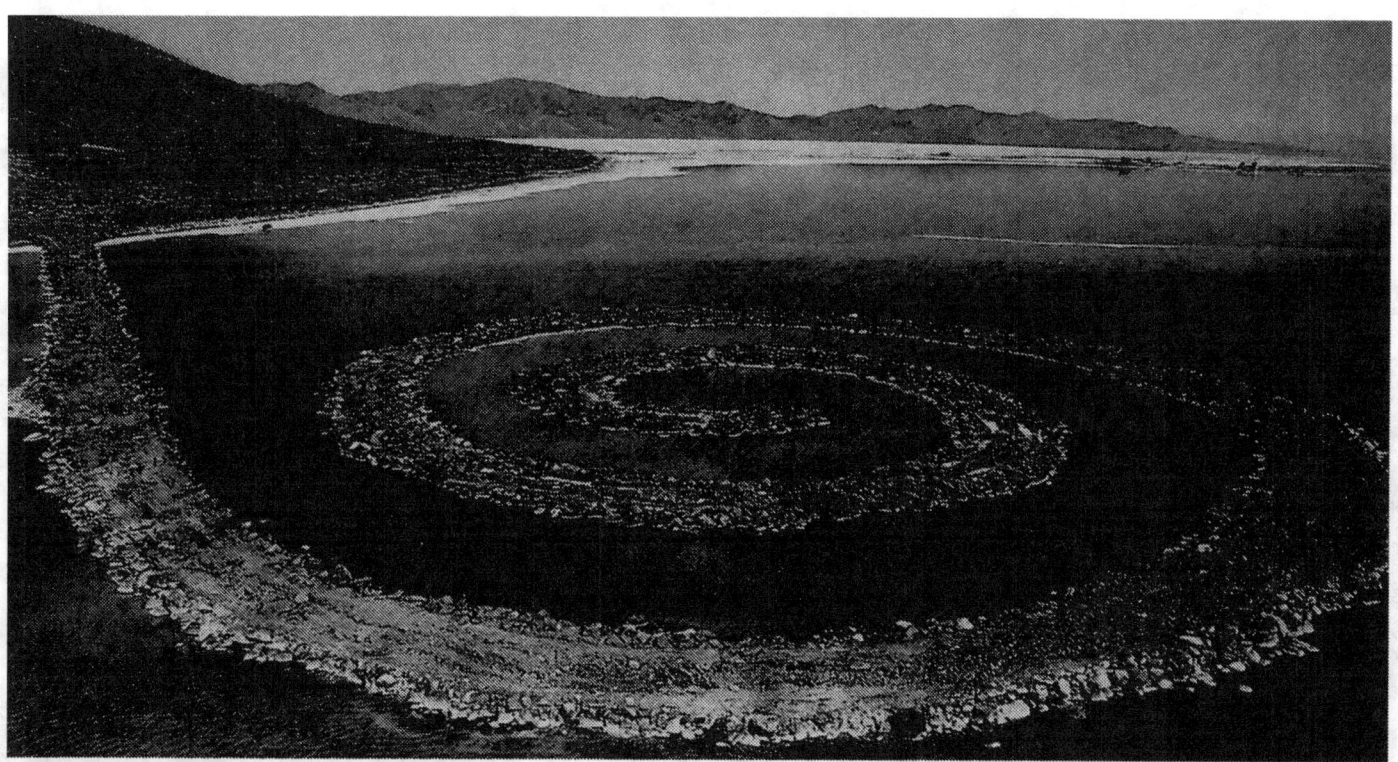

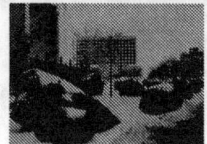 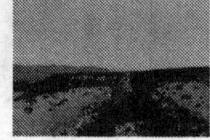 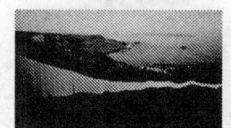 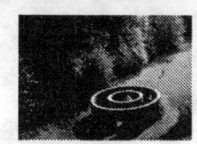 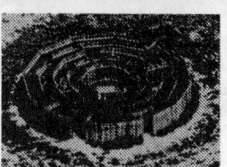

A new, special edition of our popular book on land art.
Chapters on land artists such as Robert Smithson, Walter de Maria, Christo,
Michael Heizer, Richard Long and Andy Goldsworthy.

Illustrations: 35 b/w, 2 colour. 314 pages. First edition. Paperback.

Publisher: Crescent Moon Publishing. Distributor: Gardners Books.

ISBN 1-86171-062-3 (9781861710628) £25.00 / $44.00

LAND ART IN CLOSE-UP

SPECIAL EDITION (PAPERBACK)

by William Malpas

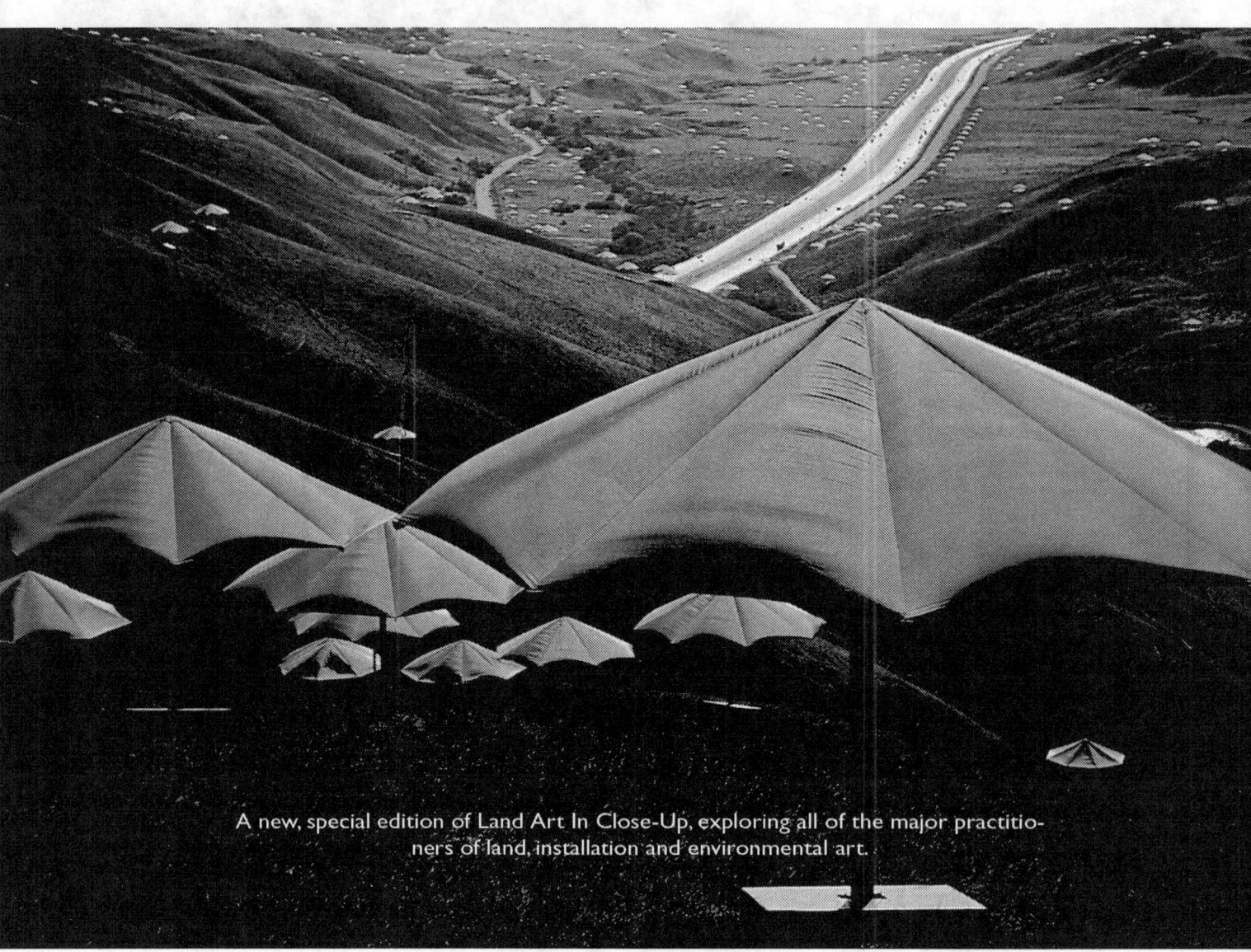

A new, special edition of Land Art In Close-Up, exploring all of the major practitioners of land, installation and environmental art.

Illustrations: 161 b/w, 2 colour. 248 pages. Second edition. Paperback.

Publisher: Crescent Moon Publishing. Distributor: Gardners Books.

ISBN 1-86171-092-5 (9781861710925) £25.00 / $44.00

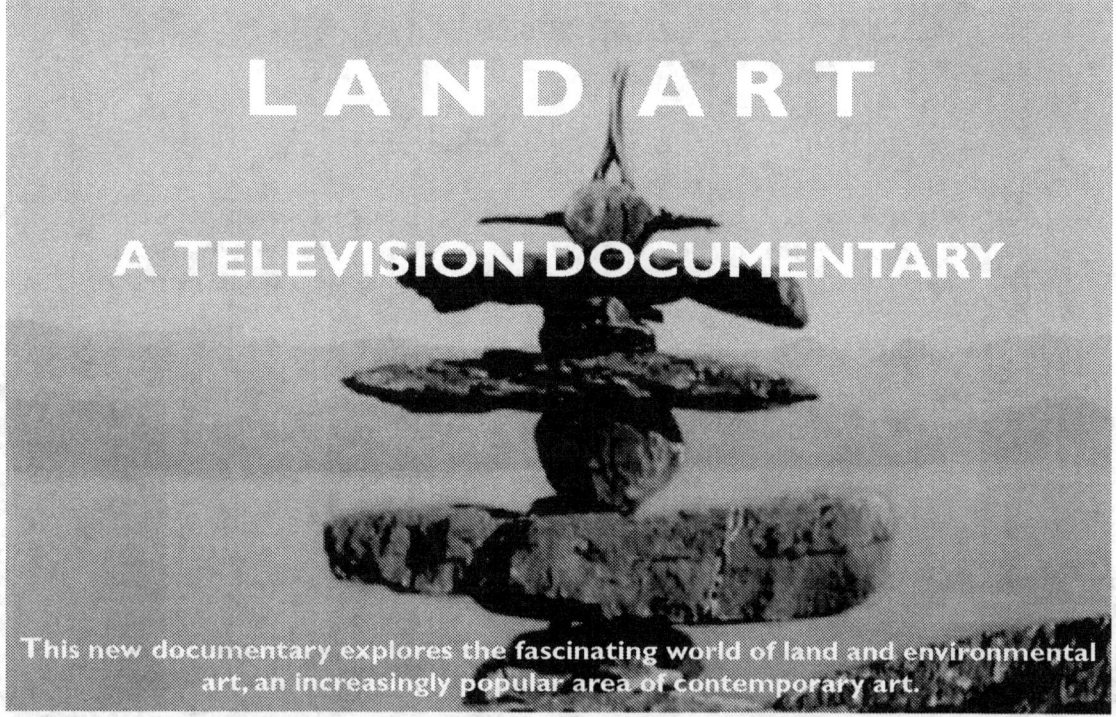

THE ART OF RICHARD LONG

COMPLETE WORKS : SPECIAL EDITION
(HARDBACK and PAPERBACK)

by William Malpas

A new study of the British artist Richard Long, an important contemporary international artist. The most detailed, in-depth exploration of Richard Long's art currently available.

Illustrations: 48 b/w, 2 colour. 439 pages.
First edition. Hardback and paperback editions.

Publisher: Crescent Moon Publishing. Distributor: Gardners Books.

ISBN 1-86171-079-8 (9781861710796) (Hardback) £60.00 / $105.00

ISBN 1-86171-081-X (9781861710819) (Paperback) £25.00 / $44.00

MINIMAL ART AND ARTISTS

FROM THE 1960S AND AFTER

by Laura Garrard

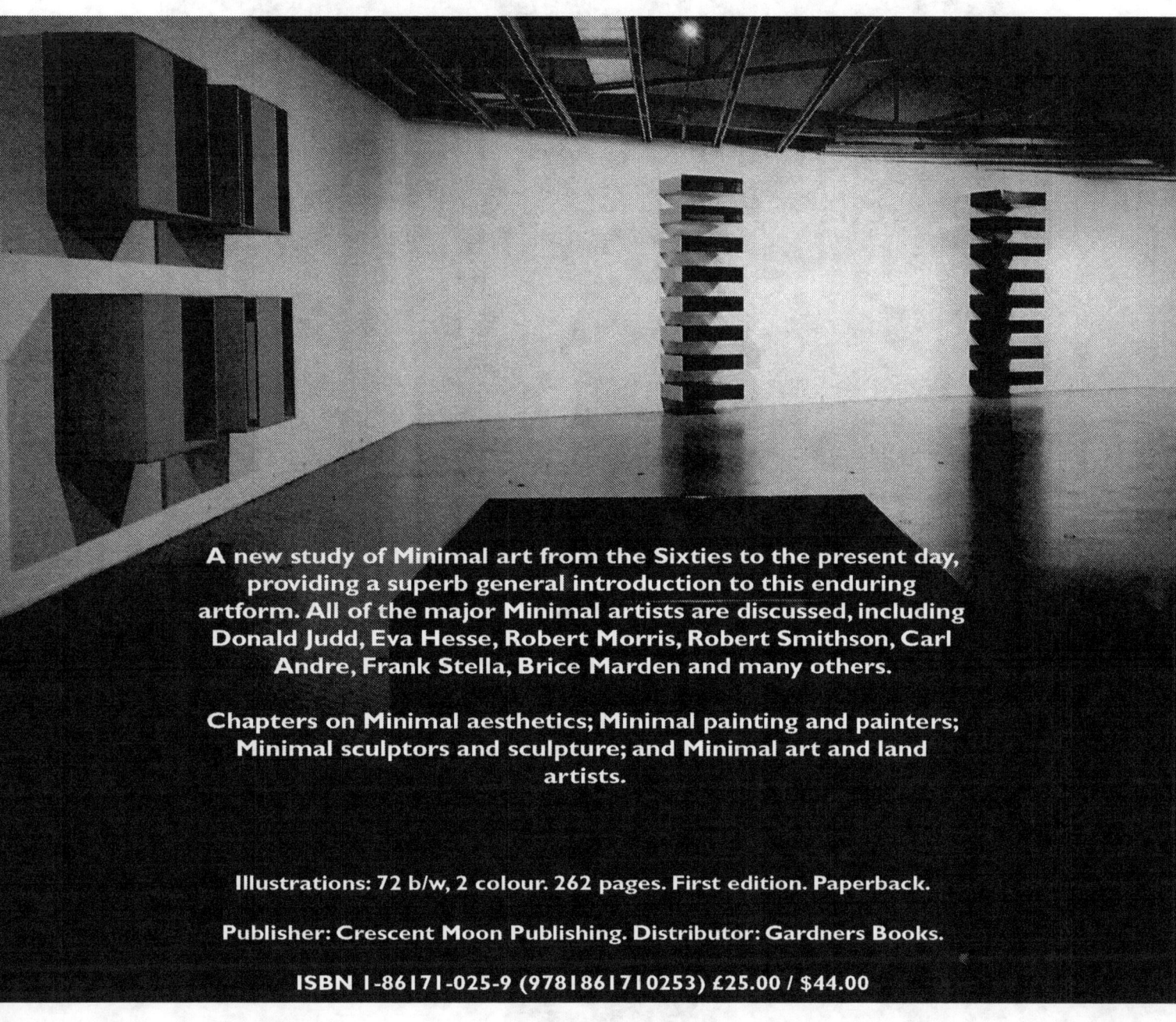

A new study of Minimal art from the Sixties to the present day, providing a superb general introduction to this enduring artform. All of the major Minimal artists are discussed, including Donald Judd, Eva Hesse, Robert Morris, Robert Smithson, Carl Andre, Frank Stella, Brice Marden and many others.

Chapters on Minimal aesthetics; Minimal painting and painters; Minimal sculptors and sculpture; and Minimal art and land artists.

Illustrations: 72 b/w, 2 colour. 262 pages. First edition. Paperback.

Publisher: Crescent Moon Publishing. Distributor: Gardners Books.

ISBN 1-86171-025-9 (9781861710253) £25.00 / $44.00

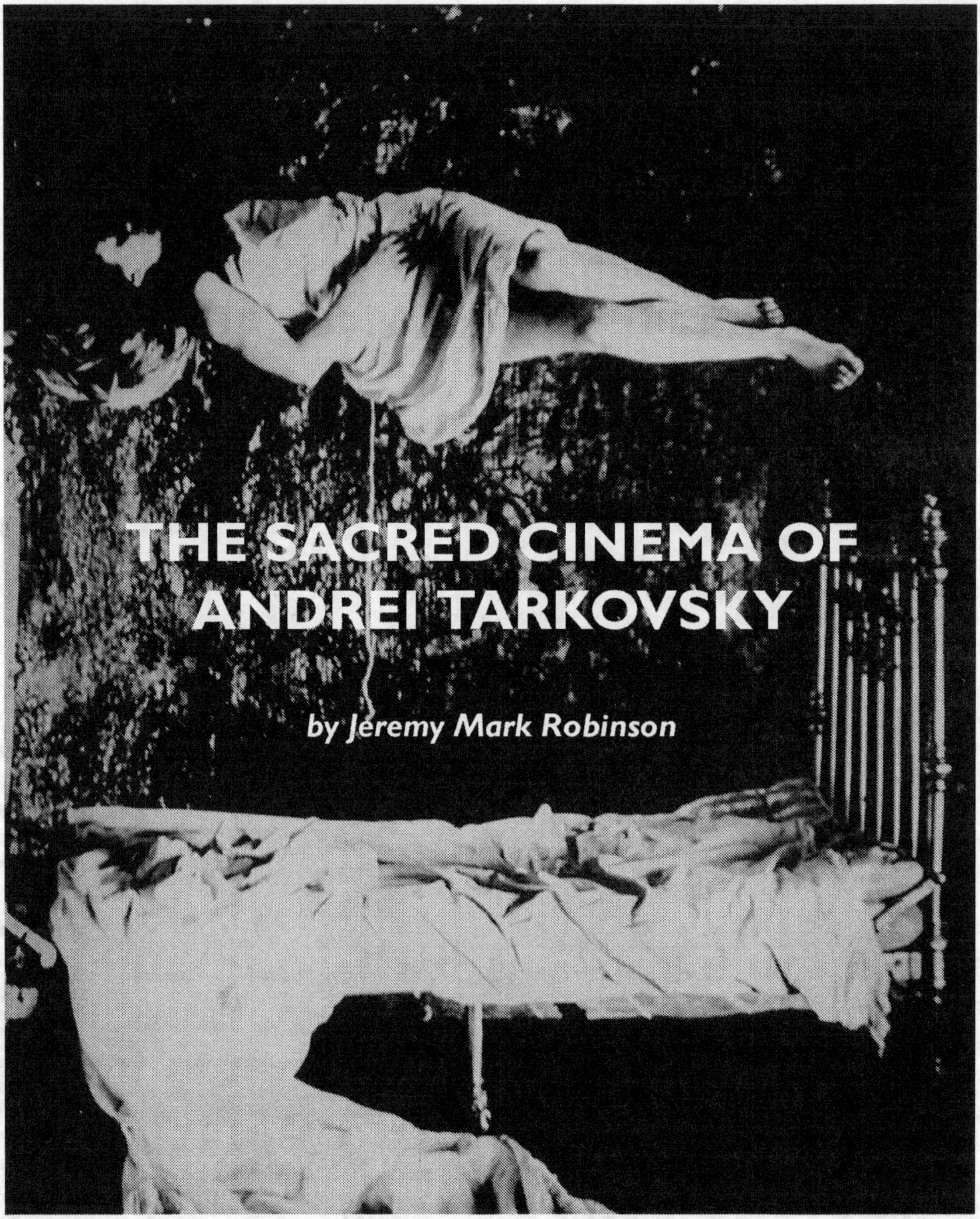

THE SACRED CINEMA OF
ANDREI TARKOVSKY

by Jeremy Mark Robinson

A new study of the Russian filmmaker Andrei Tarkovsky (1932-1986), director of seven feature films, including *Andrei Roublyov, Mirror, Solaris, Stalker* and *The Sacrifice*.
This is one of the most comprehensive and detailed studies of Tarkovsky's cinema available. Every film is explored in depth, with scene-by-scene analyses. All aspects of Tarkovsky's output are critiqued, including editing, camera, staging, script, budget, collaborations, production, sound, music, performance and spirituality. Tarkovsky is placed with a European New Wave tradition of filmmaking, alongside directors like Ingmar Bergman, Carl Theodor Dreyer, Pier Paolo Pasolini and Robert Bresson.
An essential addition to film studies.

Illustrations: 150 b/w, 4 colour. 682 pages. First edition. Hardback.

Publisher: Crescent Moon Publishing. Distributor: Gardners Books.

ISBN 1-86171-096-8 (9781861710963) £60.00 / $105.00

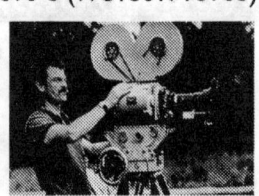

CRESCENT MOON PUBLISHING

ARTS, PAINTING, SCULPTURE

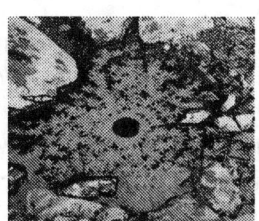

The Art of Andy Goldsworthy: Complete Works(Pbk)
The Art of Andy Goldsworthy: Complete Works (Hbk)
Andy Goldsworthy in Close-Up (Pbk)
Andy Goldsworthy in Close-Up (Hbk)
Land Art: A Complete Guide
Richard Long: The Art of Walking
The Art of Richard Long: Complete Works (Pbk)

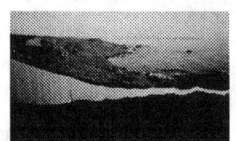

The Art of Richard Long: Complete Works (Hbk)
Richard Long in Close-Up
Land Art In the UK
Land Art in Close-Up
Installation Art in Close-Up

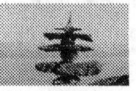

Minimal Art and Artists In the 1960s and After
Colourfield Painting
Land Art DVD, TV documentary
Andy Goldsworthy DVD, TV documentary
The Erotic Object: Sexuality in Sculpture From Prehistory to the Present Day
Sex in Art: Pornography and Pleasure in Painting and Sculpture
Postwar Art
Sacred Gardens: The Garden in Myth, Religion and Art
Glorification: Religious Abstraction in Renaissance and 20th Century Art
Early Netherlandish Painting

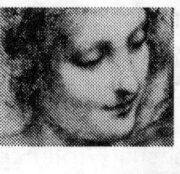

Leonardo da Vinci
Piero della Francesca
Giovanni Bellini
Fra Angelico: Art and Religion in the Renaissance
Mark Rothko: The Art of Transcendence

Frank Stella: American Abstract Artist
Jasper Johns: Painting By Numbers
Brice Marden
Alison Wilding: The Embrace of Sculpture
Vincent van Gogh: Visionary Landscapes
Eric Gill: Nuptials of God
Constantin Brancusi: Sculpting the Essence of Things
Max Beckmann

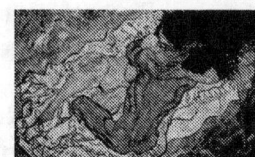

Egon Schiele: Sex and Death In Purple Stockings
Delizioso Fotografico Fervore: Works In Process I
Sacro Cuore: Works In Process 2
The Light Eternal: J.M.W. Turner
The Madonna Glorified: Karen Arthurs

LITERATURE

J.R.R. Tolkien: The Books, The Films, The Whole Cultural Phenomenon
Harry Potter
Sexing Hardy: Thomas Hardy and Feminism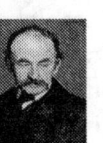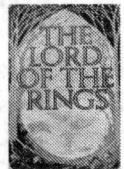
Thomas Hardy's *Tess of the d'Urbervilles*
Thomas Hardy's *Jude the Obscure*
Thomas Hardy: The Tragic Novels
Love and Tragedy: Thomas Hardy
The Poetry of Landscape in Hardy
Wessex Revisited: Thomas Hardy and John Cowper Powys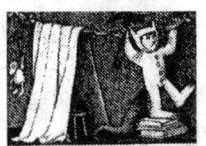
Wolfgang Iser: Essays
Petrarch, Dante and the Troubadours
Maurice Sendak and the Art of Children's Book Illustration
Andrea Dworkin
Cixous, Irigaray, Kristeva: The *Jouissance* of French Feminism
Julia Kristeva: Art, Love, Melancholy, Philosophy, Semiotics and Psychoanalysis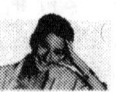
Hélene Cixous I Love You: The *Jouissance* of Writing
Luce Irigaray: Lips, Kissing, and the Politics of Sexual Difference
Peter Redgrove: Here Comes the Flood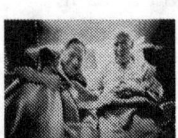
Peter Redgrove: Sex-Magic-Poetry-Cornwall
Lawrence Durrell: Between Love and Death, East and West
Love, Culture & Poetry: Lawrence Durrell
Cavafy: Anatomy of a Soul
German Romantic Poetry: Goethe, Novalis, Heine, Hölderlin, Schlegel, Schiller
Feminism and Shakespeare
Shakespeare: Selected Sonnets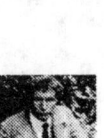
Shakespeare: Love, Poetry & Magic
The Passion of D.H. Lawrence
D.H. Lawrence: Symbolic Landscapes
D.H. Lawrence: Infinite Sensual Violence
Rimbaud: Arthur Rimbaud and the Magic of Poetry
The Ecstasies of John Cowper Powys
Sensualism and Mythology: The Wessex Novels of John Cowper Powys
Amorous Life: John Cowper Powys and the Manifestation of Affectivity (H.W. Fawkner)
Postmodern Powys: New Essays on John Cowper Powys (Joe Boulter)
Rethinking Powys: Critical Essays on John Cowper Powys
Paul Bowles & Bernardo Bertolucci
Rainer Maria Rilke
In the Dim Void: Samuel Beckett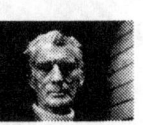
Samuel Beckett Goes into the Silence
André Gide: Fiction and Fervour
Jackie Collins and the Blockbuster Novel
Blinded By Her Light: The Love-Poetry of Robert Graves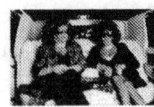
The Passion of Colours: Travels In Mediterranean Lands
Poetic Forms
The Dolphin-Boy

POETRY

The Best of Peter Redgrove's Poetry
Peter Redgrove: Here Comes The Flood
Peter Redgrove: Sex-Magic-Poetry-Cornwall
Ursula Le Guin: Walking In Cornwall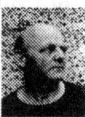
Dante: Selections From the Vita Nuova
Petrarch, Dante and the Troubadours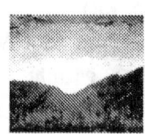
William Shakespeare: Selected Sonnets
Blinded By Her Light: The Love-Poetry of Robert Graves
Emily Dickinson: Selected Poems
Emily Brontë: Poems
Thomas Hardy: Selected Poems
Percy Bysshe Shelley: Poems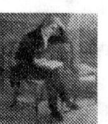
John Keats: Selected Poems
D.H. Lawrence: Selected Poems
Edmund Spenser: Poems
John Donne: Poems
Henry Vaughan: Poems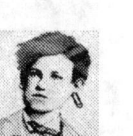
Sir Thomas Wyatt: Poems
Robert Herrick: Selected Poems
Rilke: Space, Essence and Angels in the Poetry of Rainer Maria Rilke
Rainer Maria Rilke: Selected Poems
Friedrich Hölderlin: Selected Poems
Arseny Tarkovsky: Selected Poems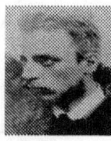
Arthur Rimbaud: Selected Poems
Arthur Rimbaud: A Season in Hell
Arthur Rimbaud and the Magic of Poetry
D.J. Enright: By-Blows
Jeremy Reed: Brigitte's Blue Heart
Jeremy Reed: Claudia Schiffer's Red Shoes
Gorgeous Little Orpheus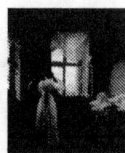
Radiance: New Poems
Crescent Moon Book of Nature Poetry
Crescent Moon Book of Love Poetry
Crescent Moon Book of Mystical Poetry
Crescent Moon Book of Elizabethan Love Poetry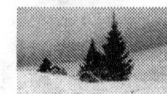
Crescent Moon Book of Metaphysical Poetry
Crescent Moon Book of Romantic Poetry
Pagan America: New American Poetry

MEDIA, CINEMA, FEMINISM and CULTURAL STUDIES

J.R.R. Tolkien: The Books, The Films, The Whole Cultural Phenomenon
Harry Potter
Cixous, Irigaray, Kristeva: The *Jouissance* of French Feminism
Julia Kristeva: Art, Love, Melancholy, Philosophy, Semiotics and   Psychoanalysis
Luce Irigaray: Lips, Kissing, and the Politics of Sexual Difference
Hélene Cixous I Love You: The *Jouissance* of Writing
Andrea Dworkin
'Cosmo Woman': The World of Women's Magazines
Women in Pop Music
Discovering the Goddess (Geoffrey Ashe)
The Poetry of Cinema
The Sacred Cinema of Andrei Tarkovsky (Pbk and Hbk)
Paul Bowles & Bernardo Bertolucci
Media Hell: Radio, TV and the Press
An Open Letter to the BBC
Detonation Britain: Nuclear War in the UK
Feminism and Shakespeare
Wild Zones: Pornography, Art and Feminism
Sex in Art: Pornography and Pleasure in Painting and Sculpture
Sexing Hardy: Thomas Hardy and Feminism

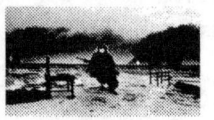
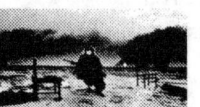
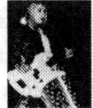
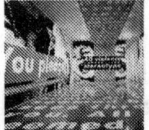
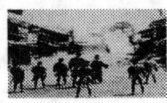
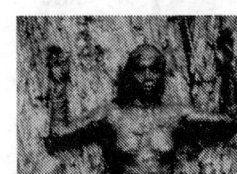
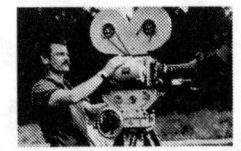
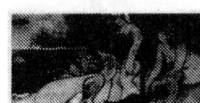

In my view *The Light Eternal* is among the very best of all the material I read on Turner. (Douglas Graham, director of the Turner Museum, Denver, Colorado)

The Light Eternal is a model monograph, an exemplary job. The subject matter of the book is beautifully organised and dead on beam. (Lawrence Durrell)

It is amazing for me to see my work treated with such passion and respect. (Andrea Dworkin)

Sex-Magic-Poetry-Cornwall is a very rich essay... It is like a brightly-lighted box. (Peter Redgrove)

CRESCENT MOON PUBLISHING
P.O. Box 393, Maidstone, Kent, ME14 5XU, United Kingdom.
01622-729593 (UK) 01144-1622-729593 (US) 0044-1622-729593 (other territories)
cresmopub@yahoo.co.uk   www.crescentmoon.org.uk

www.ingramcontent.com/pod-product-compliance
Lightning Source LLC
Chambersburg PA
CBHW081715220526
45468CB00008B/1858